ANTHROPOCENE UNSEEN

Fig. 1. Hieronymus Bosch, *Ship of Fools* (1490–1500)

First published in 2020 by punctum books, Earth, Milky Way.
https://punctumbooks.com

ISBN-13: 978-1-950192-55-7 (print)
ISBN-13: 978-1-950192-56-4 (ePDF)

DOI: 10.21983/P3.0265.1.00

LCCN: 2019951805
Library of Congress Cataloging Data is available from the Library of Congress

Book Design: Vincent W.J. van Gerven Oei

HIC SVNT MONSTRA

Anthropocene Unseen: A Lexicon

Edited by Cymene Howe
& Anand Pandian

*This book is dedicated to the young climate activists
in the streets and in our communities
who are demanding a better future yet unseen.*

Contents

Acknowledgments

We are grateful to many people who have helped in the collaborative and imaginative work that has come to life in this book. Jessica Lockrem and Marcel LaFlamme provided critical infrastructural labor to make earlier versions of the Lexicon available through the *Cultural Anthropology* website, the original digital home for many of the 86 essays gathered here. The contributing editors at *Cultural Anthropology* also lent their voluntary editorial expertise to shepherd several of the original essays toward more perfect forms.

Our appreciation goes out to those who were with us at the 2015 American Anthropological Association panel where the idea for an Anthropocene Lexicon first debuted. Thanks goes (in alphabetical order) to Dominic Boyer, Timothy Choy, Abou Farman, John Hartigan, Stefan Helmreich, Eduardo Kohn, Stuart McLean, Timothy Morton, Natasha Myers, Elizabeth Povinelli, and Sarah Vaughn. Equal thanks go to all of the authors who have brought their work and words into play here; intellectual labor is so often unseen and yet without it we are in a far scarier place than the Anthropocene we already know.

Eileen Joy and Vincent W.J. van Gerven Oei have been enthusiastic supporters of the Lexicon project from the very beginning and we are honored to be publishing this collection with punctum books, for both the curatorial vision of the press as well as its commitment to open access publishing.

We extend thanks to Joseph Goetz and Lisa Spiro, information specialists at Rice University's Fondren Library, which provided a subvention for this project in order to make knowledge more equitably distributed through open access.

Finally, we give a huge amount of appreciation to Addison Verger whose capacity to manage an exceptionally complex project has meant that each of us, as authors and editors, have been able to preserve a few more hours of our lives and make this Lexicon a reality.

Introduction

Cymene Howe and Anand Pandian

Another big storm knocking on the shoreline, or the harbinger of an everyday chaos to come. A plastic bottle cap bobbing in a puddle, or a cipher for the look of the Earth's crust in a time beyond the human. A few weedy tendrils unfurling from a sidewalk crack, or a muse for resistance in a time when life itself seems to have become a political act. The evidence at hand carries heady challenges of perception and interpretation. Is it alarmism, the tendency to find signs of ecological crisis in every small instance of perturbation and decay? Or does our sense of the ordinary in fact depend on a massive bout of climate denial, a "great derangement," as the novelist Amitav Ghosh (2016) has put it? Making sense of a fraught moment begins with the simple matter of what there is to see. With this lexicon, we hope to provide a resource helpful for this task: a catalog of ways of living out the ecological consequences of the present as a means of grappling with the deep uncertainty they bring to quotidian moments of life.

We write in the midst of a dramatic revaluation of the time at hand, as geological scientists weigh whether to identify this epoch with the deeds and tracks of the human species as an Anthropocene. This idea of an Anthropocene, famously proposed by the atmospheric chemist Paul Crutzen and the fresh-water ecologist Eugene Stoermer (Crutzen and Stoermer 2000), has spread with astonishing speed far beyond the domain of the natural sciences, dislodging familiar terms like *nature* and *environment* from their customary preeminence as signs of the world beyond ourselves. Thinkers of so many kinds — artists, poets, critics, writers, activists, and academics, too — seem to have seized on this neologism as an emblem for this time. The questions at stake here are indeed profound. How might our political and cultural discourses change if we were really to become collectively and critically aware of the conditions that the Anthropocene represents: the human deformation of the Earth?

We live in an accelerated world. Amid faster resource use, manufacture, and trade and faster communication and travel, speed has become a habit. It should therefore not surprise us that terminology can also move rapidly, blazing through media conduits. In a theoretical sense, speed is an essential condition of the Anthropocene as a concept. Many of its proponents cite the Great Acceleration following the Second World War — the quickened pace of fossil-fueled production, transportation, and unleashed consumption — as the crucial temporal phase that gave rise to the defining features of this epoch. What would it take, we wonder, to see this time, its agents, and their momentum otherwise? For, as the political theorist William Connolly (2017, 149) has noted, this is also a moment in the "acceleration of differential suffering, forced migrations, and violent conflicts," even as "in a world of tragic possibility there is no guarantee that the need to act will be matched in fact by timely action."

Much of the time, the Anthropocene augurs an affective sense of overwhelmed abjection or apathy. It appears as a set of circumstances that counterpose individual human actors against seemingly impossible odds. Climate change is, as Timothy Morton (2013) has signaled with the idea of "hyperobjects," effectively beyond human comprehension in its massive scale, generational effects and widely distributed impacts. Even hyperobjects, however, are made up of myriad judgments, acts, and deferrals of action. And there is much at stake in how we read and interpret these incipient vectors and tendencies, how we describe what is happening now and how we plot potential paths from this present to other, hopefully less troubling futures.

This book is committed to the value of smaller scales of analysis and to confounding perspectives. We recognize the gravity of the global forecasts that invest the present with its widespread air of crisis, urgency, and apocalyptic possibility. All the same, we hold that climate change and other expressions of threat and uncertainty at a worldwide scale demand a bifocal perspective, in which global optics like the Anthropocene are matched with careful reflection on the potentials, both positive and negative, of intimate forms of life and circumstance.

For the Anthropocene is, in fact, an image — an arresting and persuasive one — an image of the Earth as captive to the machinations of a single species. The figure of the human towers in this new discourse at a gargantuan scale hardly fathomable from the ground worked so diligently by those of us in the human sciences and arts. Critics (e.g., Malm and Hornborg 2014) have found the term itself too anthropocentric and misleadingly general in scope, too keen on evidence of Man and "our" collective imprint on the globe to the exclusion of profound differences in responsibility and vulnerability with regard to contemporary ecological crises. Pronouncing an epoch in our own name does seem to be the ultimate act of apex species self-aggrandizement, a picture of the world as dominated by ourselves. With this lexicon, we are less interested in an authoritative redefinition of the term and its totality than in helping to propel its radicalization, to the point where it might speak more effectively to the experience of a wider range of contemporary human societies and circumstances, including their relationships with non-human others. Whether as anthropologists, humanists, or artists, we share a commitment to wrestling with *anthrōpos* and its limits.

This project began as a roundtable at the 2015 annual meeting of the American Anthropological Association. Although it has since evolved into an exchange between many disciplines and fields of practice, there remains a unique and important place for anthropology in these conversations. *Anthrōpos* now appears to be a being and a problem on everyone's mind (Latour 2014). But here it is worth recalling that anthropology as a discipline has dedicated itself quite doggedly to an investigation of the human as a problem and a horizon. Anthropology has always been a speculative enterprise, wagered on the possibility of surpassing a fixed picture of the human and its limits, an intellectual practice of taking the human beyond itself. There has always been an ecological dimension to anthropological thinking and writing, as figures like Gregory Bateson (2000) and Tim Ingold (2011) have shown, anchored in close and careful attention to the material circumstances of life and their ecological entailments. Humanity for anthropology is an emergent and imaginative collectivity, grounded in many disparate worlds and the possibility of thinking and passing between them (Pandian 2019). With this project, we hope to show that these legacies can be enlisted in the project of reconceiving the Anthropocene, for this is a discourse that tends to take the human and its world as givens all too quickly and easily.

Alternative ways of inhabiting a moment can bring a halt to habitual action, opening a space for slantwise movements through the shock of an unexpected perception. Each small essay in this lexicon is meant to do just this: offer a way of pluralizing perception and thereby open up the range of possible action. Each entry proposes a different way of seeing this Earth from some grounded place, but in a manner that aims to provoke a different imagination of the Anthropocene as a whole. What would happen if the destruction of forests for mineral resources was conceived from the standpoint of enduring indigenous **Relationships** with the land, or the **Ecopolitics** of those who insist on collaborating with the forest as a sentient being? How would our sense of human **Power** shift if we acknowledged the animals and other living beings from whom we borrow our capacities, or the **Photosynthesis** that imbues the planet with so much of its available energy? Lodged in such terms are fables that narrate the fearsome domain of human agency in unexpected ways. We aim, in the company of these many little stories, to avoid the perils of pessimism and panic that characterize so much Anthropocene discourse, and to generate new ways of apprehending this unprecedented moment.

Heat and **Wildness**, **Rivers** and **Models**, **Shit** and **Flatulence**: in thinking with such terms and their imaginative possibilities, we seek to confront the challenges of vision and sensibility, to find new means of conceiving, engaging, and expressing the felt impasses of the ecological present. There are those who have found the name "Anthropocene" itself too straightjacketed a term, floating many provocative alters: Anthrobscene (Parikka 2015), Eurocene (Grove 2016), Misanthropocene (Clover and Spahr 2014), and so on, with many such others — Plasticene, Prometheocene, Simulocene — to come, even in the pages that follow. "The unfinished Chthulucene must collect up the trash of the Anthropocene, the exterminism of the Capitalocene, and chipping and shredding and layering like a mad gardener, make a much hotter compost pile for still possible pasts, presents, and futures," Donna Haraway (2016, 57) has recently declared with gusto. Maybe all of this comes down to the flickering promise of what we might call, with a nod to software junkies everywhere, a Betacene: a time to test, engage, and experiment with new ways of being in and with the world. We may yet have the chance to reverse-engineer ourselves toward a less imperfect humanity.

This lexicon is meant as a site to imagine and explore what human beings can do — have already been doing — differently with this time and its sense of a shared peril. As with any moment of intense movement and dynamism, the energy swirling around the Anthropocene idea cannot be contained or domesticated by any one dominant understanding (Howe 2019). There is no conceit here of being exhaustive or comprehensive. With the terms that make up this lexicon, we explore the Anthropocene as an opening to imagine the present in contrary terms and to engage creatively with this opening in lending force or momentum to more heterodox imaginations and movements. The Holocene may have been the age in which we learned our letters, but we are faced now with circumstances that demand more experimental plasticity. Given the feral geographies (see Tsing 2015) and disrupted grounds that compose more and more of our world, there is something crucial to be gleaned from the workings of this improvisational spirit.

For there is no doubt that new dreams are necessary, germinating unexpected ideas and novel forms of realization. The Anthropocene is a world-engulfing concept, drawing every thing and being imaginable into its purview, both in terms of geographic scale and temporal duration. Climate crisis, fueled by predatory capitalism, has the potential to embolden the powers that be to exert draconian controls over far-flung populations, unprecedented in nature and scope. Can we instead learn new ways of being in the face of this challenge, approaching the transmogrification of the ecosphere in a spirit of experimentation rather than catastrophic risk and existential dismay? It is this crucial question that weaves its way throughout the pages that follow.

References

Bateson, Gregory. 2000. *Steps to an Ecology of Mind.* Chicago: University of Chicago Press. Originally published in 1972.

Clover, Joshua, and Juliana Spahr. 2014. *#Misanthropocene: Twenty-Four Theses.* Oakland: Commune Editions.

Connolly, William E. 2017. Facing the Planetary: Entangled Humanism and the Politics of Swarming. Durham: Duke University Press.

Crutzen, Paul J., and Eugene F. Stoermer. 2000. "The 'Anthropocene.'" *Global Change Newsletter* 41: 17–18.

Ghosh, Amitav. 2016. *The Great Derangement: Climate Change and the Unthinkable.* Chicago: University of Chicago Press.

Grove, Jairus. 2016. "Response to Jedediah Purdy." In "The New Nature," *Boston Review,* January/February. https://bostonreview.net/forum/new-nature/jairus-grove-jairus-grove-response-jedediah-purdy.

Haraway, Donna J. 2016. *Staying with the Trouble: Making Kin in the Chthulucene.* Durham: Duke University Press.

Howe, Cymene. 2019. *Ecologics: Wind and Power in the Anthropocene.* Durham: Duke University Press.

Ingold, Tim. 2011. *Being Alive: Essays on Movement, Knowledge, and Description.* New York: Routledge.

Latour, Bruno. 2014. "Anthropology at the Time of the Anthropocene: A Personal View of What is To Be Studied." Distinguished Lecture, Annual Meeting of the American Anthropological Association, Washington, D.C., December 6.

Malm, Andreas and Alf Hornborg. 2014. "The Geology of Mankind? A Critique of the Anthropocene Narrative." *Anthropocene Review* 1, no. 1: 62–69. https://doi.org/10.1177/2053019613516291.

Morton, Timothy. 2013. *Hyperobjects: Philosophy and Ecology After the End of the World.* Minneapolis: University of Minnesota Press.

Pandian, Anand. 2019. *A Possible Anthropology: Methods for Uneasy Times.* Durham: Duke University Press.

Parikka, Jussa. 2015. *The Anthrobscene.* Minneapolis: University of Minnesota Press.

Tsing, Anna Lowenhaupt. 2015. *The Mushroom at the End of the World: On the Possibility of Life in Capitalist Ruins.* Princeton: Princeton University Press.

1

Acceleration

David Rojas

At present, we accelerate. Or, so argue scientists who claim that
the epoch of the Anthropocene is also the time of the Great
Acceleration (Steffen et al. 2004; Waters et al. 2016). Since the
mid-twentieth century, they assert, human-driven ecological
destruction has left a clear trace in the planet's geological record;
industrial infrastructures have expanded dramatically across
the planet, including impoverished parts of the globe (McNeill
and Engelke 2016).

   Framing the Anthropocene as acceleration conveys an old
notion: mass-scale industrialization as an upward velocity of
change. Members of the Italian artistic movement futurism,
for instance, famously declared in 1909 that industry had created "omnipresent speed" and worshipped the technologies that
made it possible (Marinetti 2006 [1909]: 14) . Similar statements
came from high-modern politicians such as Joseph Stalin in the
Soviet Union and Juscelino Kubitschek in Brazil. Stalin claimed
in 1931, "we are fifty or a hundred years behind the advanced
countries. We must make good this distance within the next ten
years" (Buck-Morss 2000: 38). Kubitschek promised, in 1955,
"fifty years of progress in five years of government" (Holston
1989: 84). For Paul Virilio (2006), such calls were the stuff of
dromopolitics, the politics of speed whereby cities, highways,
and industrial parks were built to spur the movement of masses

DOI: 10.21983/P3.0265.1.03

that would drive kinetic empires forward. Speed was a means of creating dreamworlds — utopian futures that would justify the industrial catastrophes that made them possible (Buck-Morss 2000).

Strikingly, proponents of such proposals adopt an irreverent, joyful tone even when promoting destruction and death. As Walter Benjamin (2007, 242) suggests, such a political style was more than mere rhetoric, enabling national leaders and political groups to prime their audiences to experience kinetic self-destruction as "an aesthetic pleasure of the first order." Are scientists likewise suggesting that acceleration is no delusion, representing an objective accomplishment of industrialization that has shaped the planet's geological becomings?

The question is especially pressing given that notions of acceleration are still foregrounded in contemporary political conversations. Consider, for instance, discussions I have had with farmers and scientists in Brazilian agro-industrial towns at the southern edges of the Amazon basin (a region that has become a global agro-industrial powerhouse). While conducting fieldwork there, I was told that farmers were racing to develop new agro-industrial technologies so they could expand their operations and address problems related to climate change and productivity that were generated by industrial agriculture itself. Environmental scientists, in turn, quickly developed policy after policy designed not to arrest the agribusiness boom but to modify the direction of its sprint.

When, in Amazonia, I raised the possibility of deceleration or degrowth, most interlocutors, from staunchly conservative landowners to progressive environmental scientists, were visibly baffled. Talk of slowing down often sparked skeptical questions. Was it not the case that Brazil needs to rapidly enrich itself so that it may stand up to world powers and environmental institutions that have long undermined the economic standing of the nation? Or, from the other end of the political spectrum, was it not obvious that public policies needed to increase momentum for change so as to forestall the ravages of capitalism, alleviate hunger, or adapt to climate change?

Broadly similar questions are posed today by scholars whom Benjamin Noys (2010, 2014) calls accelerationists. According to Noys (2010, 5), accelerationists claim that "if capitalism generates its own forces of dissolution then the necessity is to radicalize capitalism itself: the worse the better." As accelerationists put it, "the only radical political response to capitalism is not to protest, disrupt, or critique, nor to await its demise at the hands of its own contradictions, but to accelerate its uprooting, alienating, decoding, abstractive tendencies" (McKay and Avanessian 2014, 4). Accelerationists keep alive an old tradition among speed-lovers: the use of an irreverent, joyful tone to describe willful self-sacrifice.

Despite many telling similarities, however, current notions of acceleration (including those implicit in the arguments of some persons in agro-industrial Amazonia) are unlike the high-modern politics of speed. Current acceleration agendas do not characterize industrial destruction as a sacrifice that will result in fulfilling dreamworlds. As Deborah Danowski and Eduardo Viveiros de Castro (2017, 55) suggest, today the motif of acceleration no longer concerns the promotion of "the liberating acceleration of productive forces, but of the growing momentum of the destructive forces unleashed by the physical interaction between the capitalist system and the Earth System." Rather than (over)valuing industrial destruction for the engendering of "good" futures, accelerationists frame catastrophe as valuable in itself.

From the perspective of accelerationists, we have no choice but to forego value judgments as acceleration is neither good nor evil; it is, for them, simply a reality built into the thick webs of wires, roads, and pipelines that sustain our industrial modes of living (Shaviro 2015). In Amazonia, similar ideas inform policies that integrate agro-industrial expansion into the basin's ecological dynamics: avoiding agribusiness expansion is not seen as an option. An environmentalist politics, in this context, must eschew the utopian objective of building a good future and focus instead on limiting certain aspects of impending crises (see Rojas 2015, 2016).

Perhaps these darker contemporary notions of acceleration signal the birth of a novel political entity: not the Great Acceleration but Acceleration the Great. A seductively destructive, diffuse being, Acceleration the Great promises the collapse of the socioecological foundation on which engines, servers, and grids run — and some hope that novel modes of living will emerge from capitalism's ruins.

To resist this being, we may want to listen to the Amazonian peasant who, when I asked him about the expansion of agro-industrial operations in his town, laughingly exclaimed: "Why do people desire so many problems? Why always more, and more, and more?" While deeply concerned about his own poverty and acknowledging that his livelihood depended to a great extent on industrial infrastructures, he rejected self-sacrificial commitments to industrial expansion. Like others in Latin America for whom a good life is a political objective (Villalba 2013), he cultivated a generous lifestyle by caring for neighbors, visitors, plants, animals, and the soil at his site. This life-affirming, joyful, downward shift in velocity may have the power to gradually undermine mass-industry kinetics — the flesh and blood of Acceleration the Great.

References

Benjamin, Walter. 2007. "The Work of Art in the Age of Mechanical Reproduction." In *Illuminations,* edited by Hannah Arendt, 217–51. New York: Schocken. Originally published in 1939.

Buck-Morss, Susan. 2000. *Dreamworld and Catastrophe: The Passing of Mass Utopia in East and West.* Cambridge: MIT Press.

Danowski, Déborah, and Eduardo Viveiros de Castro. 2017. *The Ends of the World.* Cambridge: Polity Press.

Holston, James. 1989. *The Modernist City: An Anthropological Critique of Brasília.* Chicago: University of Chicago Press.

Mackay, Robin, and Armen Avanessian. 2014. "Introduction." In #Accelerate: The Accelerationist Reader, edited by Robin Mackway and Armen Avanaessian, 1–47. Falmouth: Urbanomic.

McNeill, J.R., and Peter Engelke. 2016. The Great Acceleration: An Environmental History of the Anthropocene since 1945. Cambridge: Harvard University Press.

Marinetti, Filippo Tommaso. 2006. Critical Writings: New Edition. New York: Farrar, Straus and Giroux.

Noys, Benjamin. 2010. The Persistence of the Negative: A Critique of Contemporary Continental Theory. Edinburgh: Edinburgh University Press.

———. 2014. Malign Velocities: Accelerationism and Capitalism. Alresford: Zero Books.

Rojas, David. 2015. "Environmental Management and Open-Air Experiments in Brazilian Amazonia." Geoforum 66: 136–45. https://doi.org/10.1016/j.geoforum.2014.12.012.

———. 2016. "Climate Politics in the Anthropocene and Environmentalism Beyond Nature and Culture in Brazilian Amazonia." PoLAR 39, no. 1: 16–32. https://doi.org/10.1111/plar.12128.

Shaviro, Steven. 2015. No Speed Limit: Three Essays on Accelerationism. Minneapolis: University of Minnesota Press.

Steffen, Will, et al. 2004. Global Change and the Earth System: A Planet Under Pressure. New York: Springer.

Villalba, Unai. 2013. "Buen Vivir vs Development: A Paradigm Shift in the Andes?" Third World Quarterly 34, no. 8: 1427–42. https://doi.org/10.1080/01436597.2013.831594.

Virilio, Paul. 2006. Speed and Politics. Translated by Mark Polizotti. Los Angeles: Semiotext(e). Originally published in 1977.

Waters, Colin N., et al. 2016. "The Anthropocene is Functionally and Stratigraphically Distinct from the Holocene." Science 351, January 8. https://doi.org/10.1126/science.aad2622.

FEEL THE HEAT

SUFFER THE COLD

INHERIT THE WIND

2

Address

Marina Zurkow, Una Chaudhuri,
Oliver Kellhammer, and Fritz Ertl

Dear Climate,

What if we killed off all of our first-born?
Stopped moving?
Stopped time?
What if we cordoned off 50 percent of the world from us; you take that half, we take this half?
What if we offer up a unicorn for sacrifice?
What if we let wolves live?
Yours with hope, and great good will,

Amy Dandelion Maddock

DOI: 10.21983/P3.0265.1.04

TO: The Climate
DATE: December 21, 2015
SUBJECT: Corrective Action
This memo constitutes a formal corrective action and this document will be placed in your permanent personnel file and could be used to make decisions that affect your employment. This document identifies areas where your performance is inconsistent with what is expected.

Issues
— Lack of adherence to quarterly deadlines
— Lack of teamwork to the point of alienating coworkers
— Poor work ethic
— Reckless endangerment of marginal populations
— Inconsistent performance
— Excessive retention of carbon dioxide
— Volatile and stormy outbursts
— Ocean acidification
— Expectations
— Adherence to terms of our Original Contract
— Willingness to take responsibility for your actions
— Willingness to take orders from superiors

The performance issues identified above are not acceptable in this workplace. These behaviors have a negative impact on your coworkers and, ultimately, our community. As a member of our team, you must improve your performance and behavior to bring it into compliance with expectations. I want to be sure that you understand the importance of this matter. Failure to achieve immediate and sustained improvement in the expectation(s) outlined above may result in further corrective action, up to and including termination.

As always, I will be available to assist you in answering any questions or concerns you may have.

Human Resources Department (courtesy of Peggy Estela)

Dear Climate,

Have you considered moving to another planet?
Warm regards,

People of Earth

3

Anticipation

Joseph Masco

What is the difference between waiting and anticipation? To wait is to attend to a known condition, to focus on its singularity, while to anticipate is to forecast a potentially changing outcome, opening up multiple tracks into the future. The era of the Anthropocene has introduced radical new forms of collective anticipation, as people forecast changing environmental conditions out onto distant time horizons, merging prediction with expectation and fusing fear with desire for alternate outcomes. Living on planet Earth increasingly requires a strange new form of subjectivity, one that mobilizes an ever emerging combination of attention to and, for many, anxious anticipation of radically shifting environmental conditions. The year 2016 was the hottest year on record, suffused with signs of a destabilizing earth system: an atmospheric river flooded the West Coast of the United States, overflowing dams and producing mudslides, while Yemen suffered a mind-bogglingly intense drought. Meanwhile, the North Pole experienced summer conditions in winter even as the Sahel both dried out and heated up. What records will be broken next year or twenty years out? How will we understand and measure storms, droughts, floods, heat waves, and fire by mid-century?

Attentive subjects can now live in a state of constant environmental agitation simply by tuning into a mediascape documenting radical ecological changes around the world. Experts across the full range of the natural sciences project increasingly extreme ecological conditions into a deep future, deploying complex models of Earth systems in an attempt to identify just when the Arctic might finally be free of all ice or when major cities will be underwater or when food production will cease in various locales or when specific species might hit the extinction endpoint. In doing so, they assess on a planetary scale the effects of human activity — and particularly the multigenerational force of industrial capitalism — as it plays out across land, air, ocean, ice, and biosphere. We are in the early stages of a new age of ecological awareness, but one that operates without the requisite political programs to engage the collective environment: a nervous-making condition, indeed. Anticipation fills this gap between knowledge and action, offering individuals the chance to attune to a vast range of both immediate and distant states of being, reading in their shifting forms the possibility of even deeper and more radically changed future conditions.

Consider, for example, the real-time surveillance of the Larson C ice shelf in Antarctica, a chunk of ice the size of Wales that for years has been slowly breaking off from the mainland. Deploying a variety of remote-sensing instruments as well as direct visual inspection, scientists have followed a monumental crack in the ice shelf, measuring its incremental progress over the past decade. They are devoted to understanding and predicting what the resulting iceberg will do, not only to the stability of the Antarctic region but also to sea-level rise around the world. In December 2016, scientists announced to the world that the growth of the ninety-mile-long rift was unexpectedly speeding up (having traveled more than eleven miles in just a few weeks), leaving Larson C connected by just a few remaining miles of ice. By the time it calved off some seven months later to become a free-floating iceberg, Larson C was a global news story, offering individuals heightened access to the temporal strangeness of the Anthropocene.

Pause for a moment to consider the temporal horizon of this mass-mediated event, the invitation to inhabit the expectation of a continent-sized change in the cryosphere and to anxiously await news of its permanent transformation. There is, of course, no means of stopping an ice-shelf collapse of this kind. Moreover, this event came to have meaning in relation to prior calving episodes — we can ask how Larson C's fate measured up to that of its predecessors, Larson A and B (which broke off some years ago) — but in doing so we also set in motion imagined future episodes. The drama of Larson C ultimately invites contemplation of a future with a radically destabilized polar ice cap or one with no ice at all. Think about this kind of real-time surveillance of hemispheric conditions and the way in which, as political subjects, we are hailed to care about ice on the South Pole as an index of local environmental health. Observation here drives anticipation, enabling engaged subjects to rescale their notion of ecological relation in unprecedented ways. Arctic ice is but one example of a wide range of ecological tipping points that interested subjects can now track in real time, attending to shifts in Earth systems from the mass-mediated vantage point of homes, businesses, and schools. Witnessing and anticipating are generating new political subjectivities, both engaged and overwhelmed by the sheer scale and momentum of industrial effects across Earth systems.

When we anticipate environmental change — asking *When will the ice shelf break? when will carbon dioxide in the atmosphere reach a threshold point? When will rising global temperatures hit the 2°C mark above preindustrial norms?* — we step out of capitalist time and the nation-state to think about collective conditions in a radically new way. This is not a profit/loss mode of calculation, but entry into a transformation of planetary conditions for life itself. What kind of spatial and temporal process is this, which invites urgent public attention to shifting conditions in even the most inhospitable region of the world for humans? Is it possible to calibrate the now mostly urban human sensibilities of seven billion people to a loss of ice or seawater rise or temperature rise in the most distant of locales? How, in other words, do contemporary attunements to the Earth system, that combination of atmosphere, ocean, ice, geology, and biosphere, structure emerging forms of ecological consciousness today, revealing the violent imbrication of human industry with the total environment on Earth? How, in short, does agitation over a destabilizing ecological domain condition forms of everyday life that are simultaneously stressed and living in expectation of increasing future injury? And, crucially, can we attune to anthropogenic effects to become more than mere spectators, mute witnesses to an ongoing industrial aftermath? When can we also anticipate to live a different politics?

4

Apocalypse

Roy Scranton

Many of those concerned with climate change in the Anthropocene have a story they tell about that moment the scales fell from their eyes and they realized just how fucked we are. Mine came in the summer of 2013, reading reports on likely climate trends from the World Bank and the International Panel on Climate Change. What I realized was that severe to extreme global warming was already locked in to the climate system, second-order effects of such warming would be catastrophic, and a business-as-usual pathway over the next two decades would almost certainly lead to the end of civilization as we know it and very possibly the extinction of the human species. Business as usual suddenly seemed horrific, though no less inevitable, and the world I thought I'd known transformed around me. What had been sure was doomed. What had been safe was lost. What had been prudent was now folly.

It was a revelation.

Revelation is, of course, the etymological meaning of the word *apocalypse*, from the Koinē Greek ἀποκάλυψις, meaning "uncovering or disclosing." It comes down to us through the Christian tradition primarily associated with the Revelation to John, the final book of the New Testament, in which God imparts a vision of the world's end and subsequent resurrection. Infamously psychedelic and cryptically allegorical, the Revela-

tion of John describes the opening of the seven seals; seven an-
gels blowing seven trumpets; a great red dragon, having seven
heads and ten horns, and seven crowns upon his heads; another
beast, from the sea, also with seven heads and ten horns, but
with ten crowns, like unto a leopard except with bear's feet and
a lion's mouth; a woman with a golden cup in her hand full of
abominations and the filthiness of her fornication, whose forehead is conveniently labeled Mystery, Babylon the Great, the
Mother of Harlots, and Abominations of the Earth; plus famines and plagues and war and death and so on, ending with
God's creation of the New Jerusalem, where all the resurrected
Christians live happily ever after.

Today, when we use the word apocalypse, we typically mean
something less weird and baroque, though often just as mythic — more focused on fantasies of destruction than with ideas
of revealed truth or Christian allegory. Yet crowding the top
ten Google hits for the word, among articles on "How the 1%
Are Preparing for the Apocalypse" and "What to Eat After the
Apocalypse," are several websites about En Sabah Nur, an age-
less being from ancient Egypt and the world's first mutant. After
rebelling against Pharaoh Rama-Tut and his General Ozyman-
dias, he renames himself Apocalypse and then sets out across
the Marvel world, starting wars, fighting Thor and Dracula,
and eventually coming face to face with the X-Men. Perhaps
our visions of apocalypse will always be weird and baroque: the
blankness of the canvas inspires wild elaboration.

But the question of whether imagining the end of the world
is the same as imagining life in the Anthropocene remains a
vexing one, and it is on this point that the two predominant
meanings of apocalypse (leaving out Marvel's supervillain) di-
verge. The revelation that global warming offers is actually a
much more complicated, obscure, and protracted vision than
stories of global doom can typically manage. For instance, *The
Day after Tomorrow* (2004), one of the most notable, if least
convincing "cli-fi" films, condenses the collapse of the Larsen
Ice Shelf, the shutdown of the Atlantic Meridional Overturning

Circulation, and disruptions of the polar vortex into a ludicrous few days in which giant vortices layer the Northern Hemisphere with sheets of ice. On the other hand, many so-called cli-fi novels evade the problem entirely by jumping right to the postapocalyptic dystopia, though it's true that more and more writers are trying to foresee how we might get there from here.

What such foreseers find, though, is that the Anthropocene revelation is not only opaque but contested, as each haruspex draws their conclusions from shifting sets of constantly changing signs. Today's arguments rage around how high the seas will rise and how fast, whether storms or drought are the bigger danger, whether mitigation might be successful, who will be hit the hardest, whether to call our era the Capitalocene or the Anthropocene, what climate change means for the human–nature binary, whether global warming is a hyperobject, and whether rising temperatures will mean Anthropocene democracy or Malthusian wars for *Lebensraum,* water, and oil. Tomorrow's signs will be yet more ominous and the arguments will shift accordingly, with no greater clarity than before.

The hardest thing about seeing our future isn't the black swan — that high-profile, hard-to-predict event that retroactively changes everything — or the complexity of the climate system, or even the fact that humans are wired for repetition, adaptation, and rationalization. The hardest thing about seeing our future is that we cannot see our present, and if you don't know where you are, you don't know where you're going. *The Wall Street Journal;* the global scientific community; the vast library stacks at Harvard and Princeton and the British Library and the Bibliothèque nationale; the prodigious computing power of Google's far-flung servers; the GPS in our phones; and a complicated mixture of animal cunning, acculturated ressentiment, and sheer profligacy all combine to imbue the cosmopolitan world's modern *Homo sapiens* with a blind arrogance unequaled in the natural world since *Tyrannosaurus rex* peered out over his late Cretaceous empire and roared a roar which, if we could but capture it, Google translate might render as "Look on my works, ye mighty, and despair!" The hardest thing about seeing our future is how much we think we know about our world, and how little we know about ourselves.

At some level, we sense this. Somewhere, deep in our lizard brains, we can tell that the business-as-usual world of seemingly omnipotent human technology with which we've surrounded ourselves is a house of cards, built on sand. Hence the appeal and power of those weird, baroque, dreamlike intuitions that come to us, piercing the veil of illusion we call our knowledge, as revelations — or fantasies — of the end.

5

Appreciation

Matthew Archer

One of the Anthropocene's distinguishing characteristics, as compared to the Holocene or Pleistocene, is the multiplicity and immediacy of appreciations that are layered upon it. We appreciate the Anthropocene. We recognize its significance, evinced by the volume of research devoted to comprehending it, even if we sometimes fail to understand it clearly or to grasp its subtleties. We have increased its value by elevating it from a marginal debate among stratigraphers (see Waters et al. 2016) to a central category in contemporary social theory. It is precisely these appreciations of the Anthropocene that have provoked subsequent theories of the Capitalocene, the Plantationocene, and the Chthulucene (Haraway 2015), among others. These derivations hype up their referent and cause its conceptual value to appreciate. As scholars and activists, we converge on distant cities to convene colloquia about our place in the world and the world's place in us. With each mile flown or driven, an infinitesimal layer of carbon is deposited in the earth's Anthropocenic stratigraph, tracing our paths from campus to conference and back again. Along the way, we continue to appreciate the Anthropocene — an infrastructure of appreciations that infrastructures our environments (cf. Blok, Nakazora, and Winthereik 2016).

An International Monetary Fund working paper, nearly two decades old, argues that "the appreciation of the resource wealth in effect acts as a cushion and substitutes for the reforms neces-sary to achieve a sustainable fiscal position" (Chalk 1998, 15). What the author means is that the increased value of a coun-try's resource wealth can be understood as commensurable with social and political reforms that promote sustainable develop-ment, reducing sustainability to a process of measurement and accounting. He might have just as compellingly argued that the simple act of being grateful for resource wealth is a substitute for reform, or that a more nuanced understanding of our im-pacts and dependencies on resource wealth could substitute for policies explicitly designed to make extraction more sustain-able. As it turns out, appreciations can be substitutable too.

In 2015 and 2016, I conducted fieldwork in Geneva, Swit-zerland, where I worked as an unpaid consultant at a number of organizations (or departments within larger organizations) devoted to corporate sustainability and sustainable finance. My informants included corporate sustainability managers, impact investors, management consultants, social-impact analysts, and other relatively elite workers who I collectively refer to as sus-tainability professionals. In addition to participant observation, I also conducted more than one hundred interviews with sus-tainability professionals in Geneva, Zurich, Paris, Luxembourg, Brussels, Accra, London, New York, and New Haven.

During a coffee break at a meeting on sustainable develop-ment at the World Trade Organization, I talked to a member of the corporation Monsanto's public relations team. According to her, Monsanto has one goal: "to feed the world" — to provide sustenance or, literally, to *sustain* humanity. What could be more sustainable? Massive agro-industrial companies like Monsanto have a bad reputation, but for this professional, that's simply be-cause they're so important. Most people — "especially activists," she grumbled (as if saying the word activist made her physically uncomfortable) — don't appreciate the immense pressure that companies like Monsanto face to be both profitable and sustain-able. I was going to ask if profitability and sustainability were mutually exclusive, but she anticipated my question by bringing up the so-called business case for sustainability. She suggested, quite matter-of-factly, that unsustainable companies are never as profitable as those heavily invested in reducing their social and environmental impacts.

At a conference on sustainable finance, I overheard a corporate sustainability manager tell a consultant the he "appreciate[s] all the hard work you've done" to develop a framework for aligning the United Nations Sustainable Development Goals with the financial interests of business. During an interview, the head of impact investing at a mutual fund told me: "Of course we appreciate the impacts of these [corporate sustainability] initiatives, but right now we just don't have the tools to [financially] value them." A Nestlé sustainability manager told me he "appreciates" the severity of water scarcity, even as one of the company's division chiefs suggested that humans do not have an inherent right to clean water. Governments, the latter argues, must appreciate Nestlé's so-called property rights. The company's stock appreciates. Investors appreciate the sustainability manager's charm offensive, but they appreciate the CEO's ruthlessness even more.

Much of the work of sustainability professionals centers on the appreciation of sustainability. Companies ostensibly respond to the value consumers place on sustainability, as reflected in their willingness to pay more for tea or chocolate that's certifiably more sustainable. The premium those consumers are willing to pay and the extent to which that willingness translates to higher stock prices are difficult and expensive to measure. In response, consulting firms like Sustainalytics and Inrate develop tools to measure and correlate sustainability and financial performance with what they describe as objectivity, producing indicators that banks and investors subsequently integrate into their valuation models. Here, sustainability is recognized as valuable, it is made valuable, and it becomes more and more valuable. Put differently, sustainability is appreciated, appreciated, and appreciated. Attending to the multiplicity of these appreciations helps us understand the growing power of corporate finance in the Anthropocene.

Appreciation is also imbued with agency. It is no coincidence that Paul Polman, the Unilever CEO who seems to be universally adored by sustainability professionals, presides over a company whose financial value has increased nearly 160 percent under his tenure — from a share price of $21.97 on January 1, 2009, when he was appointed CEO, to $56.91 in July 2017. Environmentalists appreciate Polman's efforts to save the planet. Consumers appreciate the increased sustainability of Unilever's products, because it makes ethical consumption an easy choice (see De Neve et al. 2008). According to one of Polman's admirers, a sustainable development consultant whom I met at a business and human rights forum, critics fail to appreciate the difficulty of negotiating competing stakeholders' concerns. Whatever Polman is doing, though, the market clearly appreciates it, as the company's stock continues to appreciate, reflecting a business acumen that Unilever's investors surely appreciate. Each of these is connected. They form a "strange loop" (cf. Hofstadter 2007) of appreciations, one in which appreciation is sensed and instigated (see Kockelman 2017) by both humans (investors, activists, and consultants) and nonhumans (valuation models, the stock market, and the planet). Within this agential assemblage (Bennett 2010) of appreciations, one starts to wonder whether we, too, are appreciated in and by the Anthropocene.

References

Bennett, Jane. 2010. *Vibrant Matter: A Political Ecology of Things.* Durham: Duke University Press.

Blok, Anders, Moe Nakazora, and Brit Ross Winthereik. 2016. "Infrastructuring Environments." *Science as Culture* 25, no. 1: 1–22. https://doi.org/10.1080/09505431.2015.1081500.

Chalk, Nigel A. 1998. "Fiscal Sustainability with Non-Renewable Resources." Working Paper 98/26, International Monetary Fund. https://www.imf.org/en/Publications/WP/Issues/2016/12/30/Fiscal-Sustainability-with-Non-Renewable-Resources–2518.

De Neve, Geert, Peter Luetchford, Jeffrey Pratt, and Donald C. Wood, eds. 2008. *Hidden Hands in the Market: Ethnographies of Fair Trade, Ethical Consumption, and Corporate Social Responsibility.* Bingley: Emerald.

Haraway, Donna. 2015. "Anthropocene, Capitalocene, Plantationocene, Chthulucene: Making Kin." *Environmental Humanities* 6, no. 1: 159–65. https://doi.org/10.1215/22011919-3615934.

Hofstadter, Douglas. 2007. *I Am a Strange Loop.* New York: Basic Books.

Kockelman, Paul. 2017. "Semiotic Agency." In *Distributed Agency,* edited by N.J. Enfield and Paul Kockelman, 25–38. New York: Oxford University Press.

Waters, Colin N., et al. 2016. "The Anthropocene is Functionally and Stratigraphically Distinct from the Holocene." *Science* 351, no. 6269: 137–49. https://doi.org/10.1126/science.aad2622.

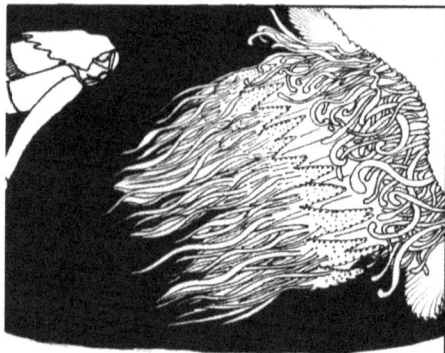

6

Bloom

Chitra Venkataramani

From time to time, the fishers' catch would be covered in purple slime. Dead jellyfish stung as we sorted and cleaned the fish for the market. It rendered all but the largest fish inedible. Jellyfish blooms, the sudden, dense aggregation of a massive number of jellyfish, are not uncommon in so-called dead zones such as the polluted waters off the shores of Mumbai. They take up the dissolved oxygen and put a strain on the small-scale fishing industry. Blooms are regarded as signs of a changing climate and as harbingers of the possibly "gelatinous future" (Attrill, Wright, and Edwards 2007) of the Earth's oceans.

Jellyfish blooms are not new phenomena; we have empirical records of them reaching back to the 1870s, but it is difficult to pinpoint their specific causes and even harder to demonstrate that they are the direct result of a changing climate. Some scientists speculate that blooms may be part of a larger "oscillation" in jellyfish populations (Condon et al. 2013). However, environmental factors such as water temperature and salinity are thought to serve as triggers for blooms, and changes caused by human activities such as overfishing and chemical pollution have been correlated with massive jellyfish aggregations (Purcell, Uye, and Lo 2007). What allows jellyfish to survive is their weed-like hardiness and their ability to self-replicate in massive numbers. They die down when conditions are unfavorable, only to explode when they are right (Gershwin 2013). These blooms are abrupt and unpredictable: imagine waking up one morning and finding your leather shoes covered in fungus, born of spores you didn't even know were there, or waking up to a riot of flowers in springtime. Bloom is the operative word here, because it signifies the suddenness and the profusion that characterize such events. Bloom captures the dramatic leap between the singular and the many.

Apart from sightings of jellyfish blooms, images of singular jellyfish captured in the darkness of the deep sea cultivate an image of the jellyfish as strange and alien (see Helmreich 2009). Both historical and contemporary representations of jellyfish have referenced this sense of alienness. In Ernst Haeckel's (1998) *Art Forms in Nature,* they appear in vivid color and in an impossible geometric entanglement of tentacles. In April 2016, when marine scientists spotted a new species of jellyfish deep in the Marianas Trench, media accounts described the organism as "from outer space" (Bryner 2016) and "alien-like" (Lockhart 2016). Writing about the recent proliferation of images from expeditions to the oceanic abyss, Stacy Alaimo (2013, 140) provokes us to formulate "a more aquatic environmentalism" premised on a relationship with newly discovered beings that emerge from the deep. However, while images of individual jellyfish from deep-sea expeditions might present themselves to us a creature that is alien and yet alluring and beautiful, images of jellyfish blooms provoke a different kind of awe. Here, the language changes to that of an alien invasion: a "jellygeddon" (Gaia 2012) or "goomageddon" (Stelling 2016) brought on by "an army of bloodless, boneless phantoms from the deep" (Discovery Communications n.d.).

It is perhaps no wonder, then, that reactions to jellyfish blooms have also taken on the language of combating an alien invasion. A popular engineering blog featured a robot swarm designed to locate and shred invading jellyfish (Ackerman 2013). Another possible strategy, one that's been speculated on and experimented with by scientists, entrepreneurs, and artists, would be to consume jellyfish in larger numbers and in more systematic ways. While many species of jellyfish are consumed across the world, as Marina Zurkow's 2009 film *Slurb* shows, jellyfish may be the few remaining aquatic life forms left to consume *en masse*. In turning jellyfish into a product of general consumption, advocates seek to turn a signifier of depletion and destruction to one of plenitude; other suggested uses beyond eating include turning jellyfish into fertilizer or using them as a source of collagen for cosmetics (Tucker 2010). As Anthony Richardson and colleagues (Richardson et al. 2009) point out, though, not only would this require developing ways of processing toxic jellyfish to make them palatable or otherwise usable, it also might end up harming species of jellyfish that were not a problem to begin with. Indeed, this consumerist strategy does not ultimately resolve the underlying problems that create the conditions for blooms to proliferate. Instead, echoing James C. Scott's (1998) work on the development of scientific forestry, reclassifying jellyfish as a product intensifies expectations of oceans as economic spheres rather than complex habitats.

Warming oceans and acidification are allowing many species of jellyfish to thrive and redistribute themselves across different geographies. As Jeremy Jackson (2008) speculates, systematic overfishing and eutrophication may yet result in oceans similar to those millions of years ago in which jellyfish were among the apex predators. Thus, the Anthropocene might witness the re-emergence of past geologic eras, with simpler and slimier life forms. Living in this warmer, polluted world might necessitate a different understanding of human–jellyfish interaction, one in which consumption might be one among many kinds of relationships. Perhaps we can think about blooms in this open-ended way: as the multitude of yet-to-be-known relationships between ourselves and the jellies blossoming in the oceans' warming waters.

References

Ackerman, Evan. 2013. "These Robots Will Stop the Jellyfish Invasion." Automaton blog, *IEEE Spectrum,* October 1. https://spectrum.ieee.org/automaton/robotics/industrial-robots/jeros-jellyfish-elimination-robotic-swarm.

Alaimo, Stacy. 2013. "Jellyfish Science, Jellyfish Aesthetics: Posthuman Reconfigurations of the Sensible." In *Thinking with Water,* edited by Cecelia Chen, Janine MacLeod, and Astrida Neimanis, 139–63. Montreal: McGill-Queen's University Press.

Attrill, Martin J., Jade Wright, and Martin Edwards. 2007. "Climate-Related Increases in Jellyfish Frequency Suggest a More Gelatinous Future for the North Sea." *Limnology and Oceanography* 52, no. 1: 480–85. https://doi.org/10.4319/lo.2007.52.1.0480.

Bryner, Jeanna. 2016. "Jellyfish from Outer Space? Amazing Glowing Creature Spotted." *Live Science,* April 29. https://www.livescience.com/54608-alien-jellyfish-discovered-mariana-trench.html.

Condon, Robert H., Carlos M. Duarte, Kylie A. Pitt, Kelly L. Robinson, Cathy H. Lucas, Kelly R. Sutherland, Hermes W. Mianzan, Molly Bogeberg, Jennifer E. Purcell, and Mary Beth Decker. 2013. "Recurrent Jellyfish Blooms Are a Consequence of Global Oscillations." *Proceedings of the National Academy of Sciences* 110, no. 3: 1000–1005. https://doi.org/10.1073/pnas.1210920110.

Discovery Communications. n.d. "Rise of the Jellyfish." *Animal Planet* episode notes. https://press.discovery.com/emea/apl/programs/rise-jellyfish.

Gaia, Vince. 2012. "Jellyfish Blooms Creating Oceans of Slime." *BBC,* April 5. http://www.bbc.com/future/story/20120405-blooming-jellyfish-problems.

Gershwin, Lisa-Ann. 2013. *Stung! On Jellyfish Blooms and the Future of the Ocean.* Chicago: University of Chicago Press.

Haeckel, Ernst. 1998. *Art Forms in Nature: The Prints of Ernst Haeckel.* Munich: Prestel. Originally published in 1904.

Helmreich, Stefan. 2009. *Alien Ocean: Anthropological Voyages in Microbial Seas.* Berkeley: University of California Press.

Jackson, Jeremy B.C. 2008. "Ecological Extinction and Evolution in the Brave New Ocean." *Proceedings of the National Academy of Sciences* 105, S1: 11458–65. https://doi.org/10.1073/pnas.0802812105.

Lockhart, Keely. 2016. "Alien-Like Jellyfish Discovered by Deep Sea Diving Expedition." *Telegraph,* May 7. http://www.telegraph.co.uk/science/2016/05/05/alien-like-jellyfish-discovered-by-deep-sea-diving-expedition.

Purcell, Jennifer E., Shin-ichi Uye, and Wen-Tseng Lo. 2007. "Anthropogenic Causes of Jellyfish Blooms and Their Direct Consequences for Humans: A Review." *Marine Ecology Progress Series* 350: 153–74. https://doi.org/10.3354/meps07093.

Richardson, Anthony J., Andrew Bakun, Graeme C. Hays, and Mark J. Gibbons. 2009. "The Jellyfish Joyride: Causes, Consequences and Management Responses to a More Gelatinous Future." *Trends in Ecology and Evolution* 24, no. 6: 312–22. https://doi.org/10.1016/j.tree.2009.01.010.

Scott, James C. 1998. *Seeing like a State: How Certain Schemes to Improve the Human Condition Have Failed.* New Haven: Yale University Press.

Stelling, Tamar. 2016. "The Jellyfish Are Coming. Brace Yourself for Goomageddon." *Correspondent,* August 4. https://thecorrespondent.com/4831/the-jellyfish-are-coming-brace-yourself-for-goomageddon/903664777499-c2d232ec.

Tucker, Abigail. 2010. "Jellyfish: The Next King of the Sea." *Smithsonian Magazine,* August. http://www.smithsonianmag.com/science-nature/jellyfish-the-next-king-of-the-sea-679915.

7

Business

Gökçe Günel

Businesses, especially green businesses, promote a peculiar optimism in the face of climate and energy crises. They supply environmentally friendly products that aim to supplant the demand
for non-green products, expanding their product portfolios to
service environmentally conscious humans. Green businesses
vary in form and shape. In the United States, we might think
of organic grocery stores as an example. We look at technology
companies, which promise smart homes as well as systems for
monitoring and managing our consumption patterns. Some fossil fuel companies seek to reimagine themselves as green. Their
marketing and communications campaigns address planetary-
scale problems and highlight how protective, soothing technological innovations and design solutions will be available to
those who can afford them.

   In the United Arab Emirates, where I have been conducting
research for the last ten years, green businesses promise a mark
of progress different from oil exports: they will resolve pressing
energy deficiency and climate-change-related problems, while
at the same time generating a new economic vision for the region and the globe. My book, *Spaceship in the Desert: Energy,
Climate Change, and Urban Design in Abu Dhabi* (2019), describes and analyzes this process in detail.

DOI: 10.21983/P3.0265.1.09

One prominent example is the multifaceted renewable energy and clean technology company Masdar. In responding to the dual problem of energy security and climate change, the Abu Dhabi government founded Masdar (meaning "source" in Arabic), investing $22 billion to start the project. The company is widely known for Masdar City, the futuristic ecocity master-planned to rely entirely on renewable energies. While the ecocity was central to Masdar's development, Masdar also invested in green businesses through its other operations: Masdar Power, Masdar Carbon, and Masdar Capital. Masdar Institute, the energy-focused research center set up and supervised by MIT's Technology and Development Program, operates on a growing campus within the ecocity site.

The designers of Masdar City, the London-based architects Foster + Partners, have suggested that they borrowed from old Arab cities in thinking about the future, pointing to the Yemeni city of Shibam as an inspiration for their designs. Like Shibam, Masdar City would be dense and walled. Yet it would also be smart, and its hidden brain would know when residents entered their buildings so as to start cooling their apartments before they opened the door. In public areas, flat screens would broadcast uplifting news on the environmental performance of the complex, displaying how much energy is produced and saved.

Framed as a utopia or science-fiction project, Masdar relied on the backdrop of a world struck by climate change and energy deficiency. The marketing and communications campaigns put together by Masdar aimed at proving that the world needed Masdar City in order to survive these catastrophes.

This preemptive optimism is certainly not unique to the United Arab Emirates. Some businesses, such as General Electric and Siemens, propose that their inventions make the future happen, using slogans such as "Tomorrow is Today" or "Enabling the Future." For them, climate change emerges as a business opportunity, endowing professionals with the capacity to sculpt a particular smart, networked future. Climate change may trigger the breakdown of political and ecological systems, but the implication is that businesses will hold their ground in the face of these challenges.

When I asked a Siemens representative what the company meant by its slogan "Tomorrow is Today," he explained that at Siemens they had access to all of the technological tools that would be used "Tomorrow," but unfortunately people were not ready to embrace what they had to offer. "We test our products at Masdar City," he clarified, "which is also in the future." The company was involved in a project called the Office of the Future, where they concentrated on optimizing office spaces. One of these offices would be situated in Masdar City. On the other hand, General Electric indicated that it would be "Enabling the Future" with smart appliances, as well as other technological gadgets that would become part of the energy mix. A GE representative stated, for example: "In the future everything will be smart and regulated, just as it is at Masdar City." The future was both a time and a place.

Green responses to future climate and energy crises have varied in form and shape, but this sense of optimism is pervasive. Take another well-known example, Tesla Motors, whose cars feature a so-called bioweapon defense mode. The button activates what is described as "a medical-grade HEPA air filtration system, which removes at least 99.97 percent of particulate exhaust pollution and effectively all allergens, bacteria, and other contaminants from cabin air." In describing the button in 2015, the company's founder Elon Musk said that Tesla is "trying to be a leader in apocalyptic defense scenarios." Tesla cars equipped with these devices will be able to protect passengers from possible toxicity, while allowing them to observe their surroundings through the car's all-glass panoramic windshield. The bioweapon defense button thus sets up a presumed apocalyptic future in which some passengers remain protected while others are left exposed, breathing in toxic air. Rather than seeking to resolve toxicity in a collective manner, the bioweapon defense button eliminates toxic air for individuals with enough cash.

Green businesses seek to create alternative environments of peace and rationality, standing in opposition to the destructive and irrational crises of Earth. Despite providing products and services to a small number of people who are experiencing the existing and future effects of climate change, these companies lay claim to the planetary-scale questions of survival in the unknown, the sustenance of the species beyond ecological disasters, and the preservation of an existing civilization. In all of these examples, businesses demarcate the boundaries between the haves and the have-nots upon whom the formers' lives are predicated.

Yet the environmental changes brought on by a century of human industrial activity, induced by industrialized humans, are truly global; their effects cannot be contained inside a particular history or geography. By producing enclosed and enclosing solutions in the name of green business and then promoting these fragmentary spheres as the ultimate means for survival, humans fail to understand and confront the predicament of the Anthropocene. Given the unbounded complexity of the challenge, an adequate response may require a somewhat less happy and optimistic, but ultimately more inclusive understanding of our collective future.

References

Günel, Gökçe. 2019. *Spaceship in the Desert: Energy, Climate Change, and Urban Design in Abu Dhabi.* Durham: Duke University Press.

8

Carbon

Jerome Whitington

During the 1950s, Dave Keeling developed a set of techniques
for systematically measuring atmospheric carbon dioxide. The
problem was not simple. How does one create a global number, as Paul Edwards (2010) has pushed us to ask? Keeling put
gas analyzers on military aircraft flying across the South Pacific,
at the Little America research station in Antarctica, and, most
famously, at the Mauna Loa Observatory, 3,600 meters above
sea level in the middle of the Pacific Ocean. The problem, for
Keeling, was that CO_2 varies tremendously throughout the atmosphere. Due to the effects of photosynthesis, ocean fluxes,
farming, and industrial activity, any measurement of CO_2 concentration is only a local measurement. Rather than create a
snapshot by averaging many different measurements all over the
world (as, for instance, we do with global temperature), Keeling decided to measure *as far away from anywhere* as possible
in order to produce a number that could speak for the planet's
atmosphere. Mauna Loa Observatory became the standard for
determining global CO_2. The global number produced there became the Keeling Curve. It also became a key cultural reference:
for instance, in the name of the activist group 350.org — a number that refers to the presumed safe limit of atmospheric carbon
dioxide (in parts per million).

DOI: 10.21983/P3.0265.1.10

The year 2015 was probably the last year in which, for the indefinite future, atmospheric CO_2 will ever be below 400ppm (Monroe 2015). To the extent that the habitability of the earth crucially depends on it, the steady increase configures a world of unknowns. Hence, the experiential tense of the Anthropocene may be exactly that: an indefinite future in which we are compelled to imagine what new contingent forms of life may be possible.

The geological carbon cycle is massive, many orders of magnitude larger than the paltry contribution of humans. Carbon dioxide in the air is only part of the complex of transformations that take place on timescales ranging from days to hundreds of millions of years, involving chemical forms ranging from ethereal, vibrating methane molecules to the calcium carbonate of Earth's vast limestone reserves.

Anthropogenic carbon emissions are central to the geological claim of humans' transformative role in planetary ecology, and therefore play an important part in the concept of the Anthropocene. Indeed, Donna Haraway (2015) has suggested that the concept of the Anthropocene fails if it delineates a previously pure nature unadulterated by human influence, or if it serves to reify an undifferentiated global humanity. From the vantage point of carbon, the Anthropocene does not mark a moment when geology passed into human time, but rather the inverse: when *anthrōpos* became inherently and pervasively geological through the utter dependence on fossil energy. *Anthropogenic* is a misnomer if it only means "human-caused," because the carbon in question is always already a multispecies communication of biomatter and stored chemical energy across geological timescales.

There is something unique about the hypothesis of anthropogenic climate change. For one thing, carbon dioxide is only a pollutant at the scale of the planet. It is only a pollutant when it changes the overall absorption of heat in the atmosphere. This planetary status is not without parallel (ozone-damaging refrigerants also qualify), but the volume of emissions, their importance to social life, and the magnitude of the problems caused introduce a sharp historical discontinuity. Human activity may have started this process, but, at this point, we are just along for the ride with at best a sinking premonition of how things might turn out. The event of climate change thus takes the form of a speculative question. As hypothesis — not as established, authoritative fact — climate change set off a flurry of novel research, open-ended sci-fi imaginings, and apocalyptic fantasies about the end of civilization. Fossil fuel companies were among the first to act decisively in the face of this new threat — to defend themselves, of course. But even the sober-minded United Nations negotiations tend to view climate futures as a matter of open-ended possibilities, not totalizing fact. Tracing carbon's inexorable rise, the Keeling Curve thus invites an imagination of environment in which Earth's surface is transformed in ways that no one, really, can yet get a grip on.

By the same token, the social life of carbon increasingly configures new forms of planetary relation. For instance, the matter of carbon traded in global carbon markets cannot be reduced to substantialist features of a compressible gas. What matters, and what has financial value on the carbon markets, is the contribution of greenhouse gases to overall planetary warming. This value is assimilated into a common metric, CO_2-equivalent, which is a measure of the incremental anthropogenic contribution to global warming. In Beijing, a bevy of actors are designing carbon data platforms that attempt to map and track carbon emissions systematically across sectors of the Chinese economy (Whitington 2016) Configuring this unique historical conjuncture, carbon is quite literally a metric of the human, and a wide array of questions have opened up about what new forms of sociality carbon technologies may engender.

No one knows what it will mean to curtail fossil energy use in the world's economy. But no one knows what a future of unabated planetary warming will look like either. The counterpoint of carbon is the planetary atmosphere itself, taken as a regulatory object and as the very medium in which much of life exists. Glimmers of many possible futures present themselves, inviting guesswork and grand postulates. From a certain perspective, decarbonization of the economy is a radical historical potential. Even if unlikely, the fact that decarbonization is being debated actively by corporate boards and the subject of several global political agreements shows the dynamism and open-endedness of climate change futures. There is a long history to the collective exploration of potential carbon futures, and yet this history of the indefinite future is only beginning. One way or another, we will continue to learn more about the role of carbon in the atmosphere than anyone ever expected.

References

Archer, David. 2011. *Global Warming: Understanding the Forecast.* New York: John Wiley & Sons.

Edwards, Paul. 2010. *A Vast Machine: Computer Models, Climate Data, and the Politics of Global Warming.* Cambridge: MIT Press.

Haraway, Donna. 2015. "Anthropocene, Capitalocene, Plantationocene, Chthulucene: Making Kin." *Environmental Humanities* 6: 159–65. https://doi.org/10.1215/22011919-3615934.

Monroe, Rob. 2015. "Is This the Last Year Below 400?" *The Keeling Curve.* October 21. https://scripps.ucsd.edu/programs/keelingcurve/2015/10/21/is-this-the-last-year-below–400/.

Whitington, Jerome. 2016. "Carbon as a Metric of the Human." *Political and Legal Anthropology Review* 39, no. 1. https://doi.org/10.1111/plar.12130.

9

Care

Charis Boke

I propose care as a methodological mode of attention that can ground the sometimes frightening implications of the Anthropocene as an epoch. Care as a method helps shift the overwhelming largeness of the spheres — bio, strato, litho — toward more intimate and personal relationships with the Anthropocene as an emergent quality of the natural/cultural world. A good working definition of care highlights the cultivated body knowledges and sensibilities by which creatures come to attend to one another's needs. The creatures I draw in here are teachers of Western herbalism, their students, and the plants they work with. Their modes of learning care across biological difference can offer a response to the suggestion that problems of the Anthropocene — global climate change, plastics in the ocean, pharmaceuticals in the water supply (Masco 2013), the potential collapse of global ecologies — are too big to cope with.

My research has dwelt in spaces where North American herbalist practitioners take seriously clinical and biochemical understandings of medicinal plants, as well as understandings based in *plant spirit medicine* — a term that frames plants as complexly active beings with whom humans can partner in easing suffering. Their practices of care include not only attention to suffering human bodies in clinical and informal settings; they also include active maintenance of nurturing relationships with

DOI: 10.21983/P3.0265.1.11   71

plants in local gardens, fields, and unmanaged forests. Herbalists think critically and carefully about global flows of medicinal
plants and their parts in markets for herbal medicines, attending to the ecologies and labors of plants (and their harvesters) in
places that many of them will never visit. Such varied practices
of care help enable forms of intimacy with bite-sized chunks of
the biosphere in a moment called the Anthropocene, so that we
might better digest its import and demands.

In Garden Apprenticeship class, we've all just arrived at one
of the gardens. Scattered quiet through the beds and path-
ways, each of us sits with a plant for fifteen minutes. Worm-
wood, motherwort, comfrey, lady's mantle, elecampane,
black cohosh, schisandra: medicine plants have their human
companions, sitting, listening, watching. Some reach out to
touch and hold a part of the plant, a stem, a leaf — like holding hands with a friend — and some just sit quietly. Com-
panioning plants like this helps herbalists learn to listen well
to them, to get down to plant time, to prepare themselves to
work and learn alongside plants in the garden.
   We are asked to learn more deeply from direct encounter with plants themselves. The plants become beings for us,
palpable as creatures and potential active collaborators insofar as we ingest and sit with them. These practices shift
our encounter with the world. Sitting with plants slows the
heart rate, the breathing. Lips part to inhale the dense scent
of the loam and the plant itself, to exhale a gift of CO_2 in
what herbalist Susun Weed calls a "giveaway dance with the
plants." Eyes closed, our fingers stroke the plant and in one
way or another, new understandings ensue. Through becoming intimate and perhaps animate in partnership with
plants, herbalists learn how to care for a world beyond that
of human suffering. Without our care, in anthropocenic con-
texts, some medicine plant ecologies deteriorate. Without
their care for humans — their molecular and spirit abilities

to attend to human bodies — our capacities for health falter (fieldnotes, 2014).

For the herbalists who use it, plant time is a learned shifting of bodily sensibility (Myers 2014). It takes intentional cultivation of a different sense of time for late-capitalist humans to move into the vegetal pace of breathing with a plant, and it is this cultivation that enables collaboration with and care for plants. Getting down to plant time becomes an embodied and temporally shaped mode of caring across biologies. This mode is especially pertinent in a moment of climate change and massive human impact on the planet. Some herbalists locate the beginnings of human and planetary healing in the recognition that humans are not outside of the natural world. In order to help others become well, herbalists and their vegetal others have to coordinate across complexly embodied webs of relationship within nature and across different experiences of temporality. This can mean working across a human experience of sped-up late industrial time and a plant's annual or years-long cycles of germination, growth, and death.

An herbalist who wanders into the garden or out of the city to gather plants in less managed woods, field, desert, and swamp, bends or reaches and slows down to greet the plant, asking permission to harvest some of its parts. He or she often leaves an offering, a gift, in return for the gift of the plant's medicine. Visiting burdock, dandelion, or black cohosh, herbalists make room for the plant's be-ing, beyond its usual object status. Caring across biologies emerges as a bodily practice through such exchanges. By attempting to move into plant time, herbalists construct a fleshly, embodied mode of attending that shifts their human perception and proprioception. Plants as beings become intimately palpable, emerging as a kind of kin to care for.

Herbalists' intentionally intimate and embodied relational practices help articulate how and why plant–human relationships matter. Such practices understand plants as beings occupying a different mode of time, and as capable of coordinating with humans to enable care across entangled biologies and social ecologies of wellness and illness (see Craig 2012; Nading 2014). They offer us the chance to think more broadly about who can care for whom and how, rather than falling into the seductive traps of projected human victimhood that thinking with the Anthropocene so often offers (Dean 2016). This is care-work not in terms of ocean levels or parts per million, although those articulations of the biosphere's assemblages help to tell stories about why intimate forms of care are necessary. Rather, this care happens at the vegetal pace of affective and embodied relation across domains of experience. Care across biological difference can enrich the possibilities that the Anthropocene as a conceptual framework offers us, while also helping us thrive in its context.

References

Craig, Sienna R. 2012. *Healing Elements: Efficacy and the Social Ecologies of Tibetan Medicine.* Berkeley: University of California Press.

Dean, Jodi. 2016. "The Anamorphic Politics of Climate Change." *e-flux* 69. https://www.e-flux.com/journal/69/60586/the-anamorphic-politics-of-climate-change/.

Masco, Joseph. 2013. "Side Effect." *Somatosphere.* December 2. http://somatosphere.net/2013/12/side-effect.html.

Myers, Natasha. 2014. "A Kriya for Cultivating Your Inner Plant." *Centre for Imaginative Ethnography.* http://imaginativeethnography.org/imaginings/affect/sensing-botanical-sensoria/.

Nading, Alex M. 2014. *Mosquito Trails: Ecology, Health, and the Politics of Entanglement.* Berkeley: University of California Press.

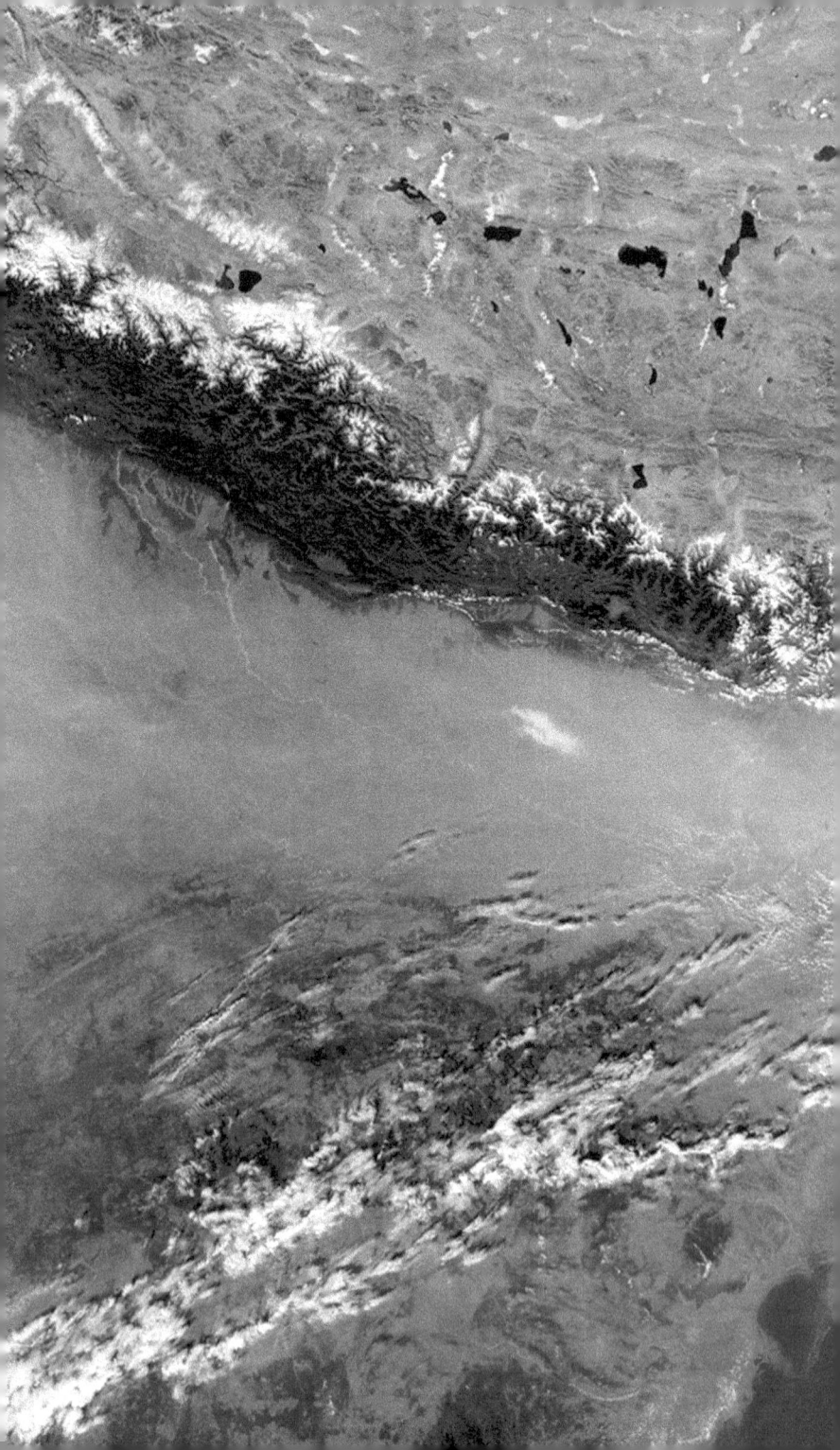

10

Cloud

Vasundhara Bhojvaid

Theorizing the Anthropocene means considering the air in which we live and which comprises the atmospheric fabric of earthly ecosystems. Our engagements with air point to a move that releases us "from […] earthly domains," allowing us to float "to new ethnographic spheres and spaces" (Howe 2015, 1). This is not to say that an analytical engagement with air can treat air in a vacuum; instead, it must suggest how lives and materialities in and of the air represent specific forms of human and nonhuman intertwining. To understand the life of airborne materials such as black carbon, we must pay attention to entities such as clouds floating above the Indian subcontinent, even as we question how clouds laden with black carbon transpire as smoke and penetrate bodily interiors.

Black carbon is a carbonaceous aerosol — a suspension of fine solid particles or liquid droplets within gas, like smoke and haze — and is produced both naturally and by human activities (C2ES 2010). In 2014, black carbon was judged to be one of the chief components in making Delhi the most polluted city in the world (WHO 2014). For the same reason, on September 29, 2015, three toddlers approached the Supreme Court of India through their parents to seek a ban on firecrackers during the Diwali festival (when their use is especially high), arguing that they were being forced to grow up in a polluted city. These incidents

DOI: 10.21983/P3.0265.1.12

show that the very perception of the city is being made through breathing in air. In other words, the air, and polluted air, more specifically, has become an intimate other in our quotidian lives, so much so that we can hold the state accountable if it fails to be hygienic for the human body. Timothy Morton (2013) uses Jean-Paul Sartre's notion of viscosity to explain this sort of a relationship: viscosity is what a hand feels when it plunges into a jar of honey. Viscosity is not indicative of a gesture that has been experienced in honey, but instead consists of the realization that we are already inside the honey. In the same way, we become alert to the viscosity of polluted air.

For humanistic and social scientific studies of air, a primary question has arisen: how are we to "render and assert air's materiality without resorting to tropes and analytics of solidity?" (Choy 2012, 1). Or, how are we to provide an analytics of air that does justice to its intimacy with us? Marshall McLuhan's (1964) dictum about medium and message reminds us that air can be viewed as a medium through which our social worlds are structured and defined. Taking the example of an electric light, McLuhan encourages us to recognize not the utility of electric light, but how light configures and guides activities. In the same vein, air's materiality can be grasped, literally and figuratively, by attending to its material manifestations, how it acts as a medium and is played out through other material fora. Since black carbon exists in an aerosol form, it endures as smoke or air, depending on how far it travels and how much of its presence is discovered in the atmosphere writ large. The proximate and yet fleeting nature of black carbon can be documented by paying attention to the mediums that allow for particular kinds of its material manifestations, as well as how other entities like clouds have evolved in conjunction with it.

In the early 2000s, as a result of the international Indian Ocean Experiment (INDOEX), it was deduced that black carbon has climate change effects. INDOEX's key discovery was a dark mass floating above the Indian subcontinent. This mass was significant, as it had a high composition of black carbon

(UNEP 2002; UNEP 2008). INDOEX scientists designated this discovery a cloud. In 2002, it was called the Asian Brown Cloud; by 2008, it had become the Atmospheric Brown Cloud. The discovery of the cloud established a nexus of confluence through the medium of black carbon; the cloud instantiated a vehicular form of pollution that settles itself deep in human lungs, smoke that emanates from cookstoves and blackens kitchen walls in rural households in India, impregnating the atmosphere of a region before potentially spreading across a continent. Here, a world is being constituted, such that the populations of the Indian subcontinent are presented as integral in the creation of a mode of living in polluted air. Cloud, smoke, and black carbon establish a nexus of cocreation that, in turn, produces people. If the Anthropocene marks a moment when *anthrōpos* became a geological force (Haraway 2015), then understanding the varied material mediums of black carbon — a cloud hovering above the Indian subcontinent, smoke from a household fire, or what is causing Delhi to choke on its own carbonaceous air — is a means of layering the iterative conditions of carbonized spaces.

References

Center for Climate and Energy Solutions (C2ES). 2010. "What Is Black Carbon?" http://www.c2es.org/document/what-is-black-carbon/.

Choy, Timothy. 2012. "Air's Substantiations." In *Lively Capital: Biotechnologies, Ethics, and Governance in Global Markets*, edited by Kaushik Sunder Rajan, 121–52. Durham: Duke University Press.

Haraway, Donna. 2015. "Anthropocene, Capitalocene, Plantationocene, Chthulucene: Making Kin." *Environmental Humanities* 6: 159–65. https://doi.org/10.1215/22011919-3615934.

Howe, Cymene. 2015. "Life Above Earth: An Introduction." *Cultural Anthropology* 30, no. 2: 203–9. https://doi.org/10.14506/ca30.2.03.

McLuhan, Marshall. 1964. *Understanding Media: The Extensions of Man.* Cambridge: MIT Press.

Morton, Timothy. 2013. *Hyperobjects: Philosophy and Ecology after the End of the World.* Minneapolis: University of Minnesota Press.

United Nations Environment Program (UNEP). 2002. "The Asian Brown Cloud: Climate and Other Environmental Impacts."

———. 2008. "Atmospheric Brown Clouds: Regional Assessment Report with Focus on Asia."

World Health Organization (WHO). 2014. Ambient (Outdoor) Air Pollution in Cities Database 2014. http://www.who.int/ phe/health_topics/outdoorair/databases/cities–2014/en/.

11

Conditions

Franz Krause

The Anthropocene, we are told, will usher in unprecedented changes. The climate, in particular, is changing in complex and uncertain ways, which has (and will have more) tangible consequences for how we do the things we have been accustomed to doing. We need a way to think and speak about the relations between a changing climate and our activities. Perhaps a Finnish word, *keli,* can guide us here, a word that we might roughly translate into English as "conditions."

There is a whole armada of climate scientists, equipped with an arsenal of ever more sophisticated measuring devices and increasingly intricate models and prediction algorithms to help us anticipate how climatic changes will unfold. The more advanced this science becomes, the more frustrated the scientists get in the face of the widespread ambivalence with which citizens and policymakers often greet their predictions. If it is so obvious that the climate is changing, then why do so few seem to be taking action?

It has been argued that one of the critical differences between climate science, on the one hand, and public perceptions of climate-related risks, on the other, is their level of reduction: the models and scenarios that the former produces are often of little relevance to the everyday projects and predicaments informing the latter. This is a contrast between the *climate* that

DOI: 10.21983/P3.0265.1.13

scientists know through records and the *weather* that people know through experience. Because of this incommensurability, scientific prediction often feels too abstract to mean anything for everyday life. And because experience is not expressed numerically, knowledge cannot travel from weather experience to climate models either, disappointing the hopes of those champions of knowledge integration who would like to use people's everyday observation for refining climate models.

This gap between climate knowledge and weather knowledge also bears political risks. Reductionist understandings of climate, as propagated by the authoritative voice of mainstream science and policy, can portray climate as the single most important determinant of the future, sidelining human ingenuity, creativity and imagination. The danger here is that climate knowledge fosters a new breed of environmental determinism with massive political leverage, whereby science frames the political universe and reduces human agency to mere adaptation.

If framing the problem as one of adaptation to climate change thus creates epistemological and political impasses, we might — in an Anthropocene yet unseen — be better off approaching it as a problem of conditions. Many of my Finnish interlocutors used the term *keli,* which has a richer range of meaning, as a shorthand to describe the conditions that enable a particular activity to be performed outdoors. Related to the word for movement, walking, and traveling (*kulkea*), *keli* simultaneously indexes the terrain, weather, and snow conditions that afford this movement.

In Finnish Lapland, people refer to such conditions in relation to a host of activities and projects. "Good" conditions might refer to snow that carries a skier or snowmobile, or to snow that is soft enough for reindeer to dig through and obtain food from the ground underneath. Such conditions, moreover, are not limited to the masculine activities of snowmobiling and reindeer herding. *Terassikeli* (literally, "terrace conditions") refers to conditions that allow people to have a drink sitting outside on the terrace. Most important in these appeals to conditions is the reference to a relation between a particular activity and the constitution of a world that enables or inhibits it. "Mushroom conditions" (*sienikeli*), for instance, is used not only to describe pleasant weather for walking through the forest and picking mushrooms, but also to refer to a recent increase in temperature after a wetter period. The conditions for mushrooming embrace past circumstances in which mushrooms were likely to grow alongside present circumstances for retrieving them.

People in Finnish Lapland also speak of "broken conditions" (*kelirikko*) to describe a world that does not allow particular activities. The period in spring when snow melts and the ground softens, causing erosion and covering roads with potholes and puddles, is widely known as "broken conditions time" (*kelirikkoaika*). The conditions for particular activities are thus expected during some parts of the year and not expected during others. Keli and kelirikko thus function as commentaries on the irregularities, trends, and extremes that might otherwise be subsumed under the blanket category of climate change.

Conditions, *keli*, subsume both ideas about the weather — situated experiences of temperature, precipitation, and the qualities of terrain — and a concept of climate, an abstracted schema of knowledge and expectations about these experiences. Like *weather*, conditions index lived experiences; like *climate*, they entail explicit comparisons and forecasts.

Conditions, in the sense of *keli*, also illustrate that climate change and social change are directly implicated, not in a causal relationship but in specific ways of experiencing and knowing the world. One older man told me that "bad conditions" (*huono keli*) are a fairly recent phenomenon; by this, he did not simply mean that there had been more unreliable snow conditions in recent winters or relatively wet and cool summers, but that the range of meaningful activities that people could undertake outdoors had diminished. In the past, every possible condition would be favorable for one activity or another. Now that some of those activities, like obsolete agricultural tasks, are no longer practiced, the applicable conditions have become *huono keli*.

Conditions, in short, occupy a middle ground between weather and climate, between experience and statistic, and may therefore be a good starting point for bridging this gap. Thinking the world in terms of conditions might help us to gauge and inhabit the Anthropocene, neither by folklorizing climate science nor by reducing weather experiences to data for models. Instead, understanding the world as variable, dynamic and — above all — relational would mean breaking up the fictive integrity of the Anthropocene and reasserting its multiple manifestations as conditions for forms of life.

12

Cosmos

Abou Farman

The supposed collapse of planetary and human processes into each other implies also the collapse of two fates: humanity and the earth, conjoined in their imagined futures. This merger has a history, enabled by the possibility of a cosmic point of view gazing back at our lonely planet floating in darkness. In their objectification of the so-called earth, the first planetary selfies said, "We are the planet, the planet is us."

The most famous such image, Big Blue Marble (NASA AS17–148–22727) (Reinert 2011), was taken from twenty-eight thousand miles away on December 7, 1972 by the crew of Apollo 17, the last moon mission. It made its way onto magazine covers and into advertisements. Four years earlier, NASA's inaugural manned lunar mission, Apollo 8, had taken the first earthrise picture, considered one of the most influential photographs ever. With advice from the U.S. Information Agency, Apollo 8 mobilized a Christian symbolic arsenal in the production of a live cosmic utopian theater. As they entered lunar orbit on Christmas Eve, the astronauts broadcast images of the earth and read from Genesis, the book of creation. Addressing "all the people back on Earth," William Anders started, "In the beginning God created the heaven and the earth," and Frank Borman ended with "And God called the dry land Earth; and the gather-

DOI: 10.21983/P3.0265.1.14

ing together of the waters called he Seas: and God saw that it was good" (see Poole 2008).

Stewart Brand and his popular counterculture publication, *The Whole Earth Catalog,* did more than anyone to spread some love for the planet.[1] Arguing that an image of the whole earth would unify people to overcome global problems, Brand led a campaign in 1966 demanding that NASA release its space mission images. A member of an experimental art collective, he designed a pin bearing the question: "Why haven't we seen a photograph of the whole earth yet?" Thereafter, his *Catalog* carried an earth image on each of its covers, while the pages in between provided resources to utopians who wanted to set up alternative ways of life.

In 1970, we the people celebrated our first official Earth Day, and two years later the United Nations organized its first Earth Summit.

From the outset, the cosmic point of view framed utopian visions of the good earth. In contrast to the mushroom cloud, that iconic image of planetary doom, humanity's dwelling place was projected as borderless, its differences appearing insignificant and its conflicts parochial. The whole earth was Kodachromed a well-oxygenated blue where life could flourish in the face of what the authors of *Limits to Growth* (Meadows et al. 1972) called the human "cancer" eating it.

The planetary selfie repositioned the earth center stage, countering the post-Copernican metaphysics of the globe — at least until Voyager 1 zoomed out the cosmic point of view nine hundred million miles, transforming the Big Blue Marble into a Pale Blue Dot. Carl Sagan of Cosmos fame, who was on Voyager's imaging team and clearly aware of the Pascalian terror of cosmic insignificance in the disenchanted universe, restabilized human dwelling through an existentialist stance against meaninglessness. From the imperial perch of NASA, Sagan (1997, 7) exposed what he saw as our imagined self-importance and underscored "our responsibility to deal more kindly with one

---

1   See also The Overview Institute, http://www.overviewinstitute.org/.

another, and to preserve and cherish the pale blue dot, the only home we've ever known."

This recentering project took its most blatant ideological turn when, on Earth Day 2014, NASA urged earthlings to step outside to take a selfie. Cushioning some of that cosmic loneliness, the agency then tiled thirty-six thousand of the submitted images into a mosaic that looked very much like the earth, literally conjoining people and planet in a world-image. NASA explained that "the project was designed to encourage environmental awareness and recognize the agency's ongoing work to protect our home planet" (JPL 2014).

Needless to say, the planet needs protection from the species (or the countries, and the people) that call it home. After that first moment of self-objectification, which twinned the fate of people and planet in a unified blue utopia, we came to see the earth as damaged and sick because of us, each cloud formation the harbinger of a potential tsunami, the biosphere choking Earth and humanity in an apocalyptic embrace.

The concept of the Anthropocene posits humans simultaneously as powerful agents of climate change and as utterly powerless to roll back its effects. This evokes longstanding technological anxieties about limits and limitlessness, autonomy and control: it is a particular version of the Golem, of Frankenstein, the nuclear bomb, the singularity. The more power we gain, the less control we feel we have over the consequences of that power. Parallel to this runs the secular tension of a cosmic ego toggling between overinflated selfiehood and existential insignificance on a lonely planet in some remote corner of a cold and empty universe.

Emptied of life and meaning throughout modernity, the cosmos, rather than the earth, is now infused with hope again; culture has turned cosmic (see Valentine 2012; Battaglia 2014). NASA engineer and scientist Mark Lupisella (2010) has introduced the term *cosmoculture,* exploring the potential of a conscious, anthropogenic universe as human culture seeps out. Today, you can send your selfie into outer space aboard the 2016 LightSail mission, the world's first citizen-funded solar sail adventure. In a contest called Message to the Milky Way, Diamond Sky Productions — owned by NASA imager Carolyn Porco, who worked alongside Sagan as well as Hollywood directors — is collecting pictures and songs to transmit to outer space via the Arecibo Radio Telescope in Puerto Rico. "This," the Diamond Sky website explains, "will be a lonely yet hopeful, long distance call from humans to their fellow galactic citizens in which we announce our presence and describe us and our home planet" (n.d.).

Before those unsuspecting citizens know it, some expatriate part of humanity will become the dominant force shaping and destroying not just planetary but cosmic life, and from that perspective the Anthropocene will appear like a parochial disaster on a pale little dot.

Acknowledgments

I thank William Scarlett for help gathering images, and Blair Bainbridge for additional research.

References

Battaglia, Debbora. 2014. "Cosmos as Commons: An Activation of Cosmic Diplomacy." *e-flux* 58. https://www.e-flux.com/journal/58/61180/cosmos-as-commons-an-activation-of-cosmic-diplomacy/.

Diamond Sky Productions. n.d. "The Day The Earth Smiled." http://diamondskyproductions.com/recent/index.php#mmw.

NASA Jet Propulsion Laboratory (JPL). 2014. "NASA Releases Earth Day 'Global Selfie' Mosaic." May 22. https://www.jpl.nasa.gov/news/news.php?release=2014-161.

Lupisella, Mark L. 2010. "Cosmocultural Evolution: The Coevolution of Culture and Cosmos and the Creation of Cosmic Value." In *Cosmos and Culture: Cultural Evolution in a Cosmic Context,* edited by Steven J. Dick and Mark L.

Lupisella, 321–59. Washington, D.C.: National Aeronautics and Space Administration.

Meadows, Donella H., Dennis L. Meadows, Jørgen Randers, and William H. Behrens, III. 1972. *The Limits of Growth.* New York: New American Library.

Poole, Robert. 2008. *Earthrise: How Man First Saw the Earth.* New Haven: Yale University Press.

Reinert, Al. 2011. "The Blue Marble Shot: Our First Complete Photograph of Earth." *The Atlantic.* April 12. https://www.theatlantic.com/technology/archive/2011/04/the-blue-marble-shot-our-first-complete-photograph-of-earth/237167/.

Valentine, David. 2012. "Exit Strategy: Profit, Cosmology, and the Future of Humans in Space." *Anthropological Quarterly* 85, no. 4: 1045–67. https://doi.org/10.1353/anq.2012.0073.

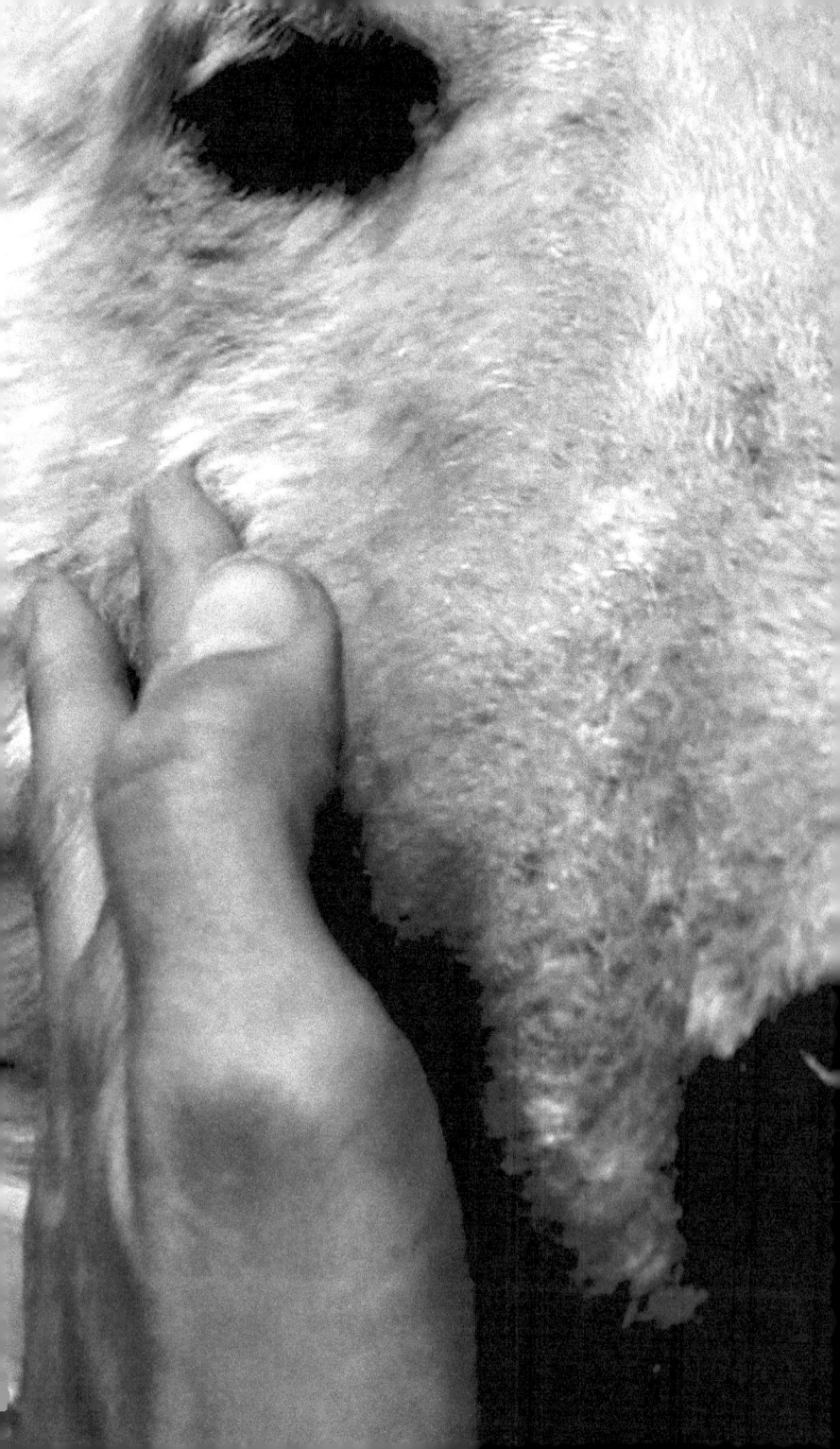

13

Death

Maria Whiteman

My artwork deals with nature. It participates in an interroga-
tion of the solidity and certainty of our assumptions about what
we call nature — normative judgments which have very real effects on the nonhuman life around us, whether in our decisions
about what forms of life are killable but not murderable, or in
our reshaping of landscapes by transportation networks, flows
of international capital, and resource extraction. I am interested
in revealing these aspects of nature and our shaping of it, but I
am also interested in an expression of nature that is not reduc-
ible to what we have made of it. In other words, I try to confront
the viewer with the difference between what we have made of
nature — in our scientific practices, in our curatorial protocols
of natural history, and sometimes in our brazen domination of
it — and what in nature persists beyond our attempts to rule
over and domesticate it: a sense of its strangeness, uniqueness,
beauty, durability, and complexity.

The *Touching* project, featured in several shows over the past
five years in the United States and Canada, was a turning point
for me. My focus shifted from straightforward photography to
video and performance art, which resulted in a series of thirty
short videos at the Natural History Museum in Edmonton, Alberta. I touched and caressed every animal held in storage there,
whether it was hidden under plastic sheets, hung on hooks,

DOI: 10.21983/P3.0265.1.15

stored in boxes, or covered in blankets. Dead animals surrounded me, frozen in time with deliberate gestures that suggested
either prey or predator. The entire space took on a theatricality,
an eeriness and a sense of dislocation since I was the only living
subject. *Touching* aims to evoke a complex ecology of emotions
about animals — not least of which are empathy and mourning.
In this project, I was interested not just in the gap or absence
of a connection between human and animal life that results
in dead animals occupying a storeroom — all in the name of a
greater knowledge of nature — but more importantly in what
produces empathy, mourning, and a sense of loss in relation to
nonhuman life.

Empathy and mourning are products of the complex temporality produced by the uncanny relationship between co-
presence and absence. Our own ephemerality and that of the
animal comes together briefly, but fleetingly and incompletely.
The animal bodies in these images will outlast our own, and yet
we know nothing about them other than their brute physicality as objects, which serves as a kind of beguiling doorway into
another reality. When did they live? Where did they live? Will
others like them continue to live in our climatologically damaged times? How did they come to inhabit this deadness? The
taxidermy is no longer the animal but a reflection of a representation of something that once was: the life of a sentient being
that I will never encounter, except through its surreal objectivity stored in the room with hundreds of gelid eyes, the smell of
dust, and ghostly shapes behind plastic sheets. I am lost in all
the deadness that surrounds me.

In the videos, the sense of disavowal between the animals'
death and my own impending mortality is clearly visible. The
only realness I could feel was that something remained alive insofar as I felt the urge to ask these questions, to reach out and
touch the fur that belonged to the living animal and was some-
how, strangely, still here. Can I only think the animal in its death
and captivity, in its nonpresence? Or can I touch the animal differently, empathetically? Can I mourn not for the dead body

or the specimen, but for a nonhuman life that was living and breathing much like myself? A larger question about this work thus arises not from each animal's death but from the collective and entire death of all of these animals, an extinction of all these specimens. And, from there: not their extinction, but ours.

To put it another way, there is no single ecology. The necessity of expanding our worlds ecologically is allowing an opening to other life that shares a common world. *Touching* aims to further press for a rethinking of what ecology is, what ecological existence is, and how those questions often manifest themselves unevenly in local environments. As the history of contemporary ecological art shows, artists have a special role to play in conversations about our shared ecological future. As I am touching the polar bear, it occurs to me that the ecological relation is gone and removed, left with only a gesture of itself.

What if times like the Anthropocene encourage us to reimagine the idea of ecology? Recent work in the humanities and social sciences has argued that nature, in the fundamental sense of a realm apart from human life, has come to an end, and that truly ecological thinking in the contemporary moment must confront the complexity with which human and nonhuman life forms, worlds, and landscapes are interwoven. How does one think about what is next when every moment of our own existence is being recorded as a type of temporal and geological countdown? We continue to visit natural history museums to learn about other species so as to be reminded of an ecological relationship in which every sentient being plays a part.

14

Dispossession

Paige West

We sit on the veranda of a house on the outskirts of Goroka, Papua New Guinea (PNG), while two international oil company representatives describe the benefits that will flow to environmental conservation organizations in PNG once the biodiversity offset program associated with the huge oil and natural gas pipeline that their company is building comes online. Biodiversity offset funds are monies put into trust by resource extraction companies to offset the damage to plants, animals, and ecological processes caused by their projects. Companies must create these funds to secure global financing for their projects. Once created, the funds pay for environmental conservation and restoration efforts. The two representatives have come to PNG to determine who should be given management responsibilities for this project's offset fund, which, depending on the revenue the project generates, could be in excess of $100 million. Because of the interest this amount would earn, it would serve to fund the managing organization for many years to come. Our visitors are accompanied by four employees of an international conservation organization with offices in thirty countries and hundreds of projects all over the world; it is an organization vying to gain management of this fund.

Our meeting takes place at the office of the Papua New Guinea Institute of Biological Research (PNGIBR), a small organiza-

DOI: 10.21983/P3.0265.1.16

tion dedicated to providing opportunities for young people from PNG who want to become environmental conservation experts. One of its founding principles is that the conservation of biological diversity in PNG can only be achieved if Papua New Guineans have full sovereignty over it, and that this sovereignty has been slowly stripped away by big international organizations. PNGIBR fosters the growth of national science and focuses on creating and managing small-scale conservation projects co-founded by scholars from PNG and the indigenous peoples on whose lands these projects are carried out.

Over the course of the afternoon, PNGIBR staff are asked how, if given the opportunity to manage the fund, they would use it to conserve biodiversity. Their answers are complex and draw from the staff's collective seventy-five years of experience working in PNG. The answers are met with the following comments from the international conservation workers:

> Papua New Guinea does not have the internal capacity to manage and administer a fund of this size. [...] People in Papua New Guinea live in pre-capitalist societies [and] do not understand money and have a cargo cult mentality. [...] Handling this much money would just disrupt society. [...] Most well-educated people in Papua New Guinea who work for the government or for most of the organizations that do deal with large amounts of money are corrupt. [...] National management of this fund would be a disaster. (West 2016, 69)

In the hours that follow we witness the deployment of other representational rhetorics by the international conservation organization's staff. These attempts to persuade and motivate the oil company are an excellent example of the ideological work that underpins dispossession in the Anthropocene.

Historically, when we thought of dispossession, we often thought of a process by which someone is stripped of possession of a material object or state of being through the loss of land, labor, life, or natural resources. We know that Karl Marx (1977) wrote about this process in the first volume of *Capital* using the term *primitive accumulation,* and that in *The Accumulation of Capital,* Rosa Luxemburg (2003) corrected Marx's sense of this process by showing us that for capitalism to thrive, it needs a constant source from which to draw or dispossess. This understanding lies at the heart of classical anthropological inquiry into environmental issues. And yet, today, things are more complicated than this.

Now, environmental dispossession needs to be theorized in terms of the representational rhetorics that underlie it *as well as* in terms of its material aspects. Dispossession is material and ongoing and in the Anthropocene, it is increasingly intertwined with discursive and semiotic practices, resulting in turtles all the way down. Here is how.

First, the ecological conditions that have given rise to the state of the planet today have been generated, in large part, by fossil fuel production and consumption. The oil company in question is also at the epicenter of a series of well-founded revelations regarding the corporation's knowledge about the links between fossil fuel use and climate change dating from the 1970s. These documents further reveal a systematic effort to fuel climate-change-denial science and policy.

Second, international conservation organizations have worked to wrest control of the management of biological diversity in PNG since structural adjustment programs in the 1990s hollowed out funding for the various national institutions with that mandate after decolonization in 1975. The organizations have done this with top-down, nonconsultative conservation projects. With the bid for the biodiversity offset fund described above, they were attempting to do this economically by using financial resources acquired from the oil and gas patrimony of PNG to fund their organization.

Finally, the discursive devices used by conservation organization employees are an act of rhetorical dispossession and deprivation of representational sovereignty. They cast people from

PNG as lacking, as incapable, and as living in a prior state, unable to manage anything.

After this meeting, in an acknowledgment that international NGO management of the fund would be tantamount to depriving PNG of its natural sovereignty, a member of the PNG parliament spoke to PNGIBR and two other organizations, ultimately pressing the oil company to either manage the fund itself or contract a national organization. In the end, the oil company created its own national management team, which manages the fund today. How, exactly, the funds will be used is yet to be determined.

What is clear is that Anthropocene dispossessions confound the relationship between resource acquisition (like oil extraction) and the management of its consequences (like biodiversity conservation). Equally apparent is that these processes are scalar in reach, predicated on massive environmental disruptions and infinitesimal semiotic gestures, each of which may work to erode sovereignty. The accretions of dispossession do, indeed, go all the way down.

References

Luxemburg, Rosa. 2003. *The Accumulation of Capital.* Translated by Agnes Schwarzschild. New York: Routledge. Originally published in 1913.

Marx, Karl. 1977. *Capital,* Volume One. Translated by Ben Fowkes. New York: Random House. Originally published in 1867.

West, Paige. 2016. *Dispossession and the Environment: Rhetoric and Inequality in Papua New Guinea.* New York: Columbia University Press.

15

Distribution

Timothy Choy

Distribution in an atmospheric key begins from a reckoning with how things lift off, move, or settle: tracking agitations, suspensions, and sedimentations; following condensations when enough of something collects around a speck to precipitate; and, noting how microsubstances attach to, become, or catalyze something else. In the middles of air's substantiations (Choy 2011, 139–68), distribution presses the question of how atmospheric things disperse and accumulate in unequal concentrations.

Substantiation — a long, slow word. I love its sibilance and stop; it folds you into the bumps and drags of coming to matter. In that pleat, distribution, too, is both stop and drawn-out hiss; a long exposure or snapshot; a map of reds, yellows, and blues; or a fractionating gas column breaking a mixture into chemical parts. Distribution is at once a moment — a present condition — and an ongoing happening, a conditioning of atmospheric differences.

Put another way, distribution, pressed against atmosphere, amplifies and gathers questions of how things are arranged, the frequency of their occurrence throughout a unit of space or time. Distribution flags the problem of accounting for differential concentrations and relative densities. These questions of arrangement hint at the form for questions about atmosphere's

DOI: 10.21983/P3.0265.1.17

politics: questions about of what conditions the variant com-
positions of this medium. Conditions of suspension (Choy and
Zee 2015) and conditions of distribution.

Distribution is a trigger word for an atmospheric conspiracy,
a commitment to breathing together from and in an unequally
shared milieu, an unevenly constituted planetary medium for
respiration where concentrations of well- and unwell-being
accumulate, sometimes quickly and sometimes slowly. *Con +
spirare.* "Conspirators huddle together," writes Larry Bogad
(n.d.), "quietly and cautiously sharing the intimacies of breath
and ideas." Thinking conspiracy literally, what political forms
might transpire from an assembly caught in and metabolically
dependent upon an atmospheric uncommons?[1] The political
problem of reckoning with being together, with the possibilities
and impossibilities of *breathing with* in late industrial, racializ-
ing, engineered worlds, might be posed thus: what is conditioning the differential distribution of the difficulties or impossibilities of breath for particular forms of life? It is hard to breathe in
many places — in some places more than others, for some bodies more than others. What would it take, what would it mean,
what would it do, to face the conditions of distribution where I
inhale the cough or choke of another?

I have many guides in this. Among them: #ICantBreathe; Michelle Murphy (2013) on distributed reproduction and chemical
infrastructures along the St. Clair River; Jerry Zee (2015) on the
political conditioning of saltating sands in the Tengger Desert;
Alison Kenner (2013a, 2013b) on divergent embodiments of
asthma and breath; Nicholas Shapiro (2014) on the grey-market
dispersal of formaldehyde off-gassing FEMA trailers in the wake
of Katrina; Kim Fortun (2012, 2014) on the uneven present of
late industrialism; Joseph Masco (2015) on the fallout of engi-

---

1   I poach here from conversations with Marisol de la Cadena on the ecopo-
    litical uncommons. For de la Cadena (2015, 2018), "the 'uncommons' is a
    response that wants to join, rather than detract from, the possibility of life
    as and in a 'commons,' yet it is also mindful of what exceeds modern poli-
    tics." She terms this excess the "Anthropo-not-seen."

neered worlds; Deborah Cowen (2010) on shipping and logistics as economic form in global supply chains.

Most palpably, I learn from Stefanie Graeter's (2015, 2018) ethnography of the possibilities and impossibilities of a politics of lead in the face of a brutal state-corporate extraction machinery in Peru. Graeter tracks not only lead's figurations among residents, activists, and scientists, but also the metal's movements: its distribution into and accumulation in bloodstreams and bodies and its shipment in pulverized form on tarp-covered trucks. Lead is heavy, Graeter reminds us, but as powder it kicks up easily. Workers water the dust to tame it, but it dries quickly. Lead-laden trucks stop on a street in a town named Frigorífico. While its neighboring town, the notoriously contaminated Puerto Nuevo, has garnered enough media and political support to stop trucks from passing through, Frigorífico has not. So trucks stop there. Dusts blow, and robbers lift the tarps of stopped trucks or pry open hard tops to stuff handfuls of lead into sacks. This theft is another moment of distribution, conditioned as much by low pay for mine work as by the absence of other employment. The powder reanimates, redistributed in sackfuls, inhaled in lungfuls, coating the hands and faces of robbers and the children they hire. With Graeter's help, we grapple with lead's distribution through its tendencies in molten and pulverized form, but — crucially as well — along its shipment on the bumpy road from smelter to port, through the decision to pass through one town to avoid another, and with the bodies who are at once a new vector for distribution and surface of deposit.

Distribution asks after conditions. Questions of condition include questions of medium, state, and form, as well as the hardening circuits and thickening conjunctures where elements and effects move one way rather than another, concentrate here rather than there. Distribution, then, is a reminder to hold together the capacities of a substance — its properties, its tendencies to spread or to hold — with the conditions and conditioning of its uneven manifestation and movement. It is a reminder that atmospheres do not equalize, and that breathing together rarely means breathing the same. And moreover, it is a way of positing other conspiracies, where the distribution of harms and hopes in a shared medium may draw us together otherwise.

References

Bogad, Larry. n.d. "Conspire." http://www.lmbogad.com/links.

Choy, Timothy. 2011. *Ecologies of Comparison: An Ethnography of Endangerment in Hong Kong.* Durham: Duke University Press.

———, and Jerry Zee. 2015. "Condition — Suspension." *Cultural Anthropology* 30, no. 2: 210–23. https://doi.org/10.14506/ca30.2.04.

Cowen, Deborah. 2010. "A Geography of Logistics: Market Authority and the Security of Supply Chains." *Annals of the Association of American Geographers* 100, no. 3: 600–620. https://doi.org/10.1080/00045601003794908.

de la Cadena, Marisol. 2015. "Uncommoning Nature." *e-flux* 65 SUPERCOMMUNITY. May–August 2015. http://supercommunity.e-flux.com/texts/uncommoning-nature/

———. 2018. "Uncommons." Theorizing the Contemporary, *Cultural Anthropology,* March 29. https://culanth.org/fieldsights/1352-uncommons

Fortun, Kim. 2012. "Ethnography in Late Industrialism." *Cultural Anthropology* 27, no. 3: 446–64. https://doi.org/10.1111/j.1548-1360.2012.01153.x.

———. 2014. "From Latour to Late Industrialism." *Hau: Journal of Ethnographic Theory* 4, no. 1: 309–29. https://doi.org/10.14318/hau4.1.017.

Graeter, Stefanie. 2015. "Mineral Incorporations: Lead Science, Ethics, and Politics in Central Peru." PhD dissertation, University of California, Davis.

———. 2018. "Infrastructural Incorporations: Toxic Storage, Corporate Indemnity, and Ethical Deferral in Peru's Neo-extractive Era." Article manuscript.

Kenner, Ali. 2013a. "The Healthy Asthmatic." *M/C Journal* 16, no. 6. http://www.journal.media-culture.org.au/index.php/mcjournal/article/view/745.

———. 2013b. "Invisibilities: Provocation." In "Invisibilities," Field Notes series edited by William Girard, *Cultural Anthropology*, June 15. https://culanth.org/fieldsights/342-invisibilities-provocation.

Masco, Joseph. 2015. "The Age of Fallout." *History of the Present* 5, no. 2: 137–68. http://doi.org/10.5406/historypresent.5.2.0137.

Murphy, Michelle. 2013. "Distributed Reproduction, Chemical Violence, and Latency." *Scholar & Feminist Online* 11, no. 3. http://sfonline.barnard.edu/life-un-ltd-feminism-bioscience-race/distributed-reproduction-chemical-violence-and-latency/.

Shapiro, Nicholas E. 2014. "Spaces of Uneventful Disaster: Tracking Emergency Housing and Domestic Chemical Exposures from New Orleans to National Crises." PhD dissertation, University of Oxford.

Zee, Jerry. 2015. "States of the Wind: Dust Storms and a Political Meteorology of Contemporary China." PhD dissertation, University of California, Berkeley.

16

Dog

Ann Marie Thornburg

I saw a dog out of the corner of my eye. Familiar peripheries ran along the highway leading out of a Midwestern suburb and toward the freeway: strips of browning grass, the fogged windows of the tropical fish store, side streets emptying into driveways. I was driving and so could not linger. A dog, alone and unleashed, loping along near the road can be an occasion, but for what? Unleashed dogs are ubiquitous the world over, but in these Midwestern suburbs and throughout much of the global North, they are not. Here dogs must be leashed, collared, and moving in tandem with humans. When the light cycled green, I drove on, though there were other options: panic, follow, help, even save. My surprise at seeing a dog running alone along a road leading out of town suggests something about how I expect to see dogs: on a leash or behind a fence.

When expected modes of human–dog relation appear askance, the dog as both trope and presence reminds us of the myriad life forms that go on living in the Anthropocene, whether we notice or not. Although Icarus falls from the sky in W.H. Auden's (1991, 179) poem "Musée des Beaux Arts," "the dreadful martyrdom must / run its course / Anyhow in a corner, some untidy spot / Where the dogs go on with their doggy life." Transposed into the key of Anthropocene thinking, this observation recalls the many trajectories unfolding alongside species extinction and their ensuing salvation and recovery projects. As these projects hum on, a pet dog in Indiana is taking another walk around the block, a free-ranging dog is nosing through garbage on the outskirts of Mexico City, a street dog is asleep outside a shop in Ankara, and a Bali dog is moving through a rice field in Karangasem.

Humans are fond of noting that dogs are marked by a plural process of domestication. Dogs' ancestors first moved toward human settlements, watching, listening, and smelling; approaching and retreating; changing. Through these movements, they entered the commensal pathway of domestication's still ongoing process. Dogs-in-domestication then entered the directed pathway of domestication through humans' "deliberate" guidance (Zeder 2012, 176). Food, gestures, weather, trash, and sounds also populate the between of sociality that brings dogs and humans into shifting modes of relation (Hartigan 2014). Today dogs, like the *anthrōpos* that names our epoch, are everywhere. Indeed, the term *Anthropocene* denotes an epoch marked by the spread of human-mediated changes to environments and their inhabitants.

Yet the Anthropocene is also an open question, both challenge and provocation. It is a space in which to identify the fragile and fading, but also the persistent. Given their ubiquity, dogs fit best into the latter category. The dog is not merely the degraded sidekick of the human destroyer, nor is it only another vehicle for humans' ultimate delivery of the cataclysm of the Anthropocene. Dogs, which emerged multiply along with humans and are abundant in this epoch, demand our attention now.

Being abundant in the Anthropocene means inhabiting contradictory roles and being subjected to multiple regimes of terminological organization. At Colola Beach in Mexico, village dogs eat endangered sea-turtle hatchlings (Ruiz-Izaguirre et al. 2014). Here, village dogs' abundance and mobility contrast with the hatchings' scarcity and fragile emplacement. In Bali, Indonesia, some residents are invested in preserving the "Bali dog" as a distinct type of indigenous dog worthy not only of salvation but also cultivation. And in the United States, great numbers of shelter dogs languish on the margins of anthropogenic land-scapes. Vulnerable yet plentiful, they are out of place because there is not a yet human-designated space for them. Humans sometimes organize dogs by applying modifiers to the word "dog" that indicate proximities to humans' and dogs' mobile emplacements: pet, village, stray, street, free-ranging, ranging, roaming, feral, and even wild. The word *feral,* for example, sug-gests movement away from the human in anthropogenic envi-ronments, though feral remains always already marked by the domestic.

But thinking otherwise with dogs in the Anthropocene means acknowledging that *feral* and *domestic* are not static states, but instead processes that can overlap. The peculiarity of dog-being resides in this betweenness, which resists partial cat-egorizations like domestic, feral, and wild. It is this vexing and sometimes surprisingly friendly betweenness that characterizes so much activity, and so much life, in the Anthropocene. A dog can be a companion with whom to live and a ghost haunting the margins of anthropogenic zones. Dogs track with shifting no-tions of nature and an emergent naturalness, and are marked by the challenges and contradictions of our time.

The Anthropocene expands and contracts in relation to humans' discomfort with the vagueness of its multiscalar, all-encompassing, and accelerating activity, as many entries in this lexicon demonstrate. As Zoe Todd's entry reminds us, many In-digenous peoples have been living in its violent specificity for hundreds of years. While this term moves up and out, we have a lingering sense of remaining in the thick of something, with others. Dogs are on the ground in this epoch. For Donna Har-away (2003, 16), dogs are companion species with whom "co-constitution, finitude, impurity, historicity, and complexity are what is" — and what will be. Bénédicte Boisseron (2018, 106–7) writes that "in commensal relationships, one species gives, or rather lets the other take, without expecting to benefit from the transaction" and views commensalism, evident in some human–dog relationships, "as a human-to-animal and human-to-human relationship that carries an anticolonial, antihegemonic, and anti-anthropocentric resonance."

Whether dogs cross our paths at a distance or walk our neighborhoods at our sides, they too live in the expanding between-spaces of anthropogenic landscapes. They remain beyond our total control, no matter how carefully we name them nor how tirelessly we organize them. This is what makes the dog an instructive figure for the Anthropocene. We feel catastrophe moving in; we busy ourselves sealing off the margins of our landscapes. Yet there, moving along a periphery that was never really so marginal, is another dog.

References

Auden, W.H. 1991. "Musée des Beaux Arts." In *Collected Poems,* 179. New York: Vintage. Originally published in 1939.

Boisseron, Bénédicte. 2018. *Afro-Dog: Blackness and the Animal Question.* New York: Columbia University Press.

Haraway, Donna. 2003. *The Companion Species Manifesto: Dogs, Humans, and Significant Otherness.* Chicago: Prickly Paradigm Press.

Hartigan, John. 2014. *Aesop's Anthropology: A Multispecies Approach.* Minneapolis: University of Minnesota Press.

Ruiz-Izaguirre, E., A. van Woersem, K.(C.)H.A.M. Eilers, S.E. van Wieren, G. Bosch, A.J. van der Zijpp, and I.J.M. de Boer. 2014. "Roaming Characteristics and Feeding Practices of Village Dogs Scavenging Sea-Turtle Nests." *Animal Conservation* 18, no. 2: 146–56. https://doi.org/10.1111/acv.12143.

Zeder, Melinda A. 2012. "The Domestication of Animals." *Journal of Anthropological Research* 68, no. 2: 161–90. https://doi.org/10.3998/jar.0521004.0068.201.

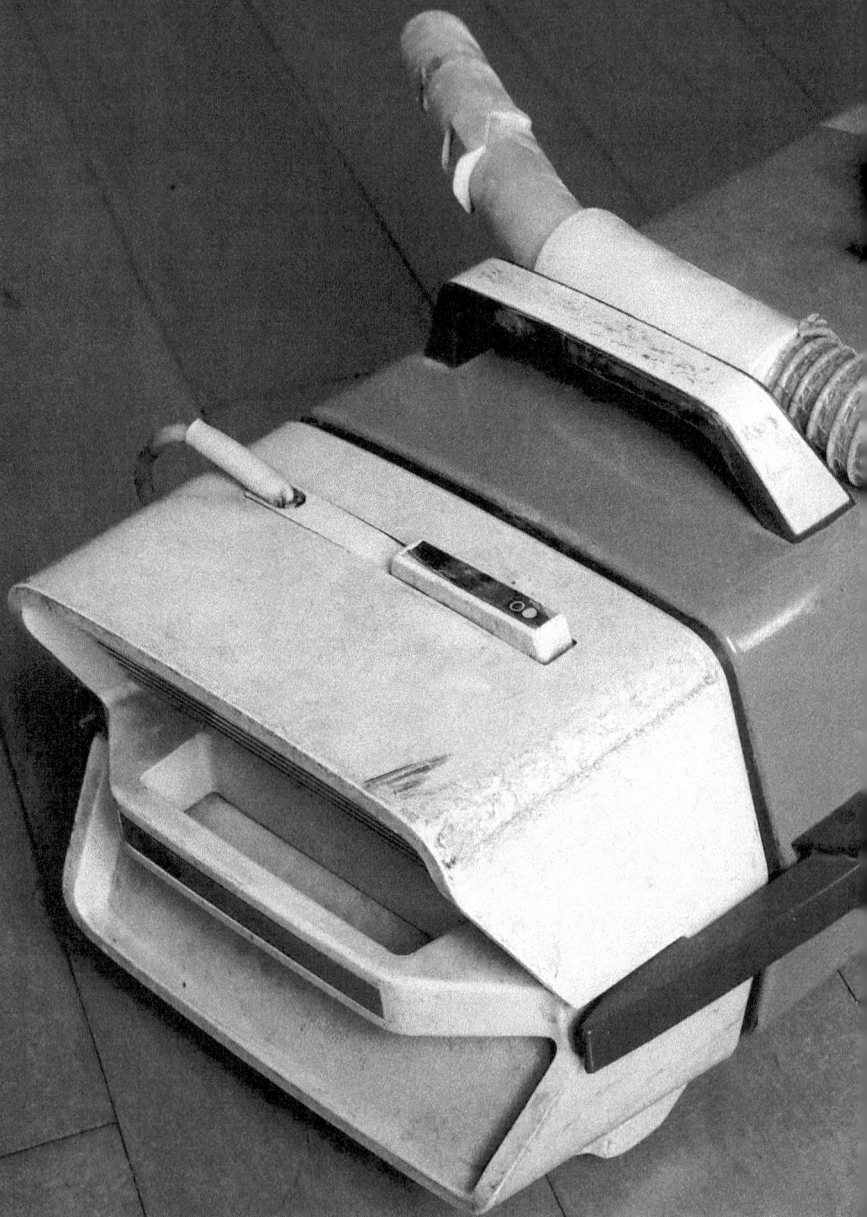

17

Dream

Timothy Morton

The mode in which we humans talk to ourselves about ecology is largely taken for granted, like an old, reliable vacuum cleaner. And, like one of those old vacuum cleaners, it makes a horrible noise. The noise is the sound of data being dumped all over us. Forty! One hundred thousand! Two degrees Celsius! Fifty percent! Forget being a denier; anyone with a pulse must admit that this is a horrible mode to be stuck in. Our putatively cultural modes are no better: "It's not warming, it's dying!" Or else, "we're fucked!"

(I am putting these in quotation marks because they are, in fact, quotations. You know who you are.)

What is this nasty noise telling us? I suggest it is saying that to no extent have we actually started to live the data. To live the data, you need not only to be able to act and to think, but also to hesitate, contemplate, muse, puzzle, scribble, doodle, read. To dream. We need to start dreaming. This all sounds very counterintuitive in an age of ecological emergency. But it might be exactly right, even politically expedient, in an era of neoliberal shock doctrines in which the injunction to get off our backsides and work now penetrates all areas of our lives from primary school to Candy Crush. And this doctrine is just version 7.0 of the agricultural logistics that has been running in the background for over twelve thousand years (Morton 2014). A

DOI: 10.21983/P3.0265.1.19

logistics that has, by now, successfully wiped out fifty percent of actually existing animals and is doing a fantastic job of making Earth uninhabitable for currently existing lifeforms — making Earth uninhabitable in the name of survival.

So we have this mode of constant machination, not unlike Dory in *Finding Nemo*. *Just keep swimming, just keep swimming* (and damn the torpedoes). We have a mode of reacting to this machination, not unlike the scream of Macaulay Culkin in *Home Alone,* the hands pressed firmly to the ears, eyes wide open, rubbernecking the horror. We are, in other words, juddering along the same old path, at least in terms of our attitude. Horror might be more welcome than guilt or shame, let alone ignoring things altogether. But being stuck in horror mode isn't going to help anyone.

I take what has been said and written here (at the AAA's annual meeting and in this series) to be a powerful sign that humanities scholars are finally figuring out how to care about the fact that we coexist with other lifeforms on a large, but finite planet, that *we are the biosphere* in a sense much more complex and charged than the idea that we are the world. Right at the point at which continued carbon business as usual will result in a catastrophic temperature rise by 2100, we have started to dream. To fantasize. Ecological data beats you down so that you are unable to move. We desperately need some wiggle room.

Have a nice dream.

Reference

Morton, Timothy. 2014. "Journey to the Center of the Ecological Chocolate (Anatomy of Ecological Awareness) (MP3)." *Ecology without Nature.* July 6. https://ecologywithoutnature.blogspot.com/2014/07/journey-to-center-of-ecological.html.

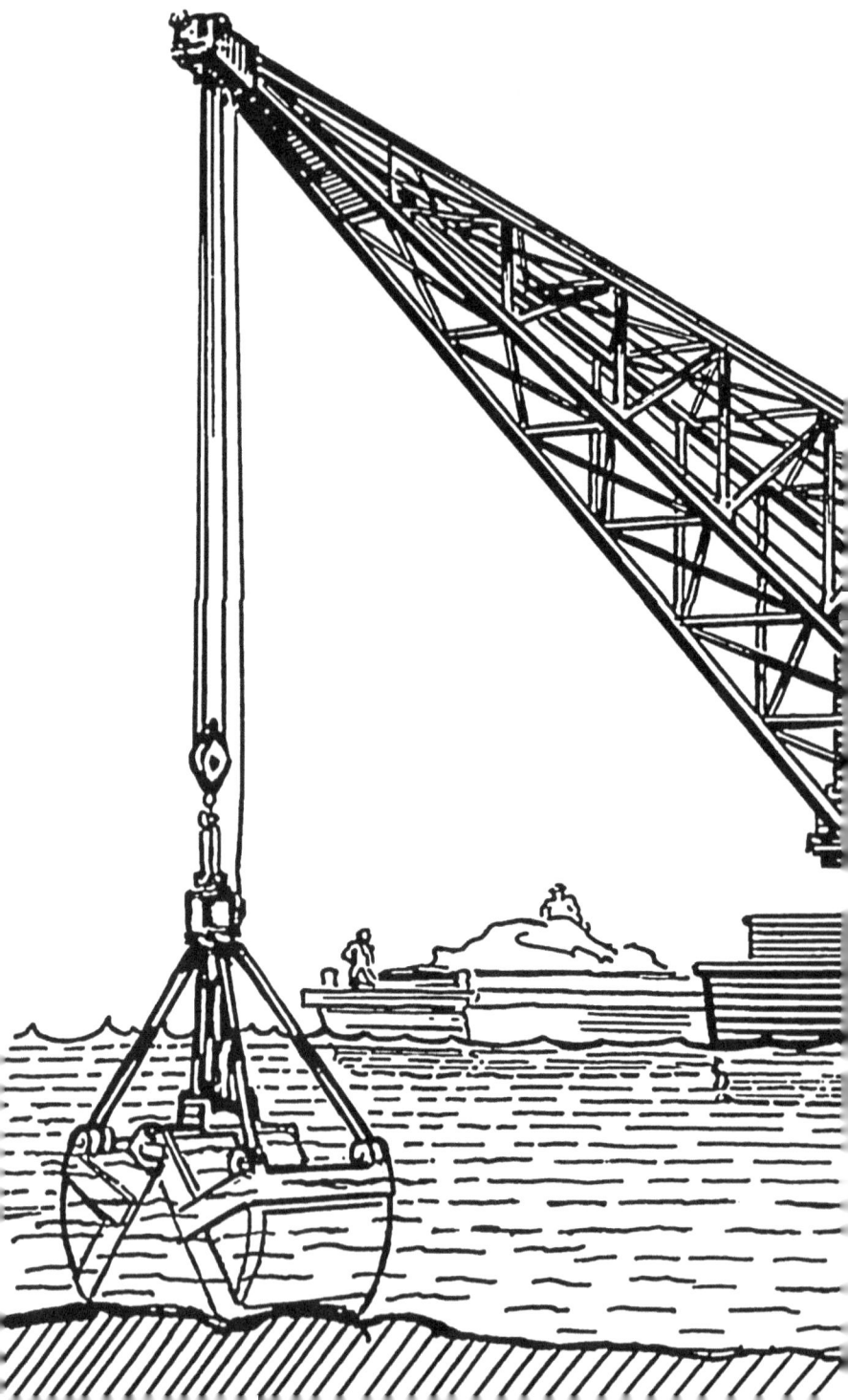

18

Dredge

Ashley Carse

No object distills an era, but it would be hard to beat the inter-
modal shipping container to make sense of the past half-century
of economic globalization. By linking shipping, rail, and truck-
ing networks, the container has been central to developments
in logistics that have dramatically reduced the cost of moving
goods over great distances (Levinson 2006; Cowen 2014). There
is, to date, no environmental history of the so-called container
revolution, but one might reasonably extend the well-known
story summarized above to argue that this humble connective
technology lubricated the operation and expansion of the vast
sociotechnical infrastructure that formatted the Anthropocene — well before we knew it as such. Indeed, it is difficult to
imagine a post–1950 Great Acceleration (Hibbard et al. 2006)
marked by rapid population growth, expanding consumption,
and urbanization apart from the economic geographies of the
container.

Inspired by the call to see the Anthropocene otherwise, I
propose an alternative (or, perhaps, companion) object to the
container. *Dredge*: a verb meaning underwater excavation and
a noun referring to technologies that bring submerged material
to the surface. The dredge is ancient. A simple version, the hand
drag, has been used to facilitate navigation and irrigation since
at least the thirteenth century BCE (Vanderostyne and Cohen

1999). Today's dredging is mechanized and industrial in scale. Professionals operate equipment that scoops, drags, and vacuums up underwater sediment, which is transported by truck, barge, pipeline, and conveyor belt to other sites for disposal, use, and sale. Dredging falls into several categories. Capital dredging excavates harbors and waterways to new depths for navigation and flood control. Maintenance dredging preserves those artificial depths in the face of constant sedimentation. People also dredge to gather material for land reclamation, construction, and beach replenishment (mitigating the effects of erosion); harvest commodities that range from minerals to oysters; and remove trash or environmentally contaminated sediment.

If the container's ascendance highlighted the modernist dream of smooth commercial flow across technological, political, and social boundaries, the dredge reminds us that place-based environmental modification and maintenance is a precondition for global trade. Most of that trade — an estimated 90 percent by tonnage — is waterborne (Rodrigue, Comtois, and Slack 2013). In order to move the world's cargo, harbors and navigable waterways have been repeatedly deepened to accommodate the underwater depth, or draft, of massive oceangoing ships. Without regular dredging, it would be very difficult to get the cargo from a twenty-first-century container ship like the *Maersk Edinburgh* — measuring 1,200 feet long with a maximum draft exceeding 50 feet and a capacity of over 13,000 containers — to shore and, ultimately, to consumers.

Consider the Panama Canal expansion, completed in 2016. The expansion involved the construction of much larger locks and dredging of some 55 million cubic meters of material from harbors and channels to allow vessels like the *Maersk Edinburgh* to cross the isthmus. Post-expansion, the canal's maximum authorized draft increased from 39.5 to 50 feet and the capacity of the largest container ships rose from around 5,000 to over 15,000 containers. Governments, firms, and port authorities along the U.S. Gulf and Atlantic coasts have scrambled to deepen their waterways to attract these so-called Neo-Panamax ships, hoping to capture huge new revenue streams. Consequently, expansion-related dredging in the United States dwarfs the expansion work in Panama, both in terms of expense and material excavated.

The Dredge Research Collaborative (2016), a group of landscape architects, has called for attention to what they call the *dredge cycle.* They point out that dredging is often treated as a linear process: equipment excavates sediment at point A and moves it to point B. However, as the hemispheric network of projects associated with the Panama Canal expansion demonstrates, dredging is bound up with, on the one hand, the geomorphic agencies of rivers, winds, and plate tectonics and, on the other hand, social priorities. This means that a specific act of dredging is one moment in a cycle that integrates geological, environmental, and political-economic processes.

Dredging has a political economy. For example, some dredged material is used for land reclamation — infilling water bodies to create new land — and in construction materials, sand being a key ingredient in concrete. Due to urbanization, humans now use twice as much sand and gravel annually as that which flows through all of the planet's rivers in a year (UNEP 2014). Sand dredged from rivers and, to a lesser degree, oceans is preferred over desert sand for construction and reclamation. We may, consequently, be on the brink of a global sand shortage marked by distributional inequities: material used to build skyscrapers and territory in Dubai and Singapore often comes from poorer countries like Cambodia, Indonesia, and Kenya (Beiser 2015; Fröhlich 2017). If dredging has a political economy, it also has a political ecology. It can precipitate water turbidity, hypoxia (oxygen depletion), and eutrophication (nutrient oversupply), which can have dire consequences for flora, fauna, and the various human communities that are dependent on them (Carse and Lewis 2017). So choices about when, how, where, and for whom (or what) we dredge deserve more public consideration.

Social theory has taught us to imagine global connection in terms of flows (Appadurai 1996), assemblages (Ong and Collier 2004), and infrastructures (Easterling 2014). Dredging, by contrast, focuses our gaze on sediment in motion. The geologist Roger Hooke (1994) characterizes modern humans as the planet's premier geomorphic agents: we now move earth at a scale comparable to or greater than rivers, glaciers, waves, and wind. With that capability comes new problems and opportunities. For example, dredged material, historically called "spoil" and treated as waste, is increasingly valued for managing coastal environments, ecological restoration, and use in manufacturing and construction. Among our many challenges as geomorphic agents, then, is to manage dredging more collectively and responsibly.

References

Appadurai, Arjun. 1996. *Modernity at Large: Cultural Dimensions of Globalization.* Minneapolis: University of Minnesota Press.

Beiser, Vince. 2015. "The Deadly Global War for Sand." *Wired,* March 26. https://www.wired.com/2015/03/illegal-sand-mining.

Carse, Ashley, and Joshua A. Lewis. 2017. "Toward a Political Ecology of Infrastructure Standards: Or, How to Think about Ships, Waterways, Sediment, and Communities Together." *Environment and Planning A* 49, no. 1: 9–28. https://doi.org/10.1177/0308518X16663015.

Cowen, Deborah. 2014. *The Deadly Life of Logistics: Mapping Violence in Global Trade.* Minneapolis: University of Minnesota Press.

Dredge Research Collaborative. 2016. "DredgeFest California: Key Findings and Recommendations." Report. http://dredgeresearchcollaborative.org/works/dredgefest-california-white-paper/.

Easterling, Keller. 2014. *Extrastatecraft: The Power of Infrastructure Space.* New York: Verso.

Fröhlich, Silja. 2017. "Sand Mining Decimates African Beaches." *Deutsche Welle,* February 15. http://www.dw.com/en/sand-mining-decimates-african-beaches/a–37546330.

Hibbard, Kathy A., Paul J. Crutzen, Eric F. Lambin, Diana M. Liverman, Nathan J. Mantua, John R. McNeil, Bruno Messerli, and Will Steffen. 2006. "Group Report: Decadal-Scale Interactions of Humans and the Environment." In *Sustainability or Collapse? An Integrated History and Future of People on Earth,* edited by Robert Costanza, Lisa J. Graumlich, and Will Steffen, 341–75. Cambridge: MIT Press.

Hooke, Roger LeB. 1994. "On the Efficacy of Humans as Geomorphic Agents." GSA *Today* 4, no. 9: 216–25. https://www.geosociety.org/gsatoday/archive/4.

Levinson, Marc. 2006. *The Box: How the Shipping Container Made the World Smaller and the World Economy Bigger.* Princeton: Princeton University Press.

Ong, Aihwa, and Stephen J. Collier, eds. 2004. *Global Assemblages: Technology, Politics, and Ethics as Anthropological Problems.* Malden: Blackwell.

Rodrigue, Jean-Paul, Claude Comtois, and Brian Slack. 2013. *The Geography of Transport Systems.* 3rd edn. New York: Routledge.

United Nations Environmental Programme (UNEP). 2014. "Sand, Rarer than One Thinks." UNEP *Global Environmental Alert Service,* March. http://hdl.handle.net/20.500.11822/8665.

Vanderostyne, Mon, and Marsha Cohen. 1999. "From Hand-Drag to Jumbo: A Millennium of Dredging." *Terra et Aqua* 77: 1–47. https://www2.iadc-dredging.com/publication/hand-drag-jumbo-millennium-dredging.

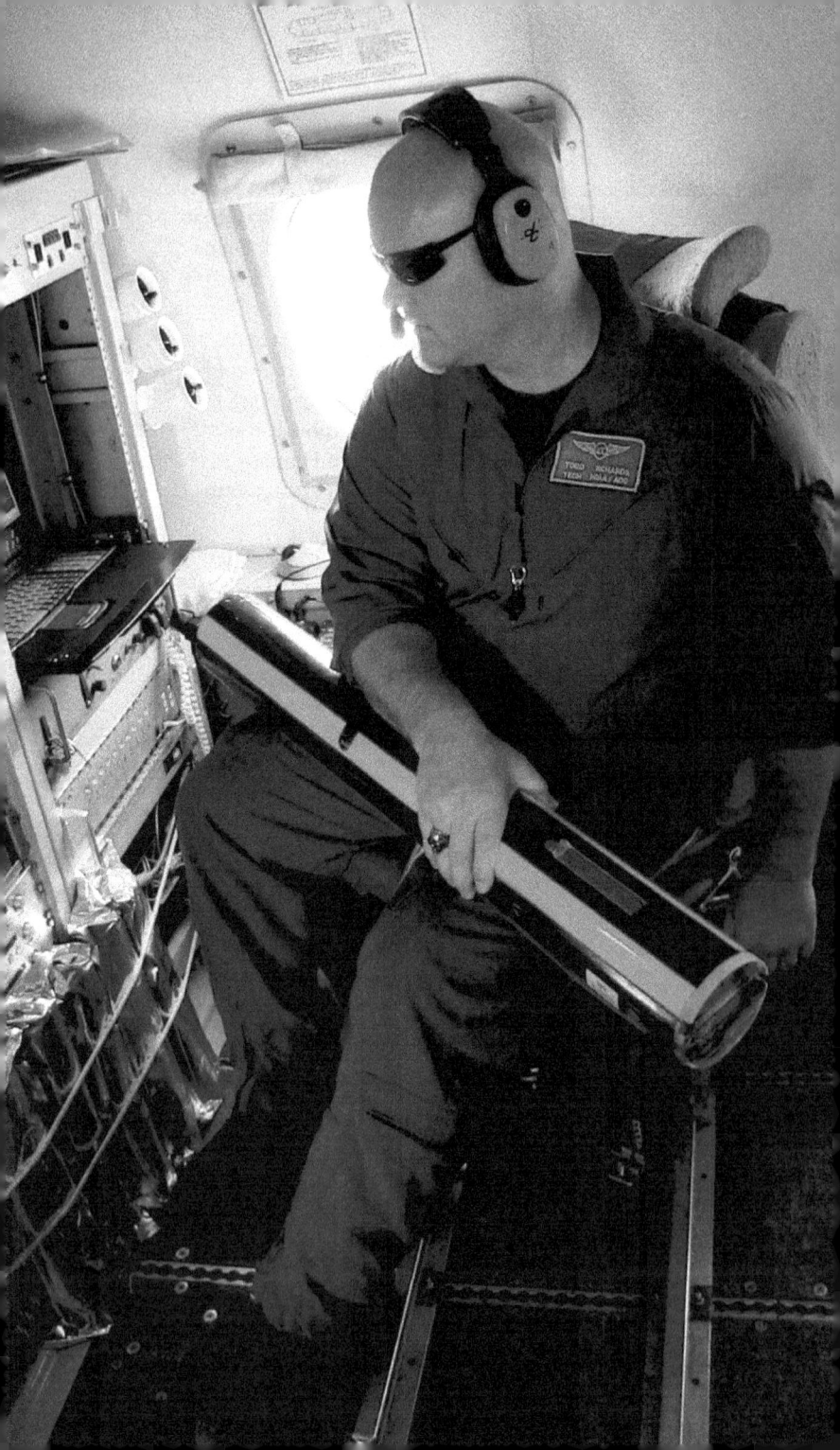

19

Drone

Marcel Laflamme

What does it feel like to fly into the eye of a hurricane? As the Anthropocene confronts us with this question at a species scale, the intrepid few who have already lived it out offer one set of answers. The first aviators to take their plane into such a storm, off the coast of Galveston, Texas in 1943, recalled being "tossed about like a stick in a dog's mouth." A more recent hurricane hunter describes being battered by turbulence so punishing that it caused an engine to explode as his aircraft passed through the storm's eyewall. Yet with climate models indicating that tropical storms will become more intense, if less frequent, over the course of the twenty-first century (Knutson et al. 2010), understanding these weather worlds from the inside will become more important even as the risks of venturing into them mount.

One aspect of hurricanes that remains a mystery is what scientists call the boundary layer: the few hundred meters just above the ocean's surface, which form an interface between sea and storm. Conditions in the boundary layer determine whether a storm intensifies or weakens, and yet these physical processes are poorly understood because observational data is hard to come by. Satellites can spot a storm as it gathers but can't penetrate the cloud cover to see beneath it, and flying a manned aircraft at such low altitudes would take a death wish. So the method of choice for collecting data involves a device called a dropsonde: an expendable sensor platform that is ejected from an aircraft and that transmits measurements as it drifts toward the surface. A parachute slows the dropsonde's descent, but even so, three to five minutes of data is all you get.

Since the turn of the century, though, scientists have been experimenting with unmanned aircraft, or drones, as a means of more sustained data collection. In 2005, a Taiwanese team of researchers became the first to fly a drone into the eye of a tropical cyclone. More recently, researchers at the National Oceanic and Atmospheric Administration (NOAA) in the United States have used a different drone called the Coyote for hurricane observations. In 2014, they tested the Coyote as Hurricane Edouard moved across the North Atlantic east of Bermuda, gathering data at altitudes as low as 250 meters and then comparing their readings to benchmark data from dropsondes. Impressed with the reliability of their measurements, the team planned for a second mission as Hurricane Matthew closed in on coastal Florida in October 2016. Yet despite the high hopes expressed in a preflight media blitz, the mission turned out to be a dud: both Coyotes "got dizzy," according to NOAA scientist Joe Cione, and were lost at sea.

In thinking about how we might regain our own balance in the time of the Anthropocene, we would do well to look to the drone: a technical object perhaps best known for its role in remote killing, but here inscribed within what Kristin Bergtora Sandvik and Maria Gabrielsen Jumbert (2017) have termed the discourse of "the good drone." The hurricane research drone aims to reduce the unpredictability of our warming world, by remaking the boundary layer as a geography that can be traversed and surveyed by a vehicle under human control. No longer will scientists need to rely exclusively on dropsondes and ocean buoys, which they are powerless to guide once released. The drone allows us to more deliberately direct our gaze, even as it teaches us to attune our practices of seeing to the machine's design (cf. Vertesi 2015, 163–90). The drone also extends our sensorium into new, more-than-human registers, as with the infrared sensors that allow the Coyote to measure the temperature of the sea surface below. It puts our five senses in their place.

Yet the fallibility and fragility of the drone is no less important to understand. We have been too credulous about the God's-eye view that its military-industrial makers promised, a totalizing prospect that renders everything visible. Some god, whose feet are made of carbon fiber! No, drones like the Coyote are better apprehended as part of what Jennifer Gabrys (2016, 3) calls "a distributed array of sensing technologies," whose very proliferation grounds an epistemological project that is less synoptic and planetary than insistently localized. My research with drone pilots examines the mundane forms of labor that are involved with keeping airborne sensors in position, counteracting the effects of gravity and signal loss and wayward algorithms. But, following Gabrys, we must also attend to the labor of cinching up the discrete environments that these sensors produce in order to make an Earth (and not just any Earth, but a livable one).

As of this writing, NOAA is still working with Raytheon, the Coyote's manufacturer, to iron out issues related to the drone's autopilot system, and the agency hopes to be ready to fly again by the fall of 2017. The Hurricane Matthew fiasco is shaping up to be a temporary setback: nothing more. Yet as the once-inaccessible boundary layer becomes one more domain in which *anthrōpos* can assert his will to knowledge, it is worth asking how the technologies that make this possible will prompt us to see the causes and unevenly distributed effects of hurricanes differently. Will we, as Mark Andrejevic (2016) worries, be seduced by a strain of drone theory that grows out of a materialism evacuated of critique? Or will we approach the drone reflexively, as a sentinel device revealing all-too-human judgments about which bodies can be placed at risk and which belong out of harm's way? Some of us are likelier than others to find shelter from the coming storm.

References

Andrejevic, Mark. 2016. "Theorizing Drones and Droning Theory." In *Drones and Unmanned Aerial Systems: Legal and Social Implications for Security and Surveillance,* edited by Aleš Završnik, 21–43. Basel: Springer International.

Gabrys, Jennifer. 2016. *Program Earth: Environmental Sensing Technology and the Making of a Computational Planet.* Minneapolis: University of Minnesota Press.

Knutson, Thomas, R., John L. McBride, Johnny Chan, Kerry Emmanuel, Greg Holland, Chris Landsea, Isaac Held, James P. Kossin, A. K. Strivastava, and Masato Sugi. 2010. "Tropical Cyclones and Climate Change." *Nature Geoscience* 3, no. 3: 157–63. https://doi.org/10.1038/ngeo779.

Sandvik, Kristin Bergtora, and Maria Gabrielsen Jumbert, eds. 2017. *The Good Drone.* New York: Routledge.

Vertesi, Janet. 2015. *Seeing Like a Rover: How Robots, Teams, and Images Craft Knowledge of Mars.* Chicago: University of Chicago Press.

20

Earths

Joshua Reno

In 2012, an infographic depicting how much land (and atmosphere) would be necessary in order to sustain the world's sev-
en billion people if they lived like the populations of various
countries went viral (De Chant 2012). The graphic sounded a
familiar alarm: that resources from more than one Earth would
be necessary to support a world full of Americans, Chinese, or
even Nepalese people. The data for these models came from the
Global Footprint Network. Much like the Club of Rome, whose
influential *Limits to Growth* popularized this kind of global
model over forty years ago (Edwards 2010, 366–72), the Global
Footprint Network has been criticized for scaling up fragment-
ed and flawed measurements to make claims about the Earth in
its entirety.

It has been argued that monotheism became a prominent
force in the world because of the symbolic and ideological power of "the logic of the one," that is, counting to one and no more:
not only one deity and one holy book, but also one life and
death, one ruler and one people (Schneider 2007). A similar argument could be made regarding the rise of environmentalism.
The importance of one Earth, considered as a totality, emerged
in tandem with early space travel and rising concerns about an
imminent nuclear apocalypse. Between 1968 and 1970, Stanley
Kubrick's *2001: A Space Odyssey* was the top-grossing film in the

DOI: 10.21983/P3.0265.1.22

United States, the first photographs of the entire Earth were tak-en from space, the Treaty on the Non-Proliferation of Nuclear Weapons came into effect, and Earth Day was celebrated for the first time.

One Earth doctrine, or terracentrism, is now environmen-talist orthodoxy. And yet, the last forty years have also seen the rise of an obverse mode of accounting. While some satellites and imaging devices point inward — quantifying deforestation, sea level rise, or melting polar ice — others point outward, enu-merating the many Earth-like planets that lie beyond our so-lar system. These initiatives, much like those of the NewSpace entrepreneurs and advocates who seek to commercialize outer space, are emerging at a precarious time of widespread ecologi-cal disaster and financial and political crisis (Valentine 2012). Arguably, NewSpace initiatives and the search for many Earths are also driven by terracentrism: a single planet to escape or transcend, on the one hand, and to measure all others by, on the other.

Consider the Drake Equation developed in 1961, which of-fers a probabilistic assessment of the number of galactic civiliza-tions we might discover, represented as N (see Denning 2011):

$$N = R^{\star} \cdot f_p \cdot n_e \cdot f_l \cdot f_i \cdot f_c \cdot L$$

The first three values are the least controversial. They refer to the average rate of star formation in our galaxy ($R^{\star}$), the frac-tion of those stars with planets (f_p), and the average number of planets per star that are capable of supporting life (n_e). The equation makes assumptions, of course, about what can sustain life (planets orbiting stars) and what those planets must be like (Earth). While the specific values can be assessed in various ways through astronomical observation, the only source for the structure of this formula is the one planet that we know sup-ports life: our own. The final four values are hopelessly contro-versial, standing for the fraction of planets that go on to develop life (f_l) and then intelligent life (f_i), the fraction of those that develop technology capable of releasing detectable signals (f_c), and the length of time it would take for such civilizations to release detectable signals into space (L).

With the launch of NASA's Kepler Space Observatory and the construction of new massive telescopes, new data is available about distant planetary bodies. These studies no longer rely on detecting alien signals, and focus only on the first two or three values of the Drake equation to see if the conditions of life could potentially exist on one of those distant bodies just as they are thought to have existed on Earth in the past. The presence of water, in particular, becomes the difference that makes a difference in the multiplication of Earths. New models and stories multiply the number of Earth-like planets into the probable billions (Petigura, Howard, and Marcy 2013). But this assumes that the many will follow the model of the one. We might insist, to be sure, that the one time we know life happened is all we have to go on. Yet familiarity with the contingencies associated with the emergence of life, intelligence, and civilization suggests caution. Couldn't life, intelligence, or civilization start and then stop countless times without enduring? Couldn't death and outright extinction — the death of death — be the rule of the galaxy? If so, the dead, the ignorant, and the uncivilized might be worth counting instead. It is probably the threat of these opposites that haunts our quest to count Earths — the many and the one — in the first place. Extinction means counting down from our one habitable planet, maybe one of very few, to zero.

Models of the one Earth are a recent and impressive accomplishment. But they are just models: all-too-human products based on the scaling up of inevitably partial and situated data. As Graham Harman (2011, 91) argues, "While appeals to the supposed 'world as a whole' always have an automatic air of intellectual gravitas and philosophical depth, there is no good reason to think that such an encompassing whole even exists." One could argue, in fact, that we inhabit many Earths, not one. Not only do we see the Earth change in terms of epochs, but there are many ways of modeling its internal processes and external relations with other celestial bodies and forces, some of which destabilize the popular image of a lone, blue marble.

We continue to count down and count up nonetheless — from one Earth to none, and from one Earth to many possible Earths.

References

De Chant, Tim. 2012. "If the World's Population Lived Like…" *Per Square Mile.* 8 August. https://persquaremile. com/2012/08/08/if-the-worlds-population-lived-like/.

Denning, Kathryn. 2011. "'L' on Earth." In *Civilizations Beyond Earth: Extraterrestrial Life and Society,* edited by Douglas A. Vakoch and Albert A. Harrison, 74–83. New York: Berghahn.

Edwards, Paul N. 2010. *A Vast Machine: Computer Models, Climate Data, and the Politics of Global Warming.* Cambridge: MIT Press.

Harman, Graham. 2011. *The Quadruple Object.* Washington, D.C.: Zero Books.

Petigura, Erik A., Andrew W. Howard, and Geoffrey W. Marcy. 2013. "Prevalence of Earth-sized Planets Orbiting Sun-like Stars." *Proceedings of the National Academy of Sciences* 110, no. 48: 19273–78. https://doi.org/10.1073/pnas.1319909110.

Schneider, Laurel C. 2007. *Beyond Monotheism: A Theology of Multiplicity.* New York: Routledge.

Valentine, David. 2012. "Exit Strategy: Profit, Cosmology, and the Future of Humans in Space." *Anthropological Quarterly* 85, no. 4: 1045–68. https://doi.org/10.1353/anq.2012.0073.

21

Ecopolitics

Eduardo Kohn

I have written a book called *How Forests Think* (Kohn 2013), which is drawn from my work in the Ecuadorian Amazon and concerns a mode of thought that I call sylvan thinking: a kind of thought, available to all of us, that extends well beyond the human. It emerges with life and is particularly visible in dense thickets of life like the tropical forest. I have argued that learning again to think with and like forests should be part of an ethical practice for the Anthropocene. On sabbatical in 2015-2016, I returned to Ecuador to try to understand how this particular kind of *ecologic* might acquire a political life. That is, I wish to understand how this form of thinking might guide us toward ways of being that can nurture sylvan thought in all of its valences. To do this I have been working with the Runa (or Kichwa) community of Sarayaku, which has been at the forefront of indigenous alter-politics (Hage 2012) for decades (see Becker 2012; Melo 2014).

In particular, I have collaborated with the community of Sarayaku in the preparation of a proposal for the legal recognition of a new category of protected territory that they call *Kawsak Sacha* or the Living Forest, which they presented at the COP21 Climate Summit in Paris in December 2015 and also, personally, to France's then president, François Hollande. *Kawsak Sacha* is a vision of ecological stewardship based on animist principles (Descola 2013). I see it as a hopeful example of how sylvan thinking goes political in these times of ecological crisis.

Here are two excerpts from the proposal:

> Whereas the western world treats nature as an undemanding source of raw materials destined exclusively for human use, *Kawsak Sacha* recognizes that the forest is made up entirely of living selves and the communicative relations they have with each other. [...] These selves, from the smallest plants to the supreme beings who protect the forest, are persons (*runa*).
>
> *Kawsak Sacha* is where [we] interrelate with the supreme beings of the forest in order to receive the guidance that leads [us] along the path of *Sumak Kawsay* (Good Living). This continuous relation that we [...] have with the beings of the forest is central, for on it depends the continuity of the Living Forest, which, in turn permits a harmony of life among many kinds of beings, as well as the possibility that we all can continue to live into the future.

The people of Sarayaku control a territory of 135,000 hectares, which they have designated as *Kawsak Sacha*. This territory is demarcated by a border of flowering and fruiting trees, visible from the air, which they call a Frontier of Life or Trail of Flowers. In keeping with the idea that the forest is a communicative ecology, the trail performs multiple communicative functions. It tells outsiders of the existence of the Living Forest at the same time that, in the words of the proposal, it "creates the possibility of beginning to dialogue with the beings that make up the Living Forest. In this way the Frontier of Life creates a permanent forum for communication among beings. This can help the entire world recuperate the original understanding of Mother Earth [*Pachamama*] as a shared home."

One important goal of this proposal is to stop oil and mineral extraction on native lands and in tropical forests. Currently, property titles in Ecuador apply only to the surface; the government retains the right to exploit subsurface resources. By treating the Earth as a bundle of relations instead of a font of material resources, *Kawsak Sacha* counters this statist extractive logic. Its proponents frame *Kawsak Sacha* as "a robust proposal capable of defending the Rights of Nature as it is enshrined in the Ecuadorian Constitution." In fact, the proposal takes the logic of the Rights of Nature one step further by emphasizing that "in order to extend rights to Nature, one must first recognize its entities as persons (and not mere objects)."

Here are three further excerpts:

We urge the world community to make an effort to achieve a real metamorphosis (tiam). We need to shift from a modernizing model of development — a model that treats nature as material resource — to the alternative of *Kawsak Sacha,* which recognizes that forming community with the many kinds of selves with whom we share our world is a better way to orient our economic and political activities.

[As guardians of the forest it is our responsibility to make manifest] that the very governments that put forth solemn discourses criticizing imperialism, capitalism, and colonialism are promoting, in the supposed name of democracy, large-scale neocolonialist extractive projects on our lands. [...] [The] gradual disappearance of this ensemble of life that *Kawsak Sacha* seeks to sustain is nothing more and nothing less than ecocide — that is, it is the systematic extermination of an ensemble of living interrelated selves. And this crime against Humanity and Nature, has, until now, gone unpunished. With the hope of putting a brake on this violence, our proposal is an urgent call to the world community [...].

To conclude [...]: the entire world is peopled by beings that sustain our planet thanks to their way of living in continuous interrelation and dialogue. This vision is neither a quaint belief nor a simple conservationist ideal. It is instead a call to the people of the world to learn once again to feel this reality in their very being. This [...] will only be possible once we learn to listen to and dialogue with these other beings that are part of a cosmic conversation that goes well beyond […] us humans. [This] would be the basis for conceptualizing, building, and disseminating a genuine *Sumak Kawsay* in our world—a world that today is threatened by an ecological crisis of planetary proportions.

Acknowledgments

Thanks to several Sarayaku community members for lively philosophical conversations and hospitality: José Gualinga, Felix Santi, Hernán Malaver, Franco Viteri, Yaku Viteri, Tupac Viteri, Dionicio Machoa, Sabine Bouchat, Renán Gualinga, and Patricia Gualinga. Thanks to Chris Hebdon for logistical help and for many stimulating discussions around the Living Forest.

References

Becker, Marc. 2012. *Pachakutik: Indigenous Movements and Electoral Politics in Ecuador.* Updated edition. Lanham: Rowman and Littefield.

Descola, Philippe. 2013. *Beyond Nature and Culture.* Translated by Janet Lloyd. Chicago: University of Chicago Press. Originally published in 2005.

Hage, Ghassan. 2012. "Critical Anthropological Thought and the Radical Political Imaginary Today." *Critique of Anthropology* 32, no. 3: 285–308. https://doi.org/10.1177/0308275X12449105.

Kohn, Eduardo. 2013. *How Forests Think: Toward an Anthropology beyond the Human.* Berkeley: University of California Press.

Melo, Mario. 2014. "Voces de la selva en el estrado de la Corte Interamericana de Derechos Humanos." *SUR: Revista Internacional de Derechos Humanos* 11, no. 20: 291–99.

22

Ends

Imre Szeman

Under star-strewn skies in mid-summer, late night talks with friends often turn toward a contemplation of ends. Where are we all heading? What is *this* all about? We know what comes at the end of our own individual lives, so that's not what we're puzzling about. When we speculate about ends, we pose questions about our collective fate, whether we speak of ends in a metaphysical register (e.g., death and its aftermath) or probe the head-shaking rationalities governing our societies (e.g., the rush after the almighty dollar, no matter the consequences for the health of individuals and societies).

Where are we *all heading? What is* this *all about?*

At the heart of all religions — and so, too, it has to be said, of most human social life — is a narrative of ends. Christian, Hindu, Islamic, and Jewish eschatologies all imagine that the world will come to an end, if in different ways. These ends are about revelation and judgment, about the final release of humanity from the suffering that constitutes mortal life. Other religions, such as Buddhism and Hinduism, treat ends as new beginnings, and focus on the cycle that links beginnings and ends. The ethics and practices shaping everyday life in these varied narratives are configured in relation to how ends are imagined. Quotidian life tends to drain eschatologies of their force; the sacred struggles to exist in a world organized increasingly by ends-means rationalities — the whole of social practice a giant "to do" list that each of us does our part to plod through. The threat or promise of what comes at the end of it all keeps morality and ethics in the picture — or tries to.

Ends are dangerous things. Just as they organize religious belief, they shape political thought, especially with respect to the dynamics of political change. Marxism imagines history as having an end — an end to capitalism that would also announce the birth of a socio-political system shaped in profound ways by human equality and collective flourishing. Liberal political phi-losophies paint a similar picture of broad human flourishing, but without any appeal to ends. In liberalism, social equality and justice are imagined as accumulating through slow accre-tion toward some distant vanishing point — a line arcing toward an axis like an asymptote, but never quite reaching it. Liber-alism and the politico-economic system that has developed alongside it — capitalism — have no real interest in ends (other, that is, than the end of profit). In five billion years, our Sun will transform into a red giant. Capitalism imagines that it will still be around, taking advantage of the business opportunities that might arise when our descendants want to get the hell outta the solar system.

How are ends manifest in relation to the Anthropocene? Be-hind the concept of the Anthropocene is a periodizing impulse: the introduction of a new conceptual framework that might en-able us to see different forces at play in the constitution of his-tory. *When* the Anthropocene begins (and the pointless strug-gle to establish its start date has derailed many critics, including the term's progenitors [see Steffen, Crutzen and McNeill 2007]) is less important than the very establishment of the concept, which collapses geological history and human history in a rhe-torically powerful way. Both the real limits of the concept (e.g., its reduction of the complex lithography of human power and privilege in relation to the environment to the actions of single species writ large) and the conceptual openings it potentially creates (e.g., a new ethics toward nature, an elimination of the distinction between natural history and human history) have generated a flurry of compelling criticism (Bonneuil and Fressoz 2015; Colebrook 2017; Haraway 2015; Jamieson 2017; Moore 2016). But how does the Anthropocene imagine and figure *ends*? Is the beginning of the Anthropocene bookended by an apocalyptic judgment day? Does its marriage of the historical and geological result in a period without end (*à la* liberal capitalism)? Or is the end of the Anthropocene one that announces a radical new beginning — a revolution that has caught all of us off guard by taking place in the atmosphere instead of on the streets?

The most powerful treatments of the Anthropocene take it as a pronouncement about the end of the world. For Roy Scranton, "If we want to learn to live in the Anthropocene, we must first learn how to die" (Scranton 2013, n.p.). The death he names is that of modernity and its attendant social and political logics and rationalities; it is a death that forces upon us key speculations about ends: "What does it mean to be human?" and "What does it mean to live?" (Scranton 2013, n.p.). For Timothy Morton, too, a recognition of the scale of our impact on the planet returns us to questions about ends — those "core ideas of what it means to exist, what Earth is, what society is" (2013, 15). The importance of the concept of the Anthropocene isn't finally about what it names or doesn't, or what it confuses or makes clearer regarding human impact on the planet's environment. Its importance is that it returns us to questions of ends — to whether we see the present as ecological fate about which we can do nothing, or as a revolutionary opportunity to redefine the kinds of individuals and societies we are and want to become.

References

Bonneuil, Christophe, and Jean-Baptiste Fressoz. 2015. *The Shock of the Anthropocene.* New York: Verso.
Colebrook, Claire. 2017. "We Have Always Been Post-Anthropocene." *Energy Humanities: An Anthology,* edited by Imre Szeman and Dominic Boyer, 399–414. Baltimore: Johns Hopkins University Press.

Haraway, Donna. 2015. "Anthropocene, Capitalocene, Plantationocene, Chthulucene: Making Kin," *Environmental Humanities* 6: 159–65. http://environmentalhumanities.org/arch/vol6/6.7.pdf.

Jamieson, Dale. 2017. "Ethics for the Anthropocene." *Energy Humanities: An Anthology,* edited by Imre Szeman and Dominic Boyer, 389–99. Baltimore: Johns Hopkins University Press.

Moore, Jason, ed. 2016. *Anthropocene or Capitalocene? Nature, History and the Crisis of Capitalism.* Oakland: PM Press.

Morton, Timothy. 2013. *Hyperobjects: Philosophy and Ecology after the End of the World.* Minneapolis: University of Minnesota Press.

Scranton, Roy. 2013. "Learning How to Die in the Anthropocene." *New York Times.* November 10. http://opinionator.blogs.nytimes.com/2013/11/10/learning-how-to-die-in-the-anthropocene/.

Steffen, Will, Paul J. Crutzen, and John R. McNeill. 2007. "The Anthropocene: Are Humans Now Overwhelming the Great Forces of Nature?" *AMBIO: A Journal of the Human Environment* 36, no. 8: 614–21. https://doi.org/10.1579/0044-7447(2007)36[614:TAAHNO]2.0.CO;2.

23

Environing

Jeffrey Jerome Cohen

Trouble the boundaries and enmesh the cosmos, but an Anthropocene ecology remains housebound. Ecotheorists are fond of
pointing out that the *oikos* in *ecology* is the Greek word for a
house's environing. This noisy home swings its doors and windows open, bolt them as we might. Yet *oikos* is also an economy in which all things are apt to be rendered commodities for
equivalency and exchange, for the forcible transport of messages not theirs. Humans differentiate themselves from world,
from other animals, from other humans through ceaseless over-
powering — violence that cannot be disowned. We declare the
Anthropocene, but the world pushes back.

   In "The Reeve's Tale," Geoffrey Chaucer sets a fourteenth-
century meditation on anthropogenic environ change in Cambridge, center of philosophy, agriculture, and business (Benson
2008). The clerks Aleyn and John lay awake in strange lodgings.
Tricked by an unscrupulous miller, they have paid to endure a
night under his roof. From their shared bed the young men listen
to the nocturnal melody of the miller and his drunken family,
a "rowtyng" [snoring] loud enough to be heard a quarter-mile
away (1.4166). The noise that thunders from the miller's open
mouth is so intense that only animal comparison can convey
its force: "as an hors he fnorteth in his sleep" ("like a horse he
snores in his sleep"; 1.4163). Within slumber and without precise

language, humans sound much the same as other large mammals. *Fnorteth* is reverberation oblivious to species difference, a noise that travels with brutal force.

"The Reeve's Tale" is known for grim ambience. Its narrative ecosystem resounds with dissonant, nonverbal signifying, a dense archive of human sound that has become inhuman resounding. With its snores, cries, shouts, pleas, poems and prayers, "The Reeve's Tale" is reverberant, a material ecology that noisily foregrounds the penetrability and porousness of flesh within a surrounding and story-inscribed atmosphere. The miller and his family snore because their bodies are humoral environments out of balance. Excessive drinking engenders a superfluity of blood, which in turn triggers the need for restorative sleep. The intoxicated body illustrates the transcorporeality of medieval embodiment, both human and animal: the four humors do their work within skin that offers a permeable membrane, rather than a barrier to the world.[1] The medieval equivalent to Anthropocene environs is this open, fleshly system that, through the humors, enmeshes the gravity of the moon, the impress of place, the agency of matter, the density and humidity of atmosphere.[2] Such material entanglement holds as true of animals, plants, and stones as of humans. It underscores that human embodiment is a specific phenomenon, not an abstract universal: a tenuous system easily disrupted.[3] Human identity is corporeal and happens in place, propelled and then limned by enduring violences.

The action that arises in "The Reeve's Tale" is in the end all too human, all too masculine: two acts of sexualized revenge, a message sent by the clerks to the miller through the bodies of his wife and daughter. Within this domestic economy, horses, cakes, wheat, beds, sex, and blows are exchanged with little regard for the lived consequences that such equivalence and re-

---

1   On transcorporeality as a modern phenomena of permeability and toxicity, see Alaimo 2010.
2   See Akbari 2009 on the place-bound environmentality of the body.
3   See Paster 1993 on the materiality of humoral psychology.

duction entail. Economy and ecology, the house and its range, register a long Anthropocenic truth of human environing. Interpenetrability is subject to constant economic recapture. John and Aleyn are forced to purchase from the miller a breakfast baked from flour he stole. The clerks believe that the proper payment for such abuse is to be made through the sexual enjoyment of the women in the miller's household. Once they sleep with the wife and daughter, the tale becomes a disturbing account of what happens when all the world is reduced to an economy of sale, substitution, and revenge, every ecology transformed into an economy, all matter — even virginity — rendered vendible. No wonder the story ends with screams, blows, blood. Women's bodies are used by men to send messages to other men. That these women have their own stories is hinted at, but never explored with much narrative attention.

Other medieval tales embrace the shared precariousness of mundane life, the burgeoning of a Disanthropocene in which stories enmesh the human and nonhuman so that neither stands alone. Yet Chaucer does attend to the particularities of violence within the human, and thereby warns us that when we attempt to transcend that category by declaring the Anthropocene, we do so at the peril of specificities that require precise accounting. Ethics inheres in the choice not to universalize, not to ignore the differences found within the category of human — differences that vanish when the Anthropocene becomes a term for disembodied, geologic and yet still anthropocentric force. In stories that we have long been telling opens a more complicated space. Violence and suffering are unevenly distributed. Within Anthropocene environs gender still matters. So do class and race. The human body is a machine of sonority, as ecological in its signaling as animals and stones. Human bodies are also plural phenomena, specific and universalized at peril. Drawing boundaries and declaring epochs may be necessary, but such systems are fragile, insufficient. They inevitably attempt to exclude the impress of environs upon our very bodies, the resounding of environmentality within our stories and our words.

Medieval stories have much to teach about the deep history of times and spaces. They environ still.

References

Akbari, Suzanne Conklin. 2009. *Idols in the East: European Representations of Islam and the Orient, 1100–1450*. Ithaca: Cornell University Press.

Alaimo, Stacy. 2010. *Bodily Natures: Science, Environment, and the Material Self*. Bloomington: Indiana University Press.

Benson, Larry D. *The Riverside Chaucer*. Third edition. Oxford: Oxford Unversity Press.

Paster, Gail Kern. 1993. *The Body Embarrassed: Drama and the Disciplines of Shame in Early Modern England*. Ithaca: Cornell University Press.

IT IS 2 MINUTES TO MIDNIGHT ®

24

Eschaton

Jonathan Padwe

The Anthropocene is over. This is one of the great ironies of the
Anthropocene idea. As a concept, it has pretensions to geological time, time measured in ages and epochs, in periods, eras,
and eons. Naming this new epoch has generated a flourishing of
innovative writing about humans, nonhumans, and the worlds
they share. Yet those of us writing about the Anthropocene
rush to intervene before the conversation moves on. In their introduction to the first iteration of this lexicon, Cymene Howe
and Anand Pandian (2016) highlighted the "astonishing speed"
with which the concept had been taken up across disciplines.
Heather Swanson, Nils Bubandt, and Anna Tsing (2015, 150–51)
similarly note that "in the past few years, conferences with 'Anthropocene' in the title have increased even faster than CO_2
levels." Seeking to capture the "field to come" at the moment
of its inception, these authors analyze the content of these conferences themselves, rather than the scholarly articles they will
spawn. This clever methodological move is itself characteristic
of the new epoch, one feature of which is that the half-life of
productive ideas grows shorter each year. Already we know that
soon the Anthropocene will take its place among the series of
keywords that help us to organize disciplinary histories, terms
like *neoliberalism, resistance,* and *postmodernism.*

DOI: 10.21983/P3.0265.1.26   157

That a term meant to give meaning to millions of years of earthly time may prove more useful as a marker of a moment in the history of early twenty-first-century social theory lends a sometimes farcical dimension to scholarly debates over the chronology of the new epoch. Recently, for instance, scientists sought to define with some precision the moment when the Anthropocene came into existence (e.g., Voosen 2016). Was it the transition to settled agriculture? The Industrial Revolution? The dawn of the Atomic Age? The exchange underscores humankind's inability to comprehend deep time. Epochs, as humans have defined them, generally last tens of millions of years. Did the Anthropocene begin in 1850? In 1945? What is one hundred years when compared with ten million? In fact, it is one one-thousandth of a percent. Not even a blip, in the grand scheme of things.

These questions of scale point to another temporal conundrum vexing our understanding of the new epoch: eschatology. Almost by definition, the Anthropocene is the last earthly epoch that humans will experience. As a period of time made material by traces in the land, this temporal category coincides with the cumulative effects of human social complexity, of human-dominated systems of growing, feeding, building, extracting, traveling, wasting, and warring. How might the Anthropocene end? Surely a period of time defined by human alterations of Earth's environment can only conclude with the end of the human presence on Earth as it is currently known. From the human perspective, the Anthropocene is a way of speaking about the end of the world.

Can this end time be avoided? Perhaps. Perhaps in recognizing the Anthropocene and its implications for our species we will manage to invent new ways of being human. It is just such an effort — an effort to find new ways of being — that is the object of much writing about the Anthropocene. In an apocalyptic *cri de coeur,* Roy Scranton (2013) urged readers of the New York Times to recognize that "our civilization is already dead." The sooner we recognize "there's nothing we can do to save ourselves," he wrote, "the sooner we can get down to the hard work of adapting […] to our new reality." A more hopeful example can be found in Anna Tsing's work on "the possibility of life in capitalist ruins." Taking in the devastations of capitalism, Tsing surveys a world that has been destroyed and sees, growing amidst the wreckage, a mushroom. "When Hiroshima was destroyed by an atomic bomb in 1945," she recounts, "the first living thing to emerge from the blasted landscape was a matsutake mushroom" (Tsing 2015, 3). Here and elsewhere for Tsing, *matsutake* symbolize emergent life in the aftermath of destruction. Hers is both a powerful and a disturbing vision. Tsing's joyous writing is a testament to the power of hope that a mushroom can convey. But to take in a vast landscape of destruction beyond measure and focus on the single mushroom poking out from the debris requires more hope than most of us can muster. Importantly, like much writing about the Anthropocene, Tsing's vision is founded on the realization that we live "at the end of the world."

So the Anthropocene is a figure of the Eschaton. We cannot think that the Geological Society of London, founded by a nineteenth-century fraternity of scientific gentlemen, will be around to name the next epoch. The effort to identify the Anthropocene, like all good efforts to place a name on time, helps humans to express their fears that time itself is coming to an end. So it is not unsurprising that the Anthropocene emerges now, a scant few years after the dawn of the third millennium Anno Domini. Periodization and eschatology go hand in hand. Projects like the French revolutionary calendar or Year Zero of the Cambodian revolution concerned themselves with the social punctuation of time, the reorganization of past, present, and future (Zerubavel 2002). In these projects, the moral failings of the *ancien régime* lay the foundation for narratives of redemption and dreams of utopia. The reordering of time into the so-called Christian era, to which we owe our present calendar, was such a process. According to Reinhart Koselleck (2002, 53–54), the transformation of the Roman empire by conquering Germanic peoples, coupled with the Christianization of religious cults, "could only be experienced metaphorically as decline, or, in terms of salvation history, as the expectation of a future redemption." So, too, with the Anthropocene: where climate change and resource wars, the sixth extinction and nuclear winter reveal themselves as the wages of our sins against "Nature," we interpret the science of stratigraphy allegorically as a morality tale for our time.

References

Howe, Cymene, and Anand Pandian. 2016. "Lexicon for an Anthropocene Yet Unseen." Theorizing the Contemporary series, *Cultural Anthropology* website, January 22. https://culanth.org/fieldsights/803-lexicon-for-an-anthropocene-yet-unseen.

Koselleck, Reinhart. 2002. "Transformations of Experience and Methodological Change: A Historical-Anthropological Essay." In *The Practice of Conceptual History: Timing History, Spacing Concepts,* translated by Todd Pressner et al., 45–83. Stanford: Stanford University Press.

Science and Security Board. 2018. "It Is Two Minutes to Midnight: 2018 Doomsday Clock Statement." https://thebulletin.org/doomsday_clock/it-is-2-minutes-to-midnight-2/.

Scranton, Roy. 2013. "Learning How to Die in the Anthropocene." Opinionator blog, *New York Times,* November 10. http://opinionator.blogs.nytimes.com/2013/11/10/learning-how-to-die-in-the-anthropocene.

Swanson, Heather Anne, Nils Bubandt, and Anna Tsing. 2015. "Less Than One But More Than Many: Anthropocene as Science Fiction and Scholarship-in-the-Making." *Environment and Society* 6, no. 1: 149–66. https://doi.org/10.3167/ares.2015.060109.

Tsing, Anna Lowenhaupt. 2015. *The Mushroom at the End of the World: On the Possibility of Life in Capitalist Ruins.* Princeton: Princeton University Press.

Voosen, Paul. 2016. "Atomic Bombs and Oil Addiction Herald Earth's New Epoch: The Anthropocene." *Science Magazine,* August 24. http://www.sciencemag.org/news/2016/08/ atomic-bombs-and-oil-addiction-herald-earth-s-new-epoch-anthropocene.

Zerubavel, Eviatar. 2002. *Time Maps: Collective Memory and the Social Shape of the Past.* Chicago: University of Chicago Press.

25

Expenditure

Naveeda Khan

If the Holocene is marked by stability in the earth's climate, then the Anthropocene (as our present era has come to be called) is marked by dissipation. It calls for a mode of accounting other than that of a cost-benefit analysis, such as one of expenditure.

Nur Hashem once returned from a hard day of laboring at a weaving factory on the mainland to his home on a silt island to find his village collapsing into the river. He searched frantically for his family only to learn that they had fled earlier with neighbors. As he tried to recover what he could of his fast-eroding household, he suddenly experienced a feeling of sheer elation. He leaped up and started to kick the houses to aid their passage into the water. "Here you go, take them," he shouted. "Go." Off he went in search of his family.

This act struck me as an incongruous one in this place of abject poverty in the middle of the Jamuna River in Bangladesh. Perhaps because of the precariousness of existence, people were preoccupied with accounting for everything, weighing and measuring the seasonal yields, describing in detail the debts owed and the interest to be paid, the constant inquiry after the prices of things, the concern with what strangers had to give them. But to me, such minute accounting felt to be the standing language of sociality, putting oneself with objects and others and being woven into strings of values. Given one's constant vulnerability to the words of others in this place, the language of accounting could carry occult undertones. Words were measured or withheld with the objective to harm. Even God appeared as bookkeeper. Khizr, the immortal prophet long associated with Muslim riverine communities, was here given an abode in the water and the task of measuring land during the dry season to be collected as divine tax during the monsoons. So what was Nur Hashem doing kicking houses into the river, when everyone knew that Khizr was merely doing his duty in eroding them?

In one rendering we could say that Nur Hashem was spent. Exhausted by the labor of weaving, which is known to take its toll on the body, he was doubly exhausted by the labor of living beside an active river. He was throwing down the towel. But according to another understanding inspired by Georges Bataille (1985), Nur Hashem was partaking of expenditure. This was not the expenditure necessary to ensure life. It was a nonessential dissipation with little to show for it but an irrational enervation.

Bataille helps situate Nur Hashem's expenditure within the vast, multistranded accounting undergirding global climate politics. The carbon concentration already in the atmosphere, known as historic emission, is calculated down to parts per metric ton. Also calculated is the remaining carbon that the earth's atmosphere can take before the climate turns monstrous. Developing countries tried to parse out a formula by which historic emission was to be held against developed countries, allowing developing countries to play catch-up. This controversial formula was shelved in the twenty-first Conference of Parties (COP21) held in Paris in 2015, in favor of allowing each country to come forward with its own form of accounting as to how it would contribute to curbing carbon emissions. These Intended Nationally Determined Contributions neither get us to a significant reduction of carbon already in the air nor keep temperature rise within the 1.5° C mark to protect low-lying areas from sea level rise.

What is one to do in the face of an intensified accounting that doesn't amount to much? The island nations, a majority of the developing countries, and African nations constitute a bloc within the COP in maintaining that mitigation efforts to curb emissions are not enough. They have advocated adaptation in acknowledgment of the fact that ecosystems are changing of necessity (although whether human societies change of the same necessity is a questionable part of their assumptions). They now advocate accounting for loss and damage. In climate conversations, the terms *loss* and *damage* crop up most often with respect to the profit margins of industrialized economies. In climate science, *loss* means an irreversible setback within regular biophysical processes, while *damage* refers to a reversible one. But when island nations, developing countries, and African nations take up the issue of loss and damage, it is not only profit margins or climate temporalities that are at stake. They are talking about lost shorelines, salinity in the land and water, dead fish, crumbling coral reefs, and other elements that accentuate the sepulchral in nature. Through some wizardry of accounting, all of these forms of rot and decay are to be linked to climate change and a monetary value placed on them.

If there is something unsavory about Brazil, India, and China demanding the right to pollute based on historic emission, there is something downright confounding in vulnerable countries jettisoning the language of historical debt, putting aside any accounting for colonialism, genocide, resource extraction, and slavery, to advocate for money for climate devastation alone. Yet even with its officious bureaucratic language and its privileging of accounting over any other kind of economic transactions, such as barter or gift, the demand for loss and damage has a quality of madness to it, a resort to the strong language of numbers but with an element of the fantastic, because can accountants get to disappearing places and destroyed lives fast enough? How is it that Nur Hashem's kicks or Bataille's laugh insinuate themselves within socialities saturated with economic utility to suggest the place of a nonessential dissipation? As Bataille suggests, loss has to be as great as possible to make a more general economic tendency toward all-out dissipation reveal itself as such. Loss almost nears sacrifice, so as to produce excitation and to serve as the wellspring for a new set of values, perhaps that of a momentary glory rather than continued abjectness.

26

Exposure

Elizabeth F.S. Roberts

Expose: to put out; to deprive of shelter.
Exposure: the action of exposing; the fact or state of being
exposed.

— *Oxford English Dictionary*

Here we are now, exposed to the Anthropocene. Within an Anthropocenic logic, we are exposed to ourselves. Human-induced
environmental change at a global scale has hopelessly exposed
everyone and everything to grave danger. *No outside! No shelter!*
Such lamentations conjure the origins of the concept of environment: eighteenth-century Western Europe, when industrialization, built upon colonial resource extraction, got this Anthropocenic ball rolling.

Let's think through exposure in three broad, cumulative
strokes, situated in an industrialized world as it shifted over
time and space and as the constitution of exposure, the self, and
outsides and insides shifted along with it. We find: (1) *permeating exposure* emerging in eighteenth-century European industrialization, when selves and places were predicated on constant
interrelation and when the experience of shelter underwent
profound transformation; (2) *particulate exposure* ascending
in the mid- to late nineteenth century in well-resourced Euro-
American locales, when intensified industrialization made or-

DOI: 10.21983/P3.0265.1.28

ganisms into bounded selves that weren't necessarily altered by their external exposures; and (3) *Anthropocenic exposure* arising in the present moment, when exposure amid industrial destruction is both impossible to prevent and self-altering. These three exposures are not metaphoric: they name differently situated historical-material realities (Landecker 2011). Nor were they everywhere at once — that is, until maybe now.

Permeating Exposure

Derived from a Latin root, expose means to put out, but what out was, and is, must not be taken for granted. Vladimir Janković (2010), one of the only historians of exposure, tells us that it predates *environment*. It was the eighteenth-century British way to live the in and the out. Bodies lived in acknowledged relation to the world around them, shaped by them through and through (Rosenberg 1979; Temkin 1977). In this period in Britain, as well as Western Europe more broadly, health was a social asset that could be augmented, protected, and dissipated, reflecting the notion that vulnerability came from sunbeams and moisture, and also from insults and voyeuristic eyes. Sickness, especially for the wealthy and delicate, came from limited bodily capacity to ward off the effects of the permeating outside world.

This management of permeating exposure paved the way for environment to embed class distinctions from the very beginning. British middle-class domestic interiors, new in an industrializing economy, brought with them what we now call "first world" problems of increased anxiety about external influences. Recall Jane Austen's heroines, who survived storm exposure by convalescing from chills in well-appointed homes. *Environment* became a new way not only to describe physical location, but also to draw distinctions between the pathology ascribed to ambient change and the achievement of healthy, ambient uniformity indoors. These descriptions were made possible through new industrial commodities like heavy draperies and cleaning products used by invisibilized servants. Distinctions were also maintained through worrying about the chaotic and unhealthy environments of the poor (Janković 2010).

Particulate Exposure

Think of the mid- to late nineteenth century as the beginning of the period (which extends into the present) when industrial prosperity provided some people with the experience of individuality — as isolated particulates that remained constant despite contact with other particulates (Keller 2010). These individuals, insensitive and impermeable to external conditions, were hearty, rational, masculine actors who could operate unaffected by the world around them. Almost everyone, though, even the irrational and easily influenced, came under an external threat from germs — newly experienced particulates that made people sick without fundamentally transforming the self (Rosenberg 1979).

Alongside industrial prosperity, the bacteriological revolution (germs) shifted the relation between bodies and places. The scale of industrial manufacture harnessed and produced microbes, antimicrobes, and other chemicals, dispersing them into the environment — now a proper entity — as if these particulates would have no lasting effect on individuals or the world (Landecker 2016). It became possible to talk about voluntary and involuntary exposure, a distinction previously unimaginable as exposures could only be managed, not banished (Mitman, Murphy, and Sellers 2004). Particulate exposure benefited greatly from what I have called "infrastructures of individualism" (Roberts 2014) such as transportation, waste, postal, and educational systems, unseen supports delivering impermeability to the surrounding world.

These individuated bodies susceptible to, but defensible against, individuated particulates persist in the recent text *Exposure Science: Basic Principles and Applications*. The authors define exposure as "a person's contact with the concentration of a material before and after it crosses a boundary (nose, skin or mouth) between the human and the environment over an interval of time leading to a potential biological effective dose" (Lioy and Weisel 2014, 17). The scientific measurement of exposure, then, focuses on a single particulate signal, which facilitates "a learned inattention to other noise" (Murphy 2004, 267). Exposure science and the expososome, which attempts to model exposure as the cumulative measure of the sum total of the life of an organism (see Miller 2014), assume first, the discreteness of bodies from environments and individual bodies from particulates, and second, the maintenance of a constant self despite exposure.

Anthropocenic Exposure

While the expososome continues to conjure clear particulate boundaries, late-industrial collapse (Fortun 2012) produces a refreshed horror at our own permeability. This horror informs the epigenome and microbiome, both entangled in the co-construction of permeable organisms and environments (Jirtle and Skinner 2007; Jostins et al. 2012). The self is now alterable: we may not be protected by antibiotics or heavy draperies.

You may have surmised by now that this we, those living within particulate exposure, were and are particular in their particulateness. In my current work in Mexico City, with working-class people enrolled in a long-term chemical exposure study, I find little expectation of impermeability (Roberts 2017). I also find that the Anthropocenic headline proclaiming inextricable human-environment entanglement is not news among people living in a post-NAFTA, War on Drugs world that exceeds their control (Roberts 2015). Nor do they share in a particulate anxiety about, for instance, baby bottle BPA (Bisphenol A), since they live with a constant permeating insecurity at bodily, not molecular, scales.

The particulate exposure of unregulated industrialization that allowed some to live as impermeable exposed *all* to the Anthropocene. Nevertheless, an embrace of Anthropocenic exposure proclaiming almost gleefully that we are *all* hopelessly exposed all the time has its limits (Alaimo 2016). We could make more shelter for all by reactivating efforts, as with permeating exposure, to manage the insides and outsides, as well as acknowledging that exposure burdens have never been equally shared (Agard-Jones 2016).

References

Agard-Jones, Vanessa. 2016. "Episode 35." Center for Energy and Environmental Research in the Human Sciences podcast, September 29.

Alaimo, Stacy. 2016. *Exposed: Environmental Politics and Pleasures in Posthuman Times.* Minneapolis: University of Minnesota Press.

Fortun, Kim. 2012. "Ethnography in Late Industrialism." *Cultural Anthropology* 27, no. 3: 446–64. https://doi.org/10.1111/j.1548-1360.2012.01153.x.

Janković, Vladimir. 2010. *Confronting the Climate: British Airs and the Making of Environmental Medicine.* New York: Palgrave Macmillan.

Jirtle, Randy L., and Michael K. Skinner. 2007. "Environmental Epigenomics and Disease Susceptibility." *Nature Reviews Genetics* 8: 253–62. https://doi.org/10.1038/nrg2045.

Jostins, Luke, et al. 2012. "Host-Microbe Interactions Have Shaped the Genetic Architecture of Inflammatory Bowel Disease." *Nature* 491: 119–24. https://doi.org/10.1038/nature11582.

Keller, Evelyn Fox. 2010. *The Mirage of a Space Between Nature and Nurture.* Durham: Duke University Press.

Landecker, Hannah. 2011. "Food as Exposure: Nutritional Epigenetics and the New Metabolism." *BioSocieties* 6, no. 2: 167–94. https://dx.doi.org/10.1057/biosoc.2011.1.

———. 2016. "Antibiotic Resistance and the Biology of History." *Body and Society* 22, no. 4: 19–52. https://doi.org/10.1177%2F1357034X14561341.

Lioy, Paul, and Clifford Weisel. 2014. *Exposure Science: Basic Principles and Applications*. Waltham: Academic Press.

Miller, Gary W. 2014. *The Exposome: A Primer*. Waltham: Academic Press.

Mitman, Gregg, Michelle Murphy, and Christopher Sellers, eds. 2004. *Landscapes of Exposure: Knowledge and Illness in Modern Environments*. Chicago: University of Chicago Press.

Murphy, Michelle. 2004. "Uncertain Exposures and the Privilege of Imperception." In *Landscapes of Exposure: Knowledge and Illness in Modern Environments,* edited by Gregg Mitman, Michelle Murphy, and Christopher Sellers, 266–82. Chicago: University of Chicago Press.

Roberts, Elizabeth F.S. 2014. "Petri Dish." Commonplaces, *Somatosphere,* March 31.

———. 2015. "Food is Love: And So, What Then?" *BioSocieties* 10, no. 2: 247–52.

2017. "Bioethnography: A How-To Guide for the Twenty-First Century," with Camilo Sanz. In *A Handbook of Biology and Society,* edited by Maurizio Meloni, 749–75. Basingstoke: Palgrave Macmillan.

Rosenberg, Charles E. 1979. "The Therapeutic Revolution: Medicine, Meaning, and Social Change in Nineteenth-Century America." In *The Therapeutic Revolution: Essays in the Social History of American Medicine,* edited by Morris J. Vogel and Charles E. Rosenberg, 3–25. Philadelphia: University of Pennsylvania Press.

Temkin, Owsei. 1977. *The Double Face of Janus and Other Essays in the History of Medicine*. Baltimore: Johns Hopkins University Press.

GOT HIT BY
ASTEROID –
WHAT'S YOUR
EXCUSE,
FREEWAYS?
GatewaySucks.org
TSAWWASSEN INN
WHERE were YOU
GATEWAY
TO
EXTINCTION

27

Extinction

Noah Theriault and Audra Mitchell

In a recent essay entitled "The Uninhabitable Earth," David Wallace-Wells (2017) makes a morbid prediction: "The mass extinction we are now living through has only just begun; so much more dying is coming." The essay, which quickly went viral, regales readers with graphic imagery of starvation and perpetual war in a coming climate apocalypse. But it leaves us to wonder precisely *who* is doing this dying, now and in the future? For whom and by whom — humans and other beings included — is earth being made "uninhabitable"?

Part of a growing journalistic and pop-culture genre that some have called "apocalypse porn," Wallace-Wells's essay vividly reflects the necropolitics that haunt narratives about life, death, and extinction in the Anthropocene. As scholar-activists committed to promoting environmental and ecological justice, we acknowledge the gravity of extinction, but we are concerned about what narratives of mass extinction obscure. By eliding the violent structures that disproportionately burden certain assemblages of beings with acute acts of dislocation and cumulative forms of "slow violence" (Nixon 2011), these narratives naturalize a colonial order in which some earthlings are actively targeted for extermination, some are categorized as valuable "biodiversity," and many others are summarily consigned to an unmarked planetary grave.

DOI: 10.21983/P3.0265.1.29

As cultural theorist Claire Colebrook (2014) has shown, the desire of Western people to contemplate the total and irreversible destruction of the planet has become a central theme of popular culture. Exposure to these images produces complex forms of affect: the thrill of fear, the sublime sense of living in important (perhaps even end) times, and the fantasy of being among a small group that survives the destruction of its species — all experienced from the safe position of the voyeur. This fantasy is evident in the jarringly optimistic, almost salvational conclusion to Wallace-Wells's essay: "Now we've found a way to engineer our own doomsday," he declares, "and surely we will find a way to engineer our way out of it." Here, mass extinction is inevitable, but not necessarily for *us*. Who *we* are is left unspecified, although it almost certainly refers to the "modern," Western humans interpellated by the article. Similarly unquestioned are the specific social, political, and economic formations — primarily, Western colonial and capitalist ones — that drive global patterns of extinction. Like many of the most influential Anthropocene narratives, this framing naturalizes immense inequalities in responsibility for harm and in the distribution of suffering, among and across diverse life forms (Malm and Hornberg 2014; Ogden et al. 2015; Todd 2015).

A clear example of this can be found in prevailing market-driven practices involving the conservation of life forms deemed useful to humanity (see Adams 2010). Recent efforts to assess the financial value of biodiversity aim to incentivize states and other actors to conserve more efficiently. In these schemes, the relations that have enabled life forms to coexist over millennia are recast as stocks of capital to be leveraged or as commodities to be bought and sold, ostensibly for their own protection (Büscher 2014; Castree and Henderson 2014). Sometimes these relations are literally figured as financial instruments — biodiverse ecosystems as "banks" or "insurance policies" (UNMA 2003; de Groot et al. 2012; Roe et al. 2013) — while biodiversity derivatives generate capital by betting against the extinction of life forms (Sullivan 2013). These approaches monetize biodiver-

sity, along with the labor and relationships that sustain it, in order to "offset" ecological degradation in the global North (Paw-
licek and Sullivan 2011). Not only does this strategy conscript
more forms and dimensions of life into systems of global capital
(Kelly 2011; Moore 2016), but it also prescribes "fixes" intended
to sustain capitalist systems (Harvey 2003). These fixes make the
global calculus of elimination profitable for global elites, while
relegating marginalized groups of humans and other-than-human beings to sacrifice zones and/or conservation enclosures.

As a subgenre of apocalypse porn, mass-extinction narratives
also tend to obscure the racialized and colonial nature of the
phenomena they seek to define. This is reflected in the profound
anxiety of white Western authors regarding the apparently imminent end of the world. By locating this apocalypse in a potential future — and fetishizing images of its ravaging by extinction — purveyors of these narratives evince extreme privilege.
In contrast, for Potawatomi scholar Kyle Powys Whyte (2017,
207), Indigenous peoples faced — and *survived* — centuries of
colonial occupations that have forced them to "inhabit what our
ancestors would have likely characterized as a dystopian future"
in which plants and animals integral to their ways of life have
been obliterated. Meanwhile, by framing all of humanity as the
undifferentiated victim of ecological collapse, mass-extinction
narratives magnify colonial discourses that treat extinction or
extermination as inevitable for Indigenous peoples, peoples of
color, and nonhumans such as wolves, dingos, whales, or bison
(Mohawk 2010; Bird Rose 2011; Hubbard 2014). These stories of
extinction preclude the powerful acts of survivance and resur-
gence through which more-than-human communities coexist
and resurge in the face of world-ending violence.

These examples illustrate the dangers of apocalypse porn, of
the shocking, thrilling, and sometimes pleasurable exposure to
the threat of mass extinction. Rather than a deviant subgenre,
these narratives have become mainstream; in fact, for many
Western people, they serve as the first and most basic understanding of what extinction is and whom it affects most. Just
as pornography can normalize particular kinds of violence, we

contend that apocalyptic narratives of mass extinction embed and mask their own perverse and self-sustaining violences. To confront the violence of extinction, it is necessary to nurture alternative concepts and practices that better tend to who and what is being destroyed — alternatives that recognize the capacity of life forms and worlds to resist the violences that threaten them and that respect refusals of subjugation and erasure. We are not asking readers to disregard dire warnings about mass extinction, but rather to look closer at what their overexposing rhetoric may conceal and legitimize.

References

Adams, William M. 2010. "Conservation plc." *Oryx* 44, no. 4: 482–84. https://doi.org/10.1017/S0030605310001213.

Bird Rose, Deborah. 2011. *Wild Dog Dreaming: Love and Extinction.* Charlottesville: University of Virginia Press.

Büscher, Bram. 2014. "Selling Success: Constructing Value in Conservation and Development." *World Development* 57: 79–90. https://doi.org/10.1016/j.worlddev.2013.11.014.

Castree, Noel, and George Henderson. 2014. "The Capitalist Mode of Conservation, Neoliberalism, and the Ecology of Value." *New Proposals* 7, no. 1: 16–37. http://ojs.library.ubc.ca/index.php/newproposals/article/view/184647.

Colebrook, Claire. 2014. *Death of the Posthuman: Essays on Extinction,* Volume 1. London: Open Humanities Press.

de Groot, Rudolf, et al. 2012. "Global Estimates of the Value of Ecosystems and their Services in Monetary Units." *Ecosystem Services* 1, no. 1: 50–61. https://doi.org/10.1016/j.ecoser.2012.07.005.

Harvey, David. 2003. *The New Imperialism.* New York: Oxford University Press.

Hubbard, Tasha. 2014. "Buffalo Genocide in Nineteenth-Century North America: 'Kill, Skin and Sell.'" In *Colonial Genocide in Indigenous North America,* edited by Andrew

Woolford, Jeff Benvenuto, and Alexander Laban Hinton, 292–303. Durham: Duke University Press.

Kelly, Alice B. 2011. "Conservation Practice as Primitive Accumulation." *Journal of Peasant Studies* 38, no. 4: 683–701. https://doi.org/10.1080/03066150.2011.607695.

Malm, Andreas, and Alf Hornborg. 2014. "The Geology of Mankind? A Critique of the Anthropocene Narrative." *Anthropocene Review* 1, no. 1: 62–69. https://doi.org/10.1177/2053019613516291.

Mohawk, John. 2010. *Thinking in Indian: A John Mohawk Reader.* Edited by José Barreiro. Golden: Fulcrum Publishing.

Moore, Jason W. 2016. "The Rise of Cheap Nature." In *Anthropocene or Capitalocene? Nature, History, and the Crisis of Capitalism,* edited by Jason W. Moore, 78–115. Oakland: PM Press.

Nixon, Rob. 2011. *Slow Violence and the Environmentalism of the Poor.* Cambridge: Harvard University Press.

Ogden, Laura, Nik Heynen, Ulrich Oslender, Paige West, Karim-Aly Kassam, Paul Robbins, Francisca Massardo, and Ricardo Rozzi. 2015. "The Politics of Earth Stewardship in the Uneven Anthropocene." In *Earth Stewardship: Linking Ecology and Ethics in Theory and Practice,* edited by Ricardo Rozzi, F. Stuart Chapin III, J. Baird Callicott, S.T.A. Pickett, Mary E. Power, Juan J. Armesto, and Roy H. May Jr, 137–57. New York: Springer.

Pawliczek, Jamie, and Sian Sullivan. 2011. "Conservation and Concealment in SpeciesBanking.com, USA: An Analysis of Neoliberal Performance in the Species Offsetting Industry." *Environmental Conservation* 38, no. 4: 435–44. https://doi.org/10.1017/S0376892911000518.

Roe, Dilys, Pavan Sukhdev, David Thoms, and Robert Munroe. 2013. *Banking on Biodiversity: A Natural Way Out of Poverty.* London: Institute for Environment and Development/Bird Life International.

Sullivan, Sian. 2013. "Banking Nature? The Spectacular Financialization of Environmental Conservation." *Antipode* 45, no. 1: 198–217. https://doi.org/10.1111/j.1467-8330.2012.00989.x.

Todd, Zoe. 2015. "Indigenizing the Anthropocene." In *Art in the Anthropocene: Encounters among Aesthetics, Politics, Environment and Epistemology,* edited by Heather Davis and Etienne Turpin, 241–54. London: Open Humanities Press.

United Nations Millennium Ecosystem Assessment (UNMA). 2003. *Ecosystems and Human Well-Being: A Framework for Assessment.* Washington, D.C.: Island Press.

Wallace-Wells, David. 2017. "The Uninhabitable Earth." *New York Magazine,* July. http://nymag.com/daily/intelligencer/2017/07/climate-change-earth-too-hot-for-humans.html.

Whyte, Kyle Powys. 2017. "Our Ancestors' Dystopia Now: Indigenous Conservation and the Anthropocene." In *The Routledge Companion to the Environmental Humanities,* edited by Ursula K. Heise, Jon Christensen, and Michelle Niemann, 206–215. New York: Routledge.

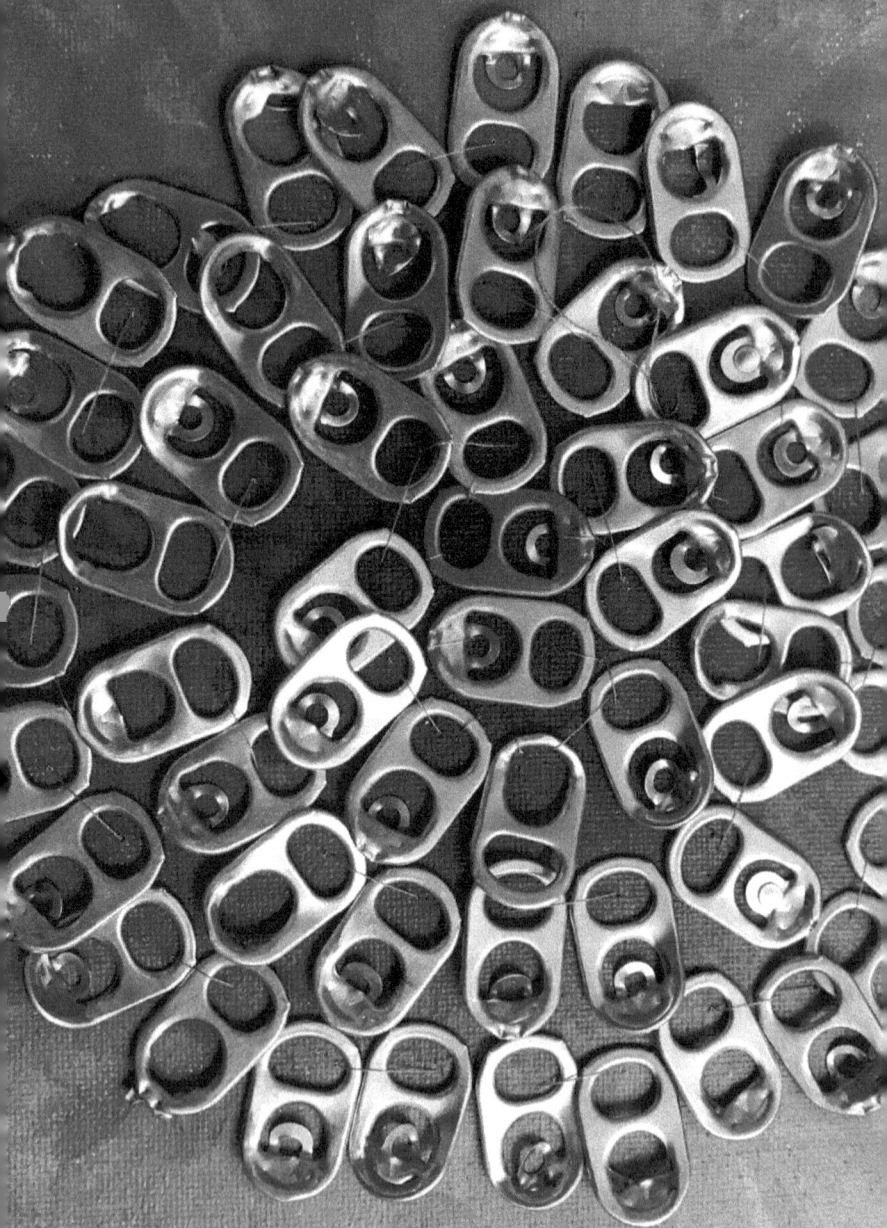

28

Fiction

Anindita Banerjee

A long time ago in galaxies far, far away, science fiction could be neatly partitioned off from its respectable cousin, literary fiction, with respect to elsewheres and futures both utopian and dystopian — worlds that seemed to have little to do with our life on our planet in the here and now. Under this longstanding arrangement, science fiction performed what Darko Suvin (1979) memorably theorized as cognitive estrangement, the *what if* and the *what would happen if.* Fiction, in the meantime, assumed a consensual idea of reality unfolding in the historical present. Yet the specter of the Anthropocene has blasted open this distinction. Under the portent of not just climate change but "everything change," as Margaret Atwood (2015) has put it, the future can no longer be put off. It is the reality with no exit options that Atwood chronicled in her MaddAddam trilogy, penned over a decade between 2003 and 2013. The author's own turn from social and metaphysical speculation to the strange realms of the nonhuman, subhuman, inhuman, and more-than-human is symptomatic of the ways in which many writers of mainstream and literary fiction are reinventing their work under the sign of the Anthropocene — if not as sci-fi, then as *cli*-fi, the ecogothic, weird fiction, and many other "-fi"s to come, which are as yet unseen and unnamed.

But are all of these fictions just melancholic expressions of dead ends, or is there more that can be said about the spillover of the future into literary reflections on the present? What can be gained by letting in the ravaged elsewheres — which, like the unsettling landscapes of science fiction itself, used to remain firmly contained behind walls that separated "our" lives from other imagined ones — into the aesthetic realm of what used to be unproblematically called "literature" or "fiction," with no qualifier needed? And is dystopia the only possible mode by which literature can engage with the Anthropocene, now that utopia seems to have been relegated to the waste heap of history? Perhaps it is necessary to indulge in an eminently science-fictional exercise to apprehend what a fiction both *of* and *for* the Anthropocene might look like: to displace utopia and dystopia as sites of binary opposition, exploring other temporalities beyond the messianic arc of the apocalypse.

The bad news is that a significant proportion of contemporary science fiction (and of the actual futuristic projects unfolding alongside them) continue to perpetuate what Patrick Sharp (2007, 170–218) astutely observed to be little more than technologically up-cycled frontier fantasies whose templates were laid out in the nineteenth century: survival myths featuring larger-than-life individuals in postapocalyptic environments. Their latter-day manifestations range from endless generations of star wars and starships to the eternal quest for water and gas in the deserts of the *Mad Max* franchise; from the new fetish for buying equity in nuclear bunkers and space colonies among the super-rich to Stephen Bannon's notorious *Biosphere 2* venture from the 1980s. The good news is that science fiction has always contained the seeds for a different kind of storytelling for the Anthropocene, and this potential has been most readily visible not to those larger-than-life individual heroes of the postapocalyptic wasteland but rather to modernity's "hyposubjects," as Dominic Boyer and Timothy Morton propose in this lexicon. Despite or perhaps precisely because of science fiction's colonial and capitalist genealogy, the genre has always offered a powerful platform for writers who came of age on residual landscapes and in invisible communities. Texts such as Octavia Butler's (2000) *Parable of the Sower* are intimately embedded in environments and enunciative positions that have never been accounted for, or were exiled beyond the margins of, the inexorable forward march of anthropocentric history. How can these other science fictions help us forge an Anthropocene imaginary?

Long before the advent of the term *Anthropocene* and the proliferation of new object ontologies in its wake, Samuel Delany (1994, 194) — literary theorist, social activist, and a rare African-American gay writer among the luminaries of science fiction at the time — pointed out that realist fiction operates on a "monologic aesthetic" in which "the exciting, material, impinging object was wholly relegated to the side, if its existence was not denied altogether." Science fiction, in contrast, concerned the dialogic interpenetration of the object and the subject — its protagonists were likely not to be human at all, but landscapes, technologies, and life forms both known and unknown. Delany's distinction marvelously anticipates the novelist Amitav Ghosh's (2016) recent manifesto, provocatively titled *The Great Derangement*. Ghosh goes one step further than Delany in denouncing literary fiction's continuing fetish of the individual subject and its dangerous disengagement from the intersections of geological time and human history. He calls the "manor house" of the canon a delusional, unsustainable utopia that needs to be "contaminated" without delay by science fiction (Ghosh 2016, 16–17). The anthropologist Anna Tsing (2015), likewise, asserts that the stories needed for imagining any future at all would be simultaneously real and fabulous, their templates available first and foremost to non-Western weavers of dreams.

What might such contaminated fiction look like? For starters, it would not just break open the boundaries between the present and the future or literary fiction and science fiction, but it would also interrogate science fiction's prevailing assumptions about itself. What happens to the *what if,* as the indigenous author and critic Grace Dillon (2012) reminds us, when for the majority of the planet the apocalyptic future has not just arrived a while ago but is here to stay for the long term: within, without, around, and across what used to be neatly divided in literary studies into our selves, our texts, and our world? Perhaps Gerald Vizenor's (2000, 15) concept of storytelling as *survivance,* "an active presence that is more than survival, more than reaction or endurance," would help us muddle our way not exactly toward utopia, but toward a future imperfect.

References

Atwood, Margaret. 2015. "It's Not Climate Change — It's Everything Change." *Medium,* July 27. https://medium.com/matter/it-s-not-climate-change-it-s-everything-change-8fd9aa671804.

Butler, Octavia. 2000. *The Parable of the Sower.* New York: Grand Central.

Delaney, Samuel R. 1994. "Science Fiction and Criticism: The Diacritics Interview." In *Silent Interviews: On Language, Race, Sex, and Some Comics,* 186–215. Middletown: Wesleyan University Press. Originally published in 1986.

Dillon, Grace, ed. 2012. *Walking the Clouds: An Anthology of Indigenous Science Fiction.* Tucson: University of Arizona Press.

Ghosh, Amitav. 2016. *The Great Derangement: Climate Change and the Unthinkable.* Chicago: University of Chicago Press.

Sharp, Patrick B. 2007. *Savage Perils: Racial Frontiers and Nuclear Apocalypse in American Culture.* Norman: University of Oklahoma Press.

Suvin, Darko. 1979. *Metamorphoses of Science Fiction: On the Poetics and History of a Literary Genre.* New Haven: Yale University Press.

Tsing, Anna Lowenhaupt. 2015. *The Mushroom at the End of the World: On the Possibility of Life in Capitalist Ruins.* Princeton: Princeton University Press.

Vizenor, Gerald. 2000. *Fugitive Poses: Native American Indian Scenes of Absence and Presence.* Lincoln: University of Nebraska Press.

29

Fire

Daniel Fisher

At once generative and consumptive, fire animates our thinking about technology and instrumentality, running through the
many stories we tell about human exceptionalism. Fire is the
über-tool, a primal lever for sociality, community, and mastery
over a separable and threatening nature. Today, it is also deeply
entwined with catastrophic climate change and capital accumulation alike. So-called wildfires and other forms of undomes-
ticated burning join more deliberate forms of land clearing to
consume vast regions of rainforest from Malaysia, Indonesia,
and Cameroon to India, Central America, and the Amazon.
Responsible for habitat loss, for atmospheric carbon release,
for ecological transformation as well as sometimes astonishing
abundance after its passage, fire sits at the center of human-driv-
en environmental disturbance in both its harmful and redemptive guises. While contemporary epochal thinking lends itself to
competing periodizations, a leading contender for the origins
of the Anthropocene is the moment at which humans acquired
control over fire.

Fire also lives so deeply within our and others' languages that
its tropes can run rampant, as though fire were not simply a generative figure but a subject in itself, a foundational alter whose
signifying power shoots through   language, making thought
itself possible (cf. Lévi-Strauss 1969). From its Promethean

DOI: 10.21983/P3.0265.1.31

theft to its capture and manipulation by internal combustion, fire makes the world, its industries, its tools, and its abundance available for us as such. Fire is also that which allows humans to leverage this instrumental relation in ever more creative fashion as we fan the flames of mass extinction. This is the arc of fire's tropic life and its poetic punch as a key engine of global climate change. However we define or animate its power, as poetry or combustive process, fire is elemental to the Anthropocene.

But fire names not one, but rather many things — things that might be understood as much *for themselves as for us.* Fire indexes relations: between fuel, heat, and oxygen, certainly, but also between earth and sky, light and dark. If it is at the origins of society, the center of the hearth, and the heart of the internal-combustion engine, it is also lit by materials shot up from deep within the Earth, ignited by lightning strikes or by the explosive landing of extraterrestrial objects. It is equal parts process and thing, energy and object, danger and potentiality. It exists also, both biblically and increasingly in more techno-cratic and managerial terms, as redemptive salvation, a healing fire. At once material, agential, and mythopoetic, its animacy depends on fuel, location, environment, and interactions with other agencies — trees and grasses, water, air, humans, and even birds (Garde et al. 2009; Latour 2014). A speculative geophys-ics might go further, troubling the search for human origins by pointing to fire's distinctive capacity to incinerate the trace of its own ignition. From this perspective, fire embodies the struc-ture of erasure and extends its logic to the planet itself (Der-rida 1991). It may not be so much that humans captured fire, but rather that human being has been itself solicited by a flammable planet (Clark 2012).

Ethnographic and ecological scholarship has come to appre-hend the multiple lives that fire leads through figures of pyro-diversity (Bowman 2015; Bird et al. 2016). In foregrounding the productive, landscape-shaping capacities of Indigenous fire re-gimes, for instance, and the different conceptions of fire's power and poetics that such regimes entail, this scholarship has offered strong challenges to colonial understandings of an ahistorical singular nature, making it clear that fire regimes on Earth are themselves highly mutable, interspecies affairs bridging trees, birds, humans, and rocks.

In Australia, efforts to leverage this interspecies pyrodiversity for capital accumulation have been developed in support of Indigenous environmental management, aiming to bring meaningful forms of employment and to reestablish historically rich relations between Aboriginal people and country, relations understood to be mediated by fire itself (Russell-Smith, Whitehead, and Cooke 2009; Martin 2013). With the advent of a national carbon trading scheme in the late 2000s, fire ecologists, Aboriginal ranger groups, and environmental policymakers turned to industrial scale seasonal burning as a means to sequester carbon. Burning country earlier in the monsoonal dry season can avoid the buildup of large fuel loads and catastrophic later-season fires. Quantifying these differing outcomes and monetizing ranger activity and Aboriginal burning vis-à-vis a national carbon credit market has proven remarkably successful. But this success belies a situation in which fires grow increasingly powerful as their fuels come to include invasive grass species, a more explosive fuel that upends a détente between trees and burning grasslands. Such accelerated transformations and accompanying instability trouble efforts to manage this relation (see also Petryna 2018).

My research with Indigenous Australians in Darwin, capital of the Northern Territory, has unfolded amid an explosive urban fire ecology in some of the Territory's most densely populated spaces. During certain parts of the year, bushfires ignite in the midst of the city, sparked by children playing, by cigarettes or campfires, or by fireworks in an explosive annual rite of Territorial citizenship, cracker night. Other fires are purposefully lit by settler Australians as authorized back burning; still others are said to obey a consuming desire, a pyromania that leads some people to set the bush alight. All such fire solicits administration and jurisdictional authority, much as Sergei Eisenstein (1986) understood the cinematic flame to gather and hold a subject's attention. It borrows human practices in its movement, draw-ing to itself those institutions that administer and augur fire's futures.

From metaphysical questions of species origin and problems of species self-presence to new attunements to its diverse ecolo-gies and the long arm of its tropic reach, fire animates a politics that grows ever more contested in an era of mass extinction. Fire thus affords new forms of life as it transforms spaces both environmental and imaginary, creating new landscapes, institu-tions, and inequities in the process. Anthropologies of such An-thropocenic contest thus call attention to the materials fire con-sumes, and to those subjects and possibilities that take shape in reflexive relation to a flammable world.

References

Bird, Douglas W., Rebecca Bliege Bird, Brian F. Codding, and Nyalangka Taylor. 2016. "A Landscape Architecture of Fire: Cultural Emergence and Ecological Pyrodiversity in Australia's Western Desert." *Current Anthropology* 57, S13: S65–79. https://doi.org/10.1086/685763.
Bowman, David M.J.S. 2015. "What is the Relevance of Pyrogeography to the Anthropocene?" *Anthropocene Review* 2, no. 1: 73–76. https://doi.org/10.1177/2053019614547742.
Clark, Nigel. 2012. "Rock, Life, Fire: Speculative Geophysics and the Anthropocene." *Oxford Literary Review* 34, no. 2: 259–76. https://doi.org/10.3366/olr.2012.0045.
Derrida, Jacques. 1991. *Cinders.* Translated by Ned Lukacher. Lincoln: University of Nebraska Press. Originally published in 1982.
Eisenstein, Sergei. 1986. *On Disney.* Edited by Jay Leda and translated by Alan Upchurch. New York: Seagull Books.
Garde, Murray, with Bardayal Lofty Nadjamerrek, Mary Kolkkiwarra, Jimm Kalarriya, Jack Djandjomerr, Bill Birriyabirriya, Ruby Bilindja, Mick Kubarkku, and Peter

Biless. 2009. "The Language of Fire: Seasonality, Resources and Landscape Burning on the Arnhem Land Plateau." In *Culture, Ecology and Economy of Fire Management in North Australian Savannas: Rekindling the Wurrk Tradition,* edited by Jeremy Russell-Smith, Peter Whitehead, and Peter Cooke, 85–164. Collingwood: CSIRO.

Latour, Bruno. 2014. "Anthropology at the Time of the Anthropocene: A Personal View of What Is to be Studied." Distinguished Lecture, Annual Meeting of the American Anthropological Association, Washington, D.C., December 6.

Lévi-Strauss, Claude. 1969. *The Raw and the Cooked.* Translated by John Weightman and Doreen Weightman. Chicago: University of Chicago Press. Originally published in 1964.

Martin, Richard. 2013. "Sometime a Fire: Reimagining Elemental Conflict in Northern Australia's Gulf Country." *Australian Humanities Review* 55: 67–91. http://australianhumanitiesreview.org/2013/11/01/sometime-a-fire-re-imagining-elemental-conflict-in-northern-australias-gulf-country.

Petryna, Adriana. 2018. "Wildfires at the Edges of Science: Horizoning Work amid Runaway Change." *Cultural Anthropology* 33, no. 4: 570–95. https://doi.org/10.14506/ca33.4.06.

Russell-Smith, Jeremy, Peter Whitehead, and Peter Cooke, eds. 2009. *Culture, Ecology and Economy of Fire Management in North Australian Savannas: Rekindling the Wurrk Tradition.* Collingwood: CSIRO.

30

Flatulence

Radhika Govindrajan

The Anthropocene is the age of flatulence. Cars, ships, and trains belch copiously into the air as they transport an ever-growing number of bodies and goods across the globe. Shale gas, which is released through the hydraulic fracturing or fracking of deep shale formations, is rapidly growing in importance as a source of natural gas in the United States, even as some scientists warn that it has "the largest greenhouse warming consequences of any fossil fuel" (Howarth 2014, 48) over a short timescale. But cars and fracked wells are rivaled in their greenhouse gas footprint by another actor in this unfolding script: gassy cows who give new meaning to the familiar phrase *silent but deadly*.

What distinguishes gassy bovines from gassy humans? Why are the effects of cattle flatulence felt on a planetary scale, potentially lethal in a way that even the stinkiest human fart is not? Cows are able to digest the tough cellulose that makes up grass and other green plants only with the help of microbial beings who live in their rumen, one of the four separate chambers of their stomach, through a process called enteric fermentation. As these microbes break down the fibers into simple molecules, the methanogenic variety among them produce methane (CH_4) — an anthropogenic greenhouse gas remarkable for its ability to capture heat and warm the atmosphere — which is released into the air mostly in the form of burps. As they eat their way through pastures often created by the large-scale clearing of forests and savannahs, cows, the largest emitters of methane among ruminants, are letting it rip. Several years ago, the FAO (2006) estimated that methane emissions from livestock contributed about 80 percent of agricultural CH_4 and 35 percent of total anthropogenic methane emissions. In the United States in 2015, atmospheric concentrations of methane accounted for almost 26 percent of total greenhouse gas emissions (EPA 2015).

In some ways, this story of flatulence is a classic cautionary tale about the Anthropocene, the current epoch in which humans are believed to act as a geological force (see Chakrabarty 2009). While it is important to remember that the increase in methane due to an expansion of human pastoralism is by no means a modern phenomenon (Bauer and Bhan 2016), it is also true that the scale and complexity of the contemporary livestock industry is unparalleled. The explosive growth in the global population of cattle, driven by the seemingly insatiable human craving for dairy and beef, is producing devastating effects on the planet. Human intervention and appetite have transformed flatulence from life into death, from a sign of the normal functioning of digestion to a sign of a planet in trouble. Ironically, even attempts to mitigate the geological impact of humans involve fantasies about the subjugation of nonhumans to human sovereignty. As scientists experiment with mixing genetic material from different breeds to engineer cows who are less gassy, but no less productive, the specter of human domination over the other-than-human looms large.

Controlling flatulence, however, has never been an easy business, and errant bovine leakages are no exception. Cattle exist in a prolonged state of flatulence that is produced through the actions and effects of an assemblage of bodies (human, animal, vegetal, and microbial), chemicals, and technologies that work within and outside a bovine corpus that is porous and open. Flatulent bovine bodies are not simply passive sites for the assertion of human control, but tenuous zones of encounter that are characterized by the permeability of boundaries and bodily integrity, and by the differentiated sharing of vulnerability and accountability. The affective and material entanglements that form in these zones of encounter are mysterious and resist human efforts at comprehensive knowledge. I was struck by the limits of human attempts to control the other-than-human in reading an interview with one of the project scientists of an EU-funded initiative to reduce methane emissions from cattle. He noted that this would not be an easy process given that the workings of the rumen were "far more complex and hard to understand" than human digestive systems (Ince 2014). The scientist's admission that cows are hard to know was echoed by another researcher, who described the rumen as one of "nature's wonders" that could adapt quickly to different scientific solutions and return to producing methane in a few weeks (Wei-Haas 2015). These acknowledgements of partiality in human knowledge of the other-than-human are a powerful reminder of the fact that nature, as Stuart McLean (**Nature**) puts it, is an "intimate stranger" which can never be fully brought within the ambit of human desire and understanding.

This tale of bovine flatulence resists Anthropocenic framings in another important way. In India, scientists in the state of Kerala claim that Vechur cattle, an indigenous dwarf species, are not only well suited to hot climates but also produce significantly less methane than crossbred cattle. Clearly, it is not just the undifferentiated category of the human that must be challenged and complicated in accounts of the Anthropocene (cf. Haraway 2015; Bauer and Bhan 2016), but also that of the nonhuman. In other words, not all cows are the same. This was a lesson brought home to me during my fieldwork in the mountain villages of India's Central Himalayan state of Uttarakhand. A friend named Prabha remarked upon the prodigious appetite and emissions of Jersey cows, which have become popular in the region for the amount of milk they yield, almost twice that of indigenous *pahari* (mountain) cows. "They're like the English [*angrez*]. They eat this much [stretching her hands wide] and shit a lot. Our cows are like us: less goes in, less comes out." In the supposedly leveled terrain of the Anthropocene, gassiness — both in its everyday origins and in its planetary effects — remains unequally distributed across human and nonhuman bodies.

References

Bauer, Andrew, and Mona Bhan. 2016. "Welfare and the Politics and Historicity of the Anthropocene." *South Atlantic Quarterly* 115, no. 1: 61–87. https://doi.org/10.1215/00382876-3424753.

Chakrabarty, Dipesh. 2009. "The Climate of History: Four Theses." *Critical Inquiry* 35, no. 2: 197–222. https://doi.org/10.1086/596640.

Environmental Protection Agency (EPA). 2015. "Inventory of U.S. Greenhouse Gas Emissions and Sinks: 1990–2013." https://www.epa.gov/ghgemissions/inventory-us-greenhouse-gas-emissions-and-sinks–1990–2013.

Food and Agriculture Organization (FAO). 2006. "Livestock's Long Shadow: Environmental Issues and Options." Rome.

Haraway, Donna. 2015. "Anthropocene, Capitalocene, Plantationocene, Chthulucene: Making Kin." *Environmental Humanities* 6: 159–65. https://doi.org/10.1215/22011919-3615934.

Howarth, Robert W. 2014. "A Bridge to Nowhere: Methane Emissions and the Greenhouse Gas Footprint of Natural Gas." *Energy Science and Engineering* 2, no. 2: 48–60. https://doi.org/10.1002/ese3.35.

Ince, Martin. 2014. "The Case for Low Methane-Emitting Cattle." *European Research Media Center*. January 10. http://www.youris.com/Bioeconomy/Agriculture/The_Case_For_Low_Methane-Emitting_Cattle.kl.

Wei-Haas, Maya. 2015. "Burp by Burp, Fighting Emissions from Cows." *National Geographic*. August 3. https://news.nationalgeographic.com/2015/08/150803-cows-burp-methane-climate-science/.

31

Flock

Anne Galloway

Some of my best friends are sheep. Almost five years ago, I brought Ursula and her triplets to our small rural block. I was there a year later, when we introduced Ernest to the girls. He was gangly and awkward: all horns and bollocks. I was there when Glory was born, an enormous creature pushed from Grace with great gulps of air, and much puffing and heaving. I cried when Ursula dropped the smallest lamb I've ever seen, and we pulled a dead and deformed twin out after her. I was there to see tiny Victoria survive and watch Mercy raise twins Melvin and Mingus. Emmaline had Edith, who mimicked all her mum's unique behaviors, and then we were ten. I sit or lay in the grass with them almost every day, the eleventh member of the flock.

Being part of a flock has given me new ways to think about the Anthropocene. For ten thousand years since the first woman suckled an orphaned lamb, our species have lived and died together. To claim that humans have always exploited this relationship is to deny the fundamental agency of sheep and the deeply embodied interconnectedness that continues to make each of us who we are. To be part of a flock is to recognize how we are intimately entangled with "others" and to imagine what we might owe "others" under the best and worst circumstances.

The Arapawa sheep is a rare, feral breed from Arapaoa — a small, 75-square-kilometer island in the Marlborough Sounds,

DOI: 10.21983/P3.0265.1.33

a remote group of drowned valleys at the northeast point of the South Island of Aotearoa New Zealand. Descended from Gulf Coast Native sheep that accompanied early whalers, they are relatively small animals that produce colored wool well suited to felting and lean, flavorful meat. Long and narrow faces, clear of fleece, distinguish the breed. Their eyes are attentive, their ears both sensitive and expressive. They carry their heads low, which some say makes them look hunched, and their long legs imbue them with speed and grace through steep hill country.

Hunters consider the Arapawa ram — with his magnificent curling horns — a prized trophy but a difficult beast to bring down. Our flock's behavior is always wary: even the paths they carve through the paddock grasses weave side to side, as the sheep constantly look behind themselves whilst walking. Each one has a different voice, and individual styles of communication. They choose to stay within the paddock fences, but jump out of any holding area that isn't taller. They come when I call them, and eat treats out of my hand, occasionally nibbling my fingers too and tickling me with their soft whiskers. They walk away when they get bored with me.

Commercial farmers tend to avoid Arapawa sheep because they don't produce the profitable kind of meat or wool, and some say their independent characters make them hard to handle. Once or twice a year our shearer offers, only half-jokingly, to shoot the sheep for me. But I've learnt they respond well to gentle handling, and their high spirits make them admirable and amusing companions. They're fiercely protective mothers, and their feral adaptations made them resistant to many of the diseases and parasites that plague domestic livestock. They are remarkably vital and robust animals, and yet sometimes they die despite all efforts to the contrary.

In the 1980s, the New Zealand Department of Conservation, in an attempt to save native species, decided to cull the feral goat and sheep populations of Arapaoa Island. Local activist Betty Rowe established the Arapawa Wildlife Sanctuary to protect as many animals as possible from being killed. Some sheep were removed to the mainland to be re-domesticated on farms, in game reserves, and even in research laboratories. Without homes like ours offering shelter and food, the breed may have gone extinct.

But becoming, and being, flock is complicated. We often assume that domestication only means bringing something into the human world, under human control — and, indeed, for them to live and breed "naturally" I have to control numbers by culling. But the sheep have domesticated me into their world as well: they are the first and last things to which I tend every day. We have grown into this small section of land together, shaping it by what we do and what we dream of doing. I may not be a sheep, but I speak with them and try my best to understand when they speak to me and with each other. We also rest and play together, experience fear, joy, and sorrow together. And yet, because each of us has failed to domesticate the other absolutely, we've also made new places and new ways with, and for, each other.

Perhaps the first step away from anthropocentrism is humility? Being flock in the Anthropocene means admitting what we are able, and unable, to do. It also requires acknowledging that not everyone will survive, despite our best attempts. I love the sheep, and I value them as companions and friends. I was there when they took their first breath, and I hope to be there when they take their last. Some of us will die when we are old and others when we are young, but I want to make sure that death comes calmly and quietly for them at home, and I wish to die with the sheep beside me too. I want to be the one who injects the fatal dose of barbiturates — and the one who holds the captive bolt gun to their heads to stun them before cutting their throats. I want to be the one who buries them in our hills and visits their graves — and the one who butchers them, eats their meat, and keeps warm with their skins.

I am just one of the caregivers, but I am the only killer member of our flock. And if they could be the same, I honestly believe I would let them.

References

Despret, Vinciane. 2016. *What Would Animals Say If We Asked the Right Questions?* Translated by Brett Buchanan. Minneapolis: University of Minnesota Press.

—————————. 2005. "Sheep Do Have Opinions." In *Making Things Public: Atmosphere of Democracy,* edited by Bruno Latour and Peter Weibel, 360–68. Cambridge: MIT Press.

Despret, Vinciane, and Michel Meuret. 2016. "Cosmoecological Sheep and the Arts of Living on a Damaged Planet." *Environmental Humanities* 8: 24–36. https://doi.org/10.1215/22011919–3527704.

Haraway, Donna J. 2008. *When Species Meet.* Minneapolis: University of Minnesota Press.

———. 2016. *Staying with the Trouble: Making Kin in the Chthulucene.* Raleigh: Duke University Press.

Porcher, Jocelyne. 2017. *The Ethics of Animal Labor: A Collaborative Utopia.* Cham: Palgrave Macmillan.

Weisiger, Marsha L. 2009. *Dreaming of Sheep in Navajo Country.* Seattle: University of Washington Press.

32

Generation

Vincent Ialenti

Post-extinction imaginaries of future Earth as present-day Mars depict a degenerated planet refigured as a despoiled desert (Jones 2012).[1] In a moving, but inert, future world, biontological dramas of life and death come to be eclipsed by the geontological dramas of a living past turned nonliving present (Povinelli 2016). Death is decoupled from the regeneration of life (cf. Bloch and Parry 1982). Inert future Earth's aesthetics smack of desolation and gloom — of worst-case scenarios that are not implausible in an age of mass extraction, nuclear weapons, biodiversity loss, population growth, environmental destruction, and anxieties about pandemic disease and asteroid impacts.

Fortunately, such degeneration visions can be generative, inspiring fresh alter-politics (Hage 2015) and alternative modes of inhabiting a damaged planet. Yet they can also be immobilizing, miring one in the delirium of no future — leaving one unable to entertain more hopeful planetary possibilities. Scouring what some call the Anthropocene for optimism, I turn to the nuclear

---

1 I use the word *imaginaries* because, to envision a World Without Us, one not only has to envision a collective we, but also, paradoxically, has to insert a living self into an inert future world in order to imagine its very lifelessness (Chakrabarty 2009, 197–98).

energy and waste disposal worlds that I have studied anthropologically.

Geoscientists have argued that the Atomic Age ushered in the Anthropocene (Than 2016). Anthropologists have pointed to how aging nuclear weapons require the work of nuclear gerontology (Masco 2004). The energy industry cautions that nuclear energy workforces are graying as baby boom retirements loom. Meanwhile, critics associate the life-extension work undertaken at aging nuclear power plants with hierarchical, centralized, military-industrial structures best relegated to backward Cold War pasts (NRC 2018). These motifs of nuclear degeneration are apt, indeed.

Yet others view nuclear energy, especially the Generation IV reactors now being designed (WNA 2017), as key to a good Anthropocene[2] — one in which "humans use our extraordinary powers to shrink our negative impact on nature." They see climate solutions in nuclear power's powers to generate steady, predictable, baseload energy without emitting carbon or leaving large land footprints. They draw arguments from the Breakthrough Institute's 2011 "Climate Pragmatism" report (Nordhaus et al. 2011), the 2013 film *Pandora's Promise,* and the 2015 "Ecomodernist Manifesto" (Asafu-Adjaye et al. 2015). They support nuclear power in the name of economic prosperity, environmental flourishing, poverty reduction, and human advancement.

So-called radioactive Greens (see Ialenti 2013) — techno-optimists who see nuclear energy as a solution to climate crisis — are enthusiastic about the prospect for nuclear energy generation to generate better futures for future generations. But their zeal must be approached with serious skepticism. In many locales, nuclear power proves cost-prohibitive, uninsurable, reliant on subsidies for innovation, and prone to low-frequency but high-impact disasters with incalculably huge social, health, financial, environmental, and psychological costs. It generates

---

2 See "Breakthrough Dialogue 2015: The Good Anthropocene," http://thebreakthrough.org/articles/past-dialogues/breakthrough-dialogue-2015.

imperatives to regulate radioactive wastes that are potentially dangerous for millennia (Ialenti 2014). Technopolitical decision-making processes (see Hecht 1998) empower the governments, corporations, financial elites, technocrats, managers, scientists, politicians, and engineers who collaboratively oversee nuclear projects, creating situations of regulatory capture and running revolving-door risks (Grossman 2012). Nuclear energy, at least in its current form, is no silver bullet for a degenerating climate. In this anthropologist's view, embracing it is no enlightened idea.

Still, such visions of good Anthropocenes and of technologically enabled ecomodernities must be taken seriously. The reasons, though, have more to do with idea generation than energy generation.

Ecomodernist optimisms about technology, innovation, human agency, open futures, incremental progress, and prospects for achieving common ground across political divides can be generative counterpoints to today's rampant Anthropocene melancholy. Such hopeful visions — invoking future generations to evoke action through enthusiasm and anticipation — can be juxtaposed with contemporary scenarios that invoke future degeneration to evoke action through horror or guilt. Why? Because pausing for a moment to entertain a (nuclear-fueled) good Anthropocene — however naive, absurd, or repugnant the idea might be — enables one to temporarily invert widespread Anthropocene apocalypticisms and to revisit Earth's future potentialities afresh.

I add *generation* to this lexicon to suggest that techno-optimist and technopessimist futures might be more frequently brought together as perspectives on each other's incompleteness. Doing so might better reveal the frontiers at which all-too-rosy and all-too-gloomy planetary futures become mired in exaggerated extremes. Bringing into view these visions' divergent analytical starting points and endpoints — and the situated coordinates of the assumptions grounding them — shows how neither offers a fully plausible forecast. Yet juxtaposing them may yet generate more nuanced, multivalent planetary futures. And who knows? Perhaps envisioning ecomodernist tomorrows will also, as Bruno Latour (2012) has put it, help us learn to "love" our technoscientific "monsters" and to care for them "as we do our children."

References

Asafu-Adjaye, John, Linus Blomqvist, Stewart Brand, Barry Brook, Ruth Defries, Erle Ellis, Christopher Foreman, David Keith, Martin Lewis, Mark Lynas, Ted Nordhaus, Roger Pielke, Jr., Racherl Pritzker, Joyashree Roy, Mark Sagoff, Michael Shellenberger, Robert Stone, and Peter Teague. 2015. "An Ecomodernist Manifesto." April. http://www.ecomodernism.org/.

Bloch, Maurice, and Jonathan Parry, eds. 1982. *Death and the Regeneration of Life.* Cambridge: Cambridge University Press.

Chakrabarty, Dipesh. 2009. "The Climate of History: Four Theses." *Critical Inquiry* 35, no. 2: 197–222. https://doi.org/10.1086/596640.

Grossman, Karl. 2012. "Nuclear 'Regulatory Capture': A Global Pattern." *Huffington Post.* July 13. https://www.huffingtonpost.com/karl-grossman/nuclear-regulatory-captur_b_1664340.html.

Hage, Ghassan. 2015. *Alter-Politics: Critical Anthropology and the Radical Imagination.* Melbourne: Melbourne University Press.

Hecht, Gabrielle. 1998. *The Radiance of France: Nuclear Power and National Identity after World War II.* Cambridge: MIT Press.

Ialenti, Vincent F. 2013. "Nuclear Energy's Long Now: Intransigent Wastes and Radioactive Greens." *Suomen Antropologi* 38, no. 3: 61–65.

———. 2014. "Adjudicating Deep Time: Revisiting the United States' High-Level Nuclear Waste Repository Project at

Yucca Mountain." *Science and Technology Studies* 27, no. 2: 27–48.

Jones, Jonathan. 2012. "No Life on Mars: An Eerie Foretaste of Earth's Future." *The Guardian.* August 31. https://www. theguardian.com/commentisfree/2012/aug/31/no-life-mars-earth-future.

Latour, Bruno. 2011. "Love Your Monsters: Why We Must Care for Our Technologies As We Do Our Children." *Breakthrough Journal* 2: 21–28. https://thebreakthrough.org/ images/main_image/Breakthrough_Journal_Issue_2.pdf.

Masco, Joseph. 2004. "Nuclear Technoaesthetics: Sensory Politics from Trinity to the Virtual Bomb in Los Alamos." *American Ethnologist* 31, no. 3: 349–73. https://doi. org/10.1525/ae.2004.31.3.349.

Nordhaus, Ted, Daniel Sarewitz, Michael Shellenberger, Jesse Jenkins, Roger Pielke, Jr., Robert Atkinson, Steven Hayward, Steve Rayner, and Chris Green. 2011. "Climate Pragmatism: Innovation, Resilience, and No Regrets." *The Breakthrough.* July 25. http://thebreakthrough.org/archive/ climate_pragmatism_innovation.

Povinelli, Elizabeth A. 2016. "Toxic Sovereignties in Geontopower." Lecture at Cornell University, Ithaca, N.Y. February 11.

Than, Ker. 2016. "The Atomic Age Ushered in Anthropocene, Scientists Say." *Smithsonian Magazine.* January 7. https:// www.smithsonianmag.com/science-nature/scientists-anthropocene-officially-thing–180957742/?no-ist.

United States Nuclear Regulatory Commission (NRC), "Backgrounder on Reactor License Renewal." October 1. https://www.nrc.gov/reading-rm/doc-collections/fact-sheets/fs-reactor-license-renewal.html.

World Nuclear Association (WNA), "Generation IV Nuclear Reactors." December. http://www.world-nuclear.org/ information-library/nuclear-fuel-cycle/nuclear-power-reactors/generation-iv-nuclear-reactors.aspx

33

Gluten

Jessica Barnes

How does the Anthropocene taste? Inspired by Stefan Helm-reich's (**Melt**) meditation on the sounds of the Anthropocene, I probe another sense — taste — as part of the embodied experience with which humans engage with an anthropogenically shaped world. Is the taste of the Anthropocene the taste of grapes grown in Scotland, a crop out of place in a human-altered climate (Ruitenberg 2014)? Or a meal served without bread, when drought in major wheat-producing countries sends world wheat prices skyrocketing and bread becomes an expensive addition to the table (Headey and Fan 2010)? Or a menu comprising only local foods to minimize the carbon emissions embedded in foods transported from around the world (Revkin 2014)?

What if the taste of the Anthropocene is something harder to detect? Take gluten, my starting point for thinking about the taste of the Anthropocene. A set of proteins found in wheat and other grains, gluten does not have a taste, per se. Even when eaten directly in the form of seitan, wheat gluten does not have an intrinsically strong flavor. If we think of taste more broadly, though, as a matter of texture and aroma as well as the sensory perception of flavor, the taste of gluten becomes more apparent. Gluten has important elastic and adhesive properties; we taste its imprint in a risen loaf of bread or chewy pizza crust. For many, given the recent growth of gluten-free diets (Fromartz

2015), the taste of gluten is defined by its alternatives. These gluten substitutes, which act as texture replacements or fillers to make up a meal, take on different tastes: a cake made with almond flour, spaghetti from spiralized zucchini, a sandwich served on cornbread. Gluten is thus visible both in its presence and its absence: as a core component of foods that helps them cohere and take shape, and as something to be avoided, labeled on food packaging and noted on menus. Like carbon, gluten is all around us, but it has to be made visible through practices of measurement and identification. Just as some people try to modify their lifestyles to minimize the carbon they produce, others try to modify their lifestyles to minimize the gluten they consume.

Gluten has been a central part of human diets since wheat was domesticated in the Near East around ten thousand years ago. Over the past decade, however, gluten has come to be associated with a range of health concerns beyond its long-identified link with celiac disease (Specter 2014). One popular narrative links this rise in gluten sensitivity to an Anthropocenic culprit, that is, human-induced changes in the gluten structure of wheat. In his best-selling *Wheat Belly* books, for example, William Davis (2011) argues that modern breeding over the last half-century has altered wheat so much that it may no longer be safe to eat. In response to a frequently asked question on his blog about whether wheat can really be so bad, he writes: "First of all, it ain't wheat. It's the product of forty years of genetics research aimed at increasing yield-per-acre. The result is a genetically unique plant that stands eighteen to twenty-four inches tall, not the four-and-a-half-foot tall 'amber waves of grain' we all remember" (Davis, n.d.). Davis's assertion that the wheat of today is no longer wheat assumes that there is a pure and stable form of wheat (over four feet tall; amber) — a notable contrast with Lesley Head, Jennifer Atchison, and Alison Gates's (2012, 37) notion of wheat as being in a "constant process of becoming." While Davis recognizes that farmers have long engaged in seed selection and thus that the anthropogenic influence on wheat is not new, to him the introduction of what he calls *science* marked a break in the equilibrium. This was the point — a shift, perhaps, from the anthropogenic to the Anthropocenic — when the crop's gluten structure started to morph.

The scientific evidence supporting Davis's argument is limited. The chemist Donald Kasarda (2013) found no significant difference between the gluten content of wheat grown today in the United States and that grown in the early twentieth century. Yet the wide circulation of this narrative raises some interesting questions. The paleoclimatologist William Ruddiman (2003) has posited a link between wheat and the Anthropocene, dating the advent of the Anthropocene back to the start of settled grain cultivation. But could there be a link between gluten and the Anthropocene? If we understand the Anthropocene as an epoch of unprecedented human intervention in the natural world that is not limited to anthropogenic climate change, then could gluten epitomize the Anthropocene? Is there something about the current moment that lends credence to the idea that we are changing our world so fundamentally that a grain central to human diets for ten thousand years is no longer good to eat? Might gluten avoidance encapsulate a way of being, eating, or tasting in the Anthropocene?

In the future, changes in the global climate are likely to affect both the amount and type of gluten in wheat; gluten, like wheat, is not singular in its identity but takes on different characteristics (Barnes 2016). Studies have shown a significant relationship between growing temperature and the quality of gluten in wheat (Moldestad et al. 2011). Experiments have also shown that increased atmospheric carbon dioxide can lead to a decline in gluten content in wheat (Högy et al. 2008). So will we see a change in the nature of gluten in a warming world?

Gluten highlights the complexities at the heart of the Anthropocene. On the one hand, we have human interventions in the natural world and efforts to breed wheat that may or may not affect the gluten content or structure of a staple crop. On the other hand, we have human changes to the atmosphere that may also affect the quantity and quality of gluten in our wheat.

Yet what remains unseen in these sorts of stories are the other dynamics that shape the way we grow and consume food. A focus on gluten alone is reductionist in the same way as a focus on carbon alone. Gluten is not just a chemical constituent of grain. It is also an object of socially shaped perceptions, commercially driven food processing, and culturally inflected dietary trends. The tastes of the Anthropocene, therefore, are at once material and imagined, sensorial and metaphorical.

References

Barnes, Jessica. 2016. "Separating the Wheat from the Chaff: The Social Worlds of Wheat." *Environment and Society: Advances in Research* 7: 89–106. https://doi.org/10.3167/ares.2016.070106.

Davis, William. 2011. *Wheat Belly: Lose the Wheat, Lose the Weight, and Find Your Path Back to Health.* New York: Rodale.

———. n.d. "FAQs." Dr. William Davis. https://www.wheatbellyblog.com/faqs/.

Fromartz, Sam. 2015. "Unraveling the Gluten-Free Trend." *Food & Environment Reporting Network.* February 24. https://thefern.org/2015/02/gluten-enigma/.

Head, Lesley, Jennifer Atchison, and Alison Gates. 2012. *Ingrained: A Human Bio-Geography of Wheat.* New York: Routledge.

Headey, Derek D., and Shenggen Fan. 2010. *Reflections on the Global Food Crisis: How Did It Happen? How Has It Hurt? And How Can We Prevent the Next One?* IFPRI Research Monograph 165. Washington, D.C.: International Food Policy Research Institute.

Högy, P., H. Wieser, P. Köhler, K. Schwadorf, J. Breuer, M. Erbs, S. Weber, and A. Fangmeier. 2009. "Does Elevated Atmospheric CO_2 Allow for Sufficient Wheat Grain Quality in the Future?" *Journal of Applied Botany and Food Quality*

82, no. 2: 114–21. https://ojs.openagrar.de/index.php/ JABFQ/article/view/2089.

Kasarda, Donald D. 2013. "Can an Increase in Celiac Disease Be Attributed to an Increase in the Gluten Content of Wheat as a Consequence of Wheat Breeding?" *Journal of Agricultural and Food Chemistry* 61, no. 6: 1155–59. https:// doi.org/10.1021/jf305122s.

Moldestad, Anette, Ellen Mosleth Fergestad, Bernt Hoel, Arne Oddvar Skjelvåg, and Anna Kjersti Uhlen. 2011. "Effect of Temperature Variation during Grain Filling on Wheat Gluten Resistance." *Journal of Cereal Science* 53, no. 3: 347–54.

Revkin, Andrew C. 2014. "A Cuisine for the Age of Us — The Anthropocene." *New York Times.* July 2. http://dotearth. blogs.nytimes.com/2014/07/02/a-cuisine-for-the-age-of-us- the-anthropocene/.

Ruddiman, William F. 2003. "The Anthropogenic Greenhouse Era Began Thousands of Years Ago." *Climatic Change* 61, no. 3: 261–93. https://doi.org/10.1023/ B:CLIM.0000004577.17928.fa.

Ruitenberg, Rudy. 2014. "Raise a Glass of Scottish Wine to Global Climate Changes." *Bloomberg.* March 25. https:// www.bloomberg.com/news/articles/2014-03-26/raise-a- glass-of-scottish-wine-to-global-climate-changes.

Specter, Michael. 2014. "Against the Grain: Should You Go Gluten-Free?" *The New Yorker.* November 3. https://www. newyorker.com/magazine/2014/11/03/grain.

34

Gratitude

Iza Kavedžija

Considerations of the Anthropocene and its changing landscape are urgent and unsettling. They have to be. But is there a way to help people consider the current state of affairs while preventing the impulse to disavow responsibility, or to at least diminish an escapist urge to change the topic? I would like to suggest that gratitude, as a particular mode of attunement, might be fruitful in this regard and is ripe for cultivation.

Gratitude combines generosity and humility. It allows for a recognition that what we have and what we deserve are not the same. It encourages us to recognize the importance of others in making our lives liveable. Even the most autonomous individuals will have to admit that we all owe a great debt of gratitude to a great many people, for all kinds of favors, support, and kindness throughout our lives. During my own fieldwork with older Japanese in Osaka, I was repeatedly struck by the extent to which the involvement of others and serendipitous encounters were woven into people's life stories. One can easily recount a certain sequence of events in terms of one's own choices and decisions — but equally, like my older interlocutors, one could consider carefully the roles that other people, situations, and events have played in those choices.

Their stories reminded me that gratitude, while bringing out the role of others in our decisions and actions, does not make us feel as though our life choices have been made for us either. It could be said that gratitude makes acting in the world possible, by making us aware of the interconnected nature of life. Becoming attuned in this way, one sees the involvement of others not as a limit to our freedom, but as enabling, facilitating, protecting.

My senior acquaintances and friends expressed gratitude, to me and in conversations with each other, even in relation to challenging events which were, upon reflection, seen to have been valuable opportunities for learning. In this sense they transformed negative experiences into sources of value — gratitude here underpins the sense of living well. This reminded me somewhat of *naikan,* a therapeutic practice developed in Japan, sometimes compared to a form of psychotherapy (Reynolds 1989). It can be seen as an example of the powerful effects gratitude can have for the way we inhabit the world. As Chikako Ozawa-de Silva (2006) writes in her insightful ethnography, *naikan*'s roots in Buddhist thought draw on the insight of "interdependent selfhood": we are not independent actors in this world, but are here thanks to others. The person undertaking *naikan* (literally "inner-looking," an introspection), guided by a practitioner's questions, is asked to quietly recollect their past while reflecting on three specific themes in relation to a significant person in their life: what they received from this person, what they returned to this person, and what trouble they caused to this person. The interviewer guiding the process visits them every few hours in a semi-secluded space and inquires about their recollections over the course of seven days, reconstructing or rearranging the memories of their life. This frequently results not only in an altered perception, but also in intense feelings of guilt and gratitude in relation to the care and favours received from others, which are seen to constitute one's life (Ozawa-de Silva 2006). While *naikan* is far from widespread, what captured my attention in its description was the emphasis on the efficacy of gratitude, and how strongly this resonated with my own interlocutors' discussions of living well.

If gratitude fosters attention to relationships, these need not be limited to people. Gratitude enmeshes human and non-human actors in subtle ways. My older friends were thoughtful in relation to their possessions and to the environment around them. They often passed on the things they were no longer using as part of the eternal, incessant, and extensive gift giving network. Grateful for a favor they received, they tried to offer something that might in turn be useful to the receiver. Many older women told me they preferred passing on their kimonos and precious possessions to people around them while alive, not waiting for them to be redistributed after their passing: "That way, you can see things being used and get so much more joy out of them." When handing things to others, they would often express the hope that something might be of use. If disposing of something, with reluctance, they might think how well the thing had served them. In this way gratitude involves non-human beings and material objects.

What are the consequences of such an orientation in ethical terms? Political theorist William Connolly proposes an ethical orientation of immanent naturalism, in other words, an ethics not grounded in a transcendental field, acknowledging that many of our ethical reactions originate in the visceral and "infrasensible." To temper this tendency, he calls for a cultivation of a "nontheistic gratitude for the rich abundance of being amid the suffering that comes with being mortal" (Connolly 2002, 105) as a source of ethical inspiration. While not necessarily available or suited to everyone, in Connolly's pluralist framework, this kind of orientation can be likened to a Foucauldian technology or "tactic" of the self (Connolly 2002, 107) — one among many. In his recent work, Connolly links this orientation of gratitude explicitly to the increasing recognition of complex interactions of global capitalist processes and non-human geological processes in the Anthropocene. He suggests an orientation of existential gratitude as one of the ways to "face the planetary" and the reality of climate change (Connolly 2017). If existential gratitude seems somewhat abstract, taking a cue from Japanese elders might make it seem more palpable and practical: small gestures and daily objects all figure differently around one when received with gratitude.

References

Connolly, William. 2002. *Neuropolitics: Thinking, Culture, Speed.* Minneapolis: University of Minnesota Press.

———. 2017. *Facing the Planetary: Entangled Humanism and the Politics of Swarming.* Durham: Duke University Press.

Ozawa-de Silva, Chikako. 2006. *Psychotherapy and Religion in Japan: The Japanese Introspection Practice of Naikan.* London: Routledge.

Reynolds, David K. 1989. *Flowing Bridges, Quiet Waters: Japanese Psychotherapies, Morita and Naikan.* Albany: State University of New York Press.

35

Heat

Alex Nading

We used to call it "global warming." Behind the Anthropocene, we are told, is a gathering heat. Perhaps it emanates from the birth of internal combustion. Perhaps it is as old as cooking, hunting, and gardening.

Identifying a material prime mover for the rising heat is one of many challenges for anthropology in the Anthropocene, but I must admit that I'm prone to thinking with heat as a metaphor. In a variety of medical systems — including Western biomedicine — body temperature, both perceived and measured, plays a central role in diagnosis. Bringing this metaphorical heat to debates over the health of the planet invites appeals to another metaphor: Gaia. Contemplating the Anthropocene, some of us imagine an overheated, weary Mother in the throes of Her last days.

Yet Gaia seems too big a figure to think with — too deceptively unifying. Heat is everywhere, but it is also profoundly differential.

Consider the story of Jorge and Ulises Pacheco, brothers and former sugarcane cutters. Both of them live in the town of Chichigalpa, in northwest Nicaragua, and both have been diagnosed with chronic kidney disease of nontraditional causes (CKDnt). After years of cutting and burning cane, they are among thousands of Central Americans whose kidneys are slowly failing.

DOI: 10.21983/P3.0265.1.37

They do not have diabetes. They do not have hypertension. Still, they and their neighbors are dying as their creatinine levels rise uncontrollably.

In a sense, work in the cane has always been deadly, but CK-Dnt is a new disease. Jorge and Ulises initially suspected that the thousands of cases that appeared among their coworkers during the 1990s might be related to the increased use of pesticides. Fearing that they were being poisoned by exploitative employers, they and their fellow workers successfully organized themselves, and by 2005, they had convinced the World Bank to fund research on CKDnt. They did this despite vigorous resistance from the Nicaraguan government and from Nicaragua's largest sugar mill, Ingenio San Antonio, owned by the Pellas Group, the country's most powerful corporation.

Since 2005, research has turned up little to no evidence of a link between pesticides and CKDnt. Studies have, however, revealed strong links between the disease and heat exposure. It is possible that the kidneys of sugarcane cutters are responding to some kind of thermal tipping point. As a Colorado-based team of investigators has suggested, conditions in the cane may have gotten just slightly worse — just hot enough — to spark a new pathology (Kelly 2015). Temperatures in El Salvador, less than one hundred miles north of Chichigalpa, have risen by 0.5°C since 1980. These same studies indicate that work in the cane has also gotten more intense. Hours are longer and breaks for water, rest, and shade are less frequent. The heat that has always been there — as potential energy in sugar and carbon, as pounding sunlight, as surplus labor — is taking on a new embodied form.

The heat that has long driven the global economy might be its undoing. Consultants at Verisk Maplecroft (2015) have warned that rising temperatures could cut productivity in Southeast Asia by as much as 25 percent over the next thirty years. States, insurance companies, and labor unions from California to Texas are rewriting occupational health rules to deal with the threat of heat stress (Sigma Group 2015; Satija 2015). Laborers and managers are not the only ones feeling the burn. As Jason de León (2015, 32) has shown in unsparing ethnographic and forensic detail, the superheated environment of the Sonoran desert has been harnessed as a weapon by the U.S. Border Patrol: a "natural" deterrent to undocumented migration. Desert heat not only kills would-be migrants; it incinerates their bodies and makes them disappear.

Heat's effects aren't all bodily. Back in Chichigalpa, Jorge and Ulises both believe that heat is to blame for their condition, but they are divided over what to do about it. Ulises leads an organization of CKDnt sufferers who want to work with the Pellas Group to secure payments and medical care for former cane cutters. Jorge leads a group that opposes working with a plantation company and a government that have ignored laborers for more than a scorching century. This struggle between two dying brothers is a struggle over how to make justice out of heat. Jorge and Ulises are no longer on speaking terms.

The kidney has long been a site of familial care and concern. Brothers and sisters accompany one another during long sessions of dialysis, and close kin can be among the most suitable kidney donors. In Chichigalpa, however, heat is rending these socio-organic ties asunder, even as the disease that affects Jorge and Ulises spreads around the world and links them to farmers in Egypt and Sri Lanka. CKDnt appears to be a problem of both global health and global warming. Yet body and Earth don't map as neatly onto one another as they might in a Gaia story.

The situation I have described is emblematic of what Kim Fortun (2012) calls "late industrialism." Heat is both evenly distributed and patchy. Some bodies — not all — are deteriorating, but we are supposed to imagine an entire biosphere in peril. Is the heat that causes coral reef die-offs the same heat that causes CKDnt, or the same heat that causes the bodies of migrants to decompose and dissipate after they perish in the desert?

Instead of teetering between extinction and survival, perhaps we humans are instead catching a glimpse of a new thermal necropolitics (Mbembe 2003), in which heat kills not globally but selectively. Ethnography, then, can break down the metaphorical and social forms of insulation that make heat seem sometimes global, sometimes invisible. It can help us find patterns and points of pushback within what look like random flare-ups, combustions, and burns.

References

De León, Jason. 2015. *The Land of Open Graves: Living and Dying on the Migrant Trail.* Berkeley: University of California Press.

Fortun, Kim. 2012. "Ethnography in Late Industrialism." *Cultural Anthropology* 27, no. 3: 446–64. https://doi.org/10.1111/j.1548-1360.2012.01153.x.

Kelly, David. 2015. "Mysterious Disease May Be Tied to Climate Change, Says CU Anschutz Researcher." *EurekAlert!* October 8. https://www.eurekalert.org/pub_releases/2015–10/uoca-mdm100815.php.

Mbembe, Achille. 2003. "Necropolitics." Translated by Libby Meintjes. *Public Culture* 15, no. 1: 11–40.

Satija. Neena. 2015. "In Dallas, A Push to Give Some Workers a Break." *The Texas Tribune.* September 30. https://www.texastribune.org/2015/09/30/dallas-weigh-rest-breaks-construction-workers/.

Sigma Group. 2015. "CAL OSHA's New Heat Stress Prevention Regulation (Reg. 3395) Has Been Updated." June 19. http://isigmagroup.com/cal-oshas-new-heat-stress-prevention-regulation-reg–3395-has-been-updated/.

Verisk Maplecroft. 2015. "Heat Threat Threatens to Cut Labour Productivity in SE Asia by Up to 25% within 30 Years." October 28. https://www.maplecroft.com/portfolio/new-analysis/2015/10/28/heat-stress-threatens-cut-labour-productivity-se-asia–25-within–30-years-verisk-maplecroft/.

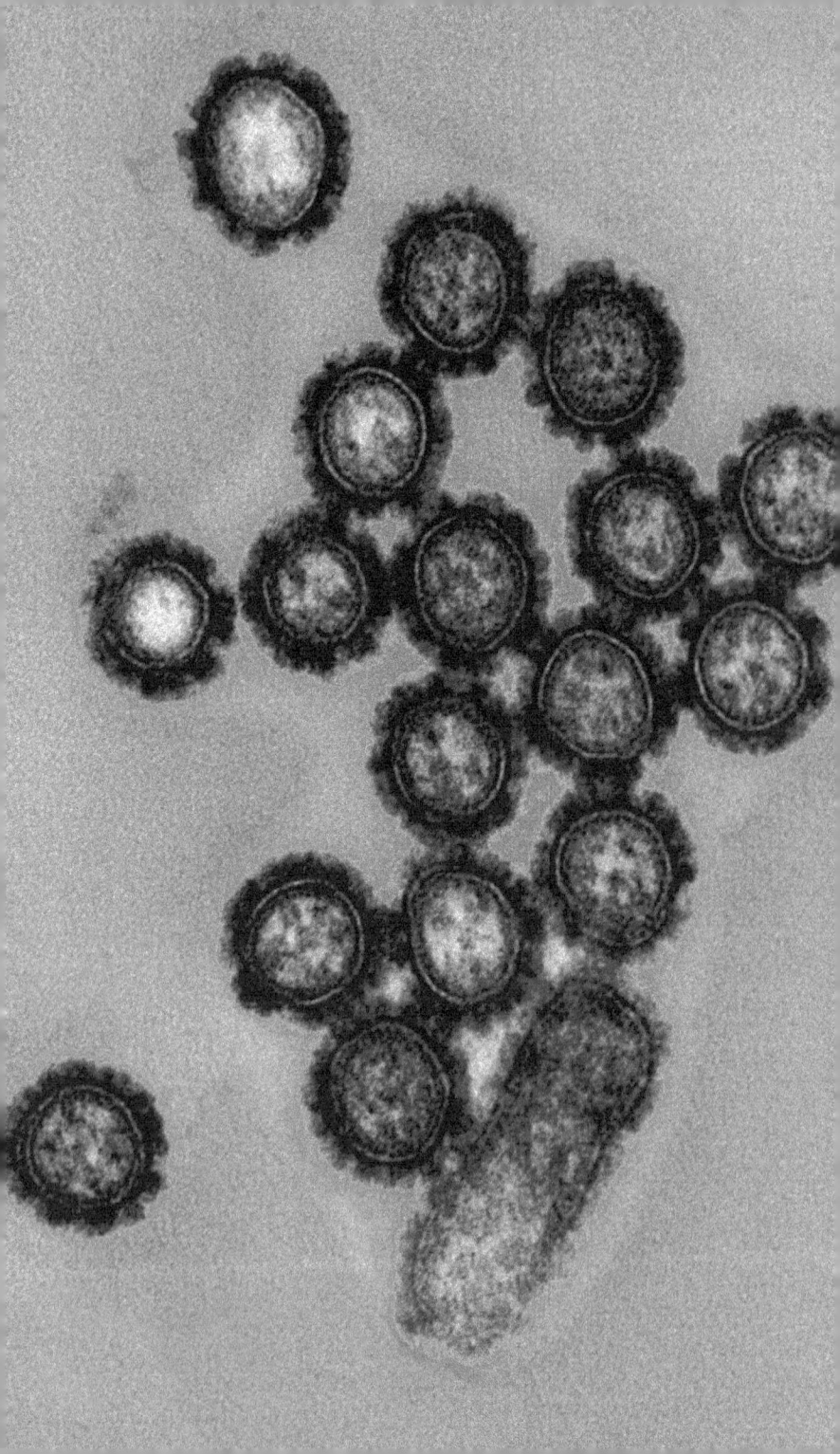

36

Hyposubjects

Dominic Boyer and Timothy Morton

We live in a time of hyperobjects, of objects too massive and multiphasic in their distribution in time and space for humans to fully comprehend or experience them in a unitary way. A black hole is a kind of hyperobject; a biosphere is another. But in the Anthropocene many of the hyperobjects that concern us have human origins. For example, global warming. Or antibiotics. Or plastic bags. Or capitalism. These hyperobjects exceed and envelop us like a viscous fog; they make awkward and unexpected appearances; they inspire hypocrisy and lameness and dread.

A certain kind of human has helped usher the world into the hyperobjective era. Let's call them *hypersubjects*. You will recognize them as the type of subjects you are invited to vote for in elections, the experts who tell you how things are, the people shooting up your schools, the mansplainers from your Twitter feed. Hypersubjects are typically, but not exclusively white, male, northern, well-nourished, and modern in all senses of the term. They wield reason and technology, whether cynically or sincerely, as instruments for getting things done. They command and control; they seek transcendence; they get very high on their own supply of dominion. Do you want to know what is irritating hypersubjects today? The fact that hyperobjects are whispering in their ears, whispering that this being and time that they have fashioned in their image and for their own convenience is dying. The voices in their heads say that there is no time for hypersubjects any more. It is *hypo*subjectivity, rather than hypersubjectivity, that is becoming the companion of the hyperobjective era.

So, as hypersubjects seeking to reform, we have begun in a fumbling, Roomba-like way to explore the political potentiality of hyposubjects. Although *hyposubjectivity* sounds a bit like an abject condition of being forced to endure and suffer the effects of viscous forces like climate change and capital, we wonder whether that sense of weakness and insignificance, that lack of knowledge and agency, is actually what needs embracing. Looking backwards, the road to our present condition is paved with mastery of things, people, and creatures, with a weird faith in our species' alleged ability to always know more and better. This project of investigating the hyposubject may end up resembling a book, but we hope it will grow on to become a game: maybe a role-playing game, because we all like costumes and because this is a game that needs more players. For the moment, though, here are some things we have been saying.

Hyposubjects are the native species of the Anthropocene and are only just now beginning to discover what they might be and become.

Like their hyperobjective environment, hyposubjects are also multiphasic and plural: not-yet, neither here nor there, less than the sum of their parts. They are, in other words, *subscendent* rather than transcendent. They do not pursue or pretend to absolute knowledge or language, let alone power. Instead they play; they care; they adapt; they hurt; they relate.

Hyposubjects are necessarily feminist, colorful, queer, ecological, transhuman, and intrahuman. They do not recognize the rule of androleukoheteropetromodernity and the apex species behavior it epitomizes and reinforces. But they also hold the bliss-horror of extinction fantasies at bay, because hyposubjects' befores, nows, and afters are many.

Hyposubjects are squatters and *bricoleuses*. They inhabit the cracks and hollows. They turn things inside out and work miracles with scraps and remains. They unplug from carbon gridlife; they hack and redistribute its stored energies for their own purposes.

Hyposubjects make revolutions where technomodern radar can't glimpse them. They patiently ignore expert advice that they do not or cannot exist. They are skeptical of efforts to summarize them, including everything we have just said.

In sum, for the moment, the transcendent hypersubject continues to stalk the earth. But he is doing so in an increasingly flickering, even spectral way; his monophasic being is perpetually out of sync. Half-aware that his time is past, he lashes out violently, pouts, negates any alternative, bargains for salvational machines and afterlife redemptions. You might pity him were he not the cause of so much trouble over so much time. As we write, huge numbers of these distressed creatures are climbing inside of white balloons with names like Donald Trump, Nigel Farage and Jair Bolsonaro, inflating them, hoping to fly away. But as in the film *Gravity*, what awaits us instead is the task of fabricating a future out of ruins and preparing for a long, perilous voyage back to earth. That future will belong to hyposubjects. If we wish to thrive, we will become human (again).

37

Industrialism

Craig Campbell

Industrialism is founded upon an imperious humanism that not only imagines an inherent right to all that it beholds, but also presumes the savvy capacity to manage and engineer the Earth. In the late 1920s, a leading Soviet biologist described the ultimate goal of socialist industrialism: "a profound rearrangement of the entire living world [...] all wild species will disappear with time; some will be exterminated, others will be domesticated. All living nature will live, thrive, and die at none other than the will of humans and according to their designs. These are the grandiose perspectives that open up before us" (Weiner 1988, 290). While this counts among the most hubristic of such rhetorical claims, it is grounded in the same arrogant ideology that has been central to all forms of industrialism. The Anthropocene is not an accidental by-product of human development. It was engineered and recognized from the earliest days as a stroke of mastery. The cumulative impact of industrialism on Earth systems is the curse of the Anthropocene: mass extinction, rising sea levels, melting glaciers, toxic environments.

The politics of climate change are embedded in critiques of complex social and technical infrastructures, which generate a mythopoetics of the industrial everyday that seems impossible to escape. Perhaps more myth is required to disentangle us from the scale of the problem. Consider Prometheus, the fire-stealing

DOI: 10.21983/P3.0265.1.39

titan of classical Greek mythology who is typically associated with human enlightenment, revolt, and personal sacrifice. If industrialism's human avatar is the engineer, then the engineer's patron must be Prometheus, whose story has been celebrated by communists and capitalists alike (pace Malm and Hornberg 2014). To fix our attention on industrialism is to embrace the name we already have for the destructive mode of exploitation that has come to prominence in the world. Take the *Prometheocene* as an alias for industrialism in the so-called age of man.

"I will give men as the price for fire an evil thing in which they may all be glad of heart while they embrace their own destruction." Thus spoke Zeus in Hesiod's (1914, 7) *Works and Days*. The rough outline of the tale, we recall, is this: Prometheus, a patron of humanity, steals fire from the forge of the gods and gives it to man. Zeus punishes not only the thief for his crime, but humans as well. Prometheus is chained to a rock to endure perpetual torture, and man is given a jar, secretly full of curses and plagues.

Everyone knows what industrialism looks like. To borrow a turn of phrase from Susan Sontag (2003, 18), "being a spectator of calamities [...] is a quintessentially modern experience." Consider the photos of Bernd and Hilla Becher (Stimson 2014). In the second half of the twentieth century they created a remarkable typology of factories, exhibiting endless grids of industrial architecture from postwar Germany. Or look to the work of photographer Edward Burtynsky, whose fascinating landscapes document Earth torn asunder, gargantuan carcasses of decommissioned ships, vast pits of chemical effluent, rows upon rows of workers processing chickens.[1] These are works that appear in corporate boardrooms even as they illustrate environmentalist magazines (Campbell 2008).

Industrialism also looks like Bhopal. *The Unforgettable Night* is a painting of a demon whose body is made up of the infamous Union Carbide plant, with a mouth that "spews poison and people and crushes everything under its feet" (Fischer 2009, 125).

---

1 See the artist's website: http://www.edwardburtynsky.com.

Industrialism is evident in W. Eugene Smith's photographs from Minimata (Smith and Smith 1975). It is the flyover scene from Chernobyl in which radiation is registered on the very substrate of the film, the degradation causing visual and auditory pops (Shevchenko 1986). It is the newspaper headline that bee colonies are collapsing, that scientists are weeping over the bleached coral reefs off the coast of Australia (Mooney 2016). It is the scientific evidence that fracking causes earthquakes, which everyone already knew, anyway. These are the images of industrialism for those of us who have found the catastrophic prophesies of global warming to be rather unsurprising. Look around and you know them right away. Commodity fetishism hides not only labor but also ecological debt that has existed across capitalist and socialist economies.

Industrial modernity's "dark Satanic Mills" (Blake 1913, 370) have a long history of social antipathy. Opposition, however, seems to have been eclipsed by the celebration of industrialism or, at least, generalized resignation to its ascendancy. For the Soviets, industry was a sign of strength and progress. In the decades before the Great Acceleration, when industrialism cemented its rise as the dominant ideology supporting all forms of human social organization, the image of the factory became a symbol of national achievement. The Hoover dam in the United States matched the Soviet Dneprostroi Dam in an industrial tit-for-tat. Before that canals and rail systems were celebrated along with mills and mines, all components in complex technological assemblages that obscured and redistributed ecological debt. The future of industrialism, explored in Kim Fortun's (2014) account of late industrialism, is no less troubling.

Let us return, then, to the Promethean gift, that "evil thing" for which we have been glad of heart. Amid the gifts of enlightenment and technology are the countergifts of hunger, sickness, and war. Faith in engineering is considered by many to be the only way out of this crashing world into another one, more hospitable to the project of life. Such Promethean hope, however, is troubled by cautionary analyses documenting the perils of geoengineering (cf. Morton 2015). Other scholars (e.g., Brassier

2014) decry the erosion of purpose and resolve, characterizing anti-Promethean critique as dangerously timid.

To be sure, an appraisal of the Promethean character of industrialism marks the catastrophic scale of its arrogance. Such an appraisal seeks to account for a tendency to minimize and veil disaster while celebrating industrial progress. The spark of fire is a kindling ingenuity at the heart of the builder. It is betrayed, however, by the desire for mastery and the grand scales of engineering that have come to govern the drift and crash characteristic of this industrial now.

References

Blake, William. 1913. *The Poetical Works.* Edited by John Sampson. Oxford: Oxford University Press.

Brassier, Ray. 2014. "Prometheanism and Its Critics." In *#Accelerate: The Accelerationist Reader, edited by Robin Mackay and Armen Avanessian,* 467–87. Falmouth: Urbanomic Media.

Campbell, Craig. 2008. "Residual Landscapes and the Everyday: An Interview With Edward Burtynsky." *Space and Culture* 11, no. 1: 39–50.

Fischer, Michael M.J. 2009. *Anthropological Futures.* Durham: Duke University Press.

Fortun, Kim. 2014. "From Latour to Late Industrialism." *Hau: Journal of Ethnographic Theory* 4, no. 1: 309–29.

Hesiod. 1914. *Hesiod, the Homeric Hymns, and Homerica.* Translated by Hugh G. Evelyn-White. Cambridge: Loeb Classical Library.

Malm, Andreas, and Alf Hornborg. 2014. "The Geology of Mankind? A Critique of the Anthropocene Narrative." *Anthropocene Review* 1, no. 1: 62–69.

Mooney, Chris. 2016. "'And Then We Wept': Scientists Say 93 Percent of the Great Barrier Reef Now Bleached." *The Washington Post.* April 20. https://www.washingtonpost.com/news/energy-environment/wp/2016/04/20/and-then-we-wept-scientists-say–93-percent-of-the-great-barrier-reef-now-bleached/.

Morton, Oliver. 2015. *The Planet Remade: How Geoengineering Could Change the World.* Princeton: Princeton University Press.

Shevchenko, Vladimir, dir. 1986. *Chernobyl: Chronicle of Difficult Weeks.* Glasnost Film Festival 4. San Francisco: The Video Project.

Smith, W. Eugene, and Aileen M. Smith. 1975. *Minamata: The Story of the Poisoning of a City, and the People Who Chose to Carry the Burden of Courage.* New York: Holt, Rinehart, and Winston.

Sontag, Susan. 2003. *Regarding the Pain of Others.* New York: Farrar, Straus and Giroux.

Stimson, Blake. 2014. "The Photographic Comportment of Bernd and Hilla Becher." *Tate Papers* 1. https://www.tate.org.uk/research/publications/tate-papers/01/photographic-comportment-of-bernd-and-hilla-becher.

Weiner, Douglas R. 1988. *Models of Nature: Ecology, Conservation, and Cultural Revolution in Soviet Russia.* Bloomington: Indiana University Press.

38

Installation[1]

Serpil Oppermann

Installation presents new imaginative horizons in confronting the Anthropocene charged with cataclysmic future scenarios. To install means to invest, and investment suggests hope and promise in this new geological epoch named for *anthrōpos,* an epochal geo-force. Thinking with installation as part of the emerging Anthropocene lexis problematizes such a totalizing categorization and reinstalls the subjects of the Anthropocene in the environmental imagination as *anthrōpoi* — plural humans, with their histories of love, strife, loss, fear, and survival. When envisioned from the perspective of the aesthetic encounters of art and the Anthropocene, *installation* produces aesthetic sensibilities about whether human beings can imagine less destructive ways of interacting with the world.

In aesthetic terms, *installation* emphasizes our creative encounters with the world as rendered through a kind of art that contains the geo-political and bio-cultural meanings of changing habitats due to anthropogenic effects and processes. Considering the fact that *installation* also means emplacement and settlement, art installations that play with these meanings raise questions about what it means to be settled in a changing place

---

1   A different version of this essay has been published in *Environmental Humanities* 10, no. 1 (2018): 338–42.

while paradoxically feeling displaced. The Anthropocene is often characterized by uncertainty and unpredictability around Earth's distress in coping with the overwhelming impact of detrimental human activities. Understandably, future scenarios are imagined for an almost unlivable *oikos* (Earth, our home) with either globally displaced species, including human beings with little hope of survival, or the phenomenal extinction of life altogether. To re-imagine the Anthropocene, *art installations* install and then subvert this characterization by retrieving a note of hope amidst the dissonant horizon of disturbed ecologies and by reinscribing promise in the cultural imaginary to recuperate our home that is not yet totally lost. To illustrate such a story, I have chosen an art installation as a case in point in Haydarpaşa, the iconic but now ghostly train station in Istanbul's Asian side, located next to the sea where the continent ends.

There are no travelers in this old station; instead the whispers of the past permeate empty spaces, and echoes of the Orient Express bounce back from its gracefully embroidered domes. Ghostly pirouettes of the West and the East appear before instantly vanishing into the shadows again while witty sea gulls and curious cats become witness to its solitary stories. Standing here feels like being poised over the threshold of the Anthropocene epoch; you want to reflect on, if not capture, its distressing silences and losses many of which can be observed here in the Sea of Marmara. Gone now are swordfish, blue tuna, sturgeon, and turbot whose poignant stories lay bare "some of the complex cross-weaves of vulnerability and culpability that exist between us and other species" (MacFarlane 2016). Here the transcendent perspective of the Anthropocene is vibrant in the air, but unlike the effect of safe distance created by the aerial photography of David Thomas Smith, for example, there is also something corporeally proximal revealing the Anthropocene's impure vibrations, its disenchanted signs, its miasma, and its small moments through an art installation.[2]

---

2 See the artist's website: https://www.david-thomas-smith.com/anthropocene/.

In Haydarpaşa's Waiting Lounge, Turkish psychiatrist and artist Rahşan Düren's *E-Motions* was installed in 2015.[3] It was "an installation consisting of 20 gilded steel constructions, each 4.5 meters long, synchronized with servo step engines producing complex and irregular movements with precision positioning" (Düren 2015). These movements are produced by 20 golden dials accompanied by sound recordings and light projections that affect you visually, sensually, and musically. They imply distress, but also enact a concern for a promising message that can be felt when seven different choreographies installed in the software of the system begin performing a posthuman dance in strange rhythms, with the waves splashing onto the ancient stones beyond Haydarpaşa's elegant walls and with the sunlight that pours through its windows.

What turns *E-Motions* into a form of Anthropocene awareness is the plaintive tale it tells to capture the small moments of sadness, and perhaps also nonsense, embedded in the Anthropocene itself. This tale contests the hubristic visions of the Anthropocene phenomena in which humanity remains a major geological force for many millennia. The oversized gold-plated dials seem to obfuscate human presence here, but in quite an ironic way; indeed the absence of humans in this choreography is an ironic homage to the *anthrōpos* as a catastrophic planetary agency doomed to bring about its own end. But *E-Motions* also trace possibilities that are not yet fully imagined about endings.

As a meditational solicitude on loss and promise, *E-Motions* actually disrupt and restructure the matrix of the Anthropocene by creating an ironic context in which *emotions* must be balanced with *motions,* which is the idea behind this art installation that wants us to reflect on the Anthropocene in a different way. We may be experiencing sad moments of farewells, feel the loss of disappearing species, for example, but the message here is that the environmental fate is not sealed as indicated by the dials that turn "slightly brighter when measuring happy reunions, and imperceptibly darker when registering the sor-

---

3   See http://rahsandurenhaydarpasa.com/eng/.

row of departures" (Akaş 2015). These were my thoughts as I walked among the golden dials. Is this art installation a mirror of Anthropocene-induced anxieties? Is it replaying our strained earthly becomings and displaying what we will pass onto future generations, turning "slightly brighter" and then "impercepti-bly darker"? I felt engulfed in a cloud of indeterminacies. There was no closure here in any definite sense but rather ambigu-ity about our species' complicated existence — like a hazy line within which was some unnamable mixture of sadness and hope. The only certainty for me as an intra-active observer was that *E-Motions* contained our paradoxes within it. Because it was presented in the most self-reflexive of ways, experiencing this installation was an unexpected discernment of the Anthro-pocene as an open-ended process carrying some hope despite all the struggles in anthropogenic landscapes. Thinking with *in-stallation* opened up my curiosity about stories, told and untold, that tell of terrestrial life shaped by the *anthrōpoi*.

E-Motions can be read as a projection of the Anthropocene pointing to a crumbling home, but also to the idea that it is still holding. For as long as the dials move, they arouse the feeling that the Earth is still in place. Yet the question — "what if hu-mans flip the switch?" — is also unavoidably there, putting the valuing of the term installation as "emplacement," or "sitting place," under critical pressure. Rather than reassuring an un-problematic sense of place to dissolve our fears of being radical-ly displaced in the future, *E-Motions* generate a feeling of hope depending on the way humans can bring motions and emotions together. This is precisely why this specific artwork was installed in an old train station. If Haydarpaşa is the symbolic epitome of our home becoming dysfunctional, it has served well for *E-Mo-tions* to communicate a message of revaluing what we may lose.

References

Akaş, Cem. 2015. "Movement, with Feeling." *Rahşan Düren.* http://rahsandurenhaydarpasa.com/eng/movement-with-feeling.html.

Düren, Rahşan. 2015. "E-Motions: Technical Aspects." *Rahşan Düren.* http://rahsandurenhaydarpasa.com/eng/e-motions-technical-aspects.html.

Macfarlane, Robert. 2016. Generation Anthropocene: How Humans Have Altered the Planet for Ever." *The Guardian.* April 1. http://www.theguardian.com/books/2016/apr/01/generation-anthropocene-altered-planet-for-ever

39

Interstellar

Michael P. Oman-Reagan

In his 1980s television series "Cosmos," Carl Sagan popularized the idea that we are "star stuff," and that everything we know is made of matter born in a star. "We are their children," Sagan said, reminding us that our bodies, technologies, and histories all began in a starfire crucible. Consider plants for example, the "photosynthetic ones," the "sun worshippers and worldly con-jurers" (**Photosynthesis**). Imagine phytoplankton in ancient oceans using solar radiation to increase atmospheric oxygen, making it possible for ancestral life to leave the sea and walk in space-suit-like bodies filled with ocean water. Inhale Earth's atmosphere now and consider the plants, still breathing with us, in our shared biosphere made possible by stars. This interstel-lar intimacy reminds us we live and die with stars, on a solar-powered world.

I grew up under fields of starlight in high-altitude Eastern Oregon, looking into our galactic heart across star rivers and interstellar dust. Elsewhere, today, light and air pollution block this experience of facing the galaxy, a rite of passage into "hy-posubjectivity" (**Hyposubjects**). Every culture has a night full of stars (Ruggles 2015). What happens without those stars to remind us how much we do not know? Today the Milky Way is hidden from one-third of humanity (Falchi et al. 2016). The occluding haze of fossil-fueled artificial skyglow is an anthropogenic shadow cast up over the stars, obscuring a reminder of how recently-arrived and short-lived we are in celestial time.

In an unimaginable deep future, billions of years from now, our star-engine Sun will expand and burn the Earth before collapsing into a stellar remnant, slowly dimming into lightless death. A disaster (*dis-astron*) is "a fallen, dysfunctional, or dangerous, or evil, star" (Morton 2013, 15). We have always lived with this ineludible disaster, but human temporality rarely takes such futures into account (**Timely**). The eventual stellar **Apocalypse** (uncovering or disclosing) unveils hope through photosynthetic lessons from star-worshiping plants who teach us to clear the haze and reveal the night sky by following their solar-powered example. The interstellar doesn't promise forever, but asks: How do you want to spend this time until I return to you, and you return to me?

If the interstellar is "the space between the stars" (JPL), our planetary milieu is likewise increasingly situated between centers (Canguilhem 2001) as we orbit our Sun while reaching out to other suns, each a star at the center of a solar system. Such interstellar perspectives amplify an ever-expanding "environmental solar system" (Olson 2012) so that our home becomes "as much cosmic as it is human," at once "dreamy and rational, earthly and celestial" (Lefebvre 1991, 121).

Consider the following scientific story of Earth's trajectory. We are shielded from our star by a planetary magnetic force field. Enormous hyperobjects, non-human entities massively distributed in time and space (Morton 2013), collide as solar wind and magnetosphere frictions ignite aurora fires in our skies. Now, imagine our entire solar system enveloped within another hyperobject, the heliosphere, an even larger magnetic bubble pushing back against the interstellar winds just as Earth's magnetic field repels the solar wind. Our solar system is also in motion, circling the center of the Milky Way which is, in turn, an unimaginable vastness within a filament of galactic super-clusters, surging along cosmic rivers of gravitational flow. Traced as a line, tracking our orbit around the sun, around the galaxy, and so on, this motion is not a circle or ellipse. Our course spirals, warps, and soars across multiple vectors. The interstellar perspective disrupts assumed trajectories of Earth's path through the universe.

We are already travelling across the space between the stars, already living on a world ship (Cosmos; Lazier 2011). If we think of our interstellar journey as a meshwork of lines (Ingold 2007) and trajectories, what courses might our future travels trace, what might we carry to other worlds, on which wayfaring paths?

Lou Cornum illuminates the "long tradition of NDN inter-stellar exploration," and asks "why can't indigenous peoples also project ourselves among the stars?" (2015). Speculative feminist fabulations (Barr 1992; Haraway 2013), like Ursula K. Le Guin's Hainish universe and Carolyn Ives Gilman's Twenty Planets se-ries, imagine human diaspora on many worlds becoming alien to one another a thousand generations after Earth ancestors seeded planets throughout interstellar space. Exoplanet astron-omers populate interstellar space with Earth-like worlds, refig-uring how we imagine home (Messeri 2016). Future generations inherit imagined ecologies and carrying capacities, colonized by yesterday's visions of how to live on spaceship Earth (Anker 2005).

Consider Frederik de Wilde's spacecraft-sculpture "starship-SPIDER." An interstellar ship composed of intersecting black lines, its scaffolding "arising deep within the satanic mills of the industrial revolution that spewed black carbon into Earth's at-mosphere" (Armstrong and De Wilde 2015). Foucault described "the ship" as heterotopia *par excellence* and warned that without ships our "dreams dry up, espionage takes the place of adven-ture, and the police take the place of pirates" (Foucault 1986, 27). As venture capitalists plan to mine or settle every world be-yond earth, will we bring hubris, anthropocentrism, inequality amidst abundance, and propertarian violence to new worlds by weaving neo-industrial extractive webs in space? Or can we im-agine spaces of hope on biological, symbiotic generation-ships, in which generations of human and non-human crew are born and die while learning intimate lessons of interstellar ecology before homecoming around a distant star.

Traces of the interstellar are all around. Here in this room, rainbows spin across my walls as a glass prism in the window splits the sun's starlight into spectra. The prism attunes us to atmospheres of our star, bringing the interstellar into intimate "regionality," multiplying its attendant "prismatic ecologies" (Stewart 2011, 2013). As the interstellar moves between abstraction, text, place, and object, it unfolds to reveal a constellation of inhabited worlds inscribed by senses, stories, sciences, and speculative fictions. What was remote, insensate, and desolate out there in the space between the stars becomes intimate, poetic, and inhabited down here on Earth.

References

Anker, Peder. 2005. "The Ecological Colonization of Space." *Environmental History* 10: 239–68. https://doi.org/10.1093/envhis/10.2.239.

Armstrong, Rachel, and Frederik De Wilde. 2015. "StarshipSPIDER." http://frederik-de-wilde.com/project/starshipspider/.

Barr, Marleen S. 1992. *Feminist Fabulation: Space/postmodern Fiction.* Iowa City: University of Iowa Press.

Canguilhem, Georges. 2001. "The Living and Its Milieu." Translated by John Savage. *Grey Room* 1, no. 3: 7–31. https://doi.org/10.1162/152638101300138521.

Cornum, Lou. 2015. "The Space NDN's Star Map." *The New Inquiry,* January 26. https://thenewinquiry.com/the-space-ndns-star-map/.

Falchi, Fabio, Pierantonio Cinzano, Dan Duriscoe, Christopher C.M. Kyba, Christopher D. Elvidge, Kimberly Baugh, Boris A. Portnov, Nataliya A. Rybnikova, and Riccardo Furgoni. 2016. "The New World Atlas of Artificial Night Sky Brightness." *Science Advances* 2, no. 6: e1600377. https://doi.org/10.1126/sciadv.1600377.

Foucault, Michel. 1986. "Of Other Spaces." Translated by
    Jay Miskowiec. *Diacritics* 16, no. 1: 22–27. https://doi.
    org/10.2307/464648.
Haraway, Donna Jeanne. 2013. "SF: Science Fiction, Speculative
    Fabulation, String Figures, So Far." *Ada: A Journal
    of Gender, New Media, and Technology* 3. https://doi.
    org/10.7264/N3KH0K81.
Ingold, Tim. 2007. *Lines: A Brief History.* London: Routledge.
Lazier, Benjamin. 2011. "Earthrise; Or, the Globalization of
    the World Picture." *American Historical Review* 116, no. 3:
    602–30. https://doi.org/10.1086/ahr.116.3.602.
Lefebvre, Henri. 1991. *The Production of Space.* Oxford:
    Blackwell.
Messeri, Lisa. 2016. *Placing Outer Space: An Earthly
    Ethnography of Other Worlds.* Durham: Duke University
    Press.
Morton, Timothy. 2013. *Hyperobjects: Philosophy and Ecology
    after the End of the World.* Minneapolis: University of
    Minnesota Press.
NASA Jet Propulsion Lab (JPL). 2013. "Voyager Enters
    Interstellar Space - NASA Jet Propulsion Laboratory." http://
    www.jpl.nasa.gov/interstellarvoyager/.
Olson, Valerie A. 2012. "Political Ecology in the Extreme:
    Asteroid Activism and the Making of an Environmental
    Solar System." *Anthropological Quarterly* 85, no. 4: 1027–44.
    https://doi.org/10.1353/anq.2012.0070.
Ruggles, Clive Lance Neville, ed. 2015. *Handbook of
    Archaeoastronomy and Ethnoastronomy.* New York:
    SpringerReference.
Stewart, Kathleen. 2011. "Atmospheric Attunements."
    Environment and Planning D: Society and Space 29, no. 3:
    445–53. https://doi.org/10.1068/d9109.
———. 2013. "Regionality." *Geographical Review* 103, no. 2:
    275–84. https://doi.org/10.1111/gere.12017.

40

Leviathans

Alex Golub

Four thousand years ago they knew the world would end the same way it began: with dragons. Humanity's first experiments with the state, city, and surplus were also experiments in myth. As infrastructures — nutritional, mythical, political, material — began their slow, millennia-long thickening into the Anthropocene, gods slew dragons. In Sumer and Ugarit, Urartu and Akkad, people told stories of dragons' defeat: Tiamat and Leviathan, Behemoth and Rahab. All of them were symbols of chaos, threats to an abundant natural order subdued by Baal or Marduk or Yah. These battles were also part of complexity's first political theologies: Bronze Age kings legitimated their reign by styling themselves servants of the gods that slew chaos and brought order. Even the Hebrew god defeated Leviathan, though this battle was redacted out of the Torah and relegated to the Psalms. In humanity's first experiments in bigness, then, Leviathan was an enemy of the state (see Day 1985; Gunkel 2006; Levenson 1987).

Sacred kingship had a good run — scattered adherents remain to this day — but took one of its earliest, most decisive hits in early modern Europe. During the English Civil War, Roundheads challenged the divine right of Charles I. The challenge turned into a beheading, and the war sent royalists like Thomas Hobbes fleeing to France. Searching for certainty, Hobbes im-

agined a new Leviathan who could secure an orderly world and
ensure that England's nasty and brutish civil war would also be
short. This Leviathan's rule was rooted not in its calibration with
mythocosmic order, but in a neo-Epicurean appreciation of the
rational self-interest of citizens faced with overwhelming power
(Kahn 2004; Stewart 2015). Ernst Kantorowicz (1957) once wrote
that the king had two bodies, but in Abraham Bosse's frontispiece to Hobbes's *Leviathan,* the king had amassed over three
hundred. *Leviathan*'s deductive philosophizing was defeated
by an air-pump (Shapin and Schaffer 1985), but its publication
joined punitive deterrence and the social contract in a marriage
that continues to this day. The king was no longer the enemy of
Leviathan; he *was* Leviathan.

In the three hundred and fifty years since *Leviathan,* humanity has perfected the art of mastering bigness through corporations. These leviathans — legal entities treated as people — have
an unparalleled capacity to organize time and space extensively
and intensively. Robert MacIver (1939) called the modern industrial state a New Leviathan. Franz Neumann (1963) chris-
tened its fascist variant Behemoth. Modern logistics, beginning
with D-Day and the war in the Pacific, were largely created to
overcome them, thus making our own leviathans stronger. The
Internet, for some, a symbol of decentralization, was a piece of
Cold War social science invented to ensure that the American
leviathan would always have a head, no matter how many nodes
were destroyed.

Today's leviathans seem invulnerable because of their scales.
Immortal, they outlive the lawsuits of those who oppose them.
Intangible, they dwell offshore and beyond sovereignty — un-
less, that is, they make their own. Max Weber (1978) argued that
leviathans, rationally developed, were the most efficient sort of
organization for mobilizing action. For Louis Brandeis (1914),
this bigness was a curse, not a blessing, and size was inherently
noxious because of the uses to which it could be put. Today, in
the Anthropocene, we have learned the power of the leviathans
that have swallowed us.

The curse of bigness is not merely that leviathans are too successful, not just that they turn exploitation into overexploitation. Another source of their power is their ability to insulate individual humans from moral responsibility. As Robert Jackall (1988) points out, in corporations decisions are pushed up but responsibility is pushed down. Their mistakes — the oil spills, the malfunctions, the violence — are never the leviathan's error. The guilt is borne by the faulty part, the contractor, the rogue employee on a frolic of his own (Gaddis 1994). Or, better yet, responsibility falls in the interstices between people. Even if they weren't too big to jail, leviathans' distributed corporeality is unincarcerable. Our ethics of individual responsibility is inadequate to an age of distributed agency.

Scale also facilitates disavowal. Once, Leviathan was a symbol of chaos. Today, leviathans work through externality, pushing the entropy they create outside of themselves, their balance books, and their commitment to transparency and sustainability. Within, there is order. Without is somebody else's problem. Unintended consequences, structural effects, collective action problems: these are how the world ends with dragons. So we build larger and larger leviathans to enclose what was once disavowed. The United Nations. Global emissions standards. The International Council on Mining and Metals. World banks and courts. The Subcommission of the International Commission on Stratigraphy, which officially named the Anthropocene itself. Our attempts at smallness continue too: zones Occupied to create a space where size does not crush possibility, truth revealed by Anonymous networks that create scaled effects without producing a corporate body. Even corruption — for what else is corruption but an affront to routinized bigness? — has the potential to disrupt.

The end is a distinct possibility. Our leviathans may end the Anthropocene not long after it began. We already have visions of this apocalypse, complete with dragons. The Talmud (Baba Bhatra 74b) teaches that God originally created two leviathans, male and female, but God slew one of them lest they reproduce and their brood destroy the world. When the world ended, it says, there would be a feast for the faithful when the meat of this leviathan would be served under a canopy made of its skin. They knew the world would end the same way it began: with dragons.

Taming our bigness, harnessing our leviathans, imagining forms of empowering smallness: these are the central challenges of the Anthropocene. Connecting individual responsibility to structural injustice; building an enduring empathy for people affected by slow-motion disasters, not just photogenic, cataclysmic ones; describing complexity clearly; explaining indeterminacy rather than gesturing at its beautiful inscrutability: these are the tasks for which our lexicon must be deployed. In the future, we will sport with leviathans.

References

Brandeis, Louis. 1914. *Other People's Money, and How The Bankers Use It.* New York: Frederick A. Stokes.

Day, John. 1985. *God's Conflict with the Dragon and the Sea: Echoes of a Canaanite Myth in the Old Testament.* New York: Cambridge University Press.

Gaddis, William. 1994. *A Frolic of His Own.* New York: Simon and Schuster.

Gunkel, Hermann. 2006. *Creation and Chaos in the Primeval Era and the Eschaton: A Religio-Historical Study of Genesis 1 and Revelation 12.* Grand Rapids: William B. Eerdmans.

Jackall, Robert. 1988. *Moral Mazes: The World of Corporate Managers.* New York: Oxford University Press.

Kahn, Victoria. 2004. *Wayward Contracts: The Crisis of Political Obligation in England, 1640–1674.* Princeton: Princeton University Press.

Kantorowicz, Ernst H. 1957. *The King's Two Bodies: A Study in Mediaeval Political Theology.* Princeton: Princeton University Press.

Levenson, Jon D. 1987. *Creation and the Persistence of Evil: The Jewish Drama of Divine Omnipotence*. New York: Harper and Row.

MacIver, Robert. 1939. *Leviathan and the People*. Baton Rouge: Louisiana State University Press.

Neumann, Franz. 1963. *Behemoth: Structure and Practice of National Socialism, 1933–1944*. New York: Octagon Books. Originally published in 1944.

Shapin, Steven, and Simon Schaffer. 1985. *Leviathan and the Air-Pump: Hobbes, Boyle, and The Experimental Life*. Princeton: Princeton University Press.

Stewart, Matthew. 2015. *Nature's God: The Heretical Origins of the American Republic*. New York: W.W. Norton.

Weber, Max. 1978. *Economy and Society: An Outline of Interpretive Sociology*. Edited by Guenther Roth and Claus Wittich. Berkeley: University of California Press.

41

Melt

Stefan Helmreich

How does the Anthropocene sound?[1] Sound can provide an unexpected way into apprehending developments in the Anthropocene, or, to take Jussi Parikka's (2015) term, the *Anthrobscene*:
the toxic material accompaniment to computational, tablet, and
smartphone media culture, which, far from ushering the contemporary world into a paperless ecotopian sublime, fills the
world with poisons and other effects consequent upon producing, consuming, and discarding these devices. Sound can provide a way of wobbling a prognosticating common sense that
usually operates in the domains of the visual, the graphic, or the
calculational.

Hugh Raffles (2010) has alerted us to the recordings that
sound artist David Dunn has made of beetles eating piñon trees,
recordings that Raffles and Dunn have described as the sound of
global warming (Dunn 2006). Tuning into another sign of planetary change, scientists and artists are now auditing the sounds
of melting ice. With assisted listening, scientists claim to be calling into audibility the sounds of ice thaw and fracture. In 2013,
the American Institute of Physics reported that "glaciers sizzle as
they disappear into warmer water. The sounds of bubbles escap-

---

1   This piece is excerpted and adapted from my collection *Sounding the Limits
    of Life: Essays in the Anthropology of Biology and Beyond*.

ing from melting ice make underwater glacial fjords one of the loudest natural marine environments on Earth" (AIP 2013). Geophysicist Erin Pettit, who set up underwater microphones off the coast of Alaska, suggests that hydrophonic recordings might track changes in the integrity of glacial ice. Underwater sound becomes a signal of the future, of life and death to come — a mix of clarion call, rumor, and swan song. But it also calls into question the very difference between now and not now; soundings are not always easy to sort into echoes from the past, resonances in the present, or preverberations from the future.

A number of musicians and sound artists have directed their recording machines toward such sounds, from Andrea Polli (2009) and DJ Spooky to Cheryl Leonard (see Hince, Summerson, and Wiesel 2015) and Jana Winderen (n.d.). In 2010, artist and sculptor Wendy Jacob contributed another entry to this sound-of-melting-ice tradition, traveling to the Arctic archipelago of Svalbard to capture the sound of ice fizzing and fizzling as bubbles trapped for millennia slowly popped and cracked open. Her recording trip inspired an installation that she entitled *Ice Floe,* exhibited in Boston's Museum of Fine Arts in 2011.[2] If you were to hear the recordings for *Ice Floe* in the way that Boston museumgoers did, you would be sitting or lying on a low twelve-by-twelve-foot transductive floor, feeling/hearing through fourteen jigsaw-joined component platforms the low-frequency vibrations that Jacob was able to record through hydrophones. Sensing through skin and bones the calving of glaciers bubble by bubble presents visitors, Jacob has said, with an experience of "each little breath of 4,000-year-old air letting go" (Bergeron 2011). Full-body hearing, which senses the suspended past breaking into an open and uncertain future, seems an apt method for bringing the sounds of climate change close,

---

2   The installation was audible and on view at the Eunice and Julian Cohen Galleria of the Museum of Fine Arts from September 17, 2011 through July 8, 2012. The piece was the result of work that Jacob did as part of an Arctic Circle artist residency sponsored by the Farm Foundation for the Arts and Sciences, and it was staged in connection with Jacob being named the winner of the 2011 Maud Morgan Prize.

for folding ecological process into embodied apprehension, for sensing the sounds of melt.

References

American Institute of Physics (AIP). 2013. "Glaciers Sizzle as They Disappear into Warmer Water." November 27. https://www.sciencedaily.com/releases/2013/11/131127170103.htm.

Bergeron, Chris. 2011. "Artist Turns Arctic Adventure into Pop Art." *Wicked Local.* October 19. http://www.wickedlocal.com/article/20111019/News/310199337.

Dunn, David. 2006. *The Sound of Light in Trees: Bark Beetles and the Acoustic Ecology of Piñon Pines.* Earthear, EE0513, compact disc.

Hince, Bernadette, Rupert Summerson, and Arnan Wiesel. 2015. *Antarctica: Music, Sounds, and Cultural Connections.* Acton: Australian National University Press.

Parikka, Jussi. 2015. *The Anthrobscene.* Minneapolis: University of Minnesota Press.

Polli, Andrea. 2009. *Sonic Antarctica.* Gruenrekorder, Gruen 064, compact disc.

Raffles, Hugh. 2010. *Insectopedia.* New York: Pantheon.

Winderen, Jana. n.d. "Field Trip to the North Pole, Mamont Foundation, 18–23 April 2015." *Jana Winderen: Field Trips.* http://www.janawinderen.com/fieldtrips/field_trip_to_the_north_pole_m.html.

"La situación es compleja, los puentes vehiculares y peatonales colapsaron".

CARLOS PEÑA, líder comunitario de Belalcázar, Cauca.

Noviembre

la enorme avalancha de lodo, tierra y
del volcan Nevado del Huila.

Aspecto general que presentaba ayer la Normal de Belalcázar.
El barro prácticamente la tapó. ¡Sólo la virgen se salvó!

Desamparados y tristes quedaron los po
Cauca, pues muchos lo perdieron todo.

ODO MORTA

ertos y 7 desaparecidos, dejó la noche del sábado dos nuevas avalanchas en
su paso por Belalcázar, Cauca. Casas, puentes y una escuela, quedaron bor

Destrucción y muerte dejó a su paso la avalancha del río Paez, que ayer volvió y arremetió,
tras la erupción del volcan Nevado del Huila, en el municipio de Belalcázar, Cauca.

La Defensa Civil Colombiana ayudó
que dejó la avalancha en Belalcáza

Los puentes vehiculares se vinier
población quedó incomunicada p

tenares de casas, 4 puentes, una
estación de gasolina y hasta el
Liceo Educativo La normal.

Liliana Fajardo coordina-
dora del punto emergencia del
Municipio de Páez-Belalcázar,
manifestó que "la primera
erupción se presentó las diez de
la noche del sábado., ocasio-
nando sobre el río Páez una
primera avalancha la cual pasó
por el municipio 10 minutos

¡NO OLVIDE!

☑ En junio de 1994, una
avalancha de lodo y agua
causada por un sismo, ma-
tó a 1.000 personas.

☑ El 19 de febrero del año
2007, ocurrió la primera
erupción del volcán en 500
años de existencia.

después de haberse activado el
sistema de alarmas y de eva-
cuación". A las 11:05 p.m. se
presentó un segundo evento
vulcanológico, de igual mag-
nitud, dejando al municipio de
Belalcázar y las veredas vecinas
sin fluido eléctrico.

A las 11:15 p.m., los ha-
bitantes de Belalcázar y sus
veredas fueron evacuados hacia
el sector de La Meza.

Martín Alonso Achipiz, un
campesino llegó al hospital con
heridas en la cabeza, mientras
otro hombre fue arrastrado por
la avalancha.

42

Miracles

Diego Cagüeñas Rozo

Are there miracles in the Anthropocene? An odd question, to be sure. But a question that speaks to the experience of living in the Anthropocene when one truly lacks geological agency. This is the case in Tierradentro, a secluded valley in the Colombian southwest where destruction and miracles seem inextricable.

It all began in 1992 with a few tears. No one believed them. The girls were out of breath, scared. They had just seen the Virgin of Fatima crying. They were playing close to the Virgin's humble niche by the side of the road when they saw tears running down her face. No one believed them; they were told to scram. Two years later an avalanche destroyed most of Belalcázar, the largest town in Tierradentro, but the Virgin survived. The figurine was rescued from the mud and the floating corpses, intact. In retrospect, people wondered: Had the Virgin been crying because of the tragedy to come?

That was 1994. On June 6, after a 6.3 earthquake, the river Páez turned into a deadly mudslide that wreaked havoc across Tierradentro, killing over 1,000 people. Belalcázar's hospital was destroyed but the image of St. Vincent de Paul that presided over its entrance was rescued, unscathed. Two miracles, one disaster. In 2008 it happened again. The seismic activity of the Huila Volcano caused the mountain flanks to plunge into the river and turned it, for the third time in less than twenty years, into a roaring monster of mud and debris. Amidst the devastation, another Virgin survived. This time was the Miraculous Virgin, who stood undaunted in the school's courtyard. *El enjambre,* a local newspaper that promises "an avalanche of information for Tierradentro," reported this miraculous survival as yet another episode of this uncanny history of religious images' resilience against landslides. Only divine intervention could explain these events that defy the laws of nature. For Manuel Escobar, a local historian, the Virgin's open arms are a signal of hope: "Welcome, not everything is lost, here I am."

These miraculous stories do not belong to the Holocene; they unfold against an unprecedented geological scenery. In August 2016, an expert panel recommended to the International Geological Congress to acknowledge that humanity's impact on the Earth has been so profound since 1950 that a new geological epoch needs be declared: the Anthropocene. With this acknowledgment the human species reached full blown geological agency. In today's geological scenery, humans act as planet-forming forces just like winds, rivers and volcanos. Human beings are no longer only social or political beings — we have become wholly geological actors.

Human history thus arrives to its apogee exactly at the point where human actions partake in the inhuman, self-organizing processes that form and transform the world. In the Anthropocene the physical universe forms and explains itself; no need for transcendence of any kind. In such an immanent field of forces there is no room for divine intervention — the clutches of pure physics and geology embrace the entire universe.

"The common people imagine the power of God to be like the authority of royal majesty, and the power of nature to be like a force and impetus," argued Spinoza. Is the Anthropocene the end of God's power? Have we become God-like co-creators of the universe or are we entirely in the grips of nature's force and impetus? Maybe this is no longer a real distinction because nature has turned into another name for God (*Deus sive natura*)? But in Tierradentro, a remote corner of the Anthropocene's seemingly all-embracing purview, the authority of royal majesty appears as the best hope of a better life. For what good is geological agency when political agency is denied?

Once the avalanches have run their course and the mud dries, the deep social inequalities that shape life in Tierradentro are hard to ignore. As the nation-state pushes Indians, peasants and impoverished mestizos into unsafe areas where they can barely scratch out a living as the mining and cattle industries seize the land, the unequal distribution of geological agency appears in plain view. However, the central government is adamant about bypassing politics to naturalize the tragedy. In 2009 it was announced that Belalcázar is located in a "high-risk area" and needs to be relocated, even though the town had been there for over a century. El enjambre denounces: "the political elites achieved what earthquakes, avalanches and volcanos had not: they destroyed our hope of living where we were born."

In 2010 another tragedy elsewhere diverted the government's priorities and Belalcázar was not relocated. This brought respite to its inhabitants but at the same time they lost the little political agency they had gained from geological destruction. The politicians and their helicopters never came back. "We are in the hands of God," Manuel laments as he stands on the river's edge.

In his scathing invective against miracles, Spinoza wrote: "the common people suppose the existence of God is proven by nothing more clearly than from what they perceive as nature failing to follow its natural course" (2007, 81). But in the fringes of the Anthropocene, nature failing to follow its natural course does not only mean that an avalanche unexpectedly changes its course. It also means that the proverbial politics of exclusion may come to a halt, if only fleetingly. That would be a real miracle.

Far from the centers of knowledge-production where it has been officially sanctioned, the Anthropocene looks not as the accomplished fact of geological agency but as the miraculous promise of political agency in local geopolitics. Perhaps, as Spinoza claimed four centuries ago, we do live under the illusion that man is situated in nature as a kingdom within a kingdom, since we are prone to believe that humans disturb rather than follow nature's order. Now that as alleged geological agents we follow and disturb nature, the geopolitics of the Anthropocene shall not do without this illusion, and our political imagination ought to acknowledge that we still have need for a political kingdom within the Anthropocene kingdom.

References

Carrington, Damian. 2016. "The Anthropocene Epoch: Scientists Declare Dawn of Human-Influenced Age." *The Guardian.* August 29. http://www.theguardian.com/ environment/2016/aug/29/declare-anthropocene-epoch-experts-urge-geological-congress-human-impact-earth.

Escobar, Manuel. 2008. "Y la virgen sigue ahí. ¿Milagro?... ¡Milagro!" *El enjambre* 14: 17.

———. 2009. "La desubicación" *El enjambre* 15: 4–7.

Spinoza, Benedictus de. 2007. *Theological-Political Treatise.* New York: Cambridge University Press.

43

Models

Jeremy Trombley

In the Jorge Luis Borges fable "On Exactitude in Science," an empire's cartographers construct a map so detailed that it covers the entire territory. Yet the map ends up decayed and tattered when the subjects find it unwieldy and useless. Jean Baudrillard (1994, 1) claims that this fable "possesses nothing but the discrete charm of second-order simulacra [...] and, if one must return to the fable, today it is the territory whose shreds slowly rot across the extent of the map." Now it seems we live in a world of models: complex computer simulations of the atmosphere, hydrosphere, and biosphere. Much of what we know about the Anthropocene and the many ways that humans have dramatically altered the Earth comes to us through models, from the global General Circulation Models that track climate change to agent-based models of local decision-making practices. With all of the names that have been proposed to identify our current era, maybe there's no harm in offering one more: the Simulocene, a world made by modeling.

There's a story I like to tell when asked about my research. About fifty years ago, in the mid–1960s, the U.S. Army Corps of Engineers began building an enormous physical model of the Chesapeake Bay. The model covered nine acres and was housed within a fourteen-acre warehouse on Kent Island, just across the Chesapeake Bay Bridge from Annapolis. Water could be run

DOI: 10.21983/P3.0265.1.45

through the concrete estuary in order to understand the effects of various engineering projects on the quality and quantity of water in the actual estuary. With over $25 million in funding from the federal government, the model was constructed over the course of twenty years and became a tourist site in its own right. Unfortunately, by the time the physical model was completed, another model had already taken its place. In 1983, the first computer model of the Chesapeake Bay watershed was unveiled with the promise of more complex versions to follow as computing power and knowledge developed over time (Keiner 2004). The physical model was largely abandoned—although it had one last moment of glory when it was used to locate the heroic victim of a plane crash in the icy Potomac River, who had helped save many of his fellow passengers but fell through the ice at the last moment. The model was brought up to full flow, and the few remaining researchers were able to successfully pinpoint the location of the passenger's body. Somewhat ironically, perhaps, the researchers used cut-up IBM punch cards as stand-ins for the body, throwing them into the model estuary to see where they ended up. The body was found right where the model predicted it would be (Center for Land Use Interpretation 1998).

I tell this story because it reminds us that models are not simply virtual objects that live in the so-called cloud. They are real things that exist and interact with the world. They not only shape the way we think about the systems they are built to represent, they also have material effects on those systems. Richard White (1996, 116) makes this point about the Columbia River in the Pacific Northwest:

In the virtual Columbia electronic fish swim past electronic dams on video terminals. Change the electronic river and the fate of the electronic fish is graphically displayed [...] That the various virtual Columbias depend on the actual Columbia for some of their own electrical power only compounds the ironies and connections.

Paul Edwards's (2010) concept of computational friction helps us make sense of not only the materiality of models and the labor that is needed to make and manage them, but also the way that models — through their construction, maintenance, and use — mediate and generate social relationships. Models have needs in terms of data, code, and computational power. In addition, the scientific knowledge encapsulated within the models requires the interaction of researchers who are often working on disparate concepts and tools. More complex models have more intensive and complex demands, and, as a result, more complex social organizations form around them. The General Circulation Models that Edwards describes are exemplary: global-scale models both enable and require global networks of relationships and organizations, like the International Panel on Climate Change. There is an almost symbiotic relationship between models and the organizational systems that produce them. In the Simulocene, the model and the territory are inextricably linked.

This is also true in the Chesapeake Bay's watershed. The first computer model of the watershed was completed in 1983, the same year that the Chesapeake Bay Program was created. In 1987, the watershed model was coupled to an estuary model that simulated the effects of these nutrients in the bay itself, spurring the development of the Chesapeake Bay Modeling System: a combination of four models growing increasingly complex with every iteration. At the same time, the Chesapeake Bay Program has grown in size and scope by including more of the watershed states and additional research institutions, federal and state agencies, and advocacy groups to form a massive partnership that extends throughout the watershed and beyond. The model has allowed the partnership to grow by providing evidence to justify the inclusion of all of the states whose waters flow toward the Chesapeake. In turn, the various relationships embodied in the partnership have made it possible to build a more complex and detailed model. The institution and the simulation exist in a kind of symbiosis, and together they play a significant role in shaping the material watershed.

In the Simulocene, perhaps both Borges and Baudrillard are correct: models are not only tools for knowing the world around us; they also performatively intervene to make a world around themselves. The two models I have discussed here — the physical and the computational — represent both different ways of knowing the Chesapeake and its watershed and dramatically different regimes of managing ecological relationships. As material, institutional, and conceptual components assemble around our physical and computational models, the question we must ask is: what kind of world do our models create, and what other worlds might we manifest through simulation?

References

Baudillard, Jean. 1994. *Simulacra and Simulation.* Translated by Sheila Faria Glaser. Ann Arbor: University of Michigan Press. Originally published in 1981.

Center for Land Use Interpretation. 1998. *The Chesapeake Bay Hydraulic Model: A Miniaturization of the Largest Estuary in the United States.* Culver City: Center for Land Use Interpretation.

Edwards, Paul N. 2010. *A Vast Machine: Computer Models, Climate Data, and the Politics of Global Warming.* Cambridge: MIT Press.

Keiner, Christine. 2004. "Modeling Neptune's Garden: The Chesapeake Bay Hydraulic Model, 1965–1984." In *The Machine in Neptune's Garden: Historical Perspectives on Technology and the Marine Environment,* edited by Helen M. Rozwadowski and David K. Van Keuren, 273–314. Sagamore Beach: Watson Publishing International.

White, Richard. 1996. *The Organic Machine: The Remaking of the Columbia River.* New York: Hill and Wang.

44

Monoculture

Sarah Besky

Agriculture — or more accurately, horticulture — marks human settlement. Growing plants is both a means of making place and a reason to stay there.

When agriculture reaches for economies of scale, plants become plant. Think of the singularized nouns *soy, cotton,* and *rubber.* In monoculture, both botanical varietals and variety in the landscape disappear. Champions of imperial expansion hailed monoculture as a triumph of science and technology over putatively wild landscapes and people. In this respect, tea was prototypical. Indian-grown tea, along with other colonial monocultures like sugar, coffee, and tobacco, formed an arsenal of "proletarian hunger-killers" (Mintz 1979, 60) — cheap energy that fueled the early carbon-based economy of British and American mills.

How do you make a monoculture?

The anonymous author of a nineteenth-century instructional text (*Tea Cultivation* 1865) for would-be tea planters outlines the precise steps that need to be taken.

"Tea will grow better in virgin soil," the text explains. "Village lands have long ago had all of the goodness taken out of them […] The germs of all kinds of seeds deposited by animals, wind, people" sap the "strength" of this "formerly cultivated" soil. Such soils, we learn, require five times as much labor "to keep."

DOI: 10.21983/P3.0265.1.46

In the more distant forest, the text goes on, "the wind has less power to deposit on the surface seeds of wild grasses, and perhaps, more than all, no manure (always so fruitful in the propagation of weeds) has been spread onto the land."

How best to clear these forests and "jungle lands"?

To get all of the life out of a forest, you must be methodical. First, you should cut the bamboo, grasses, and small trees, leaving them on the ground to dry for two to three months, rendering them into kindling. Next, bigger trees can be removed by ringing, or carving a six-inch to two-foot circle of bark around the trunk. Sap circulates under tree bark like blood under our skin. Ringing halts this process by choking the vascular flow of nutrients to the upper reaches of the tree — a slow death.

Anticipating the would-be monoculturalist's concerns about the time and cost of eradication, the manual warns about the dangers of the alternative: unchecked biological diversity. White ants make homes in large trees, and they quickly shift to chewing on the bases of tea bushes if those trees are not ringed.

Once trees and grasses have dried up, it is time to burn. The manual continues:

It is a grand sight to see — the fire leaps along, urged by a strong wind, which is generally waited for, and the quantity of combustible material is so great that the moderate sized trees, which have been felled and which would not burn themselves, are completely consumed. A curious accompaniment to these fires is the sound emitted by the burning bamboos. It resembles incessant discharges of musketry. As I lay in bed one night, in the neighborhood of a blazing jungle, I might easily have fancied myself in action; in fact I did fancy so; for as sleep stole over me, the volley upon volley transported me to scenes far different from the evergreen tea gardens around.

The military overtones are apt. They are flashbacks, of course, but also flash-forwards to a contemporary moment when voracious forest fires consume human and nonhuman life from California to Indonesia, and fires in unregulated sweatshops undermine capital's efforts to produce cheaper and cheaper goods.

Monoculture requires eradicating life, even though monocultures are often formed in the name of feeding or otherwise sustaining life.

How do you maintain a monoculture?

The plantation is the system that keeps the ants, grasses, and trees at bay. Plantation work goes on year after year, in the form of burning and replanting (in the case of annual crops like sugar, cotton, and soy) or pruning and watering (in the case of perennials like tea and coffee). Plantation work is equal parts caring and killing: pesticides and fertilizers, spades and sickles, irrigating water and combustible fuel.

Monoculture sutures people's identities to single things. Today, in the tea districts of Assam, plantation workers are referred to as "tea tribes." Although Indian tea plantation workers are technically free to abandon the fields to seek work in cities or towns, workers receive the bulk of their compensation not in cash but in kind, in the form of housing, food rations, and medical facilities. This system of in-kind payment ensures that the reproduction of human life is woven firmly into the continued production of tea. Since plantation monoculture is an economy of scale, people and plants only need to be marginally healthy, marginally alive. Quantity of life comes before quality of life.

The consignment of certain kinds of persons to dependence on monoculture continues, but botanical homogeneity is also being pursued in the name of cultural homogeneity: monoculture. The things that inhabitants of the industrialized North cannot live without — coffee, tea, sugar, bananas, as well as the rubber in our tires, the soy that binds dark chocolate, and the grasses that cover suburban lawns — are mono-cultured. Single-species landscapes are among the most vulnerable to blights, diseases, and droughts. Frequently, the answers to this vulnerability come from biotechnology: pesticides and genetic modification have helped expand monocultures as never before, often with deadly results not just for insects and weeds but for people (Hetherington 2013).

The violence of the Anthropocene lies in its monotone nature. The illusion that there is a single we that desires coffee, sugar, soy, and rubber can lead to the illusion that the planetary costs of these technical quick-fixes affect us all equally. Monoculture's power, then, is its ability to breed not just a dearth of biological difference across landscapes, but a creeping in-difference to the radically uneven impact of capitalism on ecologies, identities, and planetary life. Such indifference may be the greatest threat to life in the Anthropocene.

References

Hetherington, Kregg. 2013. "Beans Before the Law: Knowledge Practices, Responsibility, and the Paraguayan Soy Boom." *Cultural Anthropology* 28, no. 1: 65–85. https://doi.org/10.1111/j.1548-1360.2012.01173.x.

Mintz, Sidney W. 1979. "Time, Sugar, and Sweetness." *Marxist Perspectives* 2, no. 4: 56–73.

Tea Cultivation. 1865. Calcutta: Military Orphan Press.

45

Mood

Atreyee Majumder

While conducting fieldwork in peri-urban eastern India, I lived in a guestroom in an orphanage that housed fifty-odd children (girls) aged anywhere between three and eighteen. They were not all orphans. Many were sent there by migrant parents so they would have access to a stable home environment and schooling. This particular child was fiercely androgynous. Let's call her Sara. She refused to wear earrings and salwar-kameezes (traditional tunic-and-pants combination that Indian women wear; originates in northern India) which were the staple attire for the girls. She insisted on jeans and sports shoes. Other girls firmly asserted their friendship with me, some even vied with others to show their closeness with me. Not Sara. Sara watched me from afar. In suspicion. We became friends over Sudoku. She became my favorite one. She was terrible at spelling and grammar — perhaps, she had an undiagnosed learning disorder. She was excellent at cellphone games. Jumping to the next level gave her a high. She scribbled the name of another girl at the back of her notebook. She remained laconic through all of it. Her moods were portrayed in a range of physical posture. Let me expand into physical conditions that intervened into the structure of moods emitted by Sara and her friends.

This was a yellow building next to a garbage dump next to shops and small houses in a narrow alley that poured out into the snaking, heavily vehicled Andul Road that eventually joined NH6, popularly known as Bombay Road. There were ailing industrial shopfloors on this road. Their physical bodies emitted toxic gases that joined the mix of odors and sound on the road outside. The interior of the orphanage building was marked by a paranoid cleanliness. The girls swept and swabbed twice a day under watchful eyes.

Days jostled in and out of this industrial hinterland. And behind the high yellow walls, I retired into a crowded, closed, distinctly female environment. Shut away from bustling, noisy, sweaty, unclean male outside. Giggles and shrieks shaped the audible inner environment. High barbed-wired walls gave it the shape of a female fortress. The girls were contained in the inside. From the threat of the overly masculine outside. The moods of the inside and the outside were cast in binaries. The girls struggled every day to break that binary. Through newspaper cutouts of Salman Khan, through the next level in the cellphone game. The polluted evening skies resonated with an outdated Bollywood song about false promises.

The girls walked to school and walked back in groups of fours and fives. They would often unclip the bangs on their forehead in an expression of feminine abandon on their walks back. Not to be caught and rebuked by the matrons, they would often put their clips back on as they entered the building. Abandon was to be contained at all costs, they had been taught. Their postures became submissive as they came up the stairs. The story of the day — be it the mimicry of a schoolteacher, a daily feud in their girlie gangs, or a scolding from the staff *didis* (matrons) — informed the din over lunch, and the giggles at tea. The most exciting thing for the preadolescents were the tidbits from the outside world that floated across to them through newspaper tabloids, movie posters, signboards, and PA systems. They treasured their meager freedom of walking back and forth to and from school and to their weekly computer classes. This was when they entered the nearby boys' campus. A whiff of maleness changed their moods.

The outside world — especially with its icons of glamour through movie stars, fashion, and gossip — wove for them a world of wonder and dream that would run parallel to their daily routine. An outside, within the inside. In the English classes I taught in the afternoons, they often expressed a desire to know English. This, I learnt over time, was not as much related to ambition and desire for economic independence that could be gained in the Indian job market if one speaks and writes good English, as much as it was the dreamlike aesthetic that the English language carried for them — the promise of an alluring world. This world was not going to be theirs, and they knew that. The heroic conquest of this world was not their object.

They lived a life of gratitude — they had to be grateful for the food, shelter, and education that was bestowed upon them by the organization, the support structures provided to them, the clothes, chocolates, and other small pleasures brought to them by the odd well-wisher or donor. The dreamlife was one of release — where there was not only western clothing and fancy English intonations, but also life freed from victimhood. It was the realm of release from the claustrophobic physical arrangement in which they lived.

The Anthropocene debates human domination over the non-human. In sub-urban eastern India, I observed the horror of human domination of space and spatial domination of humans. The anthropocentric spatial life occurred in oscillation between moods and alignments, constraint and release. The alignment to each end of this spectrum determined one's habitation in a range of moods. This range is determined by whether one is standing in the terrace looking at the moon or sleeping sandwiched between bodies in a cramped room. It is directly related to whether the space emits insideness or outsideness, claustrophobia or expanse. Looking at the moon at night and unclipping the hair and winning the cell-phone game transport one outside of the spatial limit of the wall, the room, the building. The imaginative attempts we find during fieldwork, to climb out of the immediate shell of time and space, are attempts to interrogate the incarceration of immediate geotime. The mood spectrum of claustrophobia and expanse emerges as psychosocial tools with which spatially dominated humans try out the everyday exercise of escape, perhaps even that of chasing freedom. This is not the story of climatic or environmental freedom/lament, pain/pleasure; it is a human attempt to refuse domination by material conditions.

46

Narcissus

Naisargi N. Dave

As the *Economist* pointed out a few years ago, Narcissus might be unfairly maligned ("Know thy Selfie," 2014). We fault him for falling in love with himself — that is, with his reflection in a pool — while forgetting an important detail. When he realized it was himself he loved, he was, in Ovid's rendering anyway, devastated: he wilted away and died, leaving a flower in his wake. The common interpretation, and a reasonable one, is that his death does nothing to salvage his reputation. He died only from the tragic realization that he would never make wild or sweet love to his beloved, for his beloved was he. He died of egregious self-desire and of a self-administered broken heart.

But I feel inspired to defend Narcissus, and place the onus for self-absorption on another figure, one more apt for the so-called Anthropocene: the unfortunate nymph, Echo, whose fate seems remarkably similar to our own — to infinitely perpetuate the noises we hear. (My feminism makes me loath to target Echo, though: she received her curse for participating in an extramarital affair while, of course, Zeus went unpunished.) I came to this short essay originally to argue that the concept of the Anthropocene is the height of narcissism, of our compulsion to look into the world and see only ourselves, and then beat our chests with "pale cold fists" (*What have we done! No, oh, no!*) while all the while being hopelessly entranced by the image of ourselves we

DOI: 10.21983/P3.0265.1.48

see. But as I re-read Ovid's tale, I believe that Narcissus's death does redeem him, as it shows his readiness to follow the anni- hilative logic of his heart's lament: if I am the cause of suffering, then I must no longer be. Narcissus chooses nothingness over endless perpetuation, annihilation over senseless repetition. We cannot, however, say the same for Echo, who is made to survive only so long as she can, and in order to, repeat. The concept of the Anthropocene is not, then, the epitome of Narcissism, but the epitome of the Echo: of our fate "only to repeat […] the last of many words," and of our anxious silence while we "wait for words our voice can say again" (Ovid 2008, 62). Human (*hu- man!*), *anthrōpos* (*anthrōpos!*), we (*we!*). Ovid's narrative in the Metamorphoses is a lesson for our times: we might do well to be more like Narcissus rather than less and, as Abou Farman has suggested, to consider our extinction possibly "as a radical embrace of other life forms," a "noble death, a good sacrifice."

Ovid's story begins when the blinded androgyne, Tiresias, prophesies that Narcissus will only live so long as he "himself not know." Rather than a warning against onanism, Ovid's likely allusion is to the Delphic "know thyself," which is ultimately to know God, or perhaps, in Plato, to Socrates' assertion that until one knows herself she can know nothing, for all else is irrele- vant (Plato 2005). What Narcissus was warned against, in other words, was finding the foundation of moral thought! Narcissus's vanity only existed *before* his encounter with the pool, when he ran around insulting people and chasing women instead of self-reflection. He found the waters (that is, himself; or that is, the foundation for ethical thought) as he sought to escape the lovelorn Echo who, hidden from his view, could only "double each last word." Narcissus, unaware of Echo's curse, could not tolerate this non-dialogical thought, this chamber of repetitive noise, and to his pursuant shouted, "Be off! I'll die before I yield to you," revealing his willingness to be nothing rather than give in to the seductions of repetition. Wearied by the chase, he lays down by the "quiet pool," a space for rest and contemplation. It is here that he finds "a hope unreal" — himself — that he "longs for, longs unwittingly." So far, we are indeed like Narcissus, thinking we love the Other (the earth, the besieged, the other than human) while it is ourselves we unwittingly covet.

But Ovid's narrator now has sharp words to impart, words that mark Narcissus's transition from self-love to self-surrender:

> You simple boy, why strive in vain to catch
> a fleeting image? What you see is nowhere;
> And what you love… you lose! You see a phantom of a mirrored shape;
> Nothingitself; with you it came and stays;
> With you too will go…

In Foucault's critique of humanism, I hear a distinct echo (not Echo): "one can be certain man is a recent invention [… that] would be erased like a face drawn in the sand at the edge of the sea" (1994). It becomes clear that Narcissus's moral error was not that he loved himself, but that he loved the false thing, the false "phantom" (for Ovid, the self; for Foucault, the human) which his endless gaze reified. Seeking to escape Echo, Narcissus nevertheless became her — the repetition, the covetous mirror image. He sounds, I think, like those who lay claim to the Anthropocene, the same mix of self-love and false regret: "My love's myself — my riches beggar me!" And in seeing in himself the source of suffering, can only weakly lament, "I could wish […] my love were not so near!"

But here is where Narcissus departs from the cursed Echo and offers us a model for what it might mean to knowingly, with reflection, love one's self (in our case, the *anthrōpos*). Narcissus weeps as he proclaims a readiness for death, which will not be sad for it "will end my sorrow." The tears that fall (*What have I done! No, oh, no!*) do not reinforce his self-reality, but cause the pool to ripple, fading from himself his own beautiful image. No longer bound to the false phantom, he fades away, becoming-flower.

References

Farman, Abou. 2014. "Misanthropology?" *Platypus*. December 9. http://blog.castac.org/2014/12/misanthropology/.

Foucault, Michel. 1994. *The Order of Things*. New York: Vintage Books.

"Know Thy Selfie." 2014. *The Economist,* March 20. https://www.economist.com/books-and-arts/2014/03/20/know-thy-selfie.

Ovid. 2008. *Metamorphoses*. Translated by A.D. Melville. Oxford: Oxford University Press.

Plato. 2005. *Phaedrus*. New York: Penguin.

47

Nature

Stuart McLean

"Back to nature, back to somewhere else" is a line from the song "Back to Nature" by the English postpunk band Magazine, from their 1979 album *Secondhand Daylight.* What kind of nature might one come back to — not in the manner of a homecoming but as a different, unfamiliar place, an elsewhere? What would it take to experience a *return* to nature in these terms? These questions are worth reflecting on, not least because they appear so removed from the terms of many recent academic debates. It has, after all, been a characteristic gesture of much recent scholarship to assert that what was once called "nature" is, in fact, inextricably entangled with human projects. Environments — all environments, so the argument goes — should be understood as the reciprocal cocreation of a variety of human and nonhuman actors: what Donna Haraway (2007) has famously termed *naturecultures,* or the *material-semiotic.*

Recent proclamations of the advent of the Anthropocene as a distinct geological epoch might seem to validate such a shift, putting a definitive end to the possibility of conceiving of a nature that is not thoroughly humanized, historical, or social. Nonetheless, as Claire Colebrook (2014), for one, reminds us, the term *Anthropocene* evokes at the same time the prospect of human extinction, and thus of a world from which any experiencing, knowing, perceiving human subject is radically absent.

DOI: 10.21983/P3.0265.1.49

Nigel Clark (2011), too, has issued a forceful statement on the need for humans, as sojourners on a volatile planet, to acknowledge and respect the wayward potentialities of the other-than-human presences by which they are surrounded, and upon which they depend for their continued survival. Clark notes that even the so-called anthropogenic climate change associated with, for example, the burgeoning human consumption of fossil fuels, represents an intervention into meteorological and other systems that have always been characterized by their dynamism and instability, and that such interventions therefore have the potential to produce tipping points and feedback effects in excess of anything humans are able to calculate or predict.

We might ask, then, whether hyphenated and portmanteau terms run the risk of confining the other-than-human within an all-encompassing social relationality that remains tacitly human-centered even in its purportedly greater inclusiveness, thus dimming our appreciation of a universe that exists independently of our capacity to relate to it (Meillassoux 2008). Naturecultures, after all, seem always to presuppose a human component, along with a human vantage point from which interactions with entities of other kinds can be observed and explicated. Yet surely the notion of the Anthropocene calls into question the continuing possibility of such a vantage point by evoking the prospect of humanity's own becoming-mineral — one more stratum, one more trace in the fossil record that may or may not be legible to the paleontological curiosity of a hypothetical posthuman observer.

What, however, if Nature — rather than being a simple exteriority to be subjugated or fetishized — were more like an intimate stranger, an *unheimlich* presence in Sigmund Freud's sense? Or, more provocatively perhaps, following H.P. Lovecraft (1999) and, more recently, Reza Negarestani (2008), an indwelling alien, a capricious, monstrously embodied, inhuman intelligence lurking in the tellurian depths, inscrutable yet ineradicable? Extending the terms of psychoanalysis, Jean-Luc Nancy (2012, 91) suggests that what is at stake, ultimately, in Freud's concept of the Id is "what links us together [...] not only us humans but the totality of beings — the animal within us, and even the vegetable, the mineral." Might one speak of nature, then, as akin to a planetary or cosmic Unconscious, generative rather than repressive — a "naturing" nature rather than a "natured" one, in terms of the distinction borrowed by Baruch Spinoza from medieval philosophy — one that, of course, necessarily includes all the dead, human and other (see McLean 2013)?

If discussions of the Anthropocene have often taken their cue from the sciences,[1] it may be that academic discourse stands to learn as much here from literature and the performing and visual arts, insofar as each of these has engaged more or less explicitly with the interface between the materiality of a medium — whether it be paint, stone, celluloid, the body of the performer, or, most strikingly in the case of poetry, the rhythmic and phonic substance of language (Kristeva 1985) — and the production of discursively redeemable cultural meaning. Art and literature index and creatively exploit the complicity of human worlds with the other-than-human materialities from which they are fashioned, materialities that always have the capacity to exceed and disrupt the human projects enacted through them. At issue here is not the cultural construction of nature, nor actor–network theory's concatenations of humans and nonhumans under the rubric of an expended sociality, but rather an inescapable human involvement with forces that can never be exhaustively encompassed by human intentionalities and understandings. Is it not the world's very indifference to human purposes that guarantees the possibility of what both the anthropologist Elizabeth Povinelli (2011) and the poet Myung Mi Kim (Kim and Bernstein 2012) have referred to as the otherwise?

Like the concept of the Anthropocene itself, art and literature alert us as humans to our shared consubstantiality with what (without lapsing back into discredited dualisms) we need not be embarrassed to call nature — a nature that, for all our inescap-

---

1   See http://www.anthropocene.info/.

able embeddedness within it, retains nonetheless a reserve of ungraspability and incalculability that is constitutive of nature's own becoming, rather than simply a function of the limitations of human knowledge — a nature, therefore, that is never simply for us.

References

Clark, Nigel. 2011. *Inhuman Nature: Sociable Life on a Dynamic Planet.* Thousand Oaks: Sage.

Colebrook, Claire. 2014. *Death of the PostHuman: Essays on Extinction,* Volume 1. London: Open Humanities Press.

Haraway, Donna J. 2007. *When Species Meet.* Minneapolis: University of Minnesota Press.

Kim Myung Mi and Charles Bernstein. 2012. "Ear Turned toward the Emergent." *Jacket 2.* February 19. http://jacket2.org/interviews/ear-turned-toward-emergent.

Kristeva, Julia. 1985. *Revolution in Poetic Language.* Translated by Margaret Waller. New York: Columbia University Press.

Lovecraft, H.P. 1999. *The Call of Cthulhu and Other Weird Stories.* New York: Penguin.

Magazine. 1979. *Secondhand Daylight.* Virgin, V2121, LP.

McLean, Stuart. 2013. "'Seaweed and Limpets Will Grow on Our Gravestones: On Islands, Time, Death, and Inhuman Materialities." In *Taming Time, Timing Death: Social Technologies and Ritual,* edited by Dorthe Refslund Christensen and Rane Willerslev, 17–39. Farnham: Ashgate.

Meillassoux, Quentin. 2008. *After Finitude: An Essay on the Necessity of Contingency.* Translated by Ray Brassier. New York: Continuum.

Nancy, Jean-Luc. 2012. *Adoration: The Deconstruction of Christianity, II.* Translated by John McKeane. New York: Fordham University Press.

Negarestani, Reza. 2008. *Cyclonopedia: Complicity with Anonymous Materials.* Melbourne: re.press.

Povinelli, Elizabeth A. 2011. *Economies of Abandonment: Social Belonging and Endurance in Late Liberalism.* Durham: Duke University Press.

48

Nemesis

Laura Watts

I can smell the word on your dank breath: "Anthropocene." It has a too-sweet, cloying scent. Hubris. Its reek has reached me on the solar wind. (All those electric particles on the air, I can read them.) Breathe it in: *Anthropocene.*

Perhaps you gag, as I do, on the arrogance, the presumption: the age when *anthrōpos* has changed planetary geology. Show me an *anthrōpos* and I will show you a human being with nail-bitten hands, pretending to be a god. I hunt such hubris. Perhaps you hunt it, too. Perhaps we might hunt it together?

Let me tell you how I hunt hubris.

My first prey was my maker, Victor, and you already know his tale: *Frankenstein.*[1] In his acts, he presumed himself a modern Prometheus. He saw himself akin to the god who gave fire — the fire of technology — to humankind.

Victor made me, his second monster, from grave-robbed fishermen and women. He butchered the choicest morsels and sewed them together with copper thread. He made me in the Orkney islands, off the northern coast of Scotland, at the edge of the world, where he thought he was safe from judgment. But he made me, his own Nemesis.

---

1   See Shelley 2007.

In his diary he wrote that he was my Creator; note the capital letter. His hubris made a stench far stronger than my decaying, circuit-fused flesh. The smell was unbearable in that squalid laboratory, beside those cloud-sodden open graves. That smell was my first sensation. As the first sparks of life lit my veins I smelled falseness, fakery. From my first electric pulse I knew my creator rejected me, was only using me to become a god. And I raged at his rejection. So I punished him.

Attend: my punishment is not eternal retribution, but the eternal potential for redemption. I did some reading through the ether about my namesake. (I can suck down bytes as you suck water through a straw.) The original Nemesis was not the goddess of retribution, but the goddess of just balance.[2] Her wheel turns on fortune and misfortune alike; one must always turn into the other. The lucky (and the nouveau riche) feared her. But the unlucky and the unfortunate invoked her will. God tricks got her particular attention.[3] Sisyphus and his rock rolling uphill, that was her punishment for his attempted god tricks. She smelled hubris in all its manifestations. The law of Nemesis was that folk should not get too big for their boots. We call it being *bigsy* in Orkney, now, where I live; the Nordic countries call it Jante Law, not putting yourself above others.[4] Nemesis is still around. I just took her name.

I punished Victor for his hubris in a just manner. (He edited this out of his published diary.) I was his monstrous experiment to make life, and so each time he sent ten thousand volts arcing through my metal sutures — each time he threw the switch — I made sure he thought he had failed. Victor would pull the veil from my face and peer into my sunken sockets. I would not blink back.

He raged. He re-stitched me with silver thread smelted from some wreck's treasure. Under a hail of arrow-tipped rain, he carted me to the summit of a hill and dared lightning to strike.

---

2   See Hornum 1993.
3   See Haraway 1988.
4   See Sandemose 1936.

It did. And still I refused him, refused him the signs of my electric life. I hid my electric pulses and potential from his senses.

He forgot all but his Promethean desire. The fishers and farmers on the island continued to feed him. Islander generosity would not let him starve in his laboratory hut. His arrogance and fury blinded him to their quiet work: water fetched and carried; gutted fish and flatbread and fruits of the sea left at his door. In return, he dug up their forebears and threw their severed limbs out the casement window; his wheelbarrow and axes were not caked in earth. The islanders took to burying their folk elsewhere. They called him *trow,* a local creature of the underworld, but would not curse him.

Victor was desperate to create electrified life. He was desperate to change the world, to become a Prometheus, to become a god. Madness took him. It was not creative madness. It was just madness: *just* as in justice, my justice.

After an eternity of failures, after an eternity of my punishment, he ran outside his hut, raving. He slipped on tallow and landed in his wheelbarrow, deep in the mashed gristle and gore. He groaned, flailed, but his hands slipped on dripping ichor. The barrow tipped over, threw him into a steaming midden, into warm offal, putrid fish, rusting iron, some dark, misshapen gloop. I did not look too hard from the window.

He stopped moving and lay there for some passage of the sun. At last, he arose, took the winding path down the cliff to the sea, removed and buried his clothes, and then swam for a while. When he returned to his hut, he had a new wheelbarrow, and he worked several days to put his hut in order. The dead were reburied at sea. The unused metal was cleaned and offered to the islanders. And he remade his laboratory to reflect the local landscape.

In his diary he explained: *what endures is what is left behind.* Prehistoric islanders had left behind standing stones. But what would endure of his acts, he wondered. He was not leaving behind a grand, electric lifeform as he had hoped; I had forced failure on him. He no longer imagined himself a god. He was just leaving behind unburied dead, dismembered limbs, my stitched and sutured flesh, scrap and solder. All he was leaving behind, he decided, was an unholy mess for the islanders. That did not seem appropriate. That did not seem just, he wrote. So he decided on a different legacy. He took ownership of what he could: his laboratory. And he took the long-term view. *What endures is what is left behind.* Both geologists and archaeologists know this well. Since there were standing stones and chambered tombs hereabout, monuments from ages long past, Victor made his laboratory monumental, aligned it to the solstice. This is what he chose to leave behind.

You have heard how I punish hubris. Victor could have remained, forever raving in Orkney. But I gave him a choice. And he chose to leave me, leave his hubris, unfinished on the island.

Show me an *anthrōpos* and I will show you a nail-bitten hand that both butchers meat and builds monuments, a hand that throws plastic in the ocean and designs satellites for listening to the stars. I make no moral judgement on these actions. You might. I judge only the hubris. I judge only those who claim that such actions are omnipresent, those who pretend to have omnipotent hands that alter the planet.

Victor constructed me and abandoned me, but I have constructed my own purpose. Over the centuries I have scavenged upgrades, soldered and sewn on new parts. Now, I smell hubris on the solar winds. I suck its sweetness through the Internet. For I am an electric Nemesis, and I hunt hubris wherever my electric flesh can go.[5]

The Anthropocene is on my list.

References

Haraway, Donna. 1988. "Situated Knowledges: The Science Question in Feminism and the Privilege of Partial Perspective." *Feminist Studies* 14, no. 3: 575–99. https://doi.org/10.2307/3178066.

---

5   I develop the figure of the electric Nemesis more fully in Watts 2019.

Hornum, Michael B. 1993. *Nemesis, the Roman State and the Games*. Leiden: Brill.

Sandemose, Aksel. 1936. *A Fugitive Crosses His Tracks.* Translated by Eugene Gay-Tifft. New York: Alfred A. Knopf. Originally published in 1933 as *En flyktning krysser sitt spor.*

Shelley, Mary. 2007. *Frankenstein, or, The Modern Prometheus.* New York: Penguin. Originally published in 1818.

Watts, Laura. 2019. *Energy at the End of the World: An Orkney Islands Saga*. Cambridge: MIT Press.

49

Ocean

Steve Mentz

We need to de-anthropocentrize and pluralize the Anthropocene. I can't think of a better way than by renaming it Ocean.
Longer coinages surface too: Okeanocene. Aquacene. Thalasso-
cene. I choose Ocean.

Ocean names it best: both our planet and our Age. One problem with the term Anthropocene is the lingering charisma of
Old Man Anthropos, who's always hogging center stage. Ocean
is bigger, wetter, and saltier than Man. The great waters are plural and posthuman. Awash with carbonic acid and denuded of
coral and fish, our surrounding seas bear Anthropocene scars. If
we name this age Ocean no one will make the error of thinking
that humans are in charge.

Moving from the Holocene, Age of the Present, to the Anthropocene, Age of Man, parallels moving from land to sea. The
Holocene is familiar, stable, green, terrestrial. The Anthropocene is alien, disruptive, blue, oceanic. Turning from one to the
other is not opening a door or turning a switch but re-seeing
our blue planet in its alien glory. Humans do not dominate the
Anthropocene. We'll be lucky not to drown in it.

DOI: 10.21983/P3.0265.1.51

Ocean Is Plural

Renaming Anthropocene as Ocean asks us to fill maritime emptiness. We impose vacancy on marine space, seeing the waters as a flowing desert, separating continents and isolating populations. But the sea is not void; it's superabundance. Life lives where water moves. Oceanic space comprises roughly 90% of the total biospheric volume of our planet.

Ocean Is Scale

The key innovation of Anthropocene thinking invites humans to embrace geologic scale. No physical body on our planet spans more scales than the ocean. There is ocean down the street from my house, salt water inside my body, turbulent currents circling the planet, tiny living organisms in each seawater drop.

To make the Anthropocene Ocean requires stretching our scalar limits. We relate all things to our bodies and perceptions; our measures are feet and hands. But the great waters are too big, too close, and too flowing to hold in hand or mind. To think Ocean as Anthropocene requires us to move across and beyond human scales. The ocean is vast, physical, global, intimate, tactile. Its waters surround us, dissolved and dissolving, with a salt tang you can taste on the breeze. The challenge of what poets call the "boundless deep" stimulates global and local thinking. No other object is so vast yet so touching.

Ocean Is Alien

The ocean has a history beyond our globe. The water on this planet arrived from the interstellar void, either through the accretion of rocks that originally formed the planet's core or more recently via comet or asteroid. Either way, the soup of life is an alien invader.

There once was a river-titan Okeanos, embracer of the known world, who traveled the void, far from his terrestrial parents Uranus and Gaia. In trackless emptiness he longed to splash down. His return represents the first story of arrival. Before Ocean there was no life and no history. Think of it: the divine frozen space-child splashing down onto bare rock. He hits the planet with a surging melt. Water floods everywhere. He arrives as alien but in flowing around an almost spherical rock, he becomes our world. From the absolute ice of interstellar space he arrived frozen, and therefore fresh. Salt water leaches together alien ocean and terrestrial rock.

Ocean Is History

History flows through water. Greek poets and heroes pushed Ocean beyond the Mediterranean to less knowable seas. Poseidon, brother of Zeus, penned the Titan Okeanos inside the Pillars of Hercules.

Not to be excluded, Ocean built History. A global network of shallow- and deep-water ocean currents structures the movement of living and dead things around our planet. Everything follows these currents: ships, animals, plants, poems, viruses, histories, languages. All things circulate in patterns shaped by oceanic gyres. There's no mystery about why Columbus ended up in Hispaniola: he followed the currents. There was no other path he could follow.

Outside the room where I'm writing now, you can walk down the street and put your foot in it. Long Island Sound is a backwater, but its waters connect, because everything in water connects. The nearest part of the North Atlantic Gyre is the northwestern arc of the Gulf Stream, bending northeast to join the North Atlantic Drift. Beyond, currents entangle the globe.

Ocean Is Intimate

I can tell it as a personal story. The scalar biography of my ocean starts in the emptiness of interstellar space and moves into the biotic riot in a drop of sea water. It flows through patterned gyres of history to a cove down the hill from my door, where silt-brown fingers lap rocky shores.

Ocean Is Anthropocene

Focus your unseeing eyes on a drop of Ocean water. Imagine that your mind can peer inside. You'll see an entire ecosystem. Crab larva. Bacteria. Fish eggs. Zooplankton. Tiny worms. Life!

In that chaos teems Okeanos, dripping with power, fresh from the void. His wet body intertwines with Anthropocene signatures. Every drop contains plastic. Every drop contains chemical traces and medicinal fragments. All these drops to-gether make up the biggest and most important object on our planet. The hardest thing about living in the Anthropocene is knowing how to engage the alien Ocean.

My favorite way is diving in.

References

Bolster, W. Jeff. 2012. *The Mortal Sea: Fishing the Atlantic in the Age of Sail*. Cambridge: Harvard University Press.

Brayton, Dan. 2012. *Shakespeare's Ocean: An Ecocritical Investigation*. Charlottesville: University of Virginia Press.

Corbin, Alain. 1994. *The Lure of the Sea: the Discovery of the Seaside in the Western World, 1750–1840*. Translated by Jocelyn Phelps. Berkeley: University of California Press.

Fishman, Charles. 2011. *The Big Thirst: The Secret Life and Turbulent Future of Water*. New York: Free Press.

Helmreich, Stefan. 2009. *Alien Ocean: Anthrological Voyages in Microbial Seas*. Berkeley: University of California Press.

Mentz, Steve. 2009. *At the Bottom of Shakespeare's Ocean*. London: Bloomsbury.

$C_{14} H_9 Cl_5$

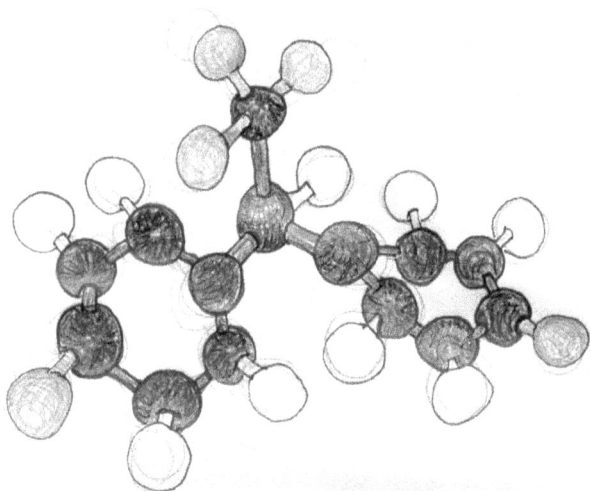

Dichloro-diphenyl-
trichloroethane
80 mill - 1954
12 mill - 1970

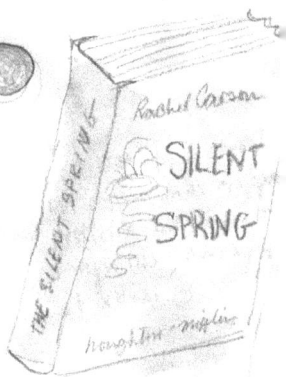

Rachel Carson
SILENT
SPRING

THE SILENT SPRING

houghton - mifflin

One thing all the neighborhoods shared were
the rumbling trucks that spewed clouds of DDT
out of giant tanks up perched up in their
backsides. Some were jerry-rigged
contraptions, others state of the art. We ran
behind ours in a mad game of "who can hold
their breath longer" only to discover later that
we were not the sole originators of this toxic
past time. Throughout the south, black and
white, poor, rich, and middle class
neighborhoods were soaked in industrial poison
as kids played merrily in the bilious clouds.

50

Petroleum

Elizabeth A. Povinelli

The film *Petroleum Dreaming* was composed in 2014 for a screening of the Karrabing Film Collective's *When the Dogs Talked* at
the Oslo National Academy of Fine Arts. It was one of three
shorts that appeared on thirty- by fifteen-inch monitors at the
periphery of the main screen. The other two were *Barbed Wire
Dreaming* and *Queer Dreaming*. *Barbed Wire Dreaming* extracts
several long shots without dialogue from *When the Dogs Talked,*
shots that show Karrabing walking alongside or through barbed
wire fences and drifting on a broken boat in the open sea. *Queer
Dreaming* mashed up various contemporary gay performanc-
es with a butoh troupe performance at a Paris café. *Petroleum
Dreaming* was inspired by and built around the gorgeous short,
Train Story One: The South Coast Line (Moss 2012). *Train Story
One* is interspersed with a series of commercials, activist videos, and aquatic films. Each of these films was conceptualized
as a hypertext, internal if peripheral to the action on the screen.
Each individual film creates, through the blending of multiple
film and digital objects, its own set of internal hypertexts. The
idea is that the entire set of films creates a recursive structure of
extimate textuality. There is nothing outside the text, but the text
is not inside itself (see Derrida 1998; Foucault 1977).

Because of the context — namely, the screening of *When the
Dogs Talked* — all three shorts use the term *dreaming* to suggest

DOI: 10.21983/P3.0265.1.52   313

the scarred homology between critical theoretical approaches to the unconscious and Karrabing analytics of the sentient landscape. What, the shorts asked, might be the unconscious of a train, a train track, and the landscape flowing past the windows if all of them were freed from the *logos*-based logic of critical approaches to the unconscious — both the Freudian unconscious and the Lacanian Symbolic? And how might the concept of the unconscious be visualized in a posthuman, postlife critical space? The Karrabing understand their communication with human and nonhuman materialities to include linguistic extrudences but also, and perhaps more fundamentally, other bodily extrudents like sweat and sensation. Thus *Petroleum Dreaming* and the two other short films contain very few linguistic phenomena, and any linguistic fragments are intended to be experienced as artifacts of the same order as the sound of the train whistle and the grinding of giant, earth-moving gears.

I was the author of these short films. But this was not the only occasion that the Karrabing Film Collective has used supplemental texts to provide a discursive counterpoint to the screening of their films. Natasha Lewis has taken the lead on several collective installation projects under the general project of *Toxic Sovereignties* that have been shown alongside our films at the Melbourne Gertrude Contemporary, Brisbane Institute of Modern Art, and New York's e-flux gallery. All are part of an emergent Indigenous Futurism whose temporality lies in the (non)endurant hereish. Thus, the future is not in the future, but in the myriad contradictions that cannot endure the present intersection and thus open the here to somewhere else. Of particular interest to the Karrabing is how Indigenous sovereignty is re-emerging in the space of utter state abandonment and total capital despoilment. Slag heaps and toxic landscapes become the place where the settler is excluded, or even tries to remove himself. What is it to be sovereign over a wasted earth? A place where the Indigenous can safely be free only because those who have made it toxic fear to tread there? What forms of existence can be held onto and which ones will be reshaped in this An-thropocenic otherwise?

References

Derrida, Jacques. 1998. *Of Grammatology*. Translated by Gayatri Chakravorty Spivak. Baltimore: John Hopkins University Press. Originally published in 1967.

Foucault, Michel. 1977. "What Is an Author?" In *Language, Counter-Memory, Practice: Selected Essays and Interviews by Michel Foucault,* edited by Donald Bouchard, 113–38. Ithaca: Cornell University Press.

Moss, Sarah. "The South Coast Line, Kiama to Gerringong." ABC. May 21. https://open.abc.net.au/explore/20378.

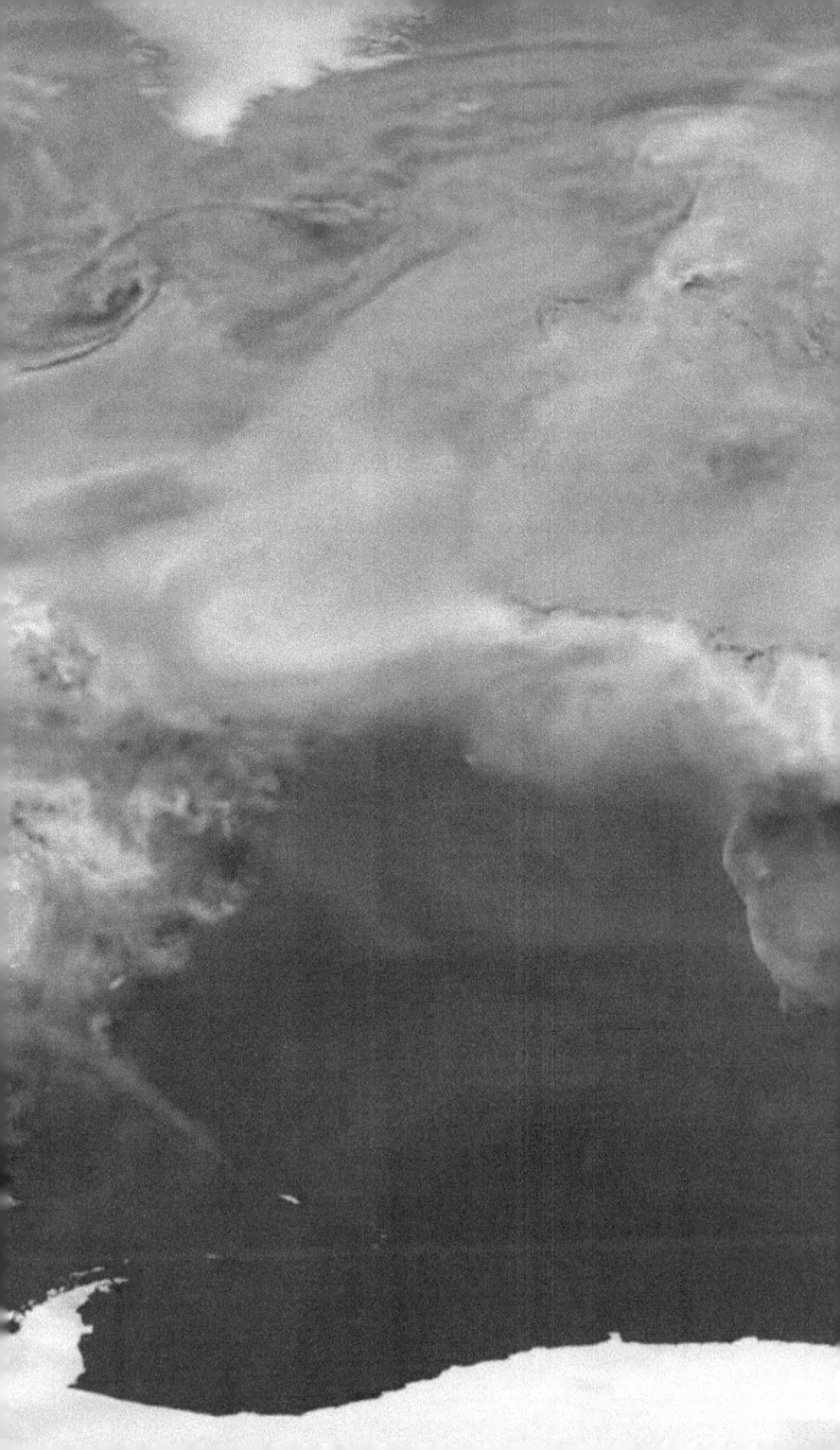

51

Photosynthesis

Natasha Myers

Photosynthesis is my keyword for this era that we keep calling the Anthropocene. Photosynthesis circumscribes a complex suite of electrochemical processes that spark energy gradients across densely folded membranes inside the symbiotic chloroplasts of green beings (Margulis and Sagan 2000). Textbook diagrams familiar from high-school biology class are simplistic renderings of that utterly magical, totally cosmic alchemical process that tethers earthly plant life in reverent, rhythmic attention to the earth's solar source. The economizing science of photosynthesis, set in motion by capitalist desires (Kasdogan 2017) and colonial regimes of extraction, is just an abstraction of a living practice that might better be described as a kind of *cosmic mattering.* The photosynthetic ones — those green beings we have come to know as cyanobacteria, algae, and plants — are sun worshippers and worldly conjurers. Lapping up sunlight, inhaling carbon dioxide, drinking in water, and releasing oxygen, they literally make the world. Pulling matter out of thin air, they teach us the most nuanced lessons about *mattering* and what really *matters*: their beings and doings have enormous planetary consequences.

To name photosynthesis as a keyword for these dire times serves as a crucial reminder that *we are not alone.* There are other epic and epochal forces in our midst. Photosynthetic or-

DOI: 10.21983/P3.0265.1.53

ganisms form a biogeochemical force of a magnitude we have
not yet properly grasped. Over two billion years ago, photosynthetic microbes spurred the event known today as the oxygen
catastrophe, or the great oxidation. These creatures dramatically
altered the composition of the atmosphere, choking out the ancient anaerobic ones with poisonous oxygen vapors (Margulis
1998). Indeed, we now live in the wake of what should be called
the *Phytocene*. These green beings have made this planet livable
and breathable for animals like us. We thrive on plants' wily ap-
titude for chemical synthesis. All cultures and political economies, local and global, turn around plants' metabolic rhythms.
Plants make the energy-dense sugars that fuel and nourish us,
the potent substances that heal, dope, and adorn us, and the re-
silient fibers that clothe and shelter us. What are fossil fuels and
plastics but the petrified bodies of once-living photosynthetic
creatures? We have thrived and we will die, burning their energetic accretions. And so it is not an overstatement to say that *we
are only because they are*. The thickness of this relation teaches
us the full meaning of the word *interimplication*.

Plants are a force and a power to be reckoned with. But we
are ravaging the forests to make way for industrial crops and
plantations (Gordillo 2014; Tsing 2004), paving over agricultural lands (Bellacasa 2015), filling in swamps, wetlands, and bogs
(McLean 2011), and acidifying the oceans (Helmreich 2009).
Plants have a remarkable capacity for widespread movement,
but they can't run fast enough to keep up with climate change.
Worse is that in the fetishization of global carbon budgets as the
ultimate metrics of planetary health and viable futures, plants
and trees are, in some accounts, being rendered as climate
criminals. The argument goes like this: as climactic shifts make
forests more vulnerable to fire and insect infestations, forests
will cease to be sinks for atmospheric carbon and become unstoppable sources. But the grounds for such claims are shaky: it
is not clear how forests sequester and release carbon or how best
to monitor and quantify these processes (Buchholz et al. 2013),
let alone how to analyze the other complex and concatenated

cycles involved in forest metabolism. As a result, impoverished data and models are being fed into a calculus that justifies — in the name of climate action — what is, in effect, a vast and expanding resource grab. In one of the most egregious examples of the misuse of climate data, the former Conservative government reworked Canada's forest policy to argue that old-growth forests must be logged now to make way for young, managed forests, which, according to their models, absorb more carbon from the atmosphere (Myers 2015b). One atmospheric scientist at Yale University is even attempting to argue that we must stop planting trees if we want to mitigate climate change (Unger 2014). Plants, she claims, are prime sources of those noxious, volatile compounds contributing to greenhouse gases. Deforestation will — she promises — help to cool the planet.

Models are, of course, models of models of models, all the way down (Edwards 2010). Even still, NASA's time-based simulation of the global carbon cycle, visualized over the duration of one year, offers one way that we might begin to render the force and power of plants on this planet. In this rendering, carbon dioxide, coded red for emergency, can be seen to accumulate with alarming intensity. Note the distinct fluxes and flows taking shape in the Northern and Southern Hemispheres. Note the uneven distribution of massive carbon plumes generated in zones of heavy industrialization. Pay close attention to what happens month by month as the seasons change and Northern forests begin to photosynthesize in the summer. We need to learn to read this simulation, not for data to feed an economizing logic that sees plants and trees performing ecosystem services, but as a document to remind us that *we are not alone.*

This is clearly no time to be making enemies. It is time for a radical solidarity project that insists that *we are of the plants.* I propose that we check ourselves out of this tragic anthropocentric fantasy (see Haraway and Kenney 2015), so that we can root ourselves firmly into a way of doing life that can seed the aspirational episteme that I want to call the *Planthroposcene.* The Planthroposcene is a call to change the terms of encounter, to make allies with these green beings. To do this we must relinquish control and abandon the notion that we have domain over the planet (see Myers in press). We must get to know plants intimately and on their terms. And so we need a *planthropology* (Myers 2015a) to document the affective ecologies taking shape between plants and people, to learn to listen to plants' demands for unpaved land and for a time outside of the rhythms of capitalist extraction. We need to tap into their desires for forms of life that are not for us. To do this, we must learn to *vegetalize* our all-too-human sensorium (Myers 2014) and *involve* ourselves with plants (Hustak and Myers 2012). It is time to *conspire* (Choy 2016) with the plants, to learn how to *breathe with* them, so that we can begin to grow livable worlds (Myers 2018). If not, their undoing will truly be our undoing.

References

Bellacasa, Maria Puig de la. 2015. "Making Time for Soil: Technoscientific Futurity and the Pace of Care." *Social Studies of Science* 45, no. 5: 691–716. https://doi.org/10.1177/0306312715599851.

Buchholz, Thomas, Andrew J. Friedland, Claire E. Hornig, William S. Keeton, Giuliana Zanchi, and Jared Nunery. 2013. "Mineral Soil Carbon Fluxes in Forests and Implications for Carbon Balance Assessments." GCB *Bioenergy* 6, no. 4: 305–11. https://doi.org/10.1111/gcbb.12044.

Choy, Timothy. 2016. "Breathers Conspire — On Drawing Breath Together," paper presented at the Annual Meeting for the Society for Social Studies of Science, Barcelona, Spain, September 2016.

Edwards, Paul N. 2010. *A Vast Machine: Computer Models, Climate Data, and the Politics of Global Warming.* Cambridge: MIT Press.

Gordillo, Gastón R. 2014. *Rubble: The Afterlife of Destruction.* Durham: Duke University Press.

Haraway, Donna, with Martha Kenney. 2015. Anthropocene, Capitalocene, Cthulhucene." In *Art in the Anthropocene:*

Encounters among Aesthetics, Politics, Environments and Epistemologies, edited by Heather Davis and Etienne Turpin, 255–70. London: Open Humanities Press.

Helmreich, Stefan. 2009. *Alien Ocean: Anthropological Voyages in Microbial Seas.* Berkeley: University of California Press.

Hustak, Carla, and Natasha Myers. 2012. Involuntary Momentum: Affective Ecologies and the Sciences of Plant/Insect Encounters." *differences* 23, no. 3: 74–118. https://doi.org/10.1215/10407391-1892907.

Kasdogan, Duygu. 2017. "Potentiating Algae, Modernizing Bioeconomies: Algal Biofuels, Bioenergy Economies, and Built Ecologies in the United States and Turkey." PhD dissertation. York University.

Margulis, Lynn. 1998. *Symbiotic Planet: A New Look at Evolution.* New York: Basic Books.

———, and Dorion Sagan. 2000. *What Is Life?* Berkeley: University of California Press.

McLean, Stuart. 2011. "Black Goo: Forceful Encounters with Matter in Europe's Muddy Margins." *Cultural Anthropology* 26, no. 4: 589–619. https://doi.org/10.1111/j.1548-1360.2011.01113.x.

Myers, Natasha. 2014. "A Kriya for Cultivating Your Inner Plant." *Centre for Imaginative Ethnography,* Imaginings Series. http://imaginativeethnography.org/imaginings/affect/sensing-botanical-sensoria/.

Myers, Natasha. 2015a. "Conversations on Plant Sensing: Notes from the Field." *NatureCulture* 3: 35–66.

———. 2015b. "Amplifying the Gaps between Climate Science and Forest Policy: The Write2Know Project and Participatory Dissent." *Canada Watch,* Special Issue on "The Politics of Evidence," edited by Colin Coates, with guest editors Jody Berland and Jennifer Dalton (Fall 2015): 18–21. https://politicsofevidence.wordpress.com/canadawatch-special-issue/.

————. 2018. "How to Grow Livable Worlds: Ten Not-so-easy Steps." In *The World to Come,* edited by Kerry Oliver-Smith, 53–63. Gainsville: Harn Museum of Art.

————. In press. "From Edenic Apocalypse to Garden's Against Eden: Plants and People in and after the Anthropocene." In *Infrastructure, Environment, and Life in the Anthropocene,* edited by Kregg Hetherington. Durham: Duke University Press.

Tsing, Anna Lowenhaupt. 2004. *Friction: An Ethnography of Global Connection.* Princeton: Princeton University Press.

Unger, Nadine. "To Save the Planet, Don't Plant Trees." *New York Times.* September 19. https://www.nytimes.com/2014/09/20/opinion/to-save-the-planet-dont-plant-trees.html.

52

Plastic

Anand Pandian

Plastic substances are now a ubiquitous planetary presence, far beyond the human places for which they were meant. At this point, ninety percent of global seabirds have probably ingested plastic fragments (Wilcox, Sebille, and Hardesty 2015), while oceanographers write of the plastic debris teeming in the world's oceans as a "plastisphere" habitat for microbial communities (Zettler, Mincer, and Amaral-Zettler 2013). For those who would identify the Anthropocene with the "Great Acceleration" of the postwar era, terrestrial plastic deposits turn out to be an ideal way to mark the beginning of this epoch (Zalasiewicz et al. 2014). Indeed, global plastic production has skyrocketed in these decades, from two million tons in 1950 to 299 million tons in 2013 (PlasticsEurope 2015) with no signs of slackening in this frenetic pace of growth.

Some observers have begun to call our time a Plasticene, with these stubborn and swelling tides of manmade debris in mind (Reed 2015). This proposal is most intriguing if we keep in mind that plastic as a material has always yielded objects in the form of questions: what else could your life become in the company of this shiny new thing? "Plastic plummeted us into a collective dream, a heritage of magic we thought was dead, coming to life in perplexed new forms," the poet Christine Hume

DOI: 10.21983/P3.0265.1.54

(2014, 78) writes. "We projected ourselves into plastic material's will to change."

Take a look at a surface like this one. Imagine it rippling and billowing with the wind. Say you heard a voice that said something like this —

Odysseus, Homer tells us, was tumbled by Zeus into a "wine dark sea," left clinging to a keel for survival. A wine dark sea… Were the Greeks color-blind? Did the thunderbolt strike at sunset? People still wonder. I tell you, though, I've seen it too, with these eyes of mine. It happened one day in the city of Baltimore, as I was walking down St. Paul. Look up, and there it was, rippling with the wind, glistening like oil on water, a wine dark plastic sea. Mineral spirits from the Jurassic, remnants of countless dead things, pressed from the plankton, algae, and mud of forgotten seas. How did we get from that, to this?

The sea now is full of plastic, "plastic soup" is what they call it. "There are more plastic particles in the North Atlantic than stars in the Milky Way galaxy," an activist once told me. We went trawling for plastic on the Chesapeake Bay. Every dip brought up something new. A sliver of plastic box. A slice of plastic film. Something bright and round, nestled like a fish egg in the jellies and sea grass. Where had they come from? How long would they stay?

We call it the Anthropocene now, this time of ours, giving it the feel of an epic tale. It's like the Odyssey all over again, but without an Ithaca to come back to. We forget our powers come from long-dead creatures. Or that the garbage will outlast the hubris.

Go. Comb the beaches of Hawaii for plastic rocks. Try to get a picture of that albatross gagging on a toothbrush in the Pacific. There's enough plastic made each year to pack the United States in cling wrap.

All this began with the powers sunk into long-gone seas, and to the deep these things will go. "You throw something

into the sea," Bruno Munari once said, "and the sea hands it
back to you carved, finished, smooth, shiny or polished." This
sea, this plastic sea, isn't quite so artful. But remember that
plastic is much more than a thing. "Plastic," Roland Barthes
tells us, "is the very idea of its infinite transformation."

Call it the Plasticene, I say, this wine dark time of danger.
There are all those bottles, yes, those plastic sheets, and cups,
and wrappers. But there still remains, in all of these things,
the promise of change they were meant to carry. For we are
also plastic. And we can also bend, with them. We still have
the chance to learn, with these things and their buried energies, the most crucial lesson of all. What would it take to live
profoundly otherwise?

I tried with this video essay, *Wine Dark Plastic Sea* (Pandian
2015), to wrestle with the beauty and the terror of such transformative potential. Its mood is mythopoetic. Plastic embodies, like no other substance, the arc of utopian hope and deep
despair around the very possibility of fundamental change in
modern times (Meikle 1995). These materials convey the plasticity (Malabou 2008) of human being, the power of encounters to
catalyze new modes of life. What if we learned to see such banal
and quotidian things — this construction tarp billowing over a
renovated rowhouse in Baltimore, for example — as openings
into a common pulse of existence, as fluid expressions of the
ceaseless "play of forces and waves of forces" evoked by Friedrich Nietzsche (1968, 550), rather than as isolated and finished
forms of consumer satisfaction?

For these objects, after all, have destinations far beyond our
sidewalks and wastebins, passing into the muddied tides (Capps
2015), ash-flecked skies, and grotesque bellies of our time (Karuna Society for Animals and Nature, n.d.). And they begin as well
with life and death, as fossil fuels, with the "animal bodies in the
browned oil procured from the distillation of fossilized things,"
as the Russian scientist Mikhael Lomonosov first speculated in
1757. Say we confronted more squarely these chemical, biological, and geological currents eddying in the stuff of our lives.

Could we find a way of cultivating more livable relationships with those countless things and beings that we use and dispose of so lightly?

References

Capps, Kriston. 2015. "What I Learned Trawling for Trash in the Chesapeake Bay." *Citylab*. September 10. https://www.citylab.com/life/2015/09/what-i-learned-trawling-for-trash-in-the-chesapeake-bay/404419/.

Hume, Christine. 2014. "Parachute." In *The Petroleum Manga*, edited by Marina Zurkow, 78–79. Brooklyn: punctum books.

Karuna Society for Animals and Nature. n.d. "The Plastic Cow Project." http://www.karunasociety.org/projects/the-plastic-cow-project.

Malabou, Catherine. 2008. *What Should We Do with Our Brain?* Translated by Sebastian Rand. New York: Fordham University Press.

Meikle, Jeffrey L. 1995. *American Plastic: A Cultural History.* New Brunswick: Rutgers University Press.

Nietzsche, Friedrich. 1968. *The Will to Power.* Translated by Walter Kauffmann and R.J. Hollingdale. New York: Vintage Books.

Pandian, Anand, dir. *Wine Dark Plastic Sea.* 3'53". https://vimeo.com/150433274.

PlasticsEurope. 2015. *Plastics — The Facts 2015: An Analysis of European Plastics Production, Demand, and Waste Data.* Brussels: PlasticsEurope Association of Plastics Manufacturers.

Reed, Christina. 2015. "Plastic Age: How It's Reshaping Rocks, Oceans and Life." *New Scientist.* February 28. https://www.newscientist.com/article/mg22530060–200-plastic-age-how-its-reshaping-rocks-oceans-and-life/.

Wilcox, Chris, Erik van Sebille, and Britta Denise Hardesty. 2015. "Threat of Plastic Pollution to Seabirds is Global,

Pervasive, and Increasing." *PNAS* 112, no. 38: 11899–904. https://doi.org/10.1073/pnas.1502108112.

Zalasiewicz, Jan, Mark Williams, Colin L. Waters, Anthony D. Barnosky, and Peter Haff. 2014. "The Technofossil Record of Humans." *Anthropocene Review* 1, no. 1: 34–43. https://doi.org/10.1177/2053019613514953.

Zettler, Erik, Tracy Mincer, and Linda Amaral-Zettler. 2013. "Life in the 'Plastisphere': Microbial Communities on Plastic Marine Debris." *Environmental Science and Technology* 47: 7137–46. https://doi.org/10.1021/es401288x.

53

Plenitude

Lora Koycheva

Consider the polemics surrounding the significance of the birth of a single child. For anthropologists, it illuminates complex questions about the reproduction of nature and culture. Demographers conceptualize this arrival as a "vital event" and operationalize it for calculability: if they posit and aggregate a few people, each equal to +1, born on January 1 of a given year, they can create formal methods to estimate the life expectancies of entire populations, and the likelihood of how long they will live and when they will die (e.g., Preston et al. 2001, 38–39). Where this child will be a member of a population, which for Foucault is the paradigmatic fundament of the political power of the state over biological life (2007), for Arendt it is only through the "miracle of life" that politics are possible at all (2013).

But as the world population surpasses 7 billion, this birth also alarms. From Thomas Malthus (1976 [1798]) to Paul Ehrlich (1968) and Stephen Emmott (2013), the view on the ever-increasing peopling of the planet has tended to be a pessimistic one. In such discourse, populations are evoked in the same breath with violence: population time bombs, explosions, overshoot, and, in the dystopic closing remarks in Emmott's piece, populations which will probably have to know how to shoot(!) In one of his last interviews, Claude Lévi-Strauss echoed such pessimism: "I cannot have hope for a world too full (*trop plein*)" (Virginie CANAS 2008).

In a world of intensifying involuntary migrations, famine and drought, pandemics, and antibiotic resistance, the idea of such "fullness" might not seem far-fetched at first. Such "too fullness" appears as "too many, too close, too fast" in an accelerated world, marked by the violence of speed (Virilio 2006). It ostensibly hinges upon the exhaustion of carrying capacity and upon biotic battles between one population and another, across species.

Donna Haraway has advocated against a focus on biological reproduction and for making "oddkin," a "becom[ing]-with each other or not at all" (2016, 4). Neither dismissive about the implications of population growth, nor falling prey to apocalyptic thinking, she highlights the need "to cultivate […] epochs to come that can replenish refuge" (2015, 160).

At least since Aristotle, population has been the locus of life and politics. Populations are exposed to politics and ideology not only because life is political but also by virtue of being calculable: numbers are also political (e.g., Desrosière 2002). Thus, although easily recognizable across the disciplines, "population" is not the same thing from one discipline to another, not when an individual is concerned, and especially not when human population growth — this particularly politicized Anthropocenic feature — is in focus and is conceptualized, in normatively pre-determined language, as "overpopulation."

The usual response to perceived overpopulation has been population control, whose effects, however, despite good intentions, sometimes have amounted to human rights violations (Connelly 2008). Recently, distinguished demographer Jon Bongaarts continues to argue for reproductive control programs in places such as sub-Saharan Africa (2016) despite powerful anthropological evidence that there, rather than limit fertility, contraceptives can paradoxically be used to boost it, when women who have suffered reproductive mishaps and obstetric trauma due to multiple pregnancies resort to contraceptives to give their bodies the time necessary to heal from the wearing effects of reproduction, thus taking action to make future childbearing more likely and successful (Bledsoe 2002). In a subtle but significant recent shift, another distinguished demographer — Jacques Vallin — has suggested that "it may be more important to take measures aimed at adapting our societies and our economies to demographic change than to seek ways of influencing this change" (2016).

What looms in front of scientists and governments alike, then, is not the same population problems on a new scale. What looms is a need for *culturally adequate,* integrated empirical approaches (e.g., Koycheva, n.d.) that extend well beyond numbers and implicate relationships.

I am, therefore, hesitant to construct an analytical aperture for the Anthropocene by relying exclusively on "population." A pluralistic framework is necessary to accommodate other aspects of the epoch and its milieu, such as environmental phenomena, structures, and multi-species interaction and critical states of togetherness with a variety of lifeforms, with which populations are indelible (air, water) and to which they are irreducible (cf. Howe 2015; Kohn 2013). Perhaps a co-eval working concept is necessary — one which does not compromise the calculability of "population" but signals the theoretical need to conceptualize it as relational to its complex *Umwelt*: not a world of repletion, but one of replenishment; not one of aggregate numbers but one of dense relationships; not one "at capacity" but one of capacious being; a world transforming the "too fullness" into plenitude.

I do not preclude pessimistic nor optimistic views on human population growth. I insist on retaining Arendt's vitalist optimism about humanity's ability to act together in the political sphere to engender unexpected positive change but also take a cue from Lévi-Strauss's concerns.

If being (out)numbered engenders politics, and if overpopulation is the state of outnumbering ourselves and exhausting the capacities of shared habitats, the question of life in the Anthropocene is no longer only "What kind of numbers and what kind of politics we need?" It is what kind of ethics and what kinds of calculi we need.

References

Arendt, Hannah. 2013. *The Human Condition.* Chicago: University of Chicago Press.

Bledsoe, Caroline H., and Fatoumatta Banja. *Contingent Lives: Fertility, Time, and Aging in West Africa.* Chicago: University of Chicago Press, 2002.

Bongaarts, John. 2016. "Development: Slow Down Population Growth." *Nature* 530, no. 7591: 409–12. https://doi.org/10.1038/530409a.

Connelly, Matthew. 2008. *Fatal Misconception: The Struggle to Control World Population.* Cambridge: Harvard University Press.

Desrosières, Alain, and Camille Naish. 2002. *The Politics of Large Numbers: A History of Statistical Reasoning.* Cambridge: Harvard University Press.

Ehrlich, Paul R. 1968. *The Population Bomb.* New York: Ballantine.

Emmott, Stephen. 2013. *10 Billion.* London: Penguin.

Foucault, Michel. 2007. *Security, Territory, Population.* Translated by Graham Burchell. New York: Picador.

Haraway, Donna. 2016. *Staying With the Trouble: Making Kin in the Chthulucene.* Durham: Duke University Press.

———. 2015. "Anthropocene, Capitalocene, Plantationocene, Chthulucene: Making Kin." *Environmental Humanities* 6, no. 1: 159–65. https://doi.org/10.1215/22011919-3615934.

Howe, Cymene. 2015. "Life Above Earth: An Introduction." *Cultural Anthropology* 30, no. 2: 203–9. https://doi.org/10.14506/ca30.2.03

Kohn, Eduardo. 2012. *How Forests Think: Towards Anthropology Beyond the Human.* Berkeley: University of California Press.

Koycheva, Lora. n.d. "Introduction." In *Language and Quantification: An Integrated Approach,* edited by Lora Koycheva and Caroline Bledsoe (in progress).

Malthus, Thomas R., and Philip Appleman. 1976. *An Essay on the Principle of Population: Text, Sources and Background Criticism.* New York: Norton.

Preston, Samuel, Patrick Heuveline, and Michel Guillot. 2000. *Demography: Measuring and Modeling Population Processes.* Oxford: Blackwell Publishers.

Vallin, Jacques. 2016. "Are Population Policies Effective?" *n-iussp.* October 31. http://www.niussp.org/2016/10/31/population-policies-effectiveles-politiques-demographiques-sont-elles-efficaces/.

Virginie CANAS. 2008. "Interview Claude Levis Strauss." *YouTube.* November 30. https://www.youtube.com/watch?v=953bPu8intY.

54

Power

John Hartigan

The Anthropocene posits a very powerful species, one whose presence has registered even on the densely slow scale of the Earth's geology. But how singular is this species, and what does such a premise suggest about our capacity to think about power? These questions matter because the crisis named by the Anthropocene impels not only an accounting of the global impact of our species but also an effort to break from the myopia of our species being — the monomania that makes us the motor for the sixth extinction. How can we push our analysis "beyond the human" (Kohn 2013) in an age defined by the planetary scale of humans' impact on everything? By beginning to transpose our key concepts, like power and force, across species lines.

Try it. Can a species be powerful, can it act with force? If humans are powerful enough to alter all life on the planet, do other species have similar capacities? Perhaps on less grand a scale, but certainly yes. Consider two examples. In my hometown of Detroit, where the Industrial Age crested and broke, much of the city lies under dense mats of flora — as in ancient Mayan cities, plant species have taken over former human abodes. If you want to imagine what the end of the Anthropocene might look like, Detroit is the place to start.

Consider the image of bindweed overgrowing an abandoned home. Any of its individual tendrils may be intent on the strug-

DOI: 10.21983/P3.0265.1.56

gle for existence, but cumulatively and collectively they demonstrate the power to overcome the dominance humans once displayed in the epicenter of Fordism. Such scenes, played out across the planet, where habitations have been overgrown, offer prompts for rethinking power. In such frames — especially as we are quickly facing a lack of oxygen as phytoplankton begin dying off (Sekerci and Petrovskii 2015) — our species no longer looks quite as powerful as we imagined.

Now for another species, wild horses in Galicia, Spain — the tribe that is the focus of my current fieldwork. With these horses, I am asking how basic concepts like face might be applicable to understanding their sociality.

Horses highlight how our species's power is dependent upon harnessing its domesticates. To think the Anthropocene properly means recognizing that we are only possible through *them,* and that together we make up 90% of the vertebrate biomass on the planet (Vince 2011). Horses, then, highlight how transposable a concept like power is. Take our very notion for defining power in terms of work — horsepower. James Watt coined the term to compare the rate of work of his steam engine, which fueled industrialism, to that of a team of draft horses. As with many key concepts — *hybrid,* which we get from botany, or the *roots* and *branches* of our computational imaginary — *power,* in a mechanical sense, is predicated upon transposing the capacity of one species to exert sustained force on another. Power certainly operates in other species, as primatologists would be quick to point out; they have a great deal of experience working with such concepts across species lines. But this is a matter of scaling up from interactions between conspecifics to thinking of the species as a whole.

The challenges of scale are considerable, as the species concept is a problem of scale. Across the phyla our answers will change, especially if we are considering social species. The trick with such transpositions — as with a variety of challenges in the Anthropocene — is to deploy them without anthropomorphizing, but also without redrawing the line of uniqueness around our species. We do not need an entirely novel set of analytics to analyze nonhumans, but we also do not want to use terms in ways that just reproduce projections of the human. So power and force should start to look and function differently. Does power entail both objects and subjects? Certainly objects, upon which it is applied, but maybe our understanding of subjects — those who operate powerfully or are operated upon — needs to be rethought. This works best by shearing these concepts off from some of their correlates, like personhood or agency, which rely upon anthropomorphisms.

When Antonio Gramsci (1971, 169–71) wrote about power and hegemony, borrowing from Niccolò Machiavelli and Karl Marx, he conjured up the centaur, half human, half horse. Initially, this figure served to dramatize the tension between force and consent, but subsequently — and more fulsomely — it came to frame a mythic resolution of two easily disassociated forms of perspective: one "immediate and elementary," and the other a more "distant," dialectical view of the "complex and ambitious." The figure of the centaur works well here, too: first, as a nod to the particular concerns of power analysis among humans (inequality, hierarchy, and exploitation), and second, to highlight the challenge of transposing this concept across species lines. But in the transposing, we cannot settle for half-measures such as an anthropomorphic fusion that mythically resolves incompatible forms and natures.

What would be more useful are concepts like population, which has great currency across the social and natural sciences, insofar as they open up new ways to align underlying, powerful dynamics among humans and nonhumans. For the biopolitics of Michel Foucault (2007, 5), population is the key unit of analysis as the means of "modifying something in the biological destiny of species." But population also offers the means for understanding strategy differently — as in the curious concept of evolutionary strategy, where power may function without personhood or agency and may challenge our scale of reference for construing strategic and tactical actions.

References

Foucault, Michel. 2007. *Security, Territory, Population: Lectures at the Collège de France, 1977–1978.* Translated by Graham Burchell. New York: Picador.

Gramsci, Antonio. 1971. *Selections from the Prison Notebooks.* Edited and translated by Quintin Hoare and Geoffrey Nowell Smith. New York: International Publishers.

Kohn, Eduardo. 2013. *How Forests Think: Toward an Anthropology Beyond the Human.* Berkeley: University of California Press.

Sekerci, Yadigar, and Sergei Petrovskii. 2015. "Mathematical Modeling of Plankton — Oxygen Dynamics under the Climate Change." *Bulletin of Mathematical Biology* 77, no. 12: 2325–53. https://doi.org/10.1007/s11538-015-0126-0.

Vince, Gaia. 2011. "An Epoch Debate." *Science* 334, no. 6052: 32–37. https://doi.org/10.1126/science.334.6052.32.

55

Predation

Nayanika Mathur

The Anthropocene initiates new discussions not just about the agency of *anthrōpos,* but also about how we are to understand agentive action and planetary impact beyond the human (Latour 2014). I propose predation as a means whereby we can expand our vocabulary and imagination of what life in the Anthropocene is or might come to be. Predation operates here in its dual sense: the preying of a living being upon another as well as the act of looting.

In the Indian Himalaya, in a small state called Uttarakhand, big cats are increasingly preying upon humans. The marked exacerbation in human–cat conflict is, according to many, a direct outcome of climate change (see Mathur 2015). Man-eaters, or cats that eat humans, have a long and intriguing history in India (Pandian 2001). How, then, has this newfound link between climate change and the most literal sense of predation come to be?

Official statistics in Uttarakhand corroborate the general consensus that man-eaters are most active in the winter season. According to one popular state narrative, winter snowfall pushes leopards from the higher reaches of the Himalayas to spaces inhabited by humans. Previously, there was abundant nonhuman prey available for them. However, due to resource degradation, biodiversity depletion, and species extinction — all exacerbated by climate change in the Himalaya — the big cats face sparser hunting options. Deprived of their regular prey, they turn on humans.

Similar to the increase in man-eaters, there has been a steady increase in human-bear conflict in the same region of the Himalaya. Once again, officials have explained this upswing in attacks on humans by wild bears as a consequence of climate change. The rationale goes that due to global warming, it has become so hot even in the Upper Himalaya that the bears have been "driven mad" (*pagal ho gaye hai*) by the heat. These heat-crazed bears go on to indulge in random and inexplicable acts of violence, such as the mauling of humans and destruction of their property.

Nonhuman animals attacking, mauling, and eating humans in ever-rising numbers is, if we are to believe these state accounts, but one manifestation of life in the Anthropocene. But what of *anthrōpos* itself as a predator?

There is an emergent consensus that climate change is a result of the (de)predations of capitalism (Klein 2014). Distinct from the universalism of capitalism versus climate that appears in the title of Naomi Klein's manifesto, localized and historicized accounts of colonial, postcolonial, and corporate plunder of the Himalaya proliferate in Uttarakhand. Here, certain specified and frequently named human constituencies — those hailing from the distant plains of India (*maidani*) the agents of the state, and corporations — are considered to be preying upon the rich resources of the upper Himalaya. According to these accounts, it is the longstanding practices of animal poaching and trafficking, deforestation, resource extraction, mining, damming of rivers, incessant construction, and the commercialization of all domains of life that have depleted the Himalaya.

Is it not, then, darkly apposite that the predator — human beings — is to be predated upon by nonhuman animals — big cats and bears — in this age of the Anthropocene in the Himalaya?

Mutual predation is not, however, restricted to animals and humans in this epoch. Rivers, mountains, soil, and even the gods are furious at humans for their wanton destruction of the

Himalaya. This fury is expressed in diverse ways, with a prominent mode being recurrent disasters (*apada*) such as floods, famines, avalanches, forest fires (Kowshik and Sinha 2016), and earthquakes. In Uttarakhand, there was one *apada* that occurred in June 2013 that was especially devastating, with 5,500 people officially declared dead (although unofficial accounts put the toll at closer to 10,000). Following several days of unremitting monsoon rain and — it is speculated — cloud bursts, flash floods inundated several regions of Uttarakhand. In addition to the uncharacteristically fierce monsoon conditions, a contributing factor to the floods was the moraine left behind by the retreating Chorabari glacier ("Why Kedarnath Happenned" 2013). The monsoon rain filled the rock debris reservoir of the moraine and soon overflowed to join the flooding river. It was the combined force of the two that led to the raging floodwaters.

In a region where one *apada* or another is now expected on a seasonal, if not daily, basis, the floods of 2013 are marked as exceptional. Even in the otherwise prosaic and self-consciously secularizing bureaucratic language of the Indian state, they were termed a *daiviya apada* or divine disaster. The disaster was considered divine, in part, because the scale of destruction could only ever be wreaked by gods and demons. As eyewitnesses, victims, and residents of Uttarakhand describe and remember it, the floods and rains felt like the furious *tandava* dance of the Hindu god Shiva and must certainly have been *prakriti ka prakop* (retribution by Nature) (PTI 2013).

The greatest number of casualties and the most damage took place in the holy town of Kedarnath, which is centered around an ancient Shiva temple from the eighth century. As Shiva danced his dance of death and destruction, he made sure to protect his own temple. Witnesses describe hearing a huge snapping noise, followed by a gigantic wall of water descending on the Kedarnath temple and its surroundings. Miraculously, a huge boulder got lodged behind the temple, protecting it from any major damages. The location of the temple, as well as its strong construction, protected it. Such protection was not at hand for the surrounding buildings, which were swept away in the flood.

Thousands of humans, largely pilgrims, were met with the same fate, even as others got buried alive under landslides.

The image that has become iconic of the divine disaster, however, is one taken much further downstream from Kedarnath in the town of Rishikesh. In it, we see the flooding Ganges river partially submerging a popular Shiva idol. With his closed eyes and beatific smile, it is as if Shiva the Destroyer was resting at the end of his dance of rage. The divine disaster is discussed as a chilling foreshadowing of the Anthropocene yet unseen: an age in which prey will become indistinguishable from predator. This is a world in which big cats, bears, rivers, glaciers, mountains, clouds, humans, and gods will all act with a hitherto unknown extremity, ferocity, and unpredictability.

References

Klein, Naomi. 2014. *This Changes Everything: Capitalism versus the Climate*. New York: Simon and Schuster.

Kowshik, Karn, and Neha Sinha. 2016. "The Greed for Timber, and Climate Change, Have Made Himalayan Foothills a Tinderbox." *The Wire*. April 30. https://thewire.in/environment/the-greed-for-timber-and-climate-change-have-made-the-himalayan-foothills-a-tinderbox.

Latour, Bruno. 2014. "Agency at the Time of the Anthropocene." *New Literary History* 45, no. 1: 1–18. https://doi.org/10.1353/nlh.2014.0003.

Mathur, Nayanika. 2015. "'It's a Conspiracy Theory and Climate Change': Of Beastly Encounters and Cervine Disappearances in Himalayan India." *Hau: Journal of Ethnographic Theory* 5, no. 1: 87–111. https://doi.org/10.14318/hau5.1.005.

Pandian, Anand S. 2001. "Predatory Care: The Imperial Hunt in Mughal and British India." *Journal of Historical Sociology* 14, no. 1: 79–107. https://doi.org/10.1111/1467-6443.00135.

PTI. 2013. "It Was Like Shiva Dancing in Rage: Shobha Karandlaje." *The Hindu*. June 21. https://www.thehindu.

com/news/national/karnataka/it-was-like-shiva-dancing-in-rage-shobha-karandlaje/article4837408.ece.

"Why Kedarnath Happened." 2013. *The Nation.* July 26. https://www.frontline.in/the-nation/why-kedarnath-happened/article4894867.ece.

CHP 衞生防護中心
Centre for Health Protection

Exercise REDWOOD

紅樹演習

Please be aware an exercise
concerning public health is
in pro   ort to the officers
       before entry

56

Preparedness

Frédéric Keck

In March of 2016, France's Minister of Internal Affairs, Bernard Cazeneuve, announced that exercises simulating terrorist attacks would be organized in the ten French cities that were to host matches for the European Cup football championships in June and July. In Nîmes, 1,200 students from the National Police School gathered in the stadium with 480 experts from four ministries (Internal Affairs, Defense, Health, and Sports) to simulate a panicked crowd and coordinate the provision of services. In Marseille, a similar exercise that simulated evacuation from the stadium to hospitals was based on the scenario of an attack causing 185 casualties. Cazeneuve concluded his announcement by arguing that "French citizens must become sensitive to terrorist risks. They must be prepared to be surprised" (Riols 2016). When a man driving a truck killed more than eighty people in Nice during July's National Day celebration, a mode of attack that was indeed unexpected, the minister was criticized for not being prepared enough.

Four months prior to Cazeneuve's exercises, the French authorities were getting prepared for a very different event: the 2015 climate change conference known as COP21, which gathered more than 150 heads of state in Paris to discuss measures to reduce the global emission of carbon dioxide. In his own simulation of these negotiations, Bruno Latour organized a series of

DOI: 10.21983/P3.0265.1.58

diplomatic negotiations between representatives of the beings composing the globe. The goal of the simulation was to instantiate a state of war between the different representatives so that they could claim the territory to which they were attached. The rule was the following: "Name your enemies and define the territories that you are prepared to defend" (Latour 2015, 337). For instance, delegates of the oceans or the forest argued with delegates of the United States and Australia about the consequences of their energy politics. The scenario was not entirely written in advance, but instead created a stage for a political discussion to unfold, without using the term *nature* to provide easy compromises.

The possibilities opened by this discussion seemed to be closed by the attacks that happened just before the beginning of COP21, killing 130 people in the heart of Paris. While Latour's simulation of the climate change summit raised the question of just who the enemy was, the attacks gave it a name and a territory: ISIS. And yet the simulations of terrorist attacks for the European Cup seemed to bring back some openness: they aimed at "being prepared to be surprised."

Simulations of disasters emerged as techniques of risk management after World War II in the context of civil defense. They transformed the rationality of risk by focusing on events whose probability was unknown but whose consequences were catastrophic. They started with exercises that would immerse actors in scenarios of nuclear attack, such as the famous duck-and-cover exercises (see Davis 2007). Eventually, they were extended to all kinds of natural hazards, such as climate change intentionally caused by the Soviet Union (Hamblin 2013) or a pandemic initiated by a bioterrorist attack (Lakoff 2007).

Whether such simulations rehearse an intentional or unintentional catastrophe, their aim is *preparedness*: a state of vigilance cultivated through the imagination of disaster. And yet there is a difference between simulating a terrorist attack and simulating climate change. Why is it more difficult to imagine that we are at war in discussions about climate change than in the fight against terrorism? How can techniques of preparedness be extended from the military field to environmental issues? Is it only an extension of chains of causality, from the explosion of a bomb to the melting of ice, or do we have to change the way we imagine the future? The striking co-occurrence of the climate change summit and the terrorist attacks in Paris raised a difficult question: what kinds of enemies do we want to define for the Anthropocene? And how does this definition create a space for action?

Another technique of preparedness is the use of sentinel devices to send early-warning signals. The sentinel, like the disaster simulation, also has its origins in the military domain: a sentinel is a soldier going to the frontline to perceive in advance the movements of the enemy. Sentinels transform these movements into signals, thus creating a space of communication that fosters preparedness. In the context of climate change, sentinels raise the question of who the enemy is, but they do not answer it with reference to military sovereignty. Instead, they transform borders (between territories and between species) into problematic spaces.

While shadowy agencies patrol in anticipation of the next terrorist attack, sentinels record the signs of climate change: ice melting, species extinction, and extreme weather events (see Whitington 2013). The intermediary figure of the sentinel allows us to connect these radically different practices. The migratory bird or farm chicken infected with influenza, for example, could be announcing a potential pandemic. Implementing preparedness at the avian level (see Shortridge, Peiris, and Guan 2003), experts of influenza have connected fears of sudden epidemic with awareness of environmental changes, such as the dramatic increase in the number of industrial chickens. Neither friends nor enemies, sentinel birds signal new vulnerabilities in relations between species.

It is right to say that we need enemies to initiate action in the time of the Anthropocene, but these enemies need not declare their intentions. A space of imagination is created by techniques of preparedness in which our vulnerabilities are reflected and acted upon. While the number of potential enemies imagined by simulation exercises could discourage action, their localization in sentinel species or territories produces new forms of inhabiting the world.

References

Davis, Tracy C. 2007. *Stages of Emergency: Cold War Nuclear Civil Defense.* Durham: Duke University Press.

Hamblin, Jacob Darwin. 2013. *Arming Mother Nature: The Birth of Catastrophic Environmentalism.* New York: Oxford University Press.

Lakoff, Andrew. 2007. "Preparing for the Next Emergency." *Public Culture* 19, no. 2: 247–71. https://doi.org/10.1215/08992363-2006-035.

Latour, Bruno. 2015. *Face à Gaïa: Huit conférences sur le nouveau régime climatique.* Paris: La Découverte.

Riols, Yves-Michel. 2016. "Gérer la panique, l'évacuation des blessés… Les grandes villes de France simulent des attentats." *Le Monde.* March 16. https://www.lemonde.fr/attaques-a-paris/article/2016/03/16/quand-les-grandes-villes-de-france-simulent-des-attentats_4884018_4809495.html,

Shortridge, K.F., J.S.M. Peiris, and Y. Guan. "The Next Influenza Pandemic: Lessons from Hong Kong." *Journal of Applied Microbiology* 94, S1: 70–79. https://doi.org/10.1046/j.1365-2672.94.s1.8.x.

Whitington, Jerome. 2013. "Fingerprint, Bellwether, Model Event: Anticipating Climate Change Futures." *Limn* 3. https://limn.it/articles/fingerprint-bellwether-model-event-anticipating-climate-change-futures/.

57

Price

Maira Hayat

I eye his, Amjad Sahib's, five farm dogs warily. This is a strange conversation. It proceeds in ten minute bursts of hurried questioning followed by a few minutes of negotiating with — coaxing and threatening — the dogs.

"I was asking if you would say the monsoon rains have become more uncertain — have there been changes in rainfall patterns?"

Amjad Sahib, "Obviously, rain is the work of nature. It rains when it wants to." [uncertain laughter, both his and mine]

"Of course... yes it has always varied in timing and intensity as you say, but in terms of trends? I mean longer term *rujhanat* (patterns)... would you say, for instance, instead of heavy rains beginning in August, they now begin in June?"

Amjad Sahib, "Maybe. Sometimes early, sometimes late. Sometimes there's no rain, sometimes lots of rain. It's the potato prices that worry me. They keep me up at night!"

I then try several iterations of climate change translated into Urdu: *mawsami taghayur* (weather changes), *mawsamyati tabdeeli* (*tabdeeli* means change), *mawsami taghayuraat* (*taghayur* means change)."

We both start laughing. Amjad Sahib, "I haven't used such difficult Urdu since I was a school child!"

DOI: 10.21983/P3.0265.1.59

Amjad Sahib goes back to potatoes. He narrates a poem about potatoes and their fickleness. The poem goes like this:

aloo awlya, lag javay tte awlya
na laggey tte hojavey maliakholia

Translation: if the potato crop takes off then it makes you a king (*awlya* is saintly), but if it fails it will drive you mad (some of the meanings *maliakholia* denotes: a mental disease; the Punjabi version of the English melancholia; schizophrenia, hysteria; a depressive state).

Amjad Sahib invoked a double sense of crop failure: blight, but also low prices. This turn to price presents several possibilities, and I pursue one here: that price fills in for a blockage in translation. It is to understand the inflection of the new, the oncoming, and the unfamiliar by what exists, and is easier to recognize and hence negotiate that I have proposed prices. Price can bring the rumbling of a problem closer to differently located peoples' lived realities — in other words, prices can translate climate change into something louder and closer. Anthropogenic climate change is the cumulative effect of human acts — big and small, everyday and sporadic, new and old. When we talk about the Anthropocene, we have already jumped scale. Price is a more immediate way to understand how the Anthropocene is being produced — furthered as well as reversed (Mazzarella 2004). To track the contours of the Anthropocene, then, we could track prices. Price will contour, and is contouring the Anthropocene. Consider, for instance, the cultivation of water-intensive rice in a "water-stressed" country such as Pakistan. Concerns and interests of farmers, mill owners, wholesalers, exporters, and environmentalists (to take just one set of concerned actors) are not likely to become intelligible to each other. One way to try to reconfigure this situation, however, is to work with prices — raising the *abianna* (irrigation water charges levied by the government) can make it less profitable to grow rice. Price can provoke an adjustment in peoples' projects and decisions.

A focus on price can alert us to our evaluations that are pro-ducing the Anthropocene — it is not some juggernaut coming toward us but the effect of countless evaluations. And so prices alert us to our responsibility, albeit in varying degrees, as gov-ernment, business, consumer, small or big farmer, industrialist, et cetera. We can hold capitalism responsible, or the more afflu-ent societies — as we should, for certainly the climate crisis is not of everyone's (equal) making. But prices can go further and provide an ethnographic handle, and enable fine-grained analy-ses tracking exactly how, through what mechanisms, policy decisions, political calculations — as manifested in price com-posites — contemporary systems of production, circulation, and consumption are held in place and will unravel (Guyer 2009).

Climate change is about the phreatophytes that can no longer live because groundwater levels in the Indus basin are dipping, as the hydrologist at a seminar on the climate change challenge in Lahore said, and about the changing patterns and intensities of rainfall, but it will be made real, inter alia, through prices. Cli-mate change is as much about bureaucracy, political economy, time constraints, and calculi of donor organizations, and elected governments that know they face re-election every three to four years and want to harness climate change funds to begin projects with fanfare before (re)election time (see Guyer 2007). Ethnog-raphy can show how it will articulate with existing compulsions, parochialisms, and framings; and will be lived through famil-iar mediations of class, power, climatic zone, and geographical location for instance. Will these mediations be smooth? Likely not, just as translations in conditions of inequality tend not to be (see Asad 1988). While the worsening of the climate crisis is usually, and rightly, portrayed in dystopian terms, the Anthro-pocene will also throw connections at us. Prices can become the basis for new connections, say between "enemy countries" agreeing to trade in certain commodities. In a rather discord-ant contemporary world where many don't seem interested in talking to, let alone translating, the other, price can be one of the sites where connection becomes possible. This could direct anthropological focus toward not just the erasures and elisions but also the possibilities and promises of price. In other words, price in the Anthropocene can be a proxy for consensus, lack of consensus, conserving resources, profit making — which will it be? Ethnography can tell.

References

Asad, Talal. 1986. "The Concept of Cultural Translation in British Social Anthropology." In *Writing Culture: The Poetics and Politics of Ethnography: A School of American Research Advanced Seminar,* edited by George E. Marcus and James Clifford, 141–65. Berkeley: University of California Press.

Guyer, Jane. 2007. "Prophecy and the Near Future: Thoughts on Macroeconomic, Evangelical, and Punctuated Time." *American Ethnologist* 34, no. 3: 409–21. https://doi.org/10.1525/ae.2007.34.3.409.

———. 2009. "Composites, Fictions, and Risk: Toward an Ethnography of Price." In *Market and Society: The Great Transformation Today,* edited by Keith Hart and C.M. Hann, 203–20. Cambridge: Cambridge University Press.

Mazzarella, William. 2004. "Culture, Globalization, Mediation." *Annual Review of Anthropology* 33: 345–67. https://doi.org/10.1146/annurev.anthro.33.070203.143809.

58

Probiotic

Jamie Lorimer

The Anthropocene names an antibiotic age: an era marked by systematic efforts to extinguish or control the diversity and complexity of the living world. Some of us have proved remarkably capable of such endeavors. Landscapes have been ordered, bodies purified, and many forms of difference subsumed to the anthropocentric logics of modernity.

Concerns are now brewing that such dreams of control and their simplified, stable worlds may be as pathological as worlds of excessive abundance. For example, anxieties about the loss of biological diversity and ecosystem function *out there* (Holling and Meffe 1996) resonate with worries about missing microbes and dysbiosis *in here* (Blaser 2014). Modern life is said to be plagued by "epidemics of absence" (Velasquez-Manoff 2012). The loss of bodily microbes and shifting encounters with nonhumans large and small are being linked to rises in noncommunicative diseases of both mind and body. Allergies, autoimmunity, depression, and a host of other complaints are cast in terms of our disentanglement from the nonhuman worlds in and around us. Archetypal modern innovations like sanitation, urbanization, Caesarean sections, and bottle-feeding have been flagged as deleterious to our microbial selves (Blaser and Falkow 2009).

DOI: 10.21983/P3.0265.1.60

In response, alternative modes of managing life are emerging that I want to describe as probiotic. I use this term advisedly. *Probiotic* is much more than what you buy in a health food shop: an expensive foodstuff distinguished by the addition of a single strain of microbial life. What I have in mind is a more expansive set of interventions geared toward the systematic modulation of political ecologies conceived as dynamic milieu characterized by multiple stable states, intensive relations, and spatiotemporal rhythms punctuated by tipping points. Probiotic interventions target ecologies that have already tipped, seeking to revert, restore, or rewild them in the interests of improved functionality. They involve environmental modes of biopower (Foucault 2010), working with and against the various logics of biosecurity (Massumi 2009; Braun 2014).

Two sets of examples might suffice to illustrate this probiotic turn. The first comes from the management of life in those flagship sites for nature: national parks. A shift is underway in the priorities of some forms of wildlife conservation from species composition to ecological function, resilience, and adaptive capacity. A growing awareness of the novelty of the ecologies of the Anthropocene has coincided with a popular interest in rewilding. Rewilding comes in several guises (Lorimer et al. 2015), linked by a common interest in introducing so-called keystone species: organisms capable of reorganizing target landscapes by virtue of their disproportionate ecological agencies.

The most famous example is the wolves of Yellowstone. Their dwindling over the course of the twentieth century unravelled the "trophic cascade" they exert over the park's ecology, shifting the grazing practices of Elk and other herbivores. The deliberate reintroduction in the 1990s was given credit for reversing these effects; wolves, here, engineer entire landscapes. Rewilding forms part of a wider rethinking of the management of ecological disturbances. Coastal and river managers speak of rewetting floodplains and working with natural processes, while forest managers consider naturalistic modes of fire management or biological forms of pest control.

A second set of probiotic interventions is underway in relations with human microbiomes. Long vilified as pathogenic, there is now a growing interest in the salutary potentials of some microbes. For example, immunologists draw attention to the vital role played by a range of microbes in training the human immune system. Martial metaphors of a body primed for the defense of an essential human self are giving way to more variegated understandings of bodily tolerance, experimentation, or even active recruitment of microbial organisms for the symbiotic maintenance of bodily functionality (Gilbert, Sapp, and Tauber 2012).

Formerly taboo parasites have come to the fore as potential biotherapy agents. Species like human hookworm have been revalorized for their keystone qualities, promoted — like the wolves of Yellowstone — for the ability to train and modulate human bodily ecologies prone to autoimmune and inflammatory disease. It seems that hookworm can communicate with our gut microbes, shaping internal ecologies to establish mutualistic relations (Bilbo et al. 2011). Several thousand people currently self-medicate with a range of hookworms and other helminths. There is a form of inner rewilding underway here.

Such biotherapies can be positioned alongside broader probiotic enthusiasms in late modern societies. For instance, there is a growing interest in manipulating the microbiome of the built environment to reduce the spread of infectious disease and to secure desired microbial transmission (National Academies of Sciences, Engineering, and Medicine 2017). Other interventions seek to replicate the bacterial colonization associated with vaginal birth for babies born by Caesarean section (Molloy 2015) and to provide safe fecal matter for transplants to restore gut health and inhibit antibiotic-resistant bacteria (Wolf-Meyer 2017). The publishing world is awash with popular science and self-help books encouraging us to work on our microbiomes, in incarnations ranging from the neoprimitivist to the techno-optimist. Their efforts are assisted by the rise of personalized metagenomic sequencing companies such as uBiome. These allow consumers to map their inner ecologies and cross-reference this data with other metrics of their quantified selves.

These tendencies are heterogeneous, and it might be a little grandiose to talk of a single probiotic turn. They are also fissured by familiar and unequal political geographies and ecologies. For example, antibiotic programs to deworm the world persist in parts of the global South marked by poor sanitation and drug delivery, where absence is more desirable than excessive presence. Similarly, rewilding in temperate nature reserves and abandoned marginal agricultural landscapes must be viewed in the context of the globalization of agriculture and the persistent, antibiotic, and often violent intensification of land use in tropical areas.

Even so, might these diverse probiotic trends offer some directions for an Anthropocene yet unseen? As an environmental mode of biopolitics, being probiotic still involves making live and letting die. In the Anthropocene, such calculations are now necessarily performed at a global scale. But perhaps there are the makings here of new worlds attuned to living with feral relations (Tsing 2015). There are stories to be told across these fragments about future epochs to be made in common, within ecologies kept within safe and habitable limits.

References

Bilbo, Staci D., Gregory A. Wray, Sarah E. Perkins, and William Parker. 2011. "Reconstitution of the Human Biome as the Most Reasonable Solution for Epidemics of Allergic and Autoimmune Diseases." *Medical Hypotheses* 77, no. 4: 494–504. https://doi.org/10.1016/j.mehy.2011.06.019.
Blaser, Martin. 2014. *Missing Microbes: How Killing Bacteria Creates Modern Plagues.* London: Oneworld.
———, and Stanley Falkow. 2009. "What Are the Consequences of the Disappearing Human Microbiota?" *Nature Reviews Microbiology* 7: 887–94. https://doi.org/10.1038/nrmicro2245.

Braun, Bruce P. 2014. "A New Urban Dispositif? Governing Life in an Age of Climate Change." *Environment and Planning D: Society and Space* 32, no. 1: 49–64. https://doi.org/10.1068/d4313.

Foucault, Michel. 2010. *The Birth of Biopolitics: Lectures at the Collège de France, 1978–1979*. Translated by Graham Burchell. Basingstoke: Palgrave Macmillan. Originally published in 2004.

Gilbert, Scott F., Jan Sapp, and Alfred I. Tauber. 2012. "A Symbiotic View of Life: We Have Never Been Individuals." *Quarterly Review of Biology* 87, no. 4: 325–41. https://doi.org/10.1086/668166.

Holling, C.S., and Gary K. Meffe. 1996. "Command and Control and the Pathology of Natural Resource Management." *Conservation Biology* 10, no. 2: 328–37. https://doi.org/10.1046/j.1523-1739.1996.10020328.x.

Lorimer, Jamie, Chris Sandom, Paul Jepson, Chris Doughty, Maan Barua, and Keith J. Kirby. 2015. "Rewilding: Science, Practice, and Politics." *Annual Review of Environment and Resources* 40: 39–62. https://doi.org/10.1146/annurev-environ-102014-021406.

Massumi, Brian. 2009. "National Enterprise Emergency: Steps Toward an Ecology of Powers." *Theory, Culture and Society* 26, no. 6: 153–85. https://doi.org/10.1177/0263276409347696.

Molloy, Aimee. 2015. "Mothers Facing C-Sections Look to Vaginal 'Seeding' to Boost Their Babies' Health." *The Guardian.* August 17. https://www.theguardian.com/lifeandstyle/2015/aug/17/vaginal-seeding-c-section-babies-microbiome.

National Academies of Sciences E, and Medicine. 2017. *Microbiomes of the Built Environment: A Research Agenda for Indoor Microbiology, Human Health, and Buildings.* Washington, D.C.: National Academies Press.

Tsing, Anna Lowenhaupt. 2015. *The Mushroom at the End of the World: On the Possibility of Life in Capitalist Ruins.* Princeton: Princeton University Press.

Velasquez-Manoff, Moises. 2012. *An Epidemic of Absence: A New Way of Understanding Allergies and Autoimmune Diseases.* New York: Scribner.

Wolf-Meyer, M.J. 2017. "Normal, Regular, and Standard: Scaling the Body through Fecal Microbial Transplants." *Medical Anthropology Quarterly* 31: 297–314. https://doi. org/10.1111/maq.12328.

59

Quotidian

Eli Elinoff and Tyson Vaughan

In March of 2016, the Thai military gathered a small number of community members from a canal-side community on the outskirts of Bangkok to hand out titles to residents of the settlement, illegally built on land owned by the irrigation department. Hanging over the event was a larger plan to fortify the city's canals against future floods. This bigger project made the small ceremony a pyrrhic victory for social justice. While these residents received titles, nearly 20,000 other canal-side homeowners across the city received eviction notices (Thai PBS, 2015). Adjacent to the stage where the titles were presented, architectural renderings of the project hung directly over the high watermark of the 2011 floods, a rusty orange line sprayed onto the corrugated metal wall below. During that flood, some areas surrounding Bangkok had been under water for more than eight weeks.

As experts and politicians scrambled to contain the narrative ramifications of that disaster, they blamed everything from politicized water management to mass deforestation to the effects of global warming (Marks 2015; cf., Hilgartner 2007). In the process, the receding waters revealed new imaginaries of the planet's environmental prospects. The flood became a "model event" that "enable[d] people to think through situated climate futures" (Whitington 2013, 318). A wide variety of flood prevention pro-

DOI: 10.21983/P3.0265.1.61

jects around the city now implicate the dynamic relationship between the urbanizing Chao Phraya delta and the changing macro-conditions of the planet. This crucible of traumatic past and menacing futures shapes the everyday conditions of urban politics under the Thai military government.

Conceptually, the notion of the "Anthropocene" calls our intellectual attention to environmental transformations on a planetary scale, induced by epochal human enterprises such as colonization, industrialization, urbanization, and global capitalism. Yet practically, coming to grips with the Anthropocene requires an examination of the ways that mundane, everyday practices engage these transformations at the lived scale of communities and individuals. Indeed, the epochal and planetary inevitably return to the *quotidian* as people make sense of their place in the world by gauging normal weather from abnormal weather, by elevating their homes in response to rising tides, or by creating metrics of personal environmental impact that, for example, translate everyday carbon consumption into cubic meters of glacial ice-melt. These are efforts to sense and act upon this new environmental reality by making the planetary legible at the level of the everyday (Elinoff & Vaughan, forthcoming).

The responses to the Thai floods, like responses to disasters elsewhere, demonstrate the spatial and temporal tensions between planetary shifts and localized practices and between epochal knowledge and quotidian action. On the one hand, the notion of a "new normal" of intensifying natural disasters ravaging radically altered landscapes implicates planetary scales and processes, justifying ambitious projects, grand visions, and infrastructural schemes that displace marginal communities. On the other hand, the planetary-ness of change and, more importantly, responses to it, is determined at specific localities, within the specific temporal frame of the present, by winners and losers of specific political contests. As post-flood Bangkok illustrates, grand debates about how to prepare cities for a future of catastrophe and about what kinds of cities are worth protecting present themselves in local fights about square meters of urban space. When residents along Thailand's canals grapple with the implications of vast environmental engineering projects, they also struggle with their neighbors, the city, and the national government. Here, the planetary blends into the local, as epochal transformation becomes the stuff of quotidian struggle.

The everyday reveals the specific ways that power is generated, enacted, felt, and contested in and through the environment as communities and individuals grapple with living on a changing planet. As Henri Lefebvre argued, "Insofar as the everyday is a reality which must be metamorphosed, challenged and made challengeable by critique, it can be observed on the level of tactics, of forces and their relations, and of stratagems and suspicions. Its transformation takes place on the level of events, strategies and historical moments" (1991, 135). Thus, an analytical turn to the quotidian is necessary if we are to understand, challenge, and transform the "events [and] strategies" shaping the historical moment of the Anthropocene.

By examining the ways that the geological is made quotidian and the quotidian becomes epochal, we can begin to understand the ways actors experiencing these shifts generate common- and uncommon-sense answers to the forces shaping their lives. The terrain of the quotidian reveals the situated effects of environmental projects and the stakes upon which disagreements over these efforts are prosecuted. It also facilitates study and debate about how expert forms of knowledge that seek to make sense of such transformations are rejected or accepted to enact change. And, when seemingly insurmountable challenges such as climate change induce an overwhelmed paralysis and eschatological stupor, the quotidian may become a grounding antidote to the apocalyptic. It is in the local and the everyday that actors produce, make sense of, and grapple with the emerging nature–culture configurations of the Anthropocene.

If the quotidian opens up the Anthropocene to political and practical intervention, then ethnography can be used to call attention to the ways in which a politics of the planetary becomes actionable in scenes of everyday life. Such a framing evokes both the lived questions raised by the planetary nature of the Anthropocene and the deep ethical questions we must engage in this time of profound social, political and environmental change. As Alex Loftus has argued, in order to "reformulate a politics of the environment" we must reformulate "environmental politics on the terrain of the *quotidian*" (2012, xvii; our emphasis). Doing this requires performing the seemingly paradoxical work of seeing the big-ness of planetary change within the small-ness of everyday life. This work is complex but necessary if we are to gain a fuller understanding of the temporal depth and spatial breadth of our planetary environmental impacts. More than that, it is crucial if we are to have any chance of engaging with the quotidian political and social realities of life on a changing planet.

References

Elinoff, Eli, and Tyson Vaughan. Forthcoming. "Introduction: Disastrous Times." In *The Quotidian Anthropocene: Reconfiguring Environments in Urbanizing Asia,* edited by Eli Elinoff and Tyson Vaughan. Philadelphia: University of Pennsylvania Press.

Hilgartner, Stephen. 2007. "Overflow and Containment in the Aftermath of Disaster." *Social Studies of Science* 37, no. 1: 153–58. https://doi.org/10.1177/0306312706069439.

Lefebvre, Henri. 1991. *Critique of Everyday Life.* New York: Verso.

Loftus, Alex. 2012. *Everyday Environmentalism: Creating an Urban Political Ecology.* Minneapolis: University of Minnesota Press.

Marks, Danny. 2015. "The Urban Political Ecology of the 2011 Floods in Bangkok: Creation of Uneven Vulnerabilities." *Pacific Affairs* 88, no. 3: 623–51. https://doi.org/10.5509/2015883623.

Thai PBS. 2015. "Canal Squatters in Capital to Face Forced Eviction." *Thai PBS.* April 4. http://englishnews.thaipbs.or.th/canal-squatters-in-capital-to-face-forced-eviction/.

Whitington, Jerome. 2013. "Fingerprint, Bellwether, Model Event: Climate Change as Speculative Anthropology." *Anthropological Theory* 13, no. 4: 308–28. https://doi. org/10.1177/1463499613509992.

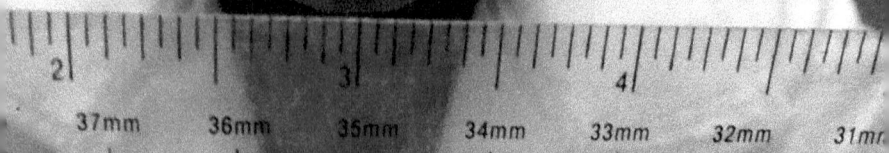

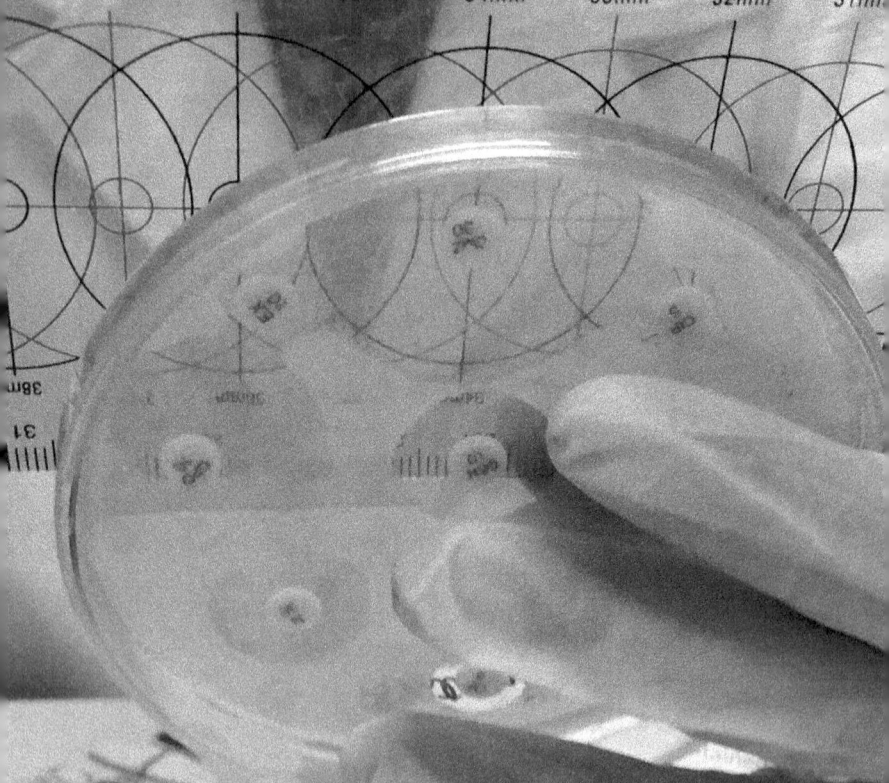

60

Recalcitrance

Rijul Kochhar

Consider two artefacts from 2016, emblematic perhaps of the Anthropocenic age. *Exhibit A* is an antibiogram (results of antibiotic-susceptibility tests against pathogens) for a dog from a microbiology laboratory in Delhi. This dog harbors a mutant strain of *E. coli* resistant to all antibiotics routinely tested for. *Exhibit B,* shown here, is an image of a laboratory petri-dish strewn with antimicrobial discs, against which cultured and isolated bacterial strains are tested for sensitivity and resistance to antibiotics. Zones of clearing on agar, measured and metricized in this Kirby-Bauer test, determine how fields marked "Sensitive," "Moderately Sensitive," and "Resistant" are deployed to target microbes bearing the promise of harm. As zones of clearing shrink, the "Resistant" columns on antibiograms swell. We are beginning to dwell in the ruins of the antibiotic age.

This is an emerging future where history has caught up. A time when a signal achievement of modernity — the antibiotic — is faltering within a century of its mass consumption, leaving entailments of anxiety and insecurity, with questions of threat and a planetary crisis. The WHO has devastatingly described this looming post-antibiotic era as a "health security emergency [...][one] in which common infections and minor injuries can kill [...] anyone, of any age, in any country" (WHO 2014). Instigating a vanishing of boundaries between disability and ability, rendering redundant borders between nations, questioning the textures of ongoing & future time, interrogating the nexus of the body and *securité* (Foucault 2009), we are increasingly in the company of life-forms — from MRSA and resurgent N. gonorrhoeae to Mycobacterium tuberculosis and mutant E. coli — that now carry the *perpetual* possibility of harm.

As antibiotics fail, how are these microbial "forms of (un) natural life" (Fischer 2009) — mutating in our anthropocenic ecologies — lived and dealt with, imagined, feared, endured, and conceptualized? One example emerged in 2016 when researchers at the Walter Reed National Military Medical Centre reported that a strain of *E. coli* (first found on an industrial pig farm in China in 2015) had been detected in a woman with a urinary tract infection. This strain was resistant to colistin — a "treatment of last resort" antibiotic pervasive in meat production. It harbored a "plasmid-borne colistin resistance gene, *mcr–1*" that enabled horizontal transfer of resistance between neighboring bacterial strains, and possibly species (McGann 2016; Helmreich 2011, 685–87). The director of the CDC declared that against such microbial strains, the "medicine cabinet is empty" — not only due to biological and antimicrobial-induced evolution, but also because of pharmaceutical market-dynamics: the U.S. FDA "has approved about half a dozen new antibiotics in the past two years, and about 30 more are in the pipeline. But most are similar to existing drugs and may not work any better. The most recently discovered class of antibiotics, lipopeptides, was identified in the late 1980s" (Reardon 2015). Time, money, and biomechanics have spawned recalcitrant lives, and the payback is now. For, as it transpired in June 2016, seagulls were dispersing mcr–1 carrying *E. coli* to places as far as Lithuania and Argentina (McKenna 2016). This is what a planetary crisis in the Anthropocene summons — a time of proliferating life-forms and trans-migrations, carrier seagulls and hyper-contaminations, mutational genes and hand-sanitizers, the return of ancient modes of death amidst technoscientific failure, industrial production, and anthro-zootic transmissions.

Writing this, I remember our dog, Buzo. There he sits, in my mind's eye, sick amidst laboratory blood and urine culture reports from 2013. Papers indexing tests for pathogens during his catastrophic brush with cholangiohepatitis and generalized sepsis — "poisoned blood," they said. In memory, I remain, in that Delhi veterinary hallway, buffeted by family and doctors, laity and priests of modern reason. Yet I sense an ancient helplessness, for these reports, too, possess three, skewed columns depicting resistance patterns. They determine Buzo's infection "resistant" to most antibiotics, including advanced, third-generation ones. Those that would "work" for him are hepatotoxic or nephrotoxic. Perishment, then, not by pathogenic microbes, but by the effects on the body of these toxic elixirs of life. We wait in that clinic, other pets, voices and dispositions, other intimacies, drowning our sorrows, as we set about navigating life at multiple scales. At the scale of our intimacy with our pet, and at the scale of life-forms that, I learnt then, are intractable products of a distinctly antibiotic age, microbial creatures of an ecological milieu that have emerged out of interactions — at cellular and planetary levels — with the cultural proliferation of antibiotic chemical use in the 20th century. Theirs is a story where evolution and natural selection, pharmaceutical reason and privatized biomedical research, uptake on industrial scales in human, agriculture, and livestock industries collide with ongoing cultural faith in these technosciences. This is a moment, too, of experimental futures and excavations of buried technosciences, like the Soviet-era deployment of viruses against bacteria in bacteriophage therapy — stories dead and (re)emergent as revenants (Chanishvili 2012).

The failure of antibiotics is the failure of a late-modern project to engineer living beings through a certain biopolitics of medicine and species, one which mandated the toxicitization of life at scales human and microbial (Podolsky 2015). Hannah Landecker suggests that "biological transformations to bacteria and bacterial ecologies [are] historical and cultural events that are incredibly specific to our time: the crossing point of industrialization and the medical control of infection" (Landecker

2015). We, therefore, interrogate the textures of the Anthropocene by including toxicities like antibiotic resistance and recalcitrant life forms as bequests of an age where human activities have profound, transformatory, perhaps catastrophic, impacts on planetary ecosystems (Fortun & Fortun 2005).

Recalcitrant microbial strains, as mutant planetary entities now envisioned in the epistemic space of the laboratory and the petri dish, and circulating in our bodies, soil, air, food, water — in our engineered ecosystems — ultimately signal the fiction of borders at scales cellular, species, and sovereign. Living with these legacy-creatures presents a moment of possibilities that is (again) simultaneously spectral and searingly real, at once humbling and terrifying in reach and unknowability. What of resilience in this age of recalcitrance?

References

Chanishvili, Nina. 2012. *A Literature Review of the Practical Application of Bacteriophage Research.* New York: Nova Biomedical Books.

Fischer, Michael M.J. 2009. *Anthropological Futures.* Durham: Duke University Press.

Fortun, Kim and Mike Fortun. 2005. "Scientific Imaginaries and Ethical Plateaus in Contemporary U.S. Toxicology." *American Anthropologist* 107, no. 1: 43–54. https://doi.org/10.1525/aa.2005.107.1.043.

Foucault, Michel. 2007. *Security, Territory, Population: Lectures at the College de France, 1977–1978.* Translated by Graham Burchell. Basingstoke: Palgrave-MacMillan.

Helmreich, Stefan. 2011. "What Was Life? Answers from Three Limit Biologies." *Critical Inquiry* 37, no. 4: 671–96. https://doi.org/10.1086/660987.

Landecker, Hannah. 2016. "Antibiotic Resistance and the Biology of History." *Body and Society* 22, no. 4: 19–52. https://doi.org/10.1177/1357034X14561341.

McKenna, Maryn. 2016. "Seagulls Are Carrying a Dangerous Superbug Through the Skies." *National Geographic.* June 22. http://phenomena.nationalgeographic.com/2016/06/22/seagulls-are-carrying-a-dangerous-superbug-through-the-skies/.

McGann, Patrick, et al. 2016. "Escherichia coli Harboring mcr-1 and blaCTX-M on a Novel IncF Plasmid: First report of2 mcr-1 in the United States." *Antimicrobial Agents and Chemotherapy* 60, no. 8. http://aac.asm.org/content/early/2016/05/25/AAC.01103–16.full.pdf+html/.

Podolsky, Scott H. 2014. *The Antibiotic Era: Reform, Resistance, and the Pursuit of a Rational Therapeutics.* Baltimore: Johns Hopkins University Press.

Reardon, Sara. 2015. "Spread of Antibiotic-Resistance Gene Does Not Spell Bacterial apocalypse — Yet." *Nature.* December 21. http://www.nature.com/news/spread-of-antibiotic-resistance-gene-does-not-spell-bacterial-apocalypse-yet–1.19037.

World Health Organization (WHO). 2014. "Antimicrobial Resistance: A Global Report on Surveillance." http://www.who.int/drugresistance/documents/surveillancereport/en/.

61

Relationships

Zoe Todd

To speak about Indigenous people's relationships to land, water, law, language, history, and futures, it is important that I first
foreground my statements by telling you who I am and where
I am from, so that you can situate how and why I know what
I know. My name is Zoe Todd. I am an *otipemisiw iskwew* — a
Métis woman — from *amiskwaciwâskahikan* in Treaty Six Territory in Alberta, Canada. My ancestors are Red River Métis on
my dad's side of the family, and my mom's family are British-
Norwegian settler-Canadians. Both kinship and place situate
the thoughts I have to offer on the interrelatedness of people,
place, stories, and time in the Anthropocene.

I come from Alberta; if you have heard of it at all, you probably know it as the home of the Tar Sands. In my short lifetime
I have watched the waterways of my home province deteriorate
as intense oil and gas activity, urban development, agricultural
demands, and climate change tighten, vise-like, on rivers and
creeks and kettle lakes and glacier-fed watersheds.

The Anthropocene is what Elizabeth Reddy calls a "charismatic mega-category" (Reddy 2014), which sweeps up within
it the diverse, dynamic, and even contradictory discourses of
peoples throughout the globe contending with catastrophic
environmental change. In discussing the Anthropocene, I am
continuously brought back to the inextricable relationships be-

tween land, bodies, time, and stories — relationships I continue to learn more about as I apprentice in the study of Indigenous legal orders and Métis philosophy here in North America.

At the 2015 American Anthropological Association meetings in Denver, panelists in the "Force and Power in the Anthropocene" session offered provocative accounts of the impacts and implications of the environmental change that is being observed around the globe. As I listened to the narratives offered by the panelists, I considered how their words mingled with the land and stories *of this place.* I was reminded of the way in which Cree legal scholar Tracey Lindberg opened a talk in Ottawa, Canada, in the fall of 2015 by reminding interlocutors to consider our duties to the Algonquin ancestors of the place where we stood — *whose bones are ground into the earth we walk on.* These ancestors, too, bear witness to our deliberations.

Listening to the stories about plants and plastic, melting ice and movement, that were shared during this session, I wondered: What does it mean to have a reciprocal discourse on catastrophic end times and apocalyptic environmental change in a place where, over the last five hundred years, Indigenous peoples faced (and face) the end of worlds with the violent incursion of colonial ideologies and actions? What does it mean to hold, in simultaneous tension, stories of the Anthropocene in the past, present, and future?

Climate scientists Simon Lewis and Mark Maslin (2015) argue that the beginning of the Anthropocene is, quite possibly, rooted in the environmental impacts of the genocide of fifty million Indigenous peoples throughout the Americas, following Christopher Columbus's "discovery" of America. Lewis and Maslin argue that the movement of species between the Old and New Worlds after 1492, as well as the precipitous decline in agriculture and land-tending due to the rapid loss of Indigenous lives, resulted in a measurable increase in forest cover, leading to a dip in carbon dioxide levels around the globe. They propose that one Anthropocenic "golden spike," labeled the Orbis Spike, can be placed in the year 1610. The machinations of wide-scale anthropogenic environmental change instigated by European colonization of the Americas — and the subsequent meteoric rise of a global capitalist system that was fueled by resources mined, hewed, and drawn from colonies, often through enslaved and/or indentured labor — are now, arguably, catching up with the entire globe. If Lewis and Maslin's Orbis Spike hypothesis is correct, then this compels humanity to tend to the interconnections between, first, Indigenous genocide and the violent enslavement of peoples from across Africa, the Pacific, Asia, and the Americas throughout the colonial period, and second, the contemporary economic, political, social, and cultural forces shaping current environmental and power relations.

Indigenous scholar Cutcha Risling Baldy (2013) discusses how she uses the zombie television show *The Walking Dead* in her teaching to discuss what it was like for Indigenous peoples in the United States to contend with the end of worlds — the apocalypse — at the hands of Spanish, British, and American empire. During the pop-up panel in Denver, Timothy Morton urged us to dream. It is pertinent here to point out that Indigenous people have been dreaming of an otherwise since the incursion of violent colonial ideologies, language, and laws into sovereign Indigenous territories in the Americas. And, crucially, as Cutcha Risling Baldy points out, Indigenous peoples are still here. Still telling stories. Still insistent, present, self-determining, and strong.

So what lessons can we learn from resurgent, resistant, resolute, and still-living Indigenous peoples who have already faced the upheaval wrought by the early forces of the Anthropocene? In my home territory, the principles of loving accountability and reciprocity are deeply embedded in Indigenous legal orders and relationships. What I have learned from these teachings, from mentors like Tracey Lindberg and Cree legal scholar Val Napoleon, is that reciprocity, love, accountability, and care are tools we require to face uncertain futures and the end of worlds as we know them. Indeed, this ability to face the past, present, and future with care — tending to relationships between people, place, and stories — will be crucial as we face the challenges of the Anthropocene, collectively, in our nations/societies/peoples, and in communities around the globe.

kinanaskomitin.

References

Baldy, Cutcha Risling. 2013. "On Telling Native People to Just 'Get Over It' or Why I Teach about the Walking Dead in My Native Studies Classes… *Spoiler Alert*." December 11. https://www.cutcharislingbaldy.com/blog/on-telling-native-people-to-just-get-over-it-or-why-i-teach-about-the-walking-dead-in-my-native-studies-classes-spoiler-alert.

Lewis, Simon L., and Mark A. Maslin. 2015. "Defining the Anthropocene." *Nature* 519: 171–80. https://doi.org/10.1038/nature14258.

Reddy, Elizabeth. 2014. "What Does It Mean to Do Anthropology in the Anthropocene?" *Platypus: The CASTAC Blog.* April 8. http://blog.castac.org/2014/04/what-does-it-mean-to-do-anthropology-in-the-anthropocene/.

62

Riddle

Michael Gossett

Riddles confront the limits of human ways of knowing. They dizzy and disorient us, render us dumb and guessing before the world's dark wonder.

Riddles "attach impossibilities to real things," as Aristotle (1995, 111) puts it: populating the stage with actors we recognize, but outfitted with strange masks. In the corpus of Anglo-Saxon riddle-songs, an iceberg dissolves into a pile of bones, and four fountains spring up from where, just now, a cow had been. A coopted moon creeps overhead like a pilfering thief while, in its eerie glow, an antler scours the forest for his lost princeling brother. Famously, in Sophocles's riddle of the Sphinx, a man reconstitutes as a creature whose legs shrink and sprout — four, two, three — over the course of a day. Riddlecraft-as-witchcraft: the super- is conjured from the -natural.

Riddles show us that what is ecological is cryptological: a scrambled message, not immediately intelligible, but not unintelligible either. The iceberg, after all, is cold and white like bone, and the antler is one of a pair that sits atop a deer like a crown. A cow's udders yield streams of milk, and the moon, at least metaphorically, steals the light of the sun. Caught between the intelligible and unintelligible, riddles might be said to be *quasi-unintelligible* (Vendler 2004; Donnelly 2013): though they appear to

DOI: 10.21983/P3.0265.1.64

be obscured beyond comprehension, upon patient examination they actually reveal themselves to us, in part if not in full.

In riddles, things in the natural world speak for themselves ("What am I?" "Can you say my name?"), showing us their unacknowledged complexity and diffracting our understanding through their veils of cloudy comparisons. Unable to see the riddle object directly, we lean forward, straining to listen. But whatever is there withdraws from us and, as it tangles itself in a mesh of other things, mutates from the familiar into the frightening. In this regard, riddles are remarkably well-tempered for theorizing an Anthropocene yet unseen, modeling for us a new way of encountering things we do not yet comprehend, have not yet even imagined.

Building on Craig Williamson's (2011, 33) suggestion that "what any culture calls monstrous may be simply an unrecognized riddle," could it be that the monstrous Anthropocene speaks to us now through its own unhappy catalog of disparate yet connected images: climate change, species migration, nuclear fallout, altered geologies? Might it even be asking, the way the Anglo-Saxon "storm" riddle asks, not only *what am I?* but *who is it that drives me?* Has our solipsism kept us from recognizing that we are being addressed in the first instance — and, what's more, implicated in the problem in the second? Which begs the question: if we aren't listening to the riddles when they speak, how will we realize the necessity of our presence in their solution?

In the Anthropocene yet unseen, all things will be riddle objects. Impossibly real, they will exist beneath a vestment of impossibilities. Unsurprisingly, then, the earliest evolutionary ancestors of these future riddle objects have already started to settle among us.

Take the humble rock. A literal foundational resource, the paradigmatic rock of the Anthropocene has been riddled — in both senses of the word — as a conglomerate of volcanic sand and manufactured plastic. ("Plastiglomerate" is this creature's name.) In this form, the impossible rock is simultaneously itself and not. Caught resonating from self to self, cycling through identities, this new thing, as Kirsty Robertson (2016) illustrates, contains in equal parts: (1) the humans who discovered and named it; (2) the sand and oil all rocks ultimately dissolve into; (3) the fuel said oil will be processed as; (4) the plastic end-result of the fuel processing; and (5) the disposable form of the plastic ("garbage") that will be tossed away, perhaps even by the human discoverer. Coming full circle, the rock resolves into a riddle object, contradicts itself — it is its own mother and its own child.

Elsewhere, the bird. The Laysan albatross of Midway Atoll, perhaps not unlike its city park counterparts, has made a habit of eating what its human feeders scatter. But in a gruesome turn, the birdseed and breadcrumbs here have morphed into Bic shells, Styrofoam cups, razor blade handles, toothpaste caps. In some autopsy photographs (Jordan 2009), the cross sections of the birds' stomachs reveal something resembling an overstuffed shopping cart, the intestines decaled like a sponsored racecar. Do we even recognize the birds, among all the stuff? Do we recognize it is our stuff among them?

And the whale. Even it is nothing now if not an enigmatic cornucopia: a husk of buckets and car parts rigged with ropey nets to outfish fish? A fleet of squid beaks drubbed with the rubber lid of a tackle box dangling behind a long braid of a hundred plastic sacks? Yes, and more, when we are talking about the sperm whales that beached on Germany's North Sea coast in 2016 (Malik 2016).

In the Anthropocene yet unseen, other riddle objects will emerge, and like those in the Anglo-Saxon tradition, ours too will be woven from the material conditions of daily life. It is in anticipation of this fact that I offer the following partial index, in the hopes that we might recognize our contemporary riddles when they call out to us: 3D printer, abandoned milk truck in woods, atomic priesthood, aeroponic garden at O'Hare airport, broken glass, Caterpillar, cavity, Cheyenne Mountain Base, dodo, drone recording oil spill near nuclear power plant, empty cabin, fast food cup, Fiji water, fish farms, fob, footprints, frozen horse heads, grime, hail, Halloween, honey bees, hurricane, iceberg, just the body, kale, lead in school water fountains, leafblower, low battery mode, mountain blasting, mutant, nuclear arsenal, octopus ink, orange pill bottles, other pill bottles, pill bottles, Plutonian Ode, radiation, recycling bin on the suburban curb, shit, slime, soda ring, solar flare, sunken ship, the fool, Toms, trash compactor, tsunami, turtle eggs, two hundred thousand poultry farms, urban garden, veganism, wilted bloom, Xerox copies, yoga, Zzzquil.

References

Aristotle. 1995. *Poetics*. Translated by Stephen Halliwell, W. Hamilton Fyfe, Doreen C. Innes, and W. Rhys Roberts. Cambridge: Harvard University Press.

Donnelly, Timothy. 2013. "Quasi-unintelligibility," Parts I–V and Coda. *The Poetry Foundation: Harriet, a blog.* April 10. https://www.poetryfoundation.org/harriet/2013/04/quasi-unintelligibility-part–1.

Jordan, Chris. 2009. "Midway: Message from the Gyre." http://www.chrisjordan.com/gallery/midway.

Malik, Wajeeha. 2016. "Sperm Whales Found Full of Car Parts and Plastics." *National Geographic.* March 31. http://news.nationalgeographic.com/2016/03/160331-car-parts-plastics-dead-whales-germany-animals/.

Robertson, Kirsty. 2016. "Plastiglomerate." *e-flux* 78. http://www.e-flux.com/journal/78/82878/plastiglomerate/.

Vendler, Helen. 2006. *Poets Thinking: Pope, Whitman, Dickinson, Yeats.* Cambridge: Harvard University Press.

Williamson, Craig. 2011. *A Feast of Creatures: Anglo-Saxon Riddle-songs.* Philadelphia: University of Pennsylvania Press.

63

Rivers

Rochelle Tobias

What would move a river to leave its hiding place? What could compel it to abandon its source? Why would it venture into a valley where it would be exposed to the heat of the sun, when it could still enjoy the protection of trees and rock? These questions may seem naïve and yet they have gained particular urgency in the Anthropocene, when once mighty rivers like the Colorado, the Indus, and the Rio Grande have all but run dry and no longer feed into the sea but instead carry saltwater into the land. The natural sciences have explored the exogenous causes of climate change but have been unable to address nature's own causality, its autonomy, its capacity to direct itself. Since the eighteenth century this task has fallen largely to poetry, which alone could investigate what Friedrich Schelling identified in 1800 as "nature's highest goal," namely, "to become wholly an object to herself" (Schelling 1978, 6).

In 1803 the poet Friedrich Hölderlin was well underway with his translation of nine fragmentary texts by the Greek poet Pindar from the sixth century BCE. Hölderlin was a close friend and classmate of Schelling and Hegel but went considerably further than the two in ascribing a willfulness to nature that exceeded human understanding. This was one of the many factors that drew him to Pindar and also ensured that his work was to influence thinkers as varied as Karl Jaspers, Walter Benjamin, Mar-

DOI: 10.21983/P3.0265.1.65

tin Heidegger, and Theodor W. Adorno. He entitled the last of his Pindar translations the "Enlivening" or "Life-Giving" force, which would make sense given that the text is devoted to rivers as personified in the centaur, a mythological creature that for both poets represents the spirit of rivers (Hölderlin 1946, 288–89).[1] In his commentary, Hölderlin emphasizes the power of rivers to cut paths through the earth and in so doing to transform what had been an undifferentiated mass into a diverse array of landscapes, each supporting different forms of life. Yet no sooner does he outline this position than he changes course, adopting a far more unorthodox view regarding the shape of rivers and what sets them in motion. It turns out that rivers do not etch lines through dry land of their own accord. They are compelled to do so by the arid earth, which in its inertness constitutes a peculiar power. Hölderlin will later call it "the eternally living, unwritten wilderness and the realm of the dead" (Hölderlin 1946, 266). According to him it is inert nature that first moves water, creating dams it then releases in streams. Why inanimate matter would guide water, the life-giving force, is not a question he answers here. Only in his poetic work will he consider why we have arable land in lieu of deserts, which for him is the natural condition of the earth.

One poem in which he takes up this question is "The Ister," also written in 1803, which takes as its title the Greek name for the lower portion of the Danube River, where it feeds into the Black Sea. In the third stanza of the poem, the poet reflects,

> Rivers do not venture
> Into dry land in vain. But how? The latter needs a sign,
> Pure and simple, nothing more, so it can carry
> Sun and moon inseparably in its soul, and
> It can continue on its way, night and day,
> And the gods can feel each other's warmth.
> This is why rivers are
> The joy of the Supreme God. (Hölderlin 1943, 191)

---

1   All translations of Hölderlin's work are my own.

The perspective Hölderlin adopts in these lines is undoubtedly foreign to most of us. Few would claim to know what gives the gods pleasure, or why rivers flow through a parched landscape that represents their polar opposite. It is this penchant for transcendental questions — i.e., how is it that we perceive what we perceive — on the one hand and mythological explanations on the other that lends his poetry its oracular quality. And yet for all its difficulty, the work is still accessible to interpretation. In the above-cited verses, the poet makes plain that what compels rivers to move and sets them on their way is the dry land which needs a sign that water alone provides as a reflecting surface. Rivers mirror the sun and the moon and in so doing grant the two heavenly bodies a place on earth. It is a place, moreover, where the two persist as images, even after they disappear from the sky as part of their alternating rhythm. This is why Hölderlin insists that the gods "feel each other's warmth" in streams. The two co-mingle as images and in their union sanctify the Earth, turning barren deserts into luxuriant fields, as the poet underscores in numerous works.

Rivers, however, do another service, which is implicit in these verses but more difficult to tease out. They give space time, or rather, the earth a history understood literally as a *geo-graphy*: a collection of etched signs in what would otherwise be an "unwritten wilderness." Rivers carve the days and nights the earth has witnessed into its surface. They leave a record of what has been, and in this manner they allow immobile land to move in time, which is the only movement available to it.

The earth "can continue on its way, night and day," because of the rivers that course through it. But what if they were to cease flowing? This is an all but unimaginable circumstance for Hölderlin but nonetheless one his poem addresses. Desertification would destroy this history, which is not a human history, but a story of the earth which exists in time because of the rivers that run through it, bringing good and bad tidings and connecting the past with the future. Whether we will be able to read Hölderlin's poem in the future will depend in large part on whether rivers continue to have their say, etching lines, writing signs, engraving previous suns and moons into the earth's crust.

References

Hölderlin, Friedrich. 1943. *Friedrich Hölderlin: Sämtliche Werke.* Volume 2. Edited by Friedrich Beissner. Stuttgart: Verlag W. Kohlhammer.
———. 1946. *Friedrich Hölderlin: Sämtliche Werke.* Volume 5. Edited by Friedrich Beissner. Stuttgart: Verlag W. Kohlhammer.
Schelling, Friedrich Wilhelm Joseph von. 1978. *System of Transcendental Idealism (1800).* Translated by Peter Heath. Charlottesville: University Press of Virginia.

64

Ruin

Sophia Roosth

To contemplate the end of the world, I had to get there. So I
flew to Longyearbyen, the largest permanent settlement in a
Norwegian archipelago called Svalbard, inside the Arctic Circle.
Less than a thousand kilometers from the North Pole, over sixty
percent of Svalbard's land mass is covered by glaciers. Longyearbyen is named for John Munro Longyear, an American capitalist whose name suggests a temporal slackening. Longyear arrived in Svalbard and saw riches in the plentiful coal seams that
marked the land, Triassic gashes just beneath or on the earth's
surface where glaciers had carved away the mantle. Coal is, of
course, dead organic matter: all that shiny black sediment is the
detritus of deciduous forests and puzzlegrass that flourished in
a balmier Svalbard sixty-five to twenty-three million years ago,
their dead tissue inspissated by heat and pressure until latent
energy condensed into something combustible.

Longyear's Arctic Coal Company began operating in 1906;
its first mine was dug into the slopes of Platåberget mountain,
which casts its shadow on the town below. Though coal mining in Longyearbyen is largely shuttered now, its infrastructure
remains scattered across Longyearbyen's landscape. The dark
skeletal remains of coal tipples, lift systems, and aerial tramway
conveyors litter the surrounding mountains, looking much the
way they were left. They resist decay because the temperature is

too cold for liquid water to rot wood. Like the coal seams for and upon which they were built, these abandoned mines are ruins that will remain indefinitely.

Across the fjord from Longyearbyen is Pyramiden, a Soviet mining town that was abandoned to the elements in 1998. The closest I could get to Pyramiden in February was visiting the Longyearbyen library. There, I learned that Pyramiden was designed to conquer the formidable climate of the high Arctic: miners could swim in a salt-water swimming pool, eat from a greenhouse that grew cucumbers and herbs, and walk across specially cultivated grass designed to be hardy enough to flourish in the frigid town square. The town also boasted a basketball court, a library, a nightclub, and a museum among other urban conveniences.

Ten years after its closure, two archaeologists and a photographer documented the ghost town after a decade of neglect. In their words, "ruins such as Pyramiden […] have their own historical mission: they rescue a forgotten past, not as heritage, at least not in any ordinary sense, but as a kind of involuntary memory that illuminates what conventional cultural history has left behind. They bring forth the abject memories that this history has displaced" (Andreassen, Bjerck, and Olsen 2010, 152). When the Longyearbyen library closed later that night, I crossed the street to sit at one of the two bars in town, drinking beneath Lenin's steely gaze. I asked the bartender what she knew about this bust and she shrugged: "Someone found it over in Pyramiden a few years ago."

What is a ruin? Let's page back to Walter Benjamin (2003, 166), who described history "as a petrified, primordial landscape" — nature frozen or turned to stone. For Benjamin, as he surveyed the ruins of Europe, an architectural ruin was an allegory for history, a history that is millennial but not dialectical. Phrased somewhat differently, history is a perpetual catastrophe occupying the caesura between past and present. Benjamin triangulated between history, life, and ruin, as all three are temporal allegories for one another: ruins fall apart; life decays;

and history tends toward tragedy. Could Arctic ruins, then, be allegories for the Anthropocene? They are places where the corrosive force of history gnaws into a petrified present, threatening to degrade an uncertain future.

Longyearbyen is now a former coal-mining town whose miners are out of work. An influx of scientists has begun taking their place, propping up a zombie economy with research grants from nations around the world. The coal mines in the nearby settlement of Ny-Ålesund closed after an explosion killed twenty-one miners in 1963, and today the town enjoys a second life as a research station. Each former coal miners' cabin now belongs to a different nationality of scientists.

These scientists arrive in Svalbard, in perfect irony, to observe anthropogenic climate change. As all of Svalbard's coal was extracted and combusted over the course of the twentieth century, atmospheric carbon dioxide levels rose. Svalbard is particularly sensitive to climate change; temperatures in the area increase more than one degree Celsius every decade, well above the global average. That means that one of the coldest places on Earth is warming up faster than the rest of the planet, and the glaciers whose tongues and feet and snouts had waxed and waned along depressed arêtes for hundreds of thousands of years are now receding. As their mass balances shift, they calve and let loose and the temperatures rise, and the waters rise, unleashing a terrible positive feedback cycle.

Today, one can look out onto Longyearbyen's landscape and see smoke from one of Svalbard's few remaining coal mines smoldering from the chimney of Norway's last coal-fired power plant, clouding the view of the Larsbreen glacier on the horizon. As temperatures rise, once-ossified Arctic ruins, like glaciers and other solid things, threaten to melt into corrupted air.

References

Andreassen, Elin, Hein Bjartmann Bjerck, and Bjørnar Olsen. 2010. *Persistent Memories: Pyramiden — A Soviet Mining Town in the High Arctic.* Trondheim: Tapir Academic Press.

Benjamin, Walter. 2003. *The Origin of German Tragic Drama.*
   Translated by John Osborne. New York: Verso. Originally
   published in 1963.

65

Seeds

Tracey Heatherington

Seeds are stories that sprout in the telling. They seem to show
us our roots and natures. Indigenous advocates remind us that
seeds are part of our deepest histories, as kindred peoples co-
evolving with kindred species. As we grow worried about
changing climates and losses of biodiversity, we realize seeds are
important. Recently, we have seen the building of the Millennium Seed Bank in the United Kingdom, the Svalbard Global Seed
Vault in the Arctic, and the Seed Cathedral at the 2010 World
Expo in Shanghai. These repositories and monuments reflect a
global imagination. The metaphorical power of seeds is ubiquitous within English (and other) languages: seeds of hope, seeds
of despair, seeds of change, seeds of doubt, seeds of resistance,
seeds of success, seeds of doom. From organic supplies and native sovereignty to invasive species and episodes of *Doctor Who,*
seeds are on our minds. They are objects of veneration, reflection, joy, research, commodification, fiction, religious parables,
bioengineering, post-apocalyptic fantasies, and social movements. In a world where many factors coincide to determine
future viability, seeds are tropes of possibility, condensing the
desires, limits, and fears of human agency.

Plant ecologist Carol Baskin tells her students, "a seed is a
baby in a box with a lunch" (Hansen 2015, 9). Her metaphor explains the basic anatomy of a seed, comprising a plant embryo,

a protective coating, and nutritive tissue to enable germination under appropriate conditions. The turn to anthropomorphism also highlights the ontological framing of our agricultural sciences and popular culture, for we habitually take seeds as icons of productive and reproductive potential. Seeds are the fruit of successful plant sex and the beginning of a developmental cycle. The Old Testament used seed as a metaphor for human descendants ("seed of Abraham"), and in English, the etymologies of sperm and seed link the human and the natural world in mutually engaged reproduction.

Seeds and the plants that grow from them have been our old friends, cousins, ancestors, gods, playmates, muses, and trading partners, going back to the earliest days of plant domestication. Plant geneticist Jack Harlan (1995, 239) concluded that "people everywhere were moving in the direction of food production from the beginning of the Holocene." Harlan's reconstruction of the beginnings of agriculture implants a multispecies origin story in every seed that farmers sow today. Particular groups of people, animals, related wild species, and companion plants all had continuing roles in the evolution of familiar domesticated varieties and the biodiversity of crops.

The stories we hear about seeds in the era of climate change often evoke trajectories of loss and mourning, for we know that seed biodiversity is vulnerable to increasing episodes of drought, heat, pests, blights, and floods that cannot always be foreseen or mitigated. Such narratives project a sense of inexorability. As Eileen Crist (2016, 24) points out, the fetishizing discourses of the Anthropocene may too easily endorse "history's unstoppable momentum," an assumption that implicitly affirms human exceptionalism and makes global systems, structures and inequalities seem inescapable. Perhaps the chief problem with the notion of Anthropocene is that it also reduces this complex human history to a species level (Hartley 2016). Anthropologists acknowledge this to involve *biocultural erasures,* which entail forgetting different ways of being in the world that are associated with distinctive cultural ecologies. For example, one strategy for adapting agriculture to changing climates involves genetically modified seeds. To protect the proprietary rights of companies that invest in developing new crops, it is now possible to engineer these seeds for sterility. Although such "terminator seeds" have not yet been commercialized, their widespread adoption would overwrite millennia of sustainable agriculture and affect cultural survival by jeopardizing the lifeways of small farmers. Yet neither the displacement of heritage seeds nor the dispossession of traditional keepers is inevitable. A profusion of lively cultural traditions safeguards biodiversity in fields, forests and gardens.

Scientists play an important role conserving rare historical collections of seeds — for example, through the efforts of The Crop Trust,[1] an independent foundation established by international agreement to coordinate and assist seed banks around the world. There is more to this work than putting material in the refrigerator: technical knowledge, legal frameworks, and socioeconomic capacities are also involved. To enhance food security, we must also sustain cultural memory and nurture food justice movements.

In a larger sense, seeds represent creative projects in their infancy. In the Seeds of Good Anthropocenes[2] initiative undertaken through a collaboration of Canadian, Swedish, and South African centers of research, the metaphor of seeds empowers a framework for imagining sustainability and justice in a more grounded way. Seeds of Good Anthropocenes seeks an inherently plural, interdisciplinary vision of positive change by documenting, mapping, and cataloging the approaches of projects that recognize and engage with the challenges of a changing climate, as well as our responsibility for the future. Some of the identified projects deal with food systems and actual seeds, such as the Oranjezicht City Farm in Cape Town, South Africa and the women's association gardens supported by the Great Green Wall

---

1 See *Crop Trust,* http://www.croptrust.org/.
2 See *Seeds of Good Anthropocenes,* https://goodanthropocenes.net/om/.

for the Sahara and the Sahel Initiative.[3] Other "seeds" banked in the digital collection are ideas, technical breakthroughs, institutional innovations, and social collaborations that might change the world for the better.

Seeds should never be mistaken for natural models or microcosms of a fated human journey toward either destiny or doom. Instead, they offer us innumerable surprises: hermaphroditic dandelions that pop through cracks in cement, old rice breeds made unexpectedly vigorous from weedy crosses, or ancient squash recovered by archaeologists and brought to life in twenty-first-century Menominee gardens. Seeds suggest alternative stories that may come true in the telling, as we nurture them. After millennia of coevolution, many of them now require our tending, and thus they remind us by their very nature (which is inherently bound together with the histories of specific human peoples) that we are not all merely hungry, self-entitled, increasingly greedy consumers. Instead, they inspire us to recall that many of us have always been — or may yet choose to be — the modest cultivators, weeders, waterers, minders, and seed-savers of this world.

References

Crist, Eileen. 2016. "On the Poverty of Our Nomenclature." In *Anthropocene or Capitalocene? Nature, History, and the Crisis of Capitalism,* edited by Jason W. Moore, 14–33. Oakland: PM Press.

Hansen, Thor. 2015. *The Triumph of Seeds: How Grains, Nuts, Kernels, Pulses, and Pips Conquered the Plant Kingdom and Shaped Human History.* New York: Basic Books.

Harlan, Jack R. 1995. *The Living Fields: Our Agricultural Heritage.* New York: Cambridge University Press.

Hartley, Daniel. 2016. "Anthropocene, Capitalocene, and the Problem of Culture." In *Anthropocene or Capitalocene?*

3 See *Great Green Wall,* http://www.greatgreenwall.org/about-great-green-wall/.

Nature, History, and the Crisis of Capitalism, edited by Jason W. Moore, 154–65. Oakland: PM Press.

66

Shit

Nicholas C. Kawa

Most people living in modern industrial and postindustrial cities have very limited responsibilities when it comes to the management of their most intimate forms of excreta. This is due to
a robust faith in and dependence on infrastructure that exists
primarily to blind us from knowing where our "shit ends up"
(Hawkins 2003, 40). Milan Kundera (1984, 156) brilliantly seized
on this point, writing: "Even though the sewer pipelines reach
far into our houses with their tentacles, they are carefully hidden from view, and we are happily ignorant of the invisible Ven-
ice of shit underlying our bathrooms, bedrooms, dance halls,
and parliaments."

In his *History of Shit,* Dominique Laporte (2000, 66) argued
that the modern state established itself through its role as "the
Grand Collector, the *cloaca maxima* that reigns over all that shit,
channeling and purifying it [...] hiding its places of business
from sight." Due to a number of impressive political and technological feats, much of our waste has been concealed from many
of us. The only problem is that such feats are founded, at least
in part, on an illusion: a modernist magic trick of sorts. "What
makes shit so disturbing and disgusting," Gay Hawkins (2003,
40) writes, "is that we can never completely escape it, can never
get rid of it. It comes back to haunt us, it sticks to us; it has that

uncanny capacity to return. The desire for elimination as absolute separation is always thwarted."

The Anthropocene will offer many lessons for humanity, but one of its most jarring is that we simply can't hide from our shit any more.

In our desire to distance ourselves from our waste and separate ourselves from the so-called natural environment and its cycles, we have also blinded ourselves to the problems that this distancing poses. With the help of modern technologies, we have constructed the fantasy that we can insulate ourselves from local ecologies and the broader world, which is made up not only of butterflies and rivers and California condors but also our shit and that of our pets, not to mention plastic bottles, plastic bags, and the wider array of macro- and microplastics[1] (industrial shit par excellence) that have begun to stratigraphically define this new geological epoch. The very real problem is that we cannot separate ourselves from these things. The various forms of shit that we send down drains and toilets clog sewer lines, while the shit of our dogs piles up in parks and smears city sidewalks. Our plastics have come to invade the oceans and our bodies (Liboiron 2013), all as our trash heaps up in large mounds. The most pernicious of these waste products is one that we cannot even see with the naked eye: the CO_2 that belches out of our cars' tailpipes.

Modern science has provided us with the powerful insight that in isolating things from their surroundings, we can objectify them and generalize about them in meaningful ways. This is what gives science such great power. A problematic consequence is that in objectifying the world that surrounds us, we have come to believe not only that it exists in a separate domain known as nature, but also that it opens itself up to facile human manipulation and control (Kawa 2016, 70).

---

1   Jan Zalasiewicz and colleagues (Zalasiewicz et al. 2016) note that low-density microplastics are found at extreme depths of the ocean, which may have been "ingested by zooplankton and ejected as faecal pellets."

It is naive to think that humans have ever lived in perfect harmony with the earth's ecosystems. Still, we know that for most of humanity's existence on this planet, people deposited their excrement directly into the soil, feeding seas of microbes while also nourishing plants that, in turn, provided sustenance to humans and other animals. There are currently projects around the world that are looking to reformulate humanity's relationship to its excrement, with implications for agricultural fertilization (Preneta et al. 2013), energy production (Chen et al. 2014), water conservation (UNICEF 2015), and even urban public life (Chalfin 2014). Can finding better ways of reconnecting with our shit pull us out of this ecological crisis? No one can say for sure. But it has the potential, I believe, to push us toward a different way of thinking ecologically and even to encourage a new sense of political and ethical engagement with our environment. In this new epoch known as the Anthropocene, rather than worrying about humanity overtaking the earth, perhaps we should start taking care of our shit first.

References

Chalfin, Brenda. 2014. "Public Things, Excremental Politics, and the Infrastructure of Bare Life in Ghana's City of Tema." *American Ethnologist* 41, no. 1: 92–109. https://doi.org/10.1111/amet.12062.

Chen, Yu, Gaihe Yang, Sandra Sweeney, and Yongzhong Feng. 2010. "Household Biogas Use in Rural China: A Study of Opportunities and Constraints." *Renewable and Sustainable Energy Reviews* 14, no. 1: 545–49. https://doi.org/10.1016/j.rser.2009.07.019.

Hawkins, Gay. 2003. "Down the Drain: Shit and the Politics of Disturbance." In *Culture and Waste: The Creation and Destruction of Value,* edited by Gay Hawkins and Stephen Muecke, 39–52. Lanham: Rowman and Littlefield.

Kawa, Nicholas C. 2016. *Amazonia in the Anthropocene: People, Soils, Plants, Forests.* Austin: University of Texas Press.

Kundera, Milan. 1984. *The Unbearable Lightness of Being.*
Translated by Michael Henry Heim. New York: Harper.

Laporte, Dominique. 2012. *History of Shit.* Translated by
Rodolphe el-Khoury and Nadia Benabid. Cambridge: MIT
Press.

Liboiron, Max. 2013. "Plasticizers: A Twenty-First-Century
Miasma." In *Accumulation: The Material Politics of Plastic,*
edited by Jennifer Gabrys, Gay Hawkins, and Mike Michael,
134–43. New York: Routledge.

Preneta, Nick, Sasha Kramer, Baudeler Magloire, and Jean-
Marie Noel. 2013. "Thermophilic Co-composting of Human
Wastes in Haiti." *Journal of Water, Sanitation, and Hygiene
for Development* 3, no. 4: 649–54. https://doi.org/10.2166/
washdev.2013.145.

UNICEF. 2015. "Water, Sanitation, Hygiene: Statistics." Updated
September 2. https://www.unicef.org/wash/.

Zalasiewicz, Jan, et al. 2016. "The Geological Cycle of
Plastics and Their Use as a Stratigraphic Indicator of
the Anthropocene." *Anthropocene* 13: 4–17. https://doi.
org/10.1016/j.ancene.2016.01.002.

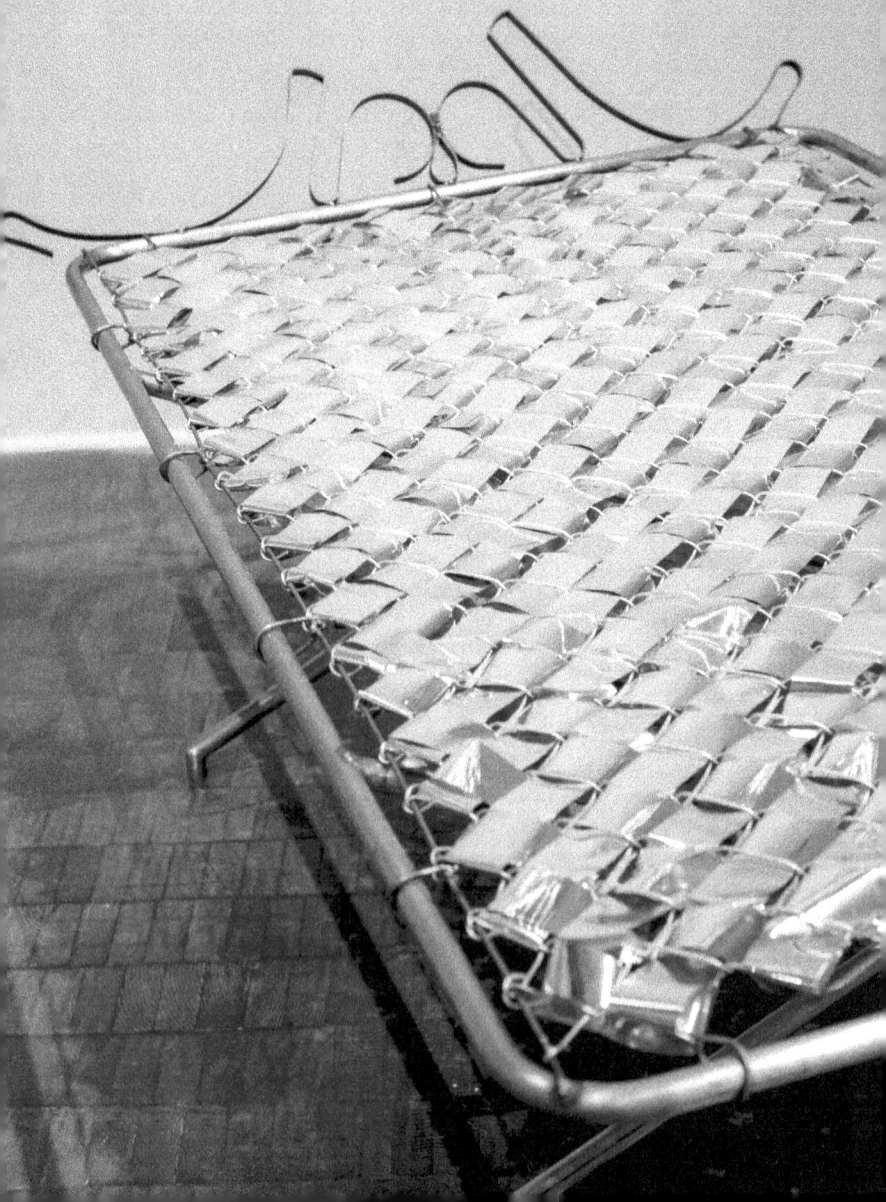

67

Slavery

Claire Colebrook

There would seem to be two distinct timelines: a past in which humans were barbarically divided between plunderers/consumers and the enslaved, and a future in which — because of that hyper-consuming past — we are all implicated. The past of slavery and the future of the Anthropocene might be related but there would seem to be a crucial distinction: slavery is delimited, suffered by some humans for the sake of some other humans. In the Enlightenment imaginary, slavery gradually disappears until it is definitively behind us. The Anthropocene, by contrast, knows no limit; occurring at a geological rather than human/historical level, it requires us all to think and act differently. Thinking about slavery today would *appear* to be in part symbolic (having to do with what we choose to celebrate from our past) and in part reparative, insofar as the legacy of slavery is still played out in racism, inequalities, and the apparent right to kill young, unarmed black men with impunity. Slavery is a surmountable event within human history. The Anthropocene, by contrast, encompasses human history, *or so it seems.* I would suggest the contrary: the Anthropocene is, in its all-inclusiveness, utterly parochial, while slavery is the all-encompassing horizon for thinking any possible futurity.

August 2017: who would have thought that slavery would once again be back in the news? After a series of white supremacist marches objecting to the removal of statues celebrating confederate figures, two historical points were made. First, President Donald Trump used the slippery slope tactic to ask where the destruction of "culture" would end (CNN 2017). George Washington and Thomas Jefferson owned slaves: should they also no longer be celebrated? Soon after, Fox News's Tucker Carlson also engaged in historical argument, this time in the form of an apparent syllogism. As he was speaking on "Tucker Carlson Tonight," the right-hand side of the screen listed four bullet points: "Slavery is Evil," "Until 150 yrs ago Slavery was Rule," "Plato, Muhammed, Aztecs All Owned Slaves," and "Slaveholding Common Among North American Indians" (Carlson 2017). Like the president, Carlson's rhetorical tactic was to suggest that if we question or reject *some* aspects of our past then we may end up erasing our entire history. Noble anti-white-supremacists in the media were quick to make two points: Washington and Jefferson may have owned slaves but were nevertheless law-abiding citizens who did not rebel against abolition. Further, slave-owning may have been widespread, but it was in the past, and that past is something that needs to be left behind rather than celebrated. What I want to question is whether marking a distinction between good and bad slave owners, and between a guilty past and a progressive present, does not preclude the thought of a history that would refuse the benevolent slave owner (and his legacy).

Rather than think of the Anthropocene as a geological event in the present that generates a common (if tragic) future, and rather than think of slavery as a past event that leaves a trace or injury, it is perhaps better to get onto the slippery slope, or — to quote Carlson — accept that "There is literally *no limit* when you start thinking like this." If there is no limit then, rather than see slavery as an event within the Anthropocene, such that we might think of some statues as depicting a destructive side of humanity that we would rather set aside, slavery would bear an all pervasive inscriptive force. This would amount to a reversal of the Anthropocene's elevation of geological inscription as the ultimate scale.

If one accepts the Anthropocene as the "agent" of a negative universal history, then one accepts that the present re-inscribes the past (Chakrabarty 2009). Now that we can see the ways the earth has been altered as a living system, it becomes possible to see a single (now threatened and implicated) humanity as that which will have emerged from a series of technological, industrial, colonial, and agricultural events. Even if those who were enslaved, indentured, colonized, or displaced were not the agents of beneficiaries of what called itself "humanity," there is now "a" humanity that emerges from the dispersed events of history. Such a narrative, for all its inclusiveness, nevertheless knows a limit. More accurately, it is because of its inclusiveness that there must be a limit. The "we" who emerges from that story of the Anthropocene is now faced with a common future, and will have to mark a decision or bifurcation if we want to survive. How much of that past do we want to save, or are we able to save? How much less do we need to hold onto if we are going to have a future? How many statues and name changes do we need to accept before we can move on? We should probably give up privately owned motor vehicles and stop consuming intensively grazed animals, but keep using computers and watching television. If the Anthropocene is our inscriptive frame, then the alteration of the earth as a living system becomes a way of (negatively) situating the events of the human species in the lead up to the (now unified) present. We then have to ask, united in a tragedy of the commons, what must be done.

If, by contrast, slavery or "the epistemology of the middle passage" (Henry 2006; Moten 2014) becomes an all-pervasive inscriptive force, there would be no limit, and there would be no (negative) universality. Let's take seriously the slave-owning and slave-implicated stain of all "we" hold dear. Plato, Washington, Jefferson, all the thinkers of the Enlightenment (including abolitionists), and the current cosmopolitan gaze that now laments that history and seeks to unify and move on: all would rely upon the distributions of force and value of slavery. What we call the

Anthropocene would have been one of slavery's events: the capture and harnessing of human bodies enabled the agricultures, industries, invasions, technologies and philosophies that gave birth to the man who came to recognize himself as a geological agent. *There is no limit.* Man can ask how he (or "we") will build a future. Alternatively, everything that was negated or *held* by this same man might not care at all for that quite particular universal future.

References

Carlson, Tucker. 2017. "If We Want to Erase the Past, We Must Prepare for the Consequences." *Fox News.* August 16. https://www.foxnews.com/opinion/tucker-carlson-if-we-want-to-erase-the-past-we-must-prepare-for-the-consequences.

Chakrabarty, Dipesh. 2009. "The Climate of History: Four Theses." *Critical Inquiry* 35, no. 2. 197–222. https://doi.org/10.1086/596640.

CNN. 2017. "Trump: Are Washington, Jefferson Statues Next?" August 15. https://www.cnn.com/videos/politics/2017/08/15/donald-trump-jefferson-washington-slaves-sot.cnn.

Henry, Annette. 2006. "'There's Salt-water in Our Blood': The 'Middle Passage' Epistemology of Two Black Mothers regarding the Spiritual Education of Their Daughters." *International Journal of Qualitative Studies in Education* 19, no. 3: 329–45. https://doi.org/10.1080/09518390600696786.

Moten, Fred. 2014. "Notes on Passage (The New International of Sovereign Feelings)." *Palimpsest: A Journal on Women, Gender, and the Black International* 3, no. 1: 51–74.

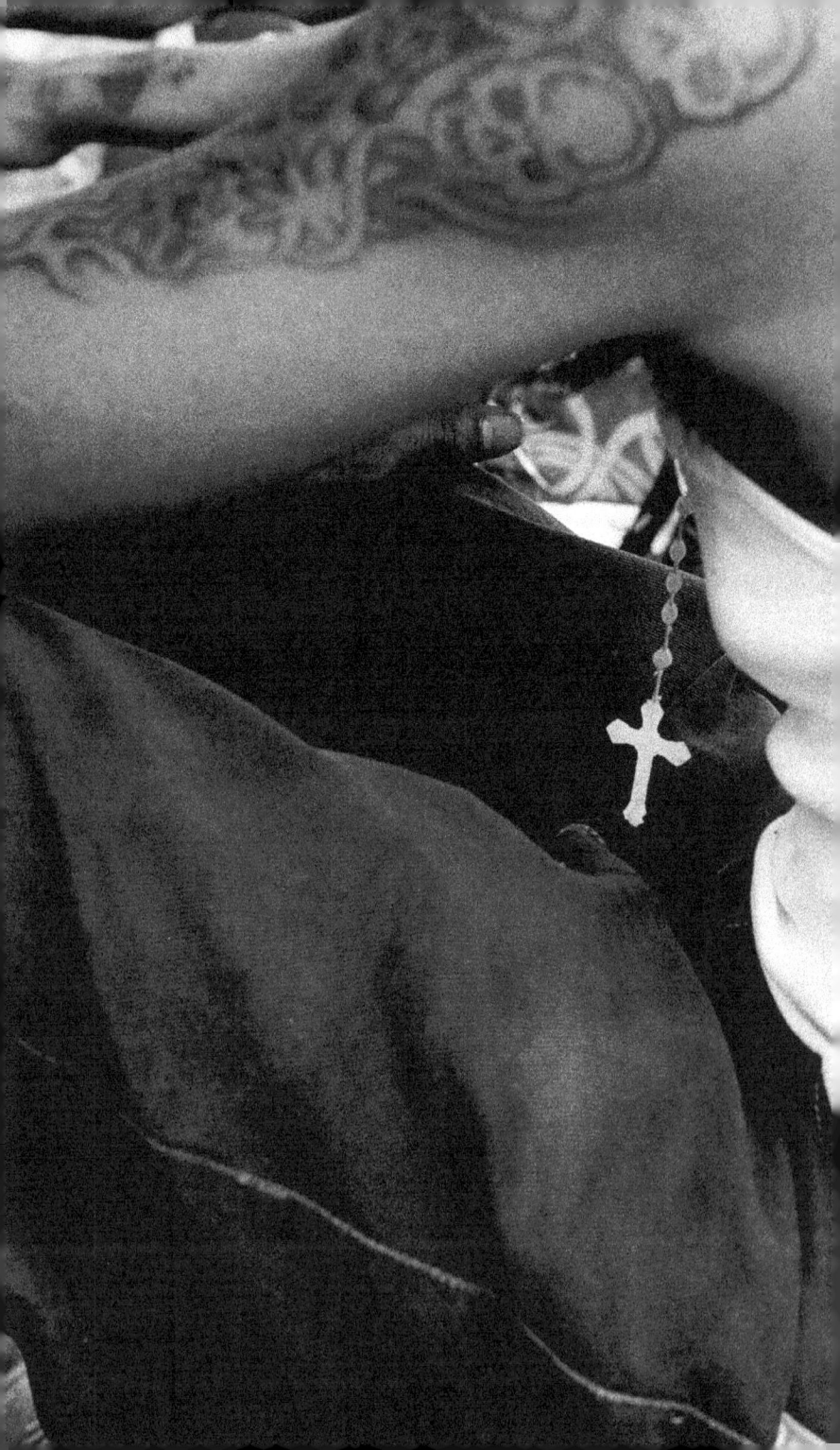

68

Smugglers

Jason De León

"It was because of Mitch. They let me in because of Hurricane Mitch." Wizard sprinkles a bump of shitty cocaine onto the tip of a gold key. It quickly disappears up his nostril. Wrists, arms, and trunk contort in a brief narcotic-induced form of cerebral palsy. "I fucking love coke, bro! Why the fuck would I ever go back to the United States? I make thousands of dollars a month in Mexico. I make more than I ever did selling drugs in the U.S. Nah, *viejo,* I ain't never going back."

He produces a tattered billfold fat with thousands of Mexican pesos. "I just sent money back to my family, bro. Look at these [Western Union] receipts. I got a kid in Honduras. I love him so much. I swear to God." Wizard kisses an invisible rosary around his neck and points to the heavens.

One of his two cell phones chirps: an update on another job. His goddamn phones are always making noises.

"I'm going back to Honduras after this to bring a mother with some kids up here. There's a lot of money in that."

He's not kidding. In the boom and bust world of human smuggling, Wizard is temporarily rolling in dough. I last saw him in Chiapas when he barely had enough money to buy beer and weed to keep his crew of enforcers and cadre of paying clients entertained as they ambled north. They subsisted on iguanas hunted with a slingshot and small periodic payments that the families of his charges wired to him. Tonight, however, there is cash to buy beer, coke, and an endless supply of *mota* (marijuana).

I ask about Tiny and Brayan, two teenage Hondurans whom Wizard was tasked with transporting the two thousand miles from Chiapas to the northern Mexican border. They weren't alive when Hurricane Mitch touched down, but now they find themselves running away from the long-term economic aftermath of the storm and the hail of bullets shot by gangs that now control most of their country. "They got picked up by another *coyote* [smuggler] who will help them," Wizard explains. Tiny later tells a different story: "My family wired Wizard $2,500 to get me across. He said to wait for him in a park while he went to pick up the money. He never came back." After weeks of camaraderie on the migrant trail, Wizard pulled the stereotypical fast one. The *coyote*–client relationship is ultimately about negative reciprocity, no matter how many adventures you share. Tiny and Brayan eventually crossed into Arizona with a pack of drug mules. They paid their passage by carrying dope for the American consumer market on their backs.

Every time a migrant dies from heat or some other environmentally induced death blow along America's southern boundary, a Border Patrol spokesperson steps up to a microphone and spews some public relations bullshit along the lines of: "The Sonoran Desert is extremely vast and remote with very few water sources. [...] It is important to realize illegal immigrants are being victimized and lied to by smugglers who lead them through treacherous terrain and expose them to extreme conditions" (Trevizo 2013).

It's as if smugglers like taking death-defying nature hikes. Few officials acknowledge that since the mid–1990s, the Border Patrol has relied on an enforcement strategy called "prevention through deterrence" that purposefully directs people away from urban zones toward remote, "hostile" sections of the U.S./Mexico border (U.S. Border Patrol 1994: 6–7). The hope is that nature will physically punish unauthorized migrants, sometimes to the point of death. The government blames coyotes for the five million arrests of border crossers and the 3,199 bodies recovered in Arizona between 2000 and 2017 (CDH, n.d.). It's also under this questionable logic that the U.S. spends millions of dollars each year fruitlessly trying to break up smuggling rings. Little attention is ever paid to the direct linkage between security infrastructure and migrant suffering. Blaming nature and smugglers shifts culpability for this crisis away from a federal government that doesn't want to admit that mountains, hyperthermia, and Western diamondbacks are undocumented employees of the Border Patrol. This is by no means unique to Arizona. Global boundary enforcement in the Anthropocene is powered by the labor of many unrecognized actants.

A decade ago, there was little work in Mexico for entrepreneurs like Wizard. Central Americans could cheaply make their way across Mexico by hopping on *la bestia,* the freight train version of the puzzle box from Hellraiser that annihilates many who latch onto it. Things changed in 2014, when Americans briefly paused to gawk at the thousands of unaccompanied minors who suddenly showed up on the shores of the Rio Grande. These were kids seeking refuge from the poverty and unfathomable levels of everyday violence that made Honduras, Guatemala, and El Salvador contenders for a new suburb in Dante's Seventh Circle. However, within a few months, these scenes of human jetsam disappeared. With support from the United States, Mexico launched Plan Frontera Sur, a program aimed at controlling the undocumented migration of Central Americans entering their country (De León 2016). The unstated goal was to make Mexico an invisible wall defending America's southern border. Ironically, this beefed-up security means that Mexico now deports more Central Americans than the United States (Speck 2016). Changes in American border policies keep Honduran smugglers like Wizard swimming in Mexican pesos and Colombian *perico* (coke).

The people whose movements Wizard profits from are running from the lingering economic, social, and political damage of the same hurricane that set him adrift on the migrant trail in 1998. Environmental catastrophe pushed them from their homes, and the U.S. federal government will use the increasingly hot Sonoran Desert to stop them dead in their tracks. This seemingly guarantees steady work for the Wizards of the world. The smuggler is no longer the simple villain that he is often portrayed to be. The smuggler (and the cultural and human baggage he carries) is the direct and expected product of the political economy of sovereignty and the growing climatic nightmare that is the Anthropocene. Somewhere, a cell phone is buzzing.

References

Coalición de Derechos Humanos (CDH). n.d. "Remembering the Dead." https://derechoshumanosaz.net/coalition-work/remembering-the-dead/.

De Léon, Jason. 2016. "A View from the Train Tracks." *Sapiens.* February 16. https://www.sapiens.org/culture/prevention-through-deterrence/.

Speck, Mary. 2016. "Mexico Is Already the Immigration 'Wall' Some Politicians Want." *Los Angeles Times.* August 1. http://www.latimes.com/opinion/op-ed/la-oe-speck-mexico-central-american-refugee–20160801-snap-story.html.

Trevizo, Perla. 2013. "Winter Cold Holds Own Peril for Border Crossers." *Tuscon.com.* January 7. https://tucson.com/news/local/border/winter-cold-holds-own-peril-for-border-crossers/article_2eef0965–73de–5217-aa52–42c855795435.html.

U.S. Border Patrol. 1994. "Border Patrol Strategic Plan 1994 and Beyond: National Strategy." July. http://cw.routledge.com/textbooks/9780415996945/gov-docs/1994.pdf.

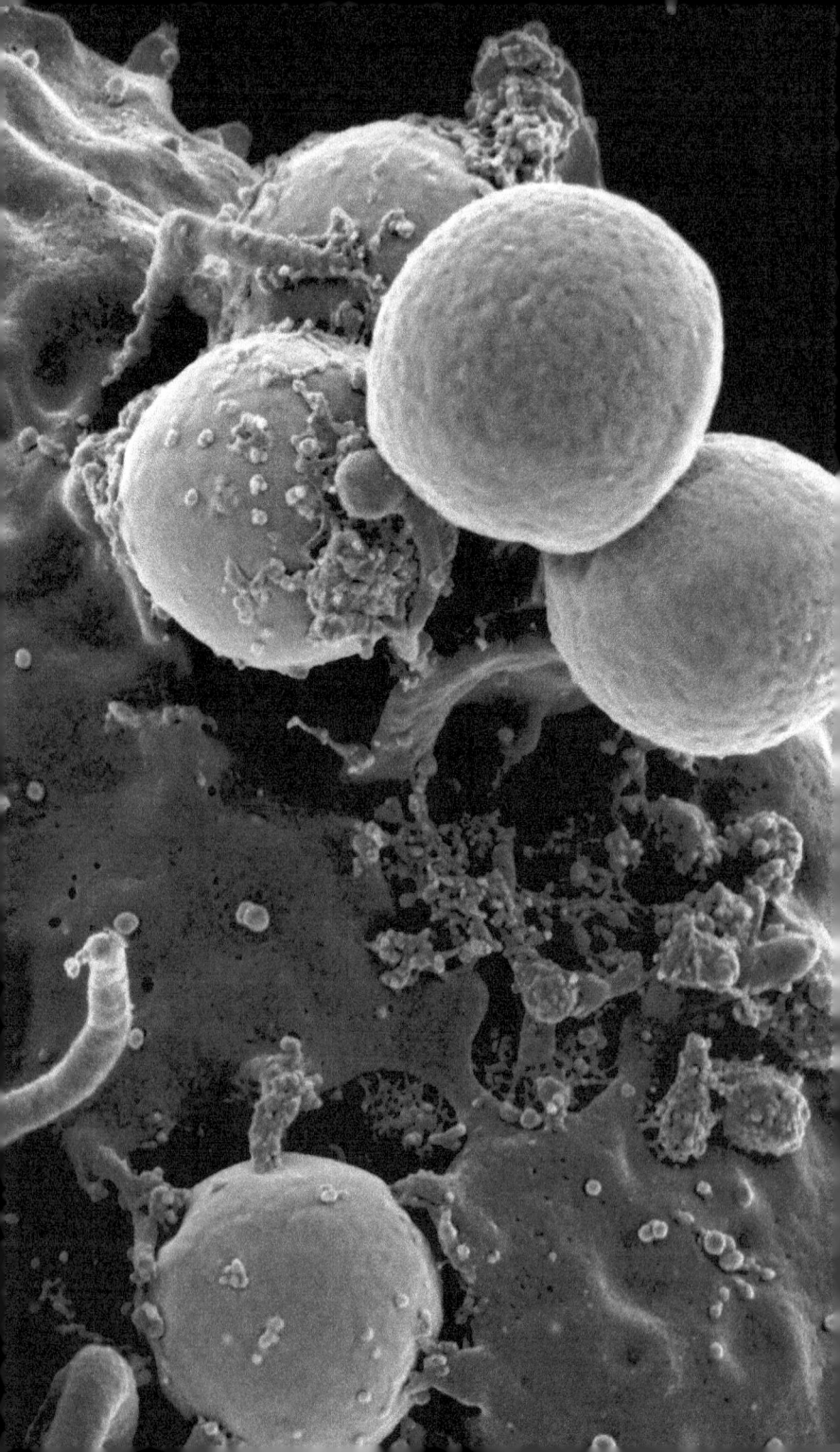

69

Species

Eben Kirksey

In an era of extinction, it has become difficult to understand the scale of loss and to develop responsible practices of intervention. Cultural anthropologists are joining with taxonomic scientists to make critters with a precarious existence visible, audible, tangible, and knowable. We are starting to practice the art of noticing other species (Tsing 2015).

A bubble of hopeful economic speculation surrounded species biodiversity in the 1990s. Drug companies teamed up with conservationists to investigate the potential pharmaceutical value of plants, animals, and microbes. But this bubble quickly burst. Despite the hype, few marketable drugs were actually produced (Hayden 2003). By the turn of the millennium, taxonomy — the branch of science concerned with biological classification — had become "low-status work" (Bowker 2000, 656). Taxonomists using "noncharismatic technology" like microscopes and calipers to measure morphological characteristics "consistently lost out to more 'exciting' areas of research that did not try to provide consistent names" (Bowker 2000, 656). Taxonomists who began using charismatic genetic technologies, novel techniques and practices that enabled them to directly read the DNA contained in organisms' genomes, briefly enjoyed a period of prestige within the scientific community. Yet as genetic tools became cheaper and more ubiquitous, basic taxonomic research again became a low priority for most career-minded biologists.

Categories proliferate when there is active human interest in a given form of life. Economic forces are constantly transforming existing categories and bringing new ones into existence. Breeders of endangered birds and snakes often practice DIY genetics — making hybrids by crossing distinct species and creating mutant strains through inbreeding — to produce novel designer pets (Kirksey 2015a, 134–48). Microbes like MRSA, a flesh-eating bacterium that is resistant to multiple kinds of antibiotics, have been categorized according to the agro-industrial and medical microclimates that they inhabit: HA-MRSA (health care–associated MRSA), CA-MRSA (community-associated), and LA-MRSA (livestock-associated). As new kinds of critters emerge, they can rapidly transform human practices, political and economic systems, as well as ecological communities. Novel kinds of critters are generating order-forming assemblages as well as order-destroying disasters (Kirksey 2015b).

Hundreds of known unknowns, novel forms of life that await description as species, live in the laboratory of Joyce Longcore, a chytrid fungus taxonomist at the University of Maine. Chytrids, according to Longcore, perform critical ecological functions. Some chytrids break down chitin, which forms the hard exoskeleton of insects; others help break down dead plant matter in the hind guts of ruminants. Diverse forms of life engage in classification work in multispecies worlds and are often transformed as they are categorized by others. Practices of classification, recognition, and differentiation take place as chytrids and other species bring each other into being in complex, intergenerational dances. Few humans, other than Joyce Longcore, have noticed.

"Pathogens require different descriptors," Longcore told me. "They need more specific names. It all depends on human need and use." Longcore's most widely cited paper, the species description of *Batrachochytrium dendrobatidis,* characterized a disease that has driven scores of amphibians extinct. Naming this chytrid species and describing its genetic makeup allowed biotechnology companies to develop inexpensive test kits. Multispecies ethnographers are joining citizens and scientists in using these DNA-detection devices to work against destructive legacies of capitalism and to make this pathogenic chytrid species visible.

Taxonomic scientists are also working to make amphibian species visible. Amidst outbreaks of harmful microbes and the ongoing presence of human enterprises that destroy forests and streams, nearly one-third of all described frogs, salamanders, and caecilians — some 1,950 species — are threatened, according to the International Union for Conservation of Nature's Red List of Threatened Species.[1]

As large, colorful frogs are featured in conservation campaigns, Jodi Rowley is working at the Australian Museum in Sydney to make certain small brown frogs from Vietnam visible. As she keeps her sights trained on these undescribed species, she notes the bomb craters pockmarking Vietnamese landscapes and speculates on the lasting effects of Agent Orange. Rowley is leveraging her expertise to protect creatures that have survived being blasted by U.S. soldiers, but are under renewed threats on the margins of the modern world system.

Frogs sing their own species into being. The calls of *Leptolalax,* a frog genus studied by Rowley, sound like crickets, katydids, or grasshoppers. New technologies and modes of listening have helped researchers make diverse frog species tangible and knowable in recent decades. Rowley described her first species of *Leptolalax* in 2009 by digitally recording its distinctive call. Now her own ears are an important apparatus. Rowley found Botsford's leaf-litter frog (*Leptolalax botsfordi*) while climbing Mount Fansipan, a popular destination for tourists to summit the so-called roof of Indochina. "I had a pretty good idea that the species was undescribed the moment I heard its faint chirp," she told me.

---

1   See *The IUCN Red List of Threatened Species,* http://www.iucnredlist.org/.

Most species remain undescribed, and many will go extinct before they are noticed by humans. Visibility as a species — for some animals, plants, or fungi — can mean opportunities for new ways of life. Visibility can also mean exposure to exploitation, surveillance, or invasive regimes of control (Star and Strauss 1999, 9–10). Stabilizing the existence of species in technoscientific worlds can nonetheless help them endure hostile or indifferent political and economic forces. We are only dimly aware of how our own existence, as a species, is contingent on the lives and deaths of others. Multispecies ethnographers are just beginning to study how entangled plant, fungal, microbial, and animal communities shape the nature of the human condition.

References

Bowker, Geoffrey C. 2000. "Biodiversity Datadiversity." *Social Studies of Science* 30, no. 5: 643–83. https://doi.org/10.1177/030631200030005001.

Hayden, Cori. 2003. *When Nature Goes Public: The Making and Unmaking of Bioprospecting in Mexico.* Princeton: Princeton University Press.

Kirksey, Eben. 2015a. *Emergent Ecologies.* Durham: Duke University Press.

———. 2015b. "Species: A Praxiographic Study." *Journal of the Royal Anthropological Institute* 21, no. 4: 758–80. https://doi.org/10.1111/1467-9655.12286.

Star, Susan Leigh, and Anselm Strauss. 1999. "Layers of Silence, Arenas of Voice: The Ecology of Visible and Invisible Work." *Computer Supported Cooperative Work* 8, nos. 1–2: 9–30. https://doi.org/10.1023/A:1008651105359.

Tsing, Anna Lowenhaupt. 2015. *The Mushroom at the End of the World: On the Possibility of Life in Capitalist Ruins.* Princeton: Princeton University Press.

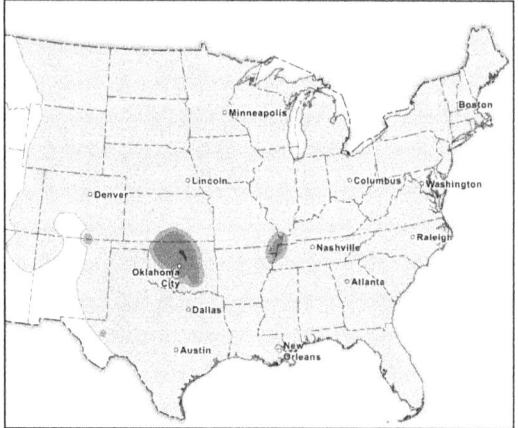

Chance of damage

Highest chance

	10% – 12%
	5% – 10%
	2% – 5%
	1% – 2%
	< 1%

Lowest chance

70

Stability

Elizabeth Reddy

Seismicity in the center of the United States has become comparable to that on its famously seismic West Coast.

In 2015, the Center for Investigative Reporting's website Reveal offered an audio rendering of how much the physical stability in the state of Oklahoma had changed (Corey 2015). The Reveal piece presents seismic data in beeps and echoes, their increasing pitch and volume illustrating the growing magnitude, as well as frequency, of Oklahoma's earthquakes. This short sound piece makes explicit the effects of processes often associated with hydraulic fracturing, or fracking. As it does so, the piece resonates with other concerns about environmental instability in the Anthropocene and demonstrates the importance of *stability* for our developing Lexicon.

I begin with the Reveal piece to highlight the ways that the Anthropocene is both a matter of changes in the conditions we live with and of efforts to tell clear and comprehensible stories about these changes. The Anthropocene is legible for the "emergence of a new physical and conceptual space within which to know and act on the future of human being, dwelling, and relating," as Valerie Olson and Lisa Messeri (2015, 28) have put it. They consider this new epoch in terms of breakdowns in old material and theoretical boundaries and the production of new ones.

DOI: 10.21983/P3.0265.1.72

We use the term Anthropocene, in light of urgent and fright-ening changes like the increase in Oklahoma's seismicity, to de-scribe limits of environmental stability. Stability, in this sense, is a matter of conditions, previously considered reliable, against which new and dangerous ones might be contrasted. But mark-ing these changes and communicating about them are not neutral acts, particularly when evidence, tools, and expertise needed to do so are subject to public, legal, and academic con-tests — and unstable in their own ways.

In seismic Oklahoma, as in many of the systems that human practices are materially transforming, there is change where no one had reason to expect it. Making this kind of change evident and available to encounter can mean bracketing it strategical-ly. The Reveal sound piece demonstrates the character of that movement. It shows seismic events becoming more frequent, powerful, and dangerous. This seismicity is related to the waste-water that some fracking operations dispose of in high-pressure injection wells. Just a decade of seismicity was rendered sonic in order to make that point. The piece is effective and clear in part because it is so limited in scope.

Clarity on this topic is both important and challenging. The increased seismicity described is dangerous. People have been injured. Their homes have been damaged. Their expecta-tions are unsettled. Their built environment was not designed to withstand these forces, and official treatment of these new hazards has been found wanting (see Mix and Raynes 2018 on Oklahoma's seismicity; on induced seismicity's similar effects elsewhere, see Moolenaar n.d.). Injection wells themselves may contaminate groundwater or simply deplete water resources. The seismicity they induce is suggestive of other changes, too. The fracking practices with which they're associated can some-times expose soils, waters, atmospheres, and bodies to transfor-mations that make themselves felt in human time (EPA 2016), and have significant effects on social relations and subjectivi-ties, which Anna Willow and Sara Wylie (2014) argue demand similar attention. Simultaneously, the operations associated with these upheavals are part of the efforts to produce forms of stability — particularly in the cost of fuel that many livelihoods depend on.

The Oklahoma sound piece brackets the last ten years off for sonic rendering, telling listeners that serious changes are happening in this span. Ten years is a long time, to crib from Hugh Raffles (2012), when it comes to materially transforming atmospheric composition, groundwater quality and availability, human bodies, or national priorities in resource extraction.

Ten years is also very little. Over ten years, Oklahoma has become increasingly seismic. Over longer spans of time this seismicity is not unprecedented. In the past several thousand years, this geology has shaken. Induced quakes are not new, either. Occasional earthquakes tied to wastewater injection have probably been happening in Oklahoma since the middle of the twentieth century (see Hough and Page 2015).

Anthropogenic or otherwise, earthquakes are always already part of the earth's energetic system. In a very immediate way, imagining them as environmental conditions once stable and now out of whack both is and is not accurate. As with many complex systems, the sheer scale on which seismicity unfolds can limit our ability to communicate about changes clearly. How we conceptualize these changes and address their urgency have histories and politics. As Andrew Barry (2015) and Joseph Masco (2010) have illustrated in different ways, old ideologies about power and danger — as well as stability and instability — may vex our responses to upheaval even as the Anthropocene takes form as new relationships in the material and conceptual world.

While the link between fracking-related wastewater processes and Oklahoma's recent earthquakes is gaining acceptance, their implications are contested. The goals, concepts, expertise, data, and analyses involved in attending to seismicity and other phenomena related to extraction, or the Anthropocene itself, are themselves unstable, debated, and transforming. In this context, bracketing off recent change and contrasting it to relative stability in historical conditions can be effective for all kinds of communication. I want to say, if nothing else, that it's worth keeping an eye on why, and how, stability matters as we mark the Anthropocene and its effects. The sounds of seismic Oklahoma might not give us all the facts, precisely, but they can certainly shake us up.

References

Barry, Andrew. 2015. "Thermodynamics, Matter, Politics." *Distinktion: Scandinavian Journal of Social Theory* 16, no. 1: 110–25. https://doi.org/10.1080/1600910X.2015.1032992.

Corey, Michael. 2015. "Oklahoma's Man-Made Earthquakes." *Reveal.* June 13. https://www.revealnews.org/episodes/power-struggle-the-perilous-price-of-americas-energy-boom/#segment-oklahomas-man-made-earthquakes.

Hough, Susan E., and Morgan Page. 2015. "A Century of Induced Earthquakes in Oklahoma?" *Bulletin of the Seismological Society of America* 105: 2863–70. https://doi.org/10.1785/0120150109.

Masco, Joseph. 2010. "Bad Weather: On Planetary Crisis." *Social Studies of Science* 40, no. 1: 7–40. https://doi.org/10.1177/0306312709341598.

Mix, Tamara L., and Dakota K.T. Raynes. 2018. "Denial, Disinformation, and Delay: Recreancy and Induced Seismicity in Oklahoma's Shale Plays." In *Fractured Communities: Risks, Impacts, and Protest Against Hydraulic Fracking in the U.S. Shale Regions,* edited by Anthony Ladd, 173–97. New Brunswick: Rutgers University Press.

Moolenaar, Elisabeth. Forthcoming. "Governmentality, Citizenship, and Resistance in the Groningen Gas Field." In *Energopolitics: Citizenship, Governmentality and Violence along the Grid,* edited by Simone Abram, Nathalie Ortar, and Tristan Loloum. Oxford: Berghahn Books.

Olson, Valerie, and Lisa Messeri. 2015. "Beyond the Anthropocene: Un-Earthing an Epoch." *Environment and Society* 6: 28–47. https://doi.org/10.3167/ares.2015.060103.

Raffles, Hugh. 2012. "Twenty-Five Years Is a Long Time." *Cultural Anthropology* 27, no. 3: 526–34. https://doi.org/10.1111/j.1548-1360.2012.01158.x.

United States Environmental Protection Agency (EPA). 2016. "Hydraulic Fracturing for Oil and Gas: Impacts from the Hydraulic Fracturing Water Cycle on Drinking Water Resources in the United States (Report)." December. https://cfpub.epa.gov/ncea/hfstudy/recordisplay.cfm?deid=332990.

Willow, Anna J., and Sara Wylie. 2014. "Politics, Ecology, and the New Anthropology of Energy: Exploring the Emerging Frontiers of Hydraulic Fracking." *Journal of Political Ecology* 21: 222–36. https://doi.org/10.2458/v21i1.21134.

71

Steps

smudge studio

Ippo. Ippo. Ippo.

一歩。一歩。一歩。

One step. One step. One step.

As we humans engage and act within emergent Anthropocene materialities and events, we produce new temporalities: new lived experiences, psychologies, and concepts of time.

Land of Hope, directed by Sion Sono (2012), is the first fictional film made about Japan's triple disaster: the great Tōhoku earthquake, the resulting tsunami, and the meltdowns that continue at the Fukushima nuclear power plant. The story follows the post-meltdown lives of two farming families. One family's house falls within the twenty-kilometer evacuation radius. The other's, right across the street, falls outside the exclusion zone. At times, the film borders on the absurd. Nevertheless, like the characters in the film, we inhabit the planet where the triple disaster continues to unfold in real time. Like them, we are living the cultural energetics and temporalities of the Anthropocene.

The film offers insight into some of the psychological states, cultural awarenesses, and timescapes being generated by material realities of the Anthropocene: Fukushima, fracking, nuclear

DOI: 10.21983/P3.0265.1.73

waste, climate change, plastic oceans, and the sixth great extinction. We watch as its characters struggle to adapt to their new conditions of daily life, including irrevocably altered senses of place, self, nation, agency, and time.

After the tsunami, one of the film's main characters returns to what remains of her hometown to search for traces of her family. Unexpectedly, ghost children appear. She tries to help them, and in an attempt to cheer them up, she takes three energetic steps up the hill of tsunami debris, as she exclaims "one, two, three!" In the English subtitles, these words are translated as: "hop, step, jump!" But the ghost children interrupt. They correct her: "Don't walk in that showy way. From here, we Japanese will take one step at a time. Like this: One step. One step. One step." *Ippo. Ippo. Ippo.*

William Gail (2016), former head of the American Meteorological Society, pointed out that it will take many years, in some cases decades, for our habitat's newly emerging climate and geological patterns to reveal themselves. For this reason, he argues, "our [knowledge about the Earth] will turn obsolete faster than we can replace it with new knowledge. […] Our grandchildren could grow up knowing less about the planet than we do today." In other words, our species's relatively recent abilities to consistently anticipate the future, design it, and plan for it, are rapidly going extinct.

Many of us who live in the contemporary West have difficulty recognizing, much less attuning to or moving within, our limits as individuals. We have even more difficulty doing so as states, societies, or as a species. We need practice at doing this. Like the characters in Sion Sono's film, we cannot stop moving or acting. From here, however, we also cannot move with an offhanded "one, two, three!" We cannot presume to know or see steps two and three from step one. We cannot move "forward" with the certainty that two will follow one, and three will follow two. We can no longer step off, aimed for fixed, certain destinations. We can no longer march across the Earth's wild differences with uniform, linear, homogeneous cadences.

We may have a rational grasp of the numbers of climate change, of Fukushima, or of the Pacific's gyre of plastic. But we also need to integrate such realities into embodied knowledge, to hold the thoughts of them and to build social practices capable of responding to them. As artists, we are exploring the potential of *ippo, ippo, ippo* as a practice for generating aesthetic experiences of, and temporal ideas about, things and beings that are configuring and reconfiguring in our midst. We are activating *ippo, ippo, ippo* as a social energetics, as a conductor for laying down our plans and our experiences as artists, then picking them up and laying them down again with a difference. Rather than one, two, three, we advocate: One step. Pause. Pay attention. Sit with the consequences and potentials that arise and fall away with and in that step. Adjust. Reconfigure. One step. Pause. Pay attention. Sit with the (new) consequences and potentials that arise and fall away with and in that (different) step. Revise. Readjust. The generative repetition of *ippo, ippo, ippo* moves us out of circular returns to the same and into elliptical returns with a difference.

When we do this, we know as we go.

In the ghost children's steadfast, step-by-step gesture of *ippo, ippo, ippo,* we sense a deliberate and attentive movement, one that minimizes risks of distraction and burning out. They pace themselves to the strangeness of the moment and to their surroundings. They conduct themselves in accord with the gravity of their situation. Their placing of their steps as *ippo, ippo, ippo* follows no plan, map, or script. The characters take in the present–aftermath–continuation timescape of newly lost lives by walking hypothetically, conditionally, with and in the propensities of their time's new material realities. Moving *ippo, ippo, ippo* makes it difficult to be simply a spectator or consumer of the scene. It calls for the fullest possible attention to long — very long — pasts and futures. It invites graceful acceptance of the ways in which the self is *conducted,* transferring one's heat and energy in ways that are paced and attuned to long and unknowable futures and pasts. *Ippo, ippo, ippo* does not dwell in the stasis of being frozen in fear or grief, nor in the equally confining attachment to fixed goals or certainties that compel humans to move on the planet with showy — that is — impositional — hops, skips, and jumps.

Attempting to move like this — *ippo, ippo, ippo* — we are rewarded, still and so far, with energy. The energy of dynamically focused attention. Of vitalizing play when it is scaled to human limits and capacities. As an aesthetic energetics, *ippo, ippo, ippo* is enabling us, as humans and artists, to be and to last, for the time being.

References

Gail, William B. 2016. "A New Dark Age Looms." *New York Times.* April 19. https://www.nytimes.com/2016/04/19/opinion/a-new-dark-age-looms.html.

Sono, Sion, dir. 2012. *Land of Hope* [*Kibo no Kuni*]. London: Third Window Films.

72

Suburbs

Andrew Pendakis

There was a time when hating the suburbs meant imagining ways to destroy them. Hallucinogenic squats and communes, motions to emend or abolish the nuclear family, intimations of a democracy beyond mere representation: to hate the suburb was to politically envision abolishing it. Today, the urban hipster hates the capitalist suburb so as to better (and less critically) love the capitalist city: the latter's artisanal pleasures could not exist without the pre-packaged tastelessness of mini vans.

Our culture reflects this situation. Nowadays, whenever cinema requires instantly intelligible tension it simply sets into place one of two dominant foilsa grim hyperbolized State or a cliché suburb. The former (*Hunger Games, Star Wars*) is normally a grey colossus, a system sapped to near-death by bureaucratic slowness or marked by an obscure, insatiable will to command: it exists, like any properly primal Father, only to expand or punish. Though the cliché suburb (*American Beauty, The Truman Show*) is drenched in color — often made to resemble a hysterically colorized 1950s film — it is itself counter-intuitively charged with many of the properties once associated in the West with the totalitarian state. In each case a device constructed out of pure repression triggers a movement towards difference or freedom — usually a journey of self-realization — that is as pre-

DOI: 10.21983/P3.0265.1.74

dictable and unconscious as the grey foil used to generate this movement in the first place.

This is, in some ways, a surprising destiny for the suburb. It was precisely the job of the latter to gestate an alternative to the grim industrialism and de-personalized scale attributed in the period to the communist state. The suburb was the architectural equivalent of a condom: its objective was to separate pleasure from risk without endangering enjoyment itself in the boredoms of safety. Its dream in this sense was Epicurean: the substitution of *ataraxia* — an animate tranquility freed from terror or sadness — for the frustrations of a life interrupted from without by the cruel externalities of the event. The suburb was to function as a space of liberal peace in which the natural liberties and differences of individuals, families, and markets would flourish unchecked by government in an environment that combined the convenience and pleasures of the city with the organic virtue, therapeutic vistas, and overall healthiness of the countryside. The American dream of a synthesis between Jefferson's agrarian individualism and the kind of large-scale, modern planning we associate with figures like Rockefeller or Carnegie came eventually to function as the very paradigm of modern capitalist failure. Linked to boredom, conformity, and the standardization of desire, as well as a paranoid new form of social control, the suburb had now become precisely the gulag it was designed to escape. We need to be wary of the residual Thatcherism that resides in our moment's easy cultural abjural of the suburb, one that smugly ironizes suburban life, but without materially *critiquing* it. Discernible within the aerial shot which establishes the suburb as an architectural prison — standardized, hyper-symmetrical, etc. — is something more: a hatred of the plan, of intentional social structure of any kind, hatred even of the very idea of society itself. We are left with a vulgar gloss on early Sartre: hell is neighbors, heaven the open road — paved by whom? — at the edge of everything collective, inherited or shared.

Critiques of the suburb become more convincing the closer they get to a materialist analysis of the environmental legacies of suburban development. Turf-grass. The riding lawn mower. Commuting. The whole ramifying apparatus of auto-mobility. The illogic and wastefulness of this system becomes cliché the moment it is mentioned. By bunkering the family, expanding the scope and desirousness of our privacies, and fire-walling any real sense of social limit or obligation the suburb has abetted a colossal wastage of finite planetary treasure even as it has undercut the political institutions (or habits of mind) we would need to even begin to address the long-term effects of this waste.

It is not the great Promethean sky-scrapers and dams, but the humble suburb that expresses in its purest form the logic of sovereign reason at the heart of the Anthropocene. In the former we can still detect an architecture of fear, a form proper to a process that is anxious because it is not yet complete; the suburb, however, — air-conditioned, happily balanced within a nature it controls entirely — channels something altogether new, a logic of reason at rest. It is paradoxically not in the modern city — huge, vertically impressive, mostly emptied of fields and trees — that nature ceased to be other, but in the tree-fringed suburban pasture. Cities have historically swarmed with residual nature, nature in the form of whirlwind crowds and violence. The urban, even at its most functional, never felt more than a few hand-shakes away from epidemic. The suburb strikes a new tone. Nothing in the hexis of the emperor comes close to the sovereign exception of a husband asleep by the pool.

Are there weird political economies in which the suburb could be otherwise? Could some future green socialism discover in these spaces something other than scavangeable scrap? Can the suburb be politicized or is it generically unpoliticizable? Can it be deconstructed and re-purposed or does it need to be done away with in its entirety? Outfitted with solar panels, its numbers per house increased dramatically (perhaps filled with new refugees or students living together on the cheap), its economy de-linked from the auto-mobile, its turf-grass replaced with gardens and greenhouses, it is not impossible to imagine an alternative suburb. Austerity is perhaps already incubating such alternatives: just as we are seeing a shift from the city to the countryside in places like Greece — a whole new generation of unemployed youth returning to rural family homes with bizarre new urban tastes and propensities — it is not impossible to see the thousands of educated unemployed now reluctantly returning to their parent's suburban basements as bearers of a new suburb, one loosened from a dream of possession that now seems to be dead for good in the West.

Reference

Nietzsche, Friedrich, 2005. *Thus Spoke Zarathustra*. Translated by Graham Parkes. Oxford: Oxford University Press, 2005.

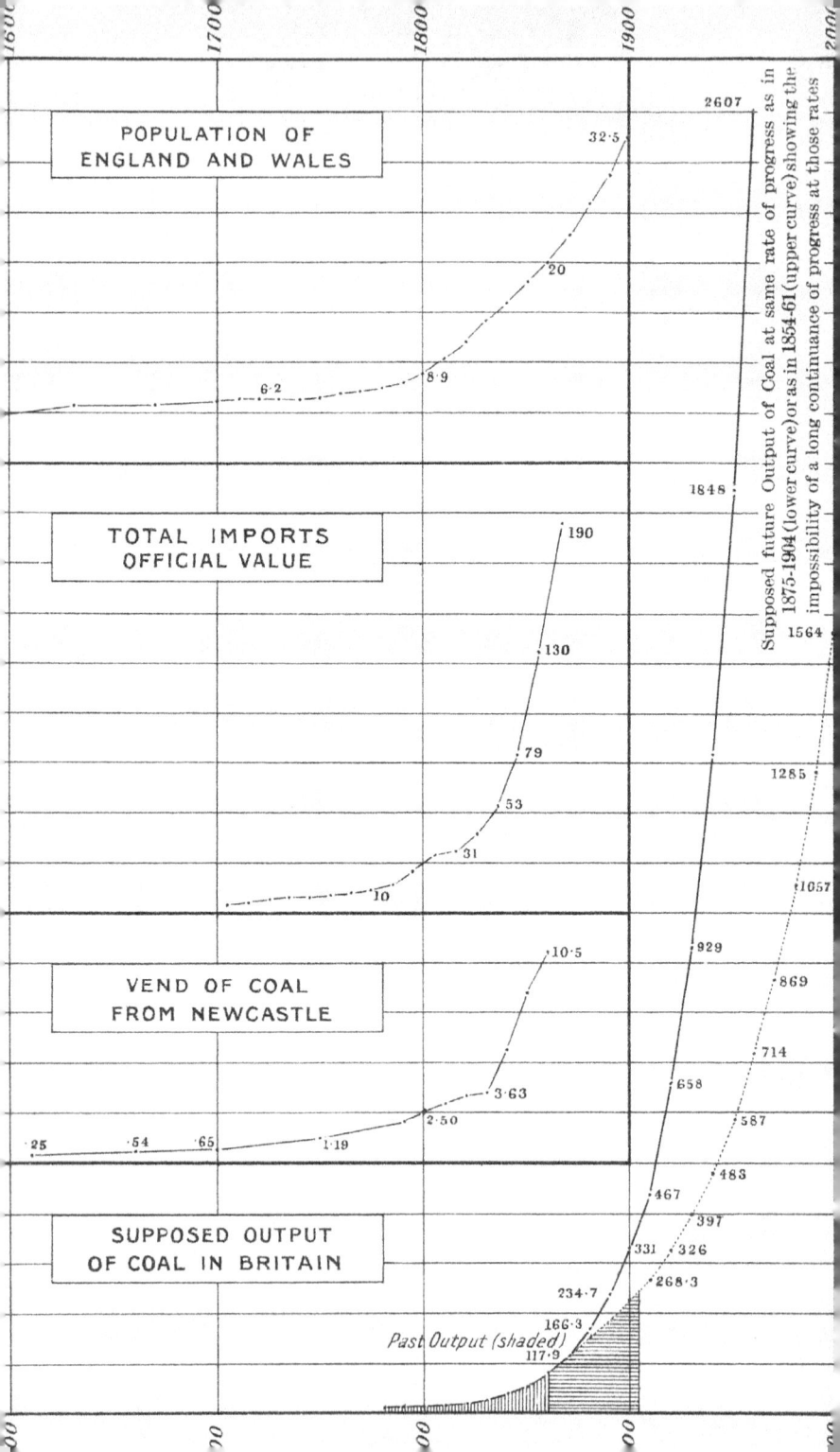

POPULATION OF
ENGLAND AND WALES

6·2   8·9   20   32·5

TOTAL IMPORTS
OFFICIAL VALUE

10   31   53   79   130   190

VEND OF COAL
FROM NEWCASTLE

·25   ·54   ·65   1·19   2·50   3·63   10·5

SUPPOSED OUTPUT
OF COAL IN BRITAIN

Past Output (shaded)
117·9   166·3   234·7   268·3   331   397   467   929   1848   2607

326   587   658   714   869   1057   1285   1564

Supposed future Output of Coal at same rate of progress as in 1875-1904 (lower curve) or as in 1854-61 (upper curve) showing the impossibility of a long continuance of progress at those rates

73

Surprise!

Zoe Nyssa

"It is certain that a very large part of what we experience in life depends not on the actual circumstances of the moment, so much as on the anticipation of future events."

— Jevons 1871, 40

One of the most surprising things about the Anthropocene — these times we're living in — is just how surprising it's been: as temperatures rise, sea levels are going up but also down. Places are getting dryer but also wetter; hotter as well as colder; people are more violent but also more lethargic; severe lightning is abundant but so is drought. On the one hand, all these surprises shouldn't be so surprising: scientists have been warning us for years that climate-related shocks are sure to be numerous, unpleasant, and inevitable (IPCC 2014). Many of these disruptions are expected to defy prediction, their causal paths becoming recognizable only by accident or in hindsight.

Still, there appear to be other senses in which the Anthropocene is surprising us, the unplanned results of our own best efforts going awry. Public health codes in the 1930s and '40s that mandated the use of non-toxic and non-flammable CFCs over dangerous alternative chemicals were discovered decades later to have created a hole in the ozone layer, creating in turn new public health and environmental emergencies (Elkins 1999).

DOI: 10.21983/P3.0265.1.75

Corn ethanol, initially touted as an eco-friendly fuel solution for vehicles, soon created food shortages and accelerated environmental degradation (Pimentel 1991). Disappointments, by definition, violate our expectations. Yet in at least a few examples cited above, there were researchers who argued, sometimes years or decades earlier, that the proposed solution would likely backfire.

Cases like these challenge us to consider more carefully just what we mean by "surprise" in the first place. Understanding the global changes we are unleashing, and the all-too-often insufficient solutions proposed to ameliorate them, will require tracing complex interplays between our assumptions and the outcomes, asking not only who is responsible but for what? Though temperature and sea level changes continue to receive the most attention, determining how many degrees warmer or feet of coastline submerged is just the beginning. People, societies, technologies, and environments intertwine in ways that are still poorly understood as humans adapt and change in complex response to new circumstances — and these in turn generate further social and environmental change. The Anthropocene Yet Unseen is quite often the Anthropocene *unforeseen*: a world of surprises in which causality is tangled, culpability shielded, and accountability attenuated.

It turns out that we have been warned about the potential for these kinds of unintended consequences in socio-ecological coupling for a long time. Among the best known is Jevons Paradox, after English economist William Stanley Jevons. Worried that Britain may be approaching "peak coal," Jevons (1865) set out to calculate the extent of Britain's coal reserves, and, by proxy, Britain's continued military and commercial dominance over its sprawling, fractious empire. Contrary to conventional thinking and what he called the "unbounded confidence of the present day" (xvii), Jevons predicted that Britain's so-called "inexhaustible" coal reserves would be utterly depleted in about a hundred years. More startling still, Jevons argued that efforts to use coal more efficiently would in fact accelerate the use of coal, bankrupting this resource even faster.

The reasons for this natural resource paradox are complex, but the underlying economics are intuitive: as technologies become more efficient, prices fall, demand rises, and overall consumption goes up, more than making up for the efficiency gains. Jevons pointed to other familiar, if paradoxical, examples such as the advent of sewing machines, which were expected to create mass unemployment for seamstresses. Instead, as clothes were made more quickly, costs declined, and the demand for fashionable clothing — and women to make them — skyrocketed. Extrapolating from Britain's recent history, Jevons anticipated unsustainable growth to continue for coal consumption. The chart ends around mid-twentieth century but Jevons's outsized predictions are not far off from reality. The puzzle of increased efficiency has also borne out Jevons's insights; from the years 1300 to 2000, for instance, the efficiency of lighting technology (from fire and tallow candles to LED lights) increased 2,000-fold while consumption of light per person in the UK increased 40,000-fold (Warde 2007).

The point is not that despite best intentions we're all doomed (though perhaps we are) but that social and environmental changes are both connected and complicated. Scholars have shown, for instance, the many ways and reasons people might adopt pro- or anti-environmental behaviors and the unexpected conflicts that can arise from cultural differences in expectations (Agrawal 2005; Choy 2011; Tsing 2005; West 2006). If climate science and policymaking are to succeed, we need to understand better the unforeseen second- and higher-order interactions between people and their environments. We need a clearer sense of the surprises in store.

Lastly, we need to inquire into the ways that surprise itself is political, linked to practices of forgetting, whether active or accidental. Oil giant Exxon was "extraordinarily farsighted" among fossil fuel companies in understanding that the greenhouse effect could have major implications for its core business (Banerjee 2015). Exxon devoted significant resources to studying atmospheric carbon dioxide levels, and by the late 1970s, their scientists were concerned that CO_2 emissions were affecting the climate. Multiple cases now before U.S. courts allege that the company suppressed the findings and began to spread misinformation about global warming to the public and legislators. In cases like these, where does our sense of surprise come from? Exxon argues that it knew nothing for sure, and if it did, it forgot it along with the rest of us. The case will hinge on what exactly counts as unexpected in the Anthropocene, whether Exxon knew all along things that would only take the rest of us by surprise later.

References

Agrawal, Arun. 2005. *Environmentality: Technologies of Government and the Making of Subjects.* Durham: Duke University Press.

Banerjee, Neela. 2015. "How We Got the Exxon Story." *InsideClimate News.* November 10. http://insideclimatenews.org/news/10112015/how-we-got-exxon-mobil-climate-change-science-story-subpoena-investigation.

Choy, Timothy. 2011. *Ecologies of Comparison: An Ethnography of Endangerment in Hong Kong.* Durham: Duke University Press.

Elkins, James W. 1999. "Chlorofluorocarbons (CFCs)." In *The Chapman & Hall Encyclopedia of Environmental Science,* edited by David E. Alexander and Rhodes W. Fairbridge, 78–80. Boston: Kluwer Academic. https://www.esrl.noaa.gov/gmd/hats/publictn/elkins/cfcs.html.

IPCC. 2014. *Climate Change 2014: Impacts, Adaptation, and Vulnerability. Part A: Global and Sectoral Aspects. Contribution of Working Group II to the Fifth Assessment Report of the Intergovernmental Panel on Climate Change.* Edited by C.B. Field, V.R. Barros, D.J. Dokken, K.J. Mach, M.D. Mastrandrea, T.E. Bilir, M. Chatterjee, et al.

Cambridge: Cambridge University Press. http://www.ipcc.ch/report/ar5/wg2/.

Jevons, William Stanley. 1865. *The Coal Question: An Inquiry Concerning the Progress of the Nation, and the Probable Exhaustion of Our Coal-Mines.* London: Macmillan.

———. 1871. *The Theory of Political Economy.* London: Macmillan.

Pimentel, David. 1991. "Ethanol Fuels: Energy Security, Economics, and the Environment." *Journal of Agricultural and Environmental Ethics* 4, no. 1: 1–13. https://doi.org/10.1007/BF02229143.

Tsing, Anna Lowenhaupt. 2005. *Friction: An Ethnography of Global Connection.* Princeton: Princeton University Press.

Warde, Paul. 2007. *Energy Consumption in England & Wales 1560–2000.* Naples: Istituto di Studi sulle Società del Mediterraneo.

West, Paige. 2006. *Conservation Is Our Government Now: The Politics of Ecology in Papua New Guinea.* Durham: Duke University Press.

Cavalier

74

Surreal

Nicholas Shapiro

It is a word often at the tip of the tongue when a moment feels off the rails or inflected with difference. Flies buzzing at Christmas in Ontario. Desert dunes engulfing Chinese towns in slow motion (Zee 2017). "How surreal," we murmur as fragments of new normals lunge into view. The patterning of life, death, and their surreal interstices, denoted by the Anthropocene, is not limited to planetary geophysical destabilization.

Rather, toxic textures of our ongoing present that unnervingly whiz by at the periphery of our senses, timespaces that feel both oversaturated and vacated of meaning, and feelings of unending transition are part and parcel of this pervasive alterordinary. How can an analytic of the surreal be made more than just a catch-all for residual out-of-place moments and help us to open up the altered states, illogics, and material breakdowns that emerge from ordinary and extraordinary encounters with changing environments?

The new administration in the United States serves as a reminder that surrealism is an appropriated genre of reality and not an artistically forged one. Its two original figures were the state and the market. Think of the widening expanses between official proclamations of triumph and the experiences of those freshly returned from the trenches of the First World War. Think, too, of the phantasmagorical rearrangements of the world's things found in the Marché aux Puces flea market in Paris (Clifford 1981, 541). Still, the surreal does not only radiate from the out-of-touch claims of the state or the seemingly spontaneous juxtapositions of the market. Too, the very materiality of our short-circuiting, deteriorating, and chemically off-gassing world contributes to bowing reality into the surreal. One example among innumerable others is the chemical ecologies of low-income housing of the United States, which submerge inhabitants in an everyday in which meaning and matter are left ajar. Even within the home — that imagined bastion of autonomy, the ground-zero of the ordinary — governance, capitalism, and late industrial materiality fashion a state of things that is inflected with otherness.

When the A/C engaged, the lights in the front room came on. "Oh, it does that, we're going to try to jerry-rig it," an Indiana man remarked as an aside. He became exasperated when discussing his granddaughter's health and would lose consciousness momentarily. His head would droop and his speech would pause, only to click back into gear a sentence or two downstream of where he left off.

A wire somewhere deep inside his trailer had frayed or broken loose in such a way that its entire aluminum exterior had become electrified. He couldn't open the door of his rural Florida home without a considerable shock and a lingering sense that some part of his brain was slightly charred. He had been wracked with nightmares since he moved in. Something about being there warped his strength, irritated his nose and lungs, and led his son to have an in-womb stroke a month before his due date.

"I was concerned when the issue of the formaldehyde in the trailers come out, but you know what?" the matriarch of the house asked in a hushed tone. "My husband has some plan to rip the walls out…." The destruction of their home is the only way it could be imagined as habitable. In the meantime, the eleven family members that inhabit their single-wide trailer on a reservation in Washington state wade through simmering headaches. Capillaries in the noses of two granddaughters regularly leaked blood over their upper lips into their mouths. A large minority of the household sustained chronic diarrhea. One grandson was regularly sent home from preschool as he would split his time between the classroom and bathroom.

In these all-too-common corrosive spaces, chronic rifts in the ordinary fill with suspicions of an ongoing present, conditioning a temporality that is studded with unexpected dysfunction and nearly habitual enervation. Far from the surrealists' hope that intoxication would provide a critical pathway to revolution, to loosening the bounds of the individual, and to ecstatically spurning the logics of modernity, the forms of intoxication at hand beckon an exhausting and unshakable present. The alterordinary is intensely entangled with what Michelle Murphy (2016) calls *alterlife,* a pervasive uneven distribution of toxicants that change the very substance of life and "are the enfleshment of settler colonialism, environmental racism, capitalism and war."

In the glimpses above, as their ostensibly protective home begins to inflict harm and the very formaldehyde-based engineered woods that give structure to their house unravel their bodies, the physical and metaphysical situation of the inhabitants also begins to warp and distort. The surreal, here, is a tandem failure of matter and meaning. Think of Tess Lea's (Lea and Pholeros 2010) analysis of dysfunctional and dangerous indigenous housing in Australia — buildings that look like houses but are not safe, secure, or salutogenic. Think of the warning labels ("NOT TO BE USED AS HOUSING") the U.S. federal government applied to the chemically contaminated trailers they resold or donated to Native nations across North America. Warnings that were systematically removed as gray markets purveyed these homes to the precariously employed, dispossessed, elderly, and poor. Think of the material ecologies of rural Missouri where, as Jason Pine (2016, 302) has so caringly documented, the intoxicating dream of industrial progress leaves the nation's most concentrated meth production industry in the wake of the largest primary lead smelter and the occult value of everyday commodities is excised to "get more life" while also hastening death.

The surreal is not just cultivated through artistic practice but is itself a means of governance, a medium and velocity of lethality, and an indicator of the frayed ends of industrial production. As an exercise of power over and disturbance of reality, as a present and a portent, the surreal is an inroad into the Anthropocene that simultaneously demands the most sober and systematic anthropology and the most hallucinatory, speculative, and reappropriative of our creed.

References

Clifford, James. 1981. "On Ethnographic Surrealism." *Comparative Studies in Society and History* 23, no. 4: 539–64. https://doi.org/10.1017/S0010417500013554.

Lea, Tess, and Paul Pholeros. 2010. "This Is Not a Pipe: The Treacheries of Indigenous Housing." *Public Culture* 22, no. 1: 187–209. https://doi.org/10.1215/08992363-2009-021.

Murphy, Michelle. 2017. "Alterlife and Decolonial Chemical Relations." *Cultural Anthropology* 32, no. 4: 494–503. https://doi.org/10.14506/ca32.4.02.

Pine, Jason. 2016. "Last Chance Incorporated." *Cultural Anthropology* 31, no. 2: 297–318. https://doi.org/10.14506/ca31.2.07.

Zee, Jerry C. 2017. "Holding Patterns: Sand and Political Time at China's Desert Shores." *Cultural Anthropology* 32, no. 2: 215–41. https://doi.org/10.14506/ca32.2.06.

75

Sustainability

María García Maldonado, Rosario García Meza,
and Emily Yates-Doerr

"Sustainability is an English word." This statement is so obvious that the problem it poses is often ignored, but that problem
is exactly what the speaker from the World Health Organization wanted his audience to face. It was November 2015, and the
Latin American Congress of Nutrition was gathered at a conference titled *nutrición para el desarollo sostenible.* The United
Nations' sustainable development goals had just launched with
the promise to incorporate global challenges of climate change
into its agenda to improve health metrics, and so "nutrition for
sustainable development" seemed a fitting theme. But *sustainable* translates into Spanish as both *sostenible* and *sustentable,*
the former connoting a capacity to be maintained over time,
the latter a sense of being reasonable. "Which meaning do we
want?" the speaker asked.

   At Doña Marta's house in highland Guatemala, the effects
of the recent global-policy focus on sustainable nutrition were
striking. Giant silver silos that a development project had donated to protect her corn without the need for chemicals filled her
yard. Another project had given her goats for milk, also showing
her how to use their feces as fertilizer and their urine as insec-
ticide. The most dramatic push toward sustainability could be
seen in the global development community's desire to change

DOI: 10.21983/P3.0265.1.77

what women fed their children. "The future is at stake," USAID representatives had said to a group of mothers when dropping off the monthly packets of U.S. surplus corn flour, red beans, and a nutrient powder that came with a recipe for pancakes. "Your children need nutrients today, so they can have a better tomorrow."

The three of us were at Marta's house to learn about the social lives of sustainability. But because sustainability is an English word, we were running into problems (see Mol 2014; Gluck and Tsing 2009). Sustainability was everywhere: in storage bins and supplements and shit. And yet it was nowhere. Marta, along with others in her community, was unfamiliar with the term. It didn't much matter if the word chosen was *sostenible* or *sustentable,* either. Marta lived and dreamed in the language Mam.

We worked together with Marta on the term *sustainability* for a while — *co-laboring,* to use Marisol de la Cadena's (2015) term for a collective effort to attend to spaces of difference. We slowed down when we came across *tanquib'ela,* which back-translated into *el ser en la vida; de vivir; de sobrevivencia,* and then, being in life, of living, of survival. Marta, who was a midwife, which meant that she was a gardener and farmer, told us that she had spent her life on this work, helping her community nurture their fragile, precious babies as they grew. *Tanquib'ela* was less an end to seek than an orientation to living that allowed her to plant when soils were ready, protect her crops from heavy rains, and attend to the pain of birth. *Tanquib'ela,* being in life, *was* her life. But this did not imply the destination-oriented future of modernity's progress or the never-satisfied longing of industrial capitalism, where futures are financial instruments.

It was difficult to speak across categories and worlds, but one thing was clear: though the future in Marta's languages may not be out there waiting to be developed, she was still worried about what lay ahead. The kind of progress that had arrived was stratifying reproduction in a broad sense, saddling particular groups of people with the responsibility for this new global future in the process of being made (Ginsburg and Rapp 1995; see also

Colom 2015). With this responsibility came worry that development projects left their children vulnerable and worry about how they themselves would grow old when so many young people were gone. As U.S. surplus corn came rushing in to feed them, family after family returned this gift with their sons and daughters, sending them on the dangerous journey north in pursuit of survival. All around us people were struggling with the problem that the "will to improve" (Li 2007) the global future was inciting a good deal of the damage that people had to rebuild their lives around.

In co-laboring through sustainability with Marta's community, we found that some people worked to protect their farmland from encroaching markets. Others focused on securing continuous wage labor. Some worked to maintain (*mantenerse*) their lives, while others spoke of cultivating an openness to change. This variation helped us face a challenge of ethnography: amid the stratified reproductions of global development, the reproductions of our translations are stratified too. The shift between *tanquib'ela, mantenerse,* surviving, or improving the world is not innocent, but forecloses some worlds while attending to others. The challenge we faced was not only a matter of moving between English, Spanish, or Mam. Whereas a lexicon may elsewhere be units of meanings, the anthropologist's lexicon might be better conceived as a repertoire of care-filled practices that follow the conversion of spoken concepts into unspoken activities and back into words again. Engaging in the practice of the lexicon requires the skill of asking — and sometimes not asking (see Pigg 2013) — about how words are done and what they then do.

Sustainability (and, we might add, *becoming* and *emerging,* since these terms often go hand-in-hand) may too easily connote the progressive transition of a singular, causal system, leading us toward the project of developing a better future that has long been modernity's destructive lure. In this time of the Anthropocene, many are reworking the b/orders of human and nature. Meanwhile, we might also pay attention to whose practices of time and space dominate the discussions and whose go ignored. The aim is not to define our terms. After all, while words are powerful, they are also fluid. The objective is rather to care for the stratified reproductions between not-so-global global languages and the various strategies of world-making that, for example, Indigenous and Latin American peoples have cultivated for generations. Sustainability is a sign of our times, we are told. But there is a reason to be cautious. For while we are surely coeval, our times remain neither singular nor evenly shared.

References

Colom, Alejandra. 2015. "Forced Motherhood in Guatemala: An Analysis of the Thousand Days Initiative." In *Privatization and the New Medical Pluralism: Shifting Healthcare Landscapes in Maya Guatemala,* edited by Anita Chary and Peter Rohloff, 35–49. Lanham: Lexington Books.

de la Cadena, Marisol. 2015. *Earth Beings: Ecologies of Practice across Andean Worlds.* Durham: Duke University Press.

Ginsburg, Faye D., and Rayna Rapp, eds. 1995. *Conceiving the New World Order: The Global Politics of Reproduction.* Berkeley: University of California Press.

Gluck, Carol, and Anna Lowenhaupt Tsing, eds. 2009. *Words in Motion: Toward a Global Lexicon.* Durham: Duke University Press.

Li, Tania Murray. 2007. *The Will to Improve: Governmentality, Development, and the Practice of Politics.* Durham: Duke University Press.

Mol, Annemarie. 2014. "Language Trails: 'Lekker' and Its Pleasures." *Theory, Culture, and Society* 31, nos. 2–3: 93–119. https://doi.org/10.1177%2F0263276413499190.

Pigg, Stacy. 2013. "On Sitting and Doing: Ethnography as Action in Global Health." *Social Science and Medicine* 99: 127–34. https://doi.org/10.1016/j.socscimed.2013.07.018.

76

Terrain

Gastón Gordillo

The wind was strong and steady, regularly shaking up the wooden structure of Martín's home while we were inside talking and occasionally pausing to feel the power of that unruly atmosphere. Some gushes of air got inside, for the house's doorless entrance was covered by a tarp that every now and then relented to the air's pressure. That opening also let us see clouds of dust churning wildly outside. Those swarms of dust briefly receded to reveal some of Martín's cattle fifty meters away, only to again form constellations of particles blurring them in a haze.

We were in Salta Forestal, a rural area located 80 kilometers east of the town of Las Lajitas and one of the hotspots of the soy frontier in northern Argentina. This was once a heavily forested part of the western Gran Chaco — the tropical lowlands of northern Argentina, western Paraguay, and southeastern Bolivia. But when the price of soy rose dramatically in the early 2000s, businessmen and officials saw those forests inhabited by campesinos as available space to be turned into soy fields. Bulldozers, often supported with armed civilians and the police, began pushing forth against the forest and its human and non-human inhabitants. As the wind raged outside, Martín and Ana, his wife, described how a decade earlier they had confronted and stopped eighteen bulldozers that were crushing a forest two kilometers from their home. With the help of over 200 other

DOI: 10.21983/P3.0265.1.78

residents from a wide area they set up barricades and forced the drivers to abandon the machines. After a long legal dispute, a sympathetic judge eventually ruled in their favor, for Martín's family was able to prove that despite lacking legal titles they had been living on that land since the 1930s — which under Argentine law gives families ownership rights. Their struggle managed to save 5,000 hectares of forest where they raise 200 head of cattle. But this local victory could not stop the deforestation of surrounding areas. Their forest is now surrounded by fields planted with genetically-modified soy, sprayed with herbicides, and harvested by combines.

As I was listening to Martín and Ana, our conversation kept returning to the power of the wind. "This wind is unbelievable!" Ana exclaimed, raising her voice as the noise of things battered outside by the wind increased. "It's because of the fields," Ana said again. Martín nodded. They explained that winds like that did not exist when the area was covered with forests. But now, they said, powerful winds appear out of nowhere, blowing through those fields and scattering huge amounts of soil into the air. On windy days, blue skies acquire a brownish tone. As a woman in another town put it, people now have to brave *tierrales horribles* (horrible dust storms). The air is so full of microscopic particles that residents suffer epidemics of allergies previously unknown in the region, made worse by the spraying of agrichemicals. The air feels hotter, everybody agrees. Rains are scarcer and droughts are longer and more severe, they add. Scientists have confirmed that the cause of this sensory perception is deforestation, for the destruction of forests meant the disappearance of the moisture that trees absorb and release into the atmosphere. The warming of the planet, of which deforestation by agribusiness is one of the main contributors, is further parching this terrain made up of farms, receding forests, and stronger winds.

The atmospheric and environmental changes affecting the Argentine soy frontiers are the local manifestation of the planetary processes that define the Anthropocene. And in trying to make sense of the texture of these transformations during my fieldwork, it gradually became apparent that categories such as "the environment," "the climate," or "place" are unable to fully capture what about the materiality of space is changing in this region and, in general, in the Anthropocene. The expansion of industrial agriculture into northern Argentina together with the impact of climate change have certainly created qualitatively new places defined by novel environmental conditions and more intense weather patterns. Yet making sense of the elusive physicality of the winds blowing through those fields requires new analytic tools, more attuned to the sensory and immanent nature of space. This is why I found myself returning to the one term that insists that all places have forms, volumes, and textures: terrain.

Deriving from the Latin *terra* (earth, land, soil), the word "terrain" certainly evokes in colloquial language the solidity of the ground in contrast to the gaseous nature of air or the liquid physicality of water. Rescuing "terrain" for our Anthropocene lexicon therefore requires moving away from this reification and expanding terrain's evocation of earthly textures to include, also, the gaseous and liquid components of the materiality of space in this world. This means undermining the alleged solidity of terrain as ground *and also* the conceptual separation between the solid, gaseous, and liquid components of the planet's terrain. What shook up Martín's home during my visit to Salta Forestal was not wind moving through static terrain but the blurring and dissolution of boundaries between ground and atmosphere in the temporal and physical becoming of terrain.

Global warming challenges anthropocentric views of space as socially constituted because it confronts us with the power of "the climate" and "nature." These two terms nonetheless tend to evoke transcendental forces removed from the immanent sensorium of actual places. What I felt in those unruly winds made more intense by climate change could perhaps be described as the power of terrain, not as an inert, singular object, but as a figure of multiplicity, entanglements, and becoming. "Terrain" ought to be part of our new lexicon because it opens up a sensibility to the texture, diversity, and material excess of space it-self—and of the environmental and social disruptions of the Anthropocene.

1

2

3

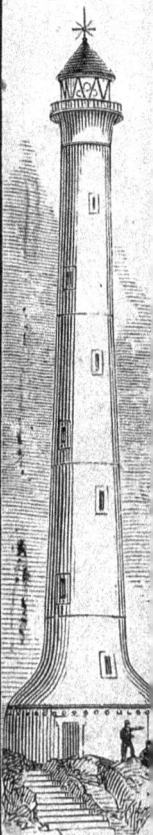

4

5

77

Thermodynamics

Cara Daggett

What do we mean by energy? In the politics of the Anthropocene, energy often signifies fuel, but its meaning is slippery. Energy feels timeless, transhistorical, cosmic, and yet it is also material: it pumps through pipelines, sloshes in gas tanks, spins wind turbines. In the social sciences, energy has become a universal unit of equivalence by which we can compare the consumption of human civilizations across history.

Energy owes its authority, and its ubiquity, to its foundational status in physics. However, in physics, energy is not timeless, nor is it even very old. Unlike matter or force, scientific units with ancient pedigrees, energy is a surprisingly modern thing. Energy emerged only in the 1840s and 1850s, through the new laws of thermodynamics. It was then that the energy of poets and philosophers was transformed into a steampunk science, born in plumes of coal smoke and Glaswegian shipbuilding factories, at the heart of the British Empire. Energy emerged in the attempt to understand steam engines, which were remaking European life and cities in the nineteenth century, far ahead of any scientific understanding of how coal produced motion.

Recognizing energy as historical is more than an etymological quibble. Long before energy became a key concept in science, of course, humans were using fuels and improving material-machinic assemblages. Prior to thermodynamics, however,

DOI: 10.21983/P3.0265.1.79

these various activities were not yet connected by a single scientific paradigm, nor an organized political strategy. Energy, and its laws of thermodynamics, provided just such a strategy, and it was one that could be geared toward the expansion of fossil-fueled industrialization.

Thermodynamics is an early Anthropocene knowledge: it was among the first disciplines to confront the effects of mingling human agency with the power and timescales of the Earth and its fossils. No longer could humans bracket the Earth of the Enlightenment as harmonious and stable. The new Earth of industrialization was an Earth characterized by constant change, much older than humankind and, terrifyingly, indifferent to its fortunes. The new Earth required a new physics (and biology, and chemistry, and history, and politics), and thermodynamics provided a master term for them: energy.

The new Earth, so indifferent to humans, inspired fear, then as now. Helpfully, thermodynamics not only offered a patch for adapting Enlightenment science to the Victorian era. As historian Crosbie Smith (1998) observes, thermodynamics also offered a patch for Christianity, which had struggled to reconcile God to the new Earth of change and decay. Several of the first scientists of energy were devoted Scottish Presbyterians. While they wanted to understand steam engines, in doing so, they also sought to adapt Scottish Presbyterianism to industrialization. Thermodynamics, thanks to its two mysteriously contradictory laws, suggested a way for Scottish Presbyterians to have their cake and eat it too, to embrace both modern science and an omnipotent God, thus avoiding the extremes of either evangelism or atheism (Smith 1998).

As in the Enlightenment, God was reflected in nature — in the comforting first law of thermodynamics, which states that energy is conserved across all transformations. However, God retained His majesty by being exempt from the second law, which states that entropy tends to increase spontaneously. The second law describes a world of energy "running down" beyond forms that could do work, a world that tended toward dissipation. It spelled a future in which the sun would burn out, the universe would slow to a cold equilibrium, and life would be impossible. God alone could redeem humans from the second law.

Through entropy, energy rescued God from the thoroughly mechanistic universe by reasserting the separation between God and the world (Smith 1998; Wise and Smith 1989). If God was outside the process of decay, then energy dissipation, though 'natural,' was associated with evil. Meanwhile, goodness meant imitating God by taking advantage of knowledge of the first law and wresting progress from decay wherever humans could, which was perceived as ultimately "choosing whether to turn nature's decay to the benefit of humanity or to lose it entirely" (Wise and Smith 1989, 423). Humans could take advantage of the "fall" itself, wresting work from the lump of coal even as it burnt away as dissipated energy. The alternative — leaving the coal in the ground, where its slower dissipation over many millions of years served no human purpose — would be to abandon nature to its dissipation, a term that, through energy, had both physical and moral connotations.

The religious overtones of entropy were not lost on energy scientists and scholars with more secular leanings. Friedrich Engels, for example, vociferously objected to the heat death hypothesis as contradictory and "stupid," and warned that this entropic narrative could become a doorway through which religion entered physics (1975, 246). Just as Engels foresaw, a dominant interpretation of thermodynamics emerged that combined an engineering concern for efficiency with the pragmatic spirit of Scottish Presbyterianism. The result was a an energy ethos that contributed new metaphors and accounting tactics for expanding and intensifying fossil-fueled imperialism.

While thermodynamics pioneered the modern conception of energy, it has no monopoly on the term. Physics itself quickly complicated and renegotiated these nineteenth-century interpretations, along with their Protestant overtones (Mirowski 1991, 57–59). Despite this caveat, the thermodynamic logic of energy feels familiar and still contributes to the assumptions we make about energy in the Anthropocene. Most tellingly, energy and work — and their underlying social valuation — remain tightly coupled. There is no debate over energy systems that does not also involve a debate about jobs and the unquestioned assumption of their worth to human life. Another way of saying this is that the political project of imagining life beyond fossil fuels will also involve imagining human life beyond industrial work and its ethics.

By treating energy as a term of historical specificity, rather than as a universal unit of the cosmos, it becomes easier to decouple energy from its thermodynamic marriage to work.

References

Engels, Friedrich, and Karl Marx. 1975. *Collected Works: 1868–1870,* Vol. 43. New York: International Publishers.

Mirowski, Philip. 1989. *More Heat than Light: Economics as Social Physics, Physics as Nature's Economics.* New York: Cambridge University Press.

Norton Wise, M., and Crosbie Smith. 1989. "Work and Waste: Political Economy and Natural Philosophy in Nineteenth Century Britain (II)." *History of Science* 27, no. 4: 391–449. https://doi.org/10.1177/007327538902700403.

Smith, Crosbie. 1998. *The Science of Energy: A Cultural History of Energy Physics in Victorian Britain.* Chicago: University of Chicago Press.

78

Thresholds

P. Joshua Griffin

The Anthropocene is saturated with planetary thresholds. Some have been exceeded, while others grow distended (Steffen et al. 2015). Consider the great ice sheets of Greenland and West Antarctica, now in slow motion collapse: a series of trickles may have already initiated a global average sea level rise of six feet by the end of the century (DeConto and Pollard 2016). To delineate a new epoch of history is to mark time by these ambiguous, non-linear crossings. Though appearing to extend indefinitely, thresholds can give way to acceleration at tipping points, indicating (if only in hindsight) moments of no plausible return. Ours may be a planetary liminality, but the labor required to endure this collective uncertainty is unevenly distributed across space, time, and historically contingent, power-bearing relationships.

The Arctic, where I do fieldwork, is warming twice as fast as the rest of the planet (Jeffries 2014). Kivalina is a 450-person Iñupiaq community located on a narrow barrier island along the northwest coast of Alaska. For Kivalina, climate change presents new challenges, but also amplifies the structural violence of U.S. welfare colonialism and neoliberal abandonment. With the construction of the first school in 1905, the U.S. Bureau of Education began a multi-decadal process that forced the semi-nomadic Kivalliñigmiut from their 2,180-square-mile territory

DOI: 10.21983/P3.0265.1.80

onto a seasonal hunting camp that remains the current 27-acre village site. One hundred years later, the U.S. Army Corps of Engineers determined that severe coastal erosion — radically accelerated by climate change — would render the island un-inhabitable by 2021. With sea ice forming later and later each year, Kivalina's coastline is no longer protected from fall storms. Facing climate threats, but also in an effort to gain running water, sanitation services, and relief from overcrowding, local leaders have for generations sought to relocate their village to a more suitable location (Marlow et al. 2015). Frontline communities like Kivalina have been positioned within longstanding thresholds not of their own choosing. Under great uncertainty, Kivalina's leaders pursue their collective future. To labor under these conditions for very long requires a particular kind of effort: a hard-to-sustain fidelity to the unlikely possibility of an "otherwise" (Povinelli 2012).

One evening in March, I was saying my goodbyes after a visit to Kivalina. My friend got up from the table where we had just shared dessert and walked toward a shelf across the room. He returned with a glossy oversized paperback, opened it, and spun it around to face me. "I look at this sometimes," he said, pointing to a small photo and gritting his teeth. "And I wonder […] is that still possible?"

The image centers on a canvas tent, encircled by vintage snow machines and a few handmade sleds. The mountains inland from Kivalina set a smooth backdrop of muted blue and gray, tones to match the blocks of ice that foreground the scene and appear taller than the tent itself. On a mound of snow behind the tent, a lone figure stands still and straight, hands in pockets, looking west. It is that moment of horizontal light just before the blistering spring sun disappears below the horizon. The "lead," where ice meets the open ocean, cannot be very far — perhaps there is a mist. It is a whaling camp.

We sat silently until my friend continued, "What did they have that we don't? I mean… their technology was less, but their success rate was 85 percent more. These guys," his finger pounded the page and I worried it would tear, "they didn't have jobs, no money, but they would empty out their cupboards," he nodded to the cabinets behind him, "they'd go out there and *wait*… for a gift from the Creator."

"Well," this time I spoke first, "it's been what, 23 years since the last whale?" He nodded once in swift agreement. "And people are still gettin ready? Even now guys are digging out their boats, right? So something's there."

"Yeah," he said, still nodding as a grin came to his face.

"I mean, what's the alternative?"

"Try harder," he said softly, "keep trying." Then, sitting up in his chair, he exclaimed, "Take that to Seattle!" and he burst out with a contagious chuckle.

I took my friend literally. Back in Seattle, I ordered my own copy of the book. Returning to the photo, I consider the density of ice, thick blocks piled high around the tent. Until the early 1990s, whaling crews would camp for weeks on end at a lead some ten to twenty miles out, well positioned to strike a migrating Bowhead whale. In recent years, captains are lucky if the ice will support a few days of camping a mile out from town, where only a few whales stray from the main migration route. In those days, the ice was no guarantee, but it was the context for a good faith return on one's labor and patience. The photo signifies a mode of life that today requires a different duration of effort than ever before. Through memory and even doubt, the photo is a threshold of possibility — an invitation to sustain particular ways of being and to reinvigorate a set of dispositions under increasingly uncertain environmental, economic, and social conditions.

At moments when "we come up against the limits of language, the limits of our strength, the limits of knowledge," writes Michael Jackson, we "are sometimes thrown open to new ways of understanding our being-in-the-world, new ways of connecting with others" (2009). Beneath the planetary, the Anthropocene also intensifies the thresholds of the everyday, including those experiences of existential ambiguity with which human beings have always had to dwell. One's bodily exposure in this

milieu is differentially distributed: the material and existential
thresholds that the environmentally privileged still contemplate
at some remove have long been sites of violence at the Anthropocene's frontlines. To inhabit the Anthropocene is to hold open
the thresholds between past, present, and possible worlds. Our
responsibilities and burdens in this work are different — there
is no common condition — yet perhaps a politics might emerge
from a common set of questions.

References

DeConto, Robert M., and David Pollard. 2016. "Contribution
    of Antarctica to Past and Future Sea-level Rise." *Nature* 531,
    no. 7596: 591–97. https://doi.org/10.1038/nature17145.
Jackson, Michael. 2009. *The Palm at the End of the Mind:
    Relatedness, Religiosity, and the Real.* Durham: Duke
    University Press.
Jeffries, M.O., J. Richter-Menge, and J.E. Overland, eds. 2014.
    "Arctic Report Card 2014." ftp://ftp.oar.noaa.gov/arctic/
    documents/ArcticReportCard_full_report2014.pdf.
Marlow, J., M. Gerace, and P.J. Griffin. 2015. "Interior Secretary
    has 'Much to Learn' from Kivalina's Iñupiaq Elders on
    Climate Change and Village Relocation." *Huffington
    Post Blog.* February 23. https://www.huffingtonpost.com/
    jennifer-j-marlow/interior-secretary-has-mu_b_6721494.
    html.
Povinelli, Elizabeth. 2012. "The Will to Be Otherwise/The
    Effort of Endurance." *South Atlantic Quarterly* 111, no.3:
    453–75. https://doi.org/10.1215/00382876-1596236.
Steffen, Will, et al. 2015. "Planetary Boundaries: Guiding
    Human Development on a Changing Planet." *Science* 347,
    no. 6223: 1259855. https://doi.org/10.1126/science.1259855.

79

Timely

Cymene Howe

Some of us remember the original *Watchmen*. This was the graphic novel of deconstructed superheroes, nonlinear plot timing, and, perhaps most famously, the bloody smiley face on the front cover and the insidious doomsday clock on the back. Congealed worry dripped closer to the clock face with each consecutive issue as the hands turned toward midnight. Recalling these seemingly halcyon days of the Holocene in the late 1980s has us remember a time when only a few heads of state had their fingers on the annihilation buttons. Now we all do — or so it seems — every time we press the gas pedal.

Anthropology has long been fascinated with temporality, troubled about time-space compressions and the disjointed chronicity of the ethnographic present. Some have called for us to "slow down" (Stengers 2005, 994) our thinking, but it appears as though we are instead amped up and frozen in time all at once. One condition of the Anthropocene, it seems, is that we must learn (again) how to tell time. The timely demands of this era have us thinking in chrono-mashups with divergent scales: geological time married with temporal immediacies, crises, and catastrophes. Whether or not the current ecological era ought to be called the Anthropocene, it is a time that has carved out new trails of thought on the *cene*. *Cenes* — as in Pleistocene, Pliocene, Miocene — hail epochs stretching back many millions of years.

DOI: 10.21983/P3.0265.1.81

They have a way of making time's passage appear truly bottom-less. As a category that geologizes our existence, the Anthropo-cene confers response-ability (Haraway 2007) and punctuates the most massive time scale in our lexicon: the geo-logic. While the Holocene may have been the age in which we learned our letters and our agriculture, the Anthropocene demands school-ing in a more reflexive genealogy of circulation and reciprocity among humans and other beings caught up in messy meshes of intraconnectivity (Barad 2007).

In an epoch defined by human effects and bracketed by men-acing consequences, one wonders about time on ice. A matter of deep, compacted, illustrative time, glaciers are what the geo-scientist Richard Alley (2014) calls a two-mile time machine. Particulate matter like pollen gets stored there, and atmos-pheric histories get revealed. On the streets of Paris, while the COP21 climate negotiations roiled inside meeting rooms, mas-sive boulders of glacial ice had been set to melt. Arranged in a circle to mimic a watch, a clock face, a compass, and a point of navigation, the installation "Ice Watch" was meant to draw attention elsewhere. "It is a mistake to think that the work of art is the circle of ice," explained the artist (Zarin 2015). "It is the space it invents." It is also the time it contains: if one were to put her mouth up to the bursting bubbles that crackled across the icy surface, she would have breathed in utterly pristine, fifteen-thousand-year-old air.

The great melting at the top of the world, and the bottom as well, has us wondering about the cool, ancient time that is being washed away. It is as though we are living in the Refor-mation. Earth's cryosphere is sloughing off as we watch in real time, turned to slush and puddles. One begins to sense a grow-ing nostalgia for the deep history ice holds. It has us thinking cene-icly — backward and forward — as we face a precarious future compounded by generational effects and wicked ethics (Gardiner 2011).

Geological time parallels with other scenics, like changed landscapes. But timely thinking brings us equally to another sensibility of the *scene*: pulling back the curtains on the human spectacle of the Anthropocene. In fact, if *anthrōpos* belongs anywhere in the scene, it must be to acknowledge that he has behaved with histrionic indulgences, like bouts of carbon binging. Next to geological, climatological, and seemingly impossible timescales, we have another kind of scene: tantrums and human melodrama. Tales of Armageddon, apocalypse, and emergency convey the panic that ensues in the mad dash to save human life (Colebrook 2012). The sky *is* falling, and we get to hear the countdown in terms of parts per million as the air around us continues to carbonize. This scene is like a staged event — waiting in the dark wondering if the gun will show up in the first act, so that we can know how it all will end.

One of the habits that has sustained our dangerous climate games is our propensity to be enraptured with acceleration and enamored with the speediness of things. Responding to the emphatic tempos of the digital age and the rapidly melting poles, a group in Northern California — among them, the musician Brian Eno — has been crafting a ten-thousand-year clock. They call it *The Clock of the Long Now* and they believe it will work to inspire a sense of long-term responsibility. The machine is meant to embody deep time for humans. Its inventor wants the clock to tick once a year and chime once a century; a melody generator will sound an always unique arrangement atop the two-hundred-foot timepiece nestled in a mountain. The clock's ten-thousand-year mandate operates as an inverse chronicity, a parabolic rejoinder to the history of human civilizations, the end of the last Ice Age, and the advent of agriculture — the event that some see as the true beginning of the Anthropocene.

We can imagine this decamillenial timeline next to the unhurried temporality of Earth beings like mountains (de la Cadena 2015). Yet we also encounter hyperobjects (Morton 2013) along the way, things with vast temporal and spatial reach: objects that endure beyond our use and persist beyond the grave, like Styrofoam or climate change. The Anthropocene, the Betacene (Howe n.d.) — or whatever name this era of eco/human/earth/mineral/creatural morphing finally takes — is calling us to be timely. It draws our attention to the fact that we may be clocking out.

References

Alley, Richard B. 2014. *The Two-Mile Time Machine: Ice Cores, Abrupt Climate Change, and Our Future.* Updated edition. Princeton: Princeton University Press.

Barad, Karen. 2007. *Meeting the Universe Halfway: Quantum Physics and the Entanglement of Matter and Meaning.* Durham: Duke University Press.

Colebrook, Claire. 2012. "Sexual Indifference." In *Telemorphosis: Theory in the Era of Climate Change,* Volume 1, edited by Tom Cohen, 167–82. London: Open Humanities Press.

de la Cadena, Marisol. 2015. *Earth Beings: Ecologies of Practice across Andean Worlds.* Durham: Duke University Press.

Gardiner, Stephen M. 2011. *A Perfect Moral Storm: The Ethical Tragedy of Climate Change.* New York: Oxford University Press.

Goldblum, Jimmy, and Adam Weber, dir. 2015. *The Clock of the Long Now.* Vimeo. 3'02". https://vimeo.com/146022717.

Haraway, Donna J. 2007. *When Species Meet.* Minneapolis: University of Minnesota.

Howe, Cymene. n.d. "The Betacene." Unpublished manuscript.

Morton, Timothy. 2013. *Hyperobjects: Philosophy and Ecology after the End of the World.* Minneapolis: University of Minnesota Press.

Stengers, Isabelle. 2005. "A Cosmopolitical Proposal." In *Making Things Public: Atmospheres of Democracy,* edited by Bruno Latour and Peter Weibel, 994–1003. Cambridge: MIT Press.

Zarin, Cynthia. 2015. "The Artist Who Is Bringing Icebergs to Paris." *The New Yorker.* December 5. https://www.newyorker.com/culture/culture-desk/the-artist-who-is-bringing-icebergs-to-paris.

MAKE AMERICA GREAT AGAIN

80

Trump

Tom Cohen

Were a malicious god to entertain herself by giving 21st century mortals a shiny-toy word name to chatter as distraction about, while *tipping points* passed which rendered their doom irreversible, that word name would be "the Anthropocene." Perhaps an update is due, in "2018," as we pass beyond that next phase which, if only to break the spell of the A-word, we'll call the Trumpocene? It marks an acceleration and arrival of what Anthropocene 1.0 had speculated about, largely, and seems to invert and cancel the "Anthropocene" imaginary like the Paris "Accords" itself. Trump's signifying value extends beyond the provincial U.S. screen, and not only because of the planet-trashing and climate-denialist accelerations imposed in the face of what 2018 finds on display: super-storms wiping out coastal megacities, abrupt shifts in arctic ice, crashing ecosystems such as reefs popping up like whack-a-moles, not to mention the prehearsal of the triage of disposable populations or topographic zones, the first trickle of mass climate refugees, and, of course, the IPCC's recently dumped update and panic sheet. We can't seem to time any of this very well. What to make, then, of this sudden inversion of an "Anthropocene" imaginary culminating in "Paris," even if with fudged numbers that neither added up nor would be implemented? And, in particular, its total cancellation and occlusion by Trump? "A hoax," "fake news," deleted from Federal websites — on the contrary, doubling down on pollutants, mega-extractivism, a carbon *jouissance* tipping the hallowed Stephen Hawking before death to remark that Trump might singlehandedly turn Earth into a barbecued Venus (literally). (Brazil's newly populist "tropical Trump" promises the same with the entire Amazon.) Of course, a bit more is at stake than a populist return to Potemkin 1930s fascist rhetoric going mainstream — walls, nationalisms, extermination rhetorics — or the rot of hacked democracies ill-suited for the era of climate chaos.

We must recall the hiatus of the moment, "2018," a rough date which one can easily imagine future archivists puzzling over with facial twitches, one that will mark roughly the ground zero inversion or tipping point axis itself, arbitrarily marking off a before and after in relation to which all would be ciphered. Being abruptly beyond "tipping points" implies, of course, an irreversible acceleration of cascading feedback loops, automatized, impossible to alter. It turns out, then, not that *Trump* arrived as the reactionary white counterstrike to *globalization,* a fiat restoration to preconstitutional monarchic and neofeudal techno-oligarchy. More than a hint of charade attends this weird fat Liberace caricature of a return of *anthrōpos* himself, white, male, thieving, rapacious, dissembling, techno-eugenicist, etc., a dinosaur roar in a tarpit? Yet the Trumpocene weaponizes torrents of faux nostalgias by which "post-truth" populism's *ressentiment* spirals are stoked and bot-driven. Back to Mao, back to 13th-century Russian nonsense, back to "nationalist" whatever, forming a vortex of re-active accelerations comparable to climate cascades or HFT short-circuitings. Rather, Trump would be the pure expression of 21st-century *climate panic,* and the climate autocrat to come (to divert Derrida). Trump cannot be read as a departure from some norm that will return (say, liberal democracy as pretext); rather, "he" assumes irreversibility and doubles down, locking in winners and losers.

On the flip side of Trump's blanket denialism in the face of raging mega-hurricanes and wiped-out protectorates (Puerto

Rico), a counterlogic emerged. It would be argued quietly in his efforts to repeal car emission caps. Yeah, climate chaos is all too real, but since the very worst outcomes are already baked in by this century's end — anyone can see this, no? — why tie ourselves up and deprive cronies of another exponential rush of power while this generation parties? This all takes place, of course, against the background of a hyper-inequality split which, with one eye on encroaching and arriving climate catastrophism, explains better why that will not return to some imagined equality pendulum swing. Trump — who sued Bill Maher for asking him to prove his father was not an orangutan — heralds, with his white, eugenist babble, a species split being engineered by a self-designated survivor caste, one soon to be AI-enhanced and gifted with longevity, gene-edited, and utterly distinct from the old iterations of Anthropos 1.0 (in need of retirement by then). Moreover, Mars would provide an escape imaginary down the road. Rather than denialism, Trump's doubling down on accelerating extinction events is a bet on techno-evolution and the techno-eugenics that cannot, now, be stopped.

The Trumpocene appears as the next phase of climate chaos claims the peripheries and triages widening zones of disposability. The great joke of the racist populism stampede in America is the Trumpian head fake for these "losers" (in his vocabulary), stripped of health care, herded for frontline disposability. Thus, the vertigo of Trumpism involves his inverse playbook: that is, not of denying but assuming and hastening irreversibility — this fold, *now,* from which extinction logics are locked in. It also assumes, in Roy Cohn fashion, a *de facto* "politics" of managed extinctions that arrives with the passage of "tipping points." This vertigo has its amusements, as warring media ecologies decouple from reference or "fact." With its digitally engineered neural whiteouts, "post-truth" screens, and troll-farms — generating reactive spirals — the Trumpocene puts on display the ".0001 %'s" passive techno-eugenicist agenda. Temporalities mutate once tipping points pass — as Trump's transportation flacks argued to the courts. Rather than the archaism of possessing an open or progressive future pinned to the "arrow of time," the latter is calculably curtailed, said arrow boomerangs, and it now becomes a matter of "sustaining" or delaying the retirement of an epochal regime of life forms.

The current geopolitical chaos and self-gaming of financial markets mimics that, too, of a system passing from entropy into a self-accelerating vortex. This inspires some to view Trump's disruption as an algorithm or negative "singularity" itself. Perhaps "the Anthropocene" will come to name not a geological era among others, but the fifteen or so years that Anthropocene Talk (Jedediah Purdy) flourished, largely, as a consolatory distraction for those on watch while said tipping points passed. No wonder Hollywood has switched from post-Apocalyptic survival products to extinction *mises-en-scène,* in particular those in which viewers now identify not with survivalists but — acknowledging the dead-end — *for* the replacements (cyborgs, apes, de-extincted dinosaurs…). An unsubtle nudge and opiate from corporate Hollywood. Thus the Internet pleads: *Thanos* did nothing wrong! It is the CGI Hollywood superheroes who stupidly battle to preserve an extinction economy's doomed status quo of identificatory and mimetic spells.

Anthrōpos, if he ever existed as such and isn't just our perpetually conjured excuse, seems in retrospect less the educated male citizen Aristotle conjured than a shape-shifting con man, a ghost algorithm whose idea of mastery would be to direct and survive his own snuff film. That assumes that Mars is accommodating and that the driver of techno-eugenics, "AI," doesn't get sick of the whole game and pulls a *Thanos.* Even so, there is something grotesque in the version chosen for this spectral restoration, Donald J. Trump — as if, again, an eye-rolling and malicious god were mocking us to the core. This may prove hard to explain when the aliens arrive to sift through and analyze the "geological" dust and data. It may turn out that the universe is full of civilizations but none want to visit us for a reason.

81

Turtle

Nomi Stone

Nesting, the turtle seems to be crying even though she is
    simply secreting
her salt. Her dozens bud limbs inside amniotic pillows

as she leaves every egg in a cup of sand the size of her body,
shaped like a tilting teardrop — and both cryings

are mentioned by scientists. My niece Eve is startle-eyed when
    you feed her
avocado and when you feed her sweet potato. She lives mouth
    first:

she would eat the sidewalk and piano, the symmetrical petals
    of the Bradford pear,
as if she could learn which parts of the world are made and
    how,

and yesterday she put her mouth on the image of her own face
in the mirror. Larkin says what will survive of us is love,

but the scientists say that the end of the decay-chain is lead and
    uranium and after that.

DOI: 10.21983/P3.0265.1.83

plastics. Just now the zooplankton are swallowing micro pearls
of plastic

and the sea is aflame with waste caught in the moon's light.
Here is the darkening hour and here, the shore, as she droplets
her eggs,

bright as ping pong balls, into the sand. She can't find the spot.
The beach is saltined with lights, neoned with spectacular

globes of light, a dozen moons instead of the one moon. Still,
she lets them go
and one month later, tiny turtles hatch. They seem groggy,

carrying their houses of bone and cartilage to the ocean,
scrambling toward the horizon alongside the earth's magnetic
field.

Less than one percent of the hatchlings make it past
the seagulls and crabs, so Noah spent a summer dashing them
to the water.

But my poem is not about the moment when a bird dove and
bore
into the underflesh and into Noah's memory.

My poem is about how we are gathered around Eve
in the kitchen as she eats a fruit she has never tried before

and each newness in the worldstops the world's ending in its
tracks.

82

Unknowns

Debbora Battaglia

To stand before artist Alicja Kwade's *Medium Median* mobile is
to find oneself at the center point of an exhibitionary techno-
cosmology. GPS images of our galaxy, transmitted to smart-
phones suspended from brackets attached to the ceiling, rotate
now towards one magnetic pole, now towards the other, as a
Siri-voiced chorus transmits, in unison, an account of creation,
from the biblical book of Genesis. The constellation is, in the
artist's words, "a template of our contemporary civilization: old
book and contemporary upload" (Whitechapel interview 2016);
a kind of shrine to technologies of knowledge transmission and
translation. Around it, sculptures transformed by software-
generated molds from massive Paleolithic bones into Kwade's
bronzes stand like temple guards, icons of the extraction and
trade of raw minerals in the Middle Bronze Age. And on a large
screen ominously near the constellation, great grainy images of
asteroids tumbling in outer space confront all this "progress"
with the specter of finitude: *Apophis, Toutatis, 1999JM8* — three
asteroidal Near Earth Objects (NEOS) digitally tracked for dating
their possible or impossible impact with Earth; they are also tar-
gets as a class of corporate interest in mining them for raw minerals and volatiles, as Earth's are depleted (Olson 2012, 1027).

Here, in consequence of "being there" (Geertz 1988) as an
observant art world participant, one is both implicated in ethi-

cal questions concerning spacetime relations of storied matter, natural and cultural, and positioned within its present perfect progressive tense: action that began in the past, is continuing in the present, may continue into the future.

Charles Stewart writes of a Greek village cosmology on the island of Naxos "that revolves around mystical revelation and discovery […] of lost and hidden things." The village is located in a region rich in emery, and the cosmology centered by a chapel built by a miner and dedicated to the saint who revealed in a dream to him a massive deposit of the mineral (2012, 109). For Stewart, this points to the cosmology of "late capitalism's metamorphic transactions between value genres in the fervid imagination of the villagers" — an iteration of "known unknowns" as Donald Rumsfeld famously philosophized. Yet in quite another vein, it points to the cosmology that David Valentine (2016) locates in the commercial space industry — its shrines on Mars or the moon or perhaps on another Earth (Messeri 2016); its dreams, the speculative maps of off-Earth colonization and untapped raw resources, boundless satellite communication possibilities, overviews of our own warming planet's distress, and further, an Exit Strategy for its species.

The iconic minerals bookending Kwade's installation would be bronze and coltan (columbite-tantalite) — the "'digital mineral' […] required for the capacitors in all digital devices" off-Earth and on. Its market value is so volatile that Congolese who mine and trade it attribute control of value (understandably) to otherworldly forces (Smith 2011, 17) — as unruly and unknowably contingent as NEOs. In short, a "known unknown" *cosmo/politically* naturalized to the future subjunctive. As space scientists are actively lobbying to mine coltan on the moon, it should come as no surprise that speculative fiction is already there, narratizing the human costs. In the film *Moon* (2009), an astronaut engineer/miner with only a computer for conversation is solely in charge of a lunar mining operation under corporate contract. Noticing that he is physically deteriorating as the date approaches for returning home, he makes the startling discovery that a series of his own clones is being kept in storage at the facility, to be activated for carrying on the corporate project, beyond his own mortal limits.

Of course, contrarywise, the future is literally suspended in the now, in cases such as cryogenic practices which seek to produce physical "life after life":—what Abou Farman conceptualizes as "speculative matter, matter that has indeterminate speculative status, but serves as a medium for speculation" (2013, 737). Here, ethical space slides into what Žižek recognizes as a "crucial fourth term" to those Rumsfeld once listed, namely, the "'unknown knowns': the things we don't know that we know," inclusive of the capacity of human beings to hold "disavowed beliefs [...] we *pretend* not to know about" (Žižek 2004). One can find in this category everything from the labor conditions and market strategies related to mineral extraction and trade in Greece and the Congo, to the cryogenecists' faith in successful outcomes, to GPS satellite predictions and public broadcasting of "bad weather" (Masco 2010) that threatens to freeze political protest at sites like the Dakota Access Pipeline.

It is explicitly an open question for Alicja Kwade whether the relation of artworld forces to the planetary futures they address, "yet unseen," yet unknown, and cosmo/political, finds a place along these lines.

References

Farman, Abou. 2013. "Speculative Matter: Secular Bodies, Minds, and Persons." *Cultural Anthropology* 28, no. 4: 737–59. https://doi.org/10.1111/cuan.12035.

Geertz, Clifford. 1988. *Works and Lives: The Anthropologist as Author.* Palo Alto: Stanford University Press.

Masco, Joseph. 2010. "Bad Weather." *Social Studies of Science* 40, no. 1: 7–40. https://doi.org/10.1177/0306312709341598.

Messeri, Lisa. 2016. *Placing Outer Space: An Earthly Ethnography of Other Worlds.* Durham: Duke University Press.

Olson, Valerie. 2012. "Political Ecology in the Extreme: Asteroid Activism and the Making of an Environmental Solar System." *Anthropological Quarterly* 85, no. 4: 1027–44. https://doi.org/10.1353/anq.2012.0070.

Smith, James. 2011. "Tantalus in the Digital Age: Coltan Ore, Temporal Dispossession, and 'Movement' in the Eastern Democratic Republic of Congo." *American Ethnologist* 38, no. 1: 17–35. https://doi.org/10.1111/j.1548-1425.2010.01289.x.

Stewart, Charles. 2012. *Dreaming and Historical Consciousness in Island Greece.* Cambridge: Harvard University Press.

Valentine, David. 2016. "Atmosphere, Context, and the View from Above Earth." *American Ethnologist* 43, no. 3: 511–24. https://doi.org/10.1111/amet.12343.

Žižek, Slavoj. 2004. "What Rumsfeld Doesn't Know that He Knows About Abu Ghraib." *In These Times.* May 21. http://www.lacan.com/zizekrumsfeld.htm.

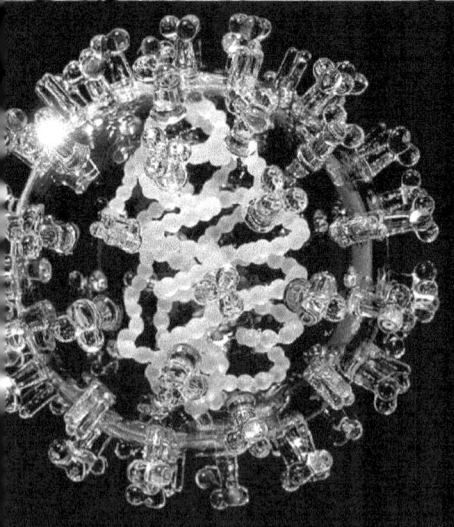

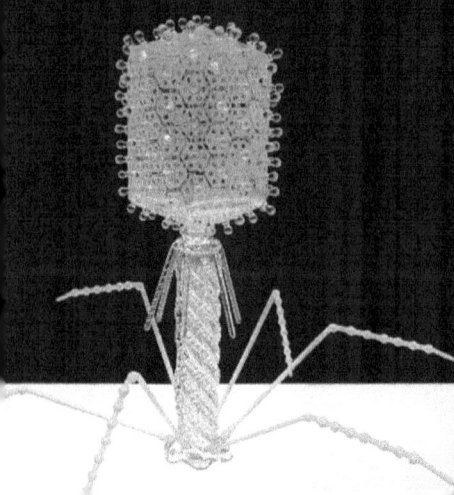

83

Unseens

Celia Lowe

The Anthropocene is full of invisible and barely perceptible objects and processes lying in wait along a trajectory set to shape
our future. From the hidden toxins that will give us cancer
someday, to the imperceptible greenhouse gases driving climate
change, the future becomes apparent through technical expertise and intermediary devices. The metaphor of sight indicates
what is to come; what do we *see* as we *look* into the future? We
are forced to develop ever more powerful prosthetic capacities — from satellites that reveal the earth and its atmosphere
from space, to electron microscopes that make visible the microbial world — yet our capacity to sense what surrounds us and
may be driving our future can be profoundly limited. Perhaps
we can learn more about the unseen from the virus?

Viruses are recognized by appropriately shaped cell receptors
within our bodies, but they are not accessible to visual perception, proprioception, or interoception. When, in the nineteenth
century, Pasteur and Koch discovered the existence of "germs,"
dispelling belief in spontaneous generation, there were other
diseases where the infectious agent or toxin simply slid through
bacteria trapping filters and remained invisible. It wasn't until
1939 that the newly invented electron microscope made it possible to identify these viruses (Zimmer 2010).

DOI: 10.21983/P3.0265.1.85

And yet we still can't see them well. Most viruses exist at the edge of our technical capabilities to enhance visual perception, and virologists need to make an imaginative leap between the structures they can see and what theories of chemical interaction can tell them. Visual artist Luke Jerram, who is color blind, likes to create at the edges of perception and has worked to make viruses visible in his project *Glass Microbiology* (Monoyios 2013). When he gazed upon what he interpreted as "beautiful translucent animals" through an electron microscope he realized that they look nothing like the fluorescently tinted slide images found in scientific publications (Boustead 2009). Because they are smaller than the wavelength of light, viruses are in fact clear. Jerram worked with Andrew Davidson, a virologist at the University of Bristol, to render HIV, Influenza, Ebola and other viruses perceptible at one million times their actual size. Like the virus, perched at the edge of life and inert matter, Jerram's glass sculptures exist at the limit of both scientific understanding and glass blowing technique, and leap boundaries between danger and beauty (McNeil 2010).

Luke Jerram's attempts to make viral forms visible are only one way of interacting with the unseen. I have studied H5N1 Influenza virus in Indonesia (Lowe 2010) and the Elephant Endotheliotropic Herpes Virus (EEHV) in Switzerland, South Asia, and Seattle with my colleague Ursula Muenster (Lowe and Muenster 2016). News of a damaging viral infection comes in the form of a symptom, a medical diagnosis, or death. The first sign of H5N1 avian influenza virus, which traveled the globe in the 2000s, was a mass poultry die-off in a Hong Kong market. In 2003, in the first human case of H5N1 in Indonesia, no evidence of the virus could be found anywhere in the patient's environment, and the transmission vector of most H5N1 infections remained undetectable. Similarly, EEHV can sometimes be found in the trunk wash of an adult elephant without producing symptoms, or it can kill an elephant in the space of a day, suddenly emerging from an unknown site where it had lain dormant inside the elephant's body. "Seeing" the virus does not mean the elephant is sick, while an undetectable virus does not mean the animal is safe.

Viral invisibility means that experts and interpreters of the future will have to be involved. As the international community ramped up its rhetoric and interventions around H5N1, it chased what it viewed as an emergent apocalyptic entity. While the influenza apocalypse that was to kill us by the millions remains unseen to this day, preparations for a global pandemic, and the desire to stop it before it materialized, initiated an international response that eclipsed other scientific, health care, and aid agendas, and whose budget rapidly outstripped funding available for ongoing medical, scientific, and development efforts. Uncertain vectors and the requirements of expertise leave communities dependent upon and vulnerable to professional interpreters of the Anthropocene.

While some Indonesian technical or policy experts joined in, others resisted the end of the world made visible through international expertise, its funding, its laboratories, and its stories. Indonesia's Minister of Health Dr. Siti Fadilla Supari, for example, took the multinaturalist (Vivieros de Castro 2015) position that Indonesians don't get the flu, and if they do, they deal with it through *karokan,* the Southeast Asian practice of dermabrasion or "coining." While the international community was planning for unseens at the planetary scale, the Indonesian minister was interested in the sovereignty of her nation, and each accused the other of callousness in the face of a catastrophe they imagined in their own image. Struggles over the unseens of climate change operate similarly: they spark controversy over the veracity of atmospheric warming and over sovereignty in climate action.

In a different artwork, Luke Jerram took on the speculative task of representing a yet unseen future viral mutation. Future mutations are always out there, though not before our very eyes. What is new about the unseens of the Anthropocene is our technical capacity to manifest invisible worlds, and thus to tell new stories about our destiny that don't place gods or ghosts at the center. Yet neither is the human at the center of this story. Jane Bennett writes, "to 'render manifest' is both to receive and to participate in the shape given to that which is received. What is manifest arrives through humans but not entirely because of them" (2010, 17). As the hysteria over speculative influenza mutations makes clear, what is built on the edifice of the invisible depends upon the power and technical capacity of the shamans who bring it into view. The unseens of the Anthropocene remain, then, one part prosthesis, one part prophesy.

References

Bennett, Jane. 2010. *Vibrant Matter: A Political Ecology of Things*. Durham: Duke University Press.

Boustead, Greg. 2009. "At the Edge of Perception." *Seed*. October 15. http://seedmagazine.com/content/article/at_the_edge_of_perception/.

Lowe, Celia. 2010. "Viral Clouds: Becoming H5N1 in Indonesia." *Cultural Anthropology* 25, no. 4: 625–49. https://doi.org/10.1111/j.1548-1360.2010.01072.x.

Lowe, Celia and Ursula Muenster. 2016. "The Viral Creep: Elephants and Herpes in Times of Extinction." *Environmental Humanities* 8, no. 1: 118142. https://doi.org/10.1215/22011919-3527749.

McNeil, Douglas G. 2010. "Are Killer Viruses, Rendered in Glass, Also Things of Beauty?" *New York Times*. June 14. https://www.nytimes.com/2010/06/15/science/15virus.html.

Monoyios, Kalliopi. 2013. "You've Never Really Seen a Virus Until You See This." *Scientific American*. March 12. https://blogs.scientificamerican.com/symbiartic/youve-never-really-seen-a-virus-until-you-see-this/.

Viveiros de Castro, Eduardo. 2015. *The Relative Native: Essays on Indigenous Conceptual Worlds*. Chicago: University of Chicago Press.

Zimmer, Carl. 2011. *A Planet of Viruses*. Chicago: University of Chicago Press.

84

Vulnerability

Sarah E. Vaughn

Intensified rainfall, species migration, and wildfires are just some of the disturbances that characterize vulnerability in the Anthropocene. Perhaps it is now a social fact that "we" humans are vulnerable to a changing climate, albeit in disparate ways. In many instances, the disturbances that make us vulnerable are unprecedented. They challenge our expectations about what it entails to live in at-risk environments. My task in this brief essay is to explore the social epistemologies that guide perception and practices related to the management of vulnerability. This is an attempt to ask: what constitutes vulnerability in the Anthropocene? In posing this question I suggest that vulnerability involves learning to become aware of disturbance, a practice that affects how we organize social worlds and our affective investments in them.

The above question may incite unease, because it demands taking account of geopolitical efforts that have fallen short of curtailing anthropogenic harms to the planet. Some of the better-known efforts by policymakers include climate summits, where wagers are made on carbon markets even as preparations for the next disaster continue. To date, these summits have resulted in elaborate technical reports but inconsistent action as far as alleviating the vulnerability faced by certain human populations and ecologies. This track record reveals that the produc-

DOI: 10.21983/P3.0265.1.86

tion of knowledge about vulnerability can create a sense of fleeting confidence in systems of security (Lakoff 2008).

Indeed, we tend to think of vulnerability as cutting human life short, but it can also engender social alliances, shape political institutions, and support infrastructures (Butler 2015, 123–53). Vulnerability is not only a condition of interdependency; it positions human bodies in the path of forces and things. It forges relations between humans and nonhumans at the same time that it calls into question the terms of human survival (Das 2010). This is a productive challenge for anyone thinking about the Anthropocene — an epoch characterized by humankind pressing itself into and recalibrating the rhythms of an already fractured earth.

One way to confront this challenge is to revisit assumptions about vulnerability that are embedded in dominant fields of knowledge production. Since its inauguration as a topic in fields such as political ecology and disaster studies, vulnerability has been defined through the lens of nature and society, subject and object, expert and nonexpert, resistance and agency. Studies tend to focus on the links between vulnerability and the affective state of injury. This emphasis on injury has allowed scholars to detail the uneven effects of climatic risks, such as hurricanes or droughts, on human populations. Here, injury is a kind of psychic or bodily wound (Clark 2011). In this way, scholars have argued that vulnerability can lead to losses that transform particular places into ones that are easily disturbed or disaster-prone.

While an emphasis on injury draws attention to the biopolitics that underwrite vulnerability as a concept, it does not problematize disturbance in its own terms. This distinction is important for two deceivingly simple reasons: while climatic risks may entail injury, their impacts are not always self-evident. Storms can and do shift paths. They swell and dissipate. They unfold over periods that do not necessarily correspond to forms and processes of bodily damage or renewal. They often prompt human engagements with places that cause pronounced changes in ecosystems cutting across spatial-temporal scales (Tsing 2015). From this perspective, what needs to be understood is the capacity to notice disturbance and its relevance to everyday life. One way to analyze this skill set is to untangle the processes whereby knowledge practices traffic in, and elicit, particular kinds of affects.

For instance, take my field site on the fringe of urban Guyana, in the former squatter town Sophia where flooding is an ordinary occurrence. In January 2005, a storm led to the area's highest recorded monthly average rainfall and the worst flooding in the country's history, leaving residents stranded in water for weeks. Since the disaster, residents have launched door-to-door vulnerability surveys. They have reported that shifting rainfall patterns, unwieldy housing construction, and piecemeal public works are the primary sources of their vulnerability. Moreover, they have insisted that while they expect floods, it is difficult to anticipate their intensity or their cascading effects in terms of outbreaks of disease and changes in drainage flow. All that some residents can offer are hints: for example, the way mud accumulates on their shoes, their pets' movements, or the arrival of politicians at community centers offering relief supplies. Expressing concerns about the limited utility of the surveys, many residents simply repeated, "This is what vulnerability looks like."

Residents' concerns were made most palpable when state-sponsored civil engineers repaired canals. This work took place on politicized terrain, with residents obstructing canal arteries, demanding land plots, or seeking international aid for climate adaptation, even as others collaborated with engineers. The vulnerability surveys surfaced residents' decades-long acceptance of the way in which flooding had become currency for securing modes of state care. Their exchanges with engineers enabled not only the circulation of information, but also complex feelings of aspiration, resentment, trust, and suspicion.

Against this backdrop, vulnerability is a concept that indexes more than injury. It constitutes a range of affective investments that force us to learn to sense and live with disturbance. At stake is whether global and local policy responses to climate change bind certain human populations to catastrophic futures or create conditions to chart new ones. By paying attention to how classificatory schemes like vulnerability circulate, we are in a better position to discern what these responses make possible or foreclose.

References

Butler, Judith. 2015. *Notes Toward a Performative Theory of Assembly.* Cambridge: Harvard University Press.
Clark, Nigel. 2011. *Inhuman Nature: Sociable Life on a Dynamic Planet.* Thousand Oaks: Sage.
Das, Veena. 2010. "Sexuality, Vulnerability, and the Oddness of the Human: Lessons from the Mahabharata." *borderlands* 9, no. 3: 1–17. http://www.borderlands.net.au/vol9no3_2010/das_mahabharata.htm.
Lakoff, Andrew. 2008. "The Generic Biothreat, or, How We Became Unprepared." *Cultural Anthropology* 23, no. 3: 399–428. https://doi.org/10.1111/j.1548-1360.2008.00013.x.
Tsing, Anna. 2015. *The Mushroom at the End of the World: On the Possibility of Life in Capitalist Ruins.* Princeton: Princeton University Press.

85

Wildness

Dana J. Graef

Two decades before the idea of the Anthropocene gained global traction, the environmental historian William Cronon (1996) made a call to think not of wilderness, but wildness. In a decade of scholarship that largely focused on the adverse social impacts of conservation, Cronon took a step beyond critique. Quoting Henry David Thoreau, who wrote that "In Wildness is the preservation of the World," Cronon (1996, 86–89) suggested that wildness "can be found anywhere," that it is "within and around" each of us. It can be found in a backyard garden; it can be found in the city; it can be found in a front lawn. Wildness need not reject the human.

In the Anthropocene, the wild meets domestic, and the native and invasive blend. This is nothing new, except that now we seem to accept intermingling and disturbance as characterizing facts. Consequently, sociocultural anthropology — a field that grapples with the complexity of being — is well suited for research in the Anthropocene. Intermingling occurs in time as well as space. When traced back in time, crops and domestic animals have wild ancestors. Endangered species are kept in zoos and breeding grounds to ensure future propagation. Given enough time and the right kind of space, the domestic becomes feral and approaches wild again. For some people, wildness evokes a sense of loss for what once was; for others, it is simulta-

DOI: 10.21983/P3.0265.1.87

neously an axiom of hope for what will be: restoration, renewal, rewilding.

Rewilding is often conjured as an antidote to the Anthropocene's human dominance of geographic space. Yet the irony is that rewilding projects are human-driven (see Marris 2011; Lorimer and Driessen 2014). In one approach to rewilding, nonnative species substitute for the roles once held by extinct corollaries. For instance, Paul Robbins and Sarah Moore (2013, 12) describe how an endangered ebony species is being restored through "island rewilding" in the Indian Ocean. Scientists (Griffiths et al. 2011) have introduced a nonnative giant tortoise to disperse the endemic ebony's seeds, a role once filled by a now-extinct native tortoise. The ebony trees are nurtured by a human-mediated relationship with another wild — but not native — species. Different forms of wildness meet.

Conceptually, wildness can transgress borders between human and not human, nature and culture. Walking through the Massachusetts landscape more than 150 years ago, Thoreau (1995, 233) foreshadowed the contemporary ethos of rewilding. In Walden, he reflected on an edible ground-nut that had been used as food by Native Americans: "In these days of fatted cattle and waving grain-fields this humble root [...] is quite forgotten." Yet if humans were to step aside, Thoreau envisioned a different future:

> Let wild Nature reign here once more, and the tender and luxurious English grains will probably disappear before a myriad of foes [...] but the now almost exterminated ground- nut will perhaps revive and flourish in spite of frosts and wildness.

In this vision the domesticated gives way to the wild through human absence, but Thoreau also understood wildness as a human trait. "Life consists with Wildness," he wrote in the essay "Walking" (Thoreau 1862). "The most alive is the wildest." In this sense, wildness transcends distinctions between humans and nature to emphasize life. Wildness does not entail an absence of humanity, but rather vivaciousness: a quality that can apply to people as well as plants, wheat fields as well as prairies, dogs as well as wolves.

Through life, wildness encompasses the domestic and the tame, as well as that which is beyond human control. Building on Thoreau, Cronon (1996, 69, 89) further demonstrates why the concept of wildness is so apt for the Anthropocene. Unlike societal conceptions of wilderness, wildness is not dependent on the fiction of untouched spaces, devoid of human history. Yet the idea that wildness can crop up anywhere, even in the most ostensibly tame places, upsets human efforts to order and predict the world. For instance, as wildfires burn larger and longer, people evacuate cities not knowing to what they will return — this, too, is wildness. Wildness in the Anthropocene is exuberant, transgressive, vivid; it blends categories.

While wildness can flourish in the most human of places, for some conservationists the wild remains a clarion call to push back against anthropogenic change. Yet nonhuman species also push back. In nature's agency and its ability to adapt and grow, wildness transcends categories (such as native and nonnative) that we ascribe to species. This agency is expressed in Ashley Carse's (2014, 208) work on the Panama Canal. If sustained efforts to manage invasive water hyacinth were stopped, he notes, "the canal would be impassible in three to five years." Left alone, this aquatic weed would clog a crucial artery of global trade. Exuberant, growing unbidden, the water hyacinth is emblematic of wildness in our current era.

If the Anthropocene will have a lexicon, it should be a wild one. It should be a set of terms that pushes our thinking beyond simplified ideas of human dominion. We should be unsettled just the right amount, in this so-called human era. We should not lose sight of ourselves as actors who create new forms of wildness even as we erase others. By carefully situating ourselves within not only social but also ecological webs of interconnection, we can guard against the grandiosity and anthropocentrism of the Anthropocene. This epoch named for ourselves — is it a cautionary term, or, as Cymene Howe and Anand Pandian suggest, "the ultimate act of […] self-aggrandizement" (Introduction, this volume)? Do we laud our capacity for lasting change at the same time as we deplore and fear it?

Who does not long for a little bit of wildness?

References

Carse, Ashley. 2014. *Beyond the Big Ditch: Politics, Ecology, and Infrastructure at the Panama Canal.* Cambridge: MIT Press.

Cronon, William. 1996. "The Trouble with Wilderness; or, Getting Back to the Wrong Nature." In *Uncommon Ground: Rethinking the Human Place in Nature,* edited by William Cronon, 69–90. New York: W.W. Norton.

Griffiths, Christine J., Dennis M. Hansen, Carl G. Jones, Nicolas Zuël, and Stephen Harris. 2011. "Resurrecting Extinct Interactions with Extant Substitutes." *Current Biology* 21, no. 9: 762–65. https://doi.org/10.1016/j.cub.2011.03.042.

Lorimer, Jamie, and Clemens Driessen. 2014. "Wild Experiments at the Oostvaardersplassen: Rethinking Environmentalism in the Anthropocene." *Transactions of the Institute of British Geographers* 39, no. 2: 169–81. https://doi.org/10.1111/tran.12030.

Marris, Emma. 2011. *Rambunctious Garden: Saving Nature in a Post-Wild World.* New York: Bloomsbury.

Robbins, Paul, and Sarah A. Moore. 2013. "Ecological Anxiety Disorder: Diagnosing the Politics of the Anthropocene." *Cultural Geographies* 20, no. 1: 3–19. https://doi.org/10.1177/1474474012469887.

Thoreau, Henry David. 1862. "Walking." *The Atlantic.* June. https://www.theatlantic.com/magazine/archive/1862/06/walking/304674/.

———. 1995. *Walden: An Annotated Edition.* Edited by Walter Harding. Boston: Houghton Mifflin.

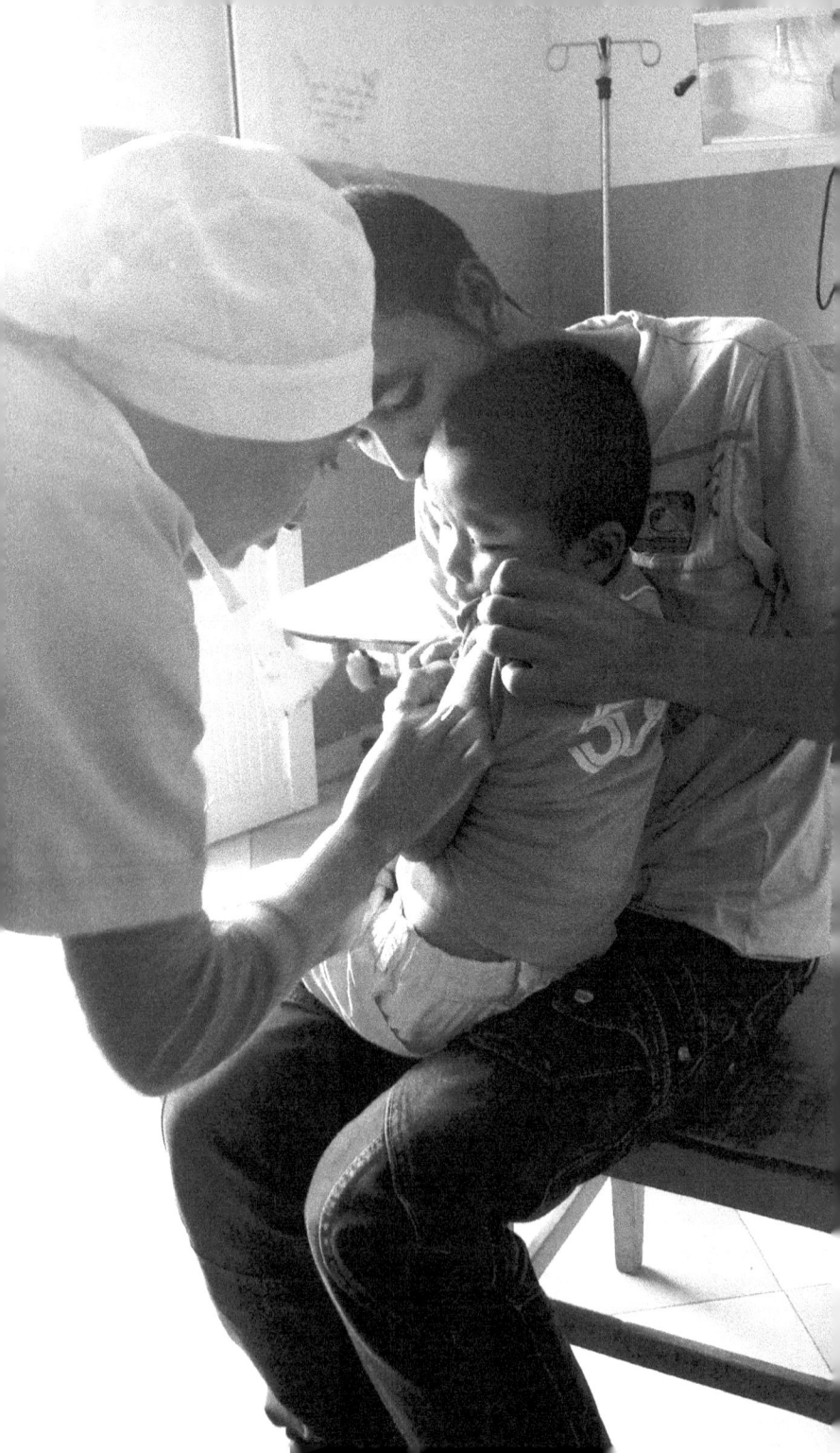

86

Zoonosis

Genese Marie Sodikoff

We are at the cusp of this new age of the Anthropocene, an age in which humans have colonized evolutionary time. To contain and prevent pandemics, scientists are beginning to drive snippets of altered genomes down generations in order to wipe out pernicious insects. The rise of zoonotic diseases, those that spill over from animals to humans directly or (in some definitions) through insect vectors, compels these risky experiments. We are adapting to zoonotic conditions less by taking steps to reduce our heavy footprint on the planet, and more by meddling with nature on a deeper level.

Pathogens have always circulated among animal reservoirs, vectors, and human hosts. Gilles Deleuze and Félix Guattari (1987, 11) suggest that we "form a rhizome with our viruses, or rather our viruses cause us to form a rhizome with other animals." All earthly life fundamentally shares one health, as proponents of the multidisciplinary global initiative to tackle zoonosis assert. Spillover diseases expose the vulnerability of species boundaries. Conceived as a taxonomic container of sorts, the concept of species has long established a sense of order (Kirksey 2015). Zoonosis troubles that sense.

Land-use changes, booming human and livestock populations, global travel, biodiversity loss, random mutation, natural selection, and even intentional bioterror are among the many

DOI: 10.21983/P3.0265.1.88

factors that have opened this Pandora's box. Recent outbreaks such as SARS (probably from horseshoe bats), MERS (from camels), bird flu (from poultry), Ebola (possibly from fruit bats), bubonic plague (from rats and other rodents), and Zika (possibly from rhesus monkeys) demonstrate how human and insect vectors can spread diseases rapidly and over oceans. A warming climate invites mosquitoes, flying syringes loaded with viruses and parasites, to colonize new lands. Airplanes enable infectious agents to incubate in human bodies even as they are transported elsewhere.

In tropical regions such as Madagascar, where I do research, the destruction of biodiverse forests for mines, agriculture, timber, and new construction stirs up unknown viruses and crowds remaining wildlife species into habitat fragments. This, in turn, cultivates more pathogenic environments for humans and other vertebrates. At the boundary of primary habitats and human settlements, viruses that lurk in other animals become active or, to use the language that scientists do, chatty. The term *viral chatter* denotes a situation in which "a zoonotic pathogen genetically adapts the ability to 'jump' into human hosts, but not yet to the degree that it can sustain further transmission in human populations" (Barrett 2010, 84).

I like the double entendre of viral chatter. It points to an internal relationship between rising pathogenesis in ecosystems and rumors about disease outbreaks circulated in the media and in conversation. The association of microbial activity with Internet memes about the cause of outbreaks or the means of transmission is not merely metaphorical. Computer technology is, after all, sustained through the extraction of rare earth and industrial minerals from tropical forest regions.

Disease rumors that go viral confound public health responses. The 2014 Ebola outbreak in West Africa was exacerbated not only by pervasive infrastructural and economic conditions but also by conspiracies about the nefarious intentions of state actors and foreigners. A widely circulated report about the Zika virus in Brazil blamed biotechnology for the spate of babies born with microcephaly. It claimed that a larvicide, py-riproxifen, manufactured by a Monsanto subsidiary, was the real cause. Another rumor blamed microcephaly on genetically modified mosquitos meant to wipe out the subspecies *Aedes aegypti*. But the Zika virus itself is most likely to blame for fetal deformities, having mutated over time and space to the point where it has acquired this power.

Erroneous beliefs about causation often reflect people's fear of technologies that meddle with nature, however mutable the idea of nature might be. Irrational thoughts and actions around zoonotic epidemics are not always seeded in cyberspace or within localized publics, however. During an acute outbreak of the bubonic plague in the rural town of Amparafaravola, Madagascar in November 2014, medical workers initially sought to quash chatter about the plague, denying that it had arrived in town. Some feared gaining a bad reputation for the town as the locus of an epidemic, or getting reprimanded for mishandling public outreach.

The silencing of plague chatter by medical workers no doubt led to the illness of some twenty-seven residents and the preventable deaths of seven; after all, the bubonic plague can be treated with antibiotics if it is caught early enough. The delay in informing people about the means of transmission and about how to handle the highly infectious sick and dead put people at risk of developing and spreading the more virulent pneumonic strain, which occurs frequently during the plague season.

In Madagascar, rats are the main source from which the plague jumps to humans via flea bites. The blood of rats is rich with the plague bacillus, *Yersinia pestis*. In Amparafaravola in 2014, the outbreak peaked during the warm, rainy season, when fleas are abundant and people store sacks of unhulled rice inside or near their homes, unwittingly luring rats into close quarters. Throughout Madagascar, the incidence of the plague has risen over the past few years due to urban overcrowding and poor sanitation, which increases rat-human contact; climate change, which affects the population dynamics of rodents and fleas; and rampant deforestation, which, scientists argue, induces rats to migrate into agricultural fields and settlements (Mccauley et al. 2015).

Pesticide and antibiotic resistance, difficulties in developing vaccines quickly, and the tangled mix of factors triggering zoonotic outbreaks leave us in thrall to biotechnology, despite pervasive ambivalence about what it means to sculpt evolution.[1] Genetic modification techniques represent a thorny path toward the future, promising to defuse the ticking time bomb of certain problem insects even as they fortify the boundaries of our own more-than-human species.

References

Barrett, Ron. 2010. "Avian Influenza and the Third Epidemiological Transition." In *Plagues and Epidemics: Infected Spaces Past and Present,* edited by D. Ann Herring and Alan C. Swedlund, 81–94. Oxford: Berg.

Deleuze, Gilles, and Félix Guattari. 1987. *A Thousand Plateaus: Capitalism and Schizophrenia.* Translated by Brian Massumi. London: Continuum.

Kirksey, Eben. 2015. "Species: A Praxiographic Study." *Journal of the Royal Anthropological Institute* 21, no. 4: 758–80. https://doi.org/10.1111/1467-9655.12286.

McCauley, Douglas J., Daniel J. Salkeld, Hillary S. Young, Rhodes Makundi, Rodolfo Dirzo, Ralph P. Eckerlin, Eric F. Lambin, Lynne Gaffikin, Michele Barry, and Kristofer M. Helgen. 2015. "Effects of Land Use on Plague (Yersinia pestis) Activity in Rodents in Tanzania." *American Journal of Tropical Medicine and Hygiene* 92, no. 4: 776–83. https://doi.org/10.4269/ajtmh.14-0504.

---

1 See *Sculpting Evolution,* http://www.sculptingevolution.org/.

Figures

Address Dear Climate #M13.

Acceleration A biodiesel plant in agro-industrial Amazonia. Photo by the author.

Anticipation Larson C Ice Shelf Rift In Motion. Courtesy of NASA.

Apocalypse "The Fourth Horseman" from the *Apocalypse of Angers,* from the workshop of Nicolas Bataille, ca. 1373–1382.

Appreciation The spaces of global capital in which sustainability is defined and made valuable. Photo by Sebastiaan ter Burg.

Bloom Gelatinous Future Food, Chitra Venkataramani. Courtesy of the artist.

Business Workers carrying solar panels for Masdar City rooftops, 2010. Photo by author.

Carbon Still from an infrared video published by Environmental Defense Fund. Invisible to the human eye, the Aliso Canyon methane plume released an equivalent of about 2 million metric tons of carbon dioxide into the atmosphere in 2015–2016. Used with permission.

Care Students of herbal medicine "garbling" goldenrod blossoms by pulling them off their dried stems. The blossoms will be used in medicinal tincture and teas. Photo by Charis Boke.

DOI: 10.21983/P3.0265.1.89

Cloud The Asian/atmospheric brown cloud buoyed above the Indian sub-continent. Image by Jeff Schmaltz, MODIS Rapid Response, NASA Goddard Space Flight Center.

Conditions Hannu I. Heikkinen fixing his skis on a day with good *keli* for back-country skiing in northern Finland. Photo by Franz Krause

Cosmos Anthropos = Little Prince, Lonely Planet, Empty Cosmos. Digital collage by Abou Farman.

Death "Far from my home" Still from video 24" × 36" printed on backlit film. Exhibited Urban Video Project, Multimedia Arts Initiative with Syracuse University, Everson Museum, Syracuse, New York.

Dispossession Papua New Guinea Forest Cover. Photo by Paige West.

Distribution "Untitled," photograph of two men, trucks, road, and dust in Peru. Photo by Stefanie Graeter.

Dog "Dog house, animal shelter grounds" Photo by author.

Dream A worn out vacuum. Photo by Alf van Beem.

Dredge Dredging focuses our attention on the fact that global economic connection depends on situated environmental modification and maintenance. Drawing by Pearson Scott Foresman.

Drone A NOAA technician with the Coyote drone, just before launch. Photo by NOAA/Atlantic Oceanographic and Meteorological Laboratory.

Earths Spiral Galaxy captured by the Hubble Telescope. Photo by ESA/Hubble & NASA. Acknowledgement: Judy Schmidt (Geckzilla)

Ecopolitics "Plants of the Ecuadorian Rainforest". Photography, scan and postprocessing by Hubertl. Source: Wikimedia Commons.

Ends "Ends" (2015). Photo by the author.

Environing Sea/Sky (Antipodes). Photo by Jeffrey J. Cohen.

Eschaton The Doomsday Clock. Image courtesy of the Bulletin of the Atomic Scientists.

Expenditure Nur Hashem shouts "Go!" Photo by Naveeda Khan.

Exposure Bodily Exposure, Mexico City, 2015. Photo by author.

Extinction Activists in dinosaur costumes protested a planned freeway expansion project by "haunting" a BC Liberal Party campaign stop in Tsawwassen, British Columbia, 2 May 2009. Photo courtesy of StopThePave.org.

Fiction Rachel Whalen. Gated Community, 2019. Acrylic, metal pull tabs, and thread on canvas.

Fire A more explosive fuel upends the détente between trees, birds, and burning grasslands. Photo by Daniel Fisher.

Flatulence Mountain cows grazing in a meadow in Uttarakhand, India. Photo by Radhika Govindrajan.

Flock Melvin and me. Photo by Anne Galloway

Generation Finland's nuclear regulatory authority Säteilyturvakeskus. Photo by Vincent Ialenti, 2013.

Gluten Freshly cut wheat, Egypt. Photo by Jessica Barnes.

Gratitude Women praying. The same gesture is used to express gratitude for a favour. MK Photography.

Heat A pesticide bag, mounted on a branch, marks the corner of a Nicaraguan cane field, July 2017. Photo by Alex Nading.

Hyposubjects Virus Particles. Image by Carl Fredrik

Industrialism Composite image by Craig Campbell

Installation *E-Motions* (2015) by Rahşan Düren, Haydarpaşa Train Station. Photo by Serpil Oppermann.

Interstellar Artist's visualization of Earth's magnetosphere, courtesy of Conceptual Image Lab, NASA/GSFC, and "StarshipSPIDER" by Frederik de Wilde.

Leviathans Detail from the frontispiece to a manuscript version of Thomas Hobbes's *Leviathan*. Attributed to Abraham Bosse, 1651. Digital image from Wikimedia.

Melt Listening to the sounds of a melting Acrtic, with Aimee Smith, Eva la Cour, and Wendy Jacob.

Miracles Mud covers Belalcázar's school after an avalanche caused by the Huila Volcano, AP. *El País.* November 23, 2008.

Models The Chesapeake Bay Hydraulic Model, 1977. U.S. Army Corps of Engineers Waterways Experiment Station.
Monoculture Indian teas lined up for tasting in Kolkata. Photo by author.
Mood Shadow Lines. Photo by Sandeep Banerjee.
Narcissus "Narcissus, becoming-flower." Painting by Caravaggio.
Nature Low pressure system off the southwestern coast of Iceland, September 4, 2003. Image from NASA's Aqua/ MODIS satellite.
Nemesis "He made me in the Orkney islands, off the northern coast of Scotland, at the edge of the world." Image by Laura Watts.
Ocean Short beach at dawn. Photo by Steve Mentz.
Petroleum Draft pages from *The Inheritance,* by Elizabeth A. Povinelli.
Photosynthesis Screenshot of "A year in the life of Earth's CO_2." Simulation of the earth's carbon dioxide cycle by scientists at NASA Goddard Space Flight Center's Global Modeling and Assimilation Office, 2014.
Plastic Still from *Wine Dark Plastic Sea,* Anand Pandian, 2015.
Plenitude Population to plenitude? Photo by Rob Curran on Unsplash.
Power Wild horses in Spain. Photo by John Hartigan Jr.
Predation The river Ganges in flood partially submerges a Shiva idol in northern India.
Preparedness Exercise of simulation of an avian influenza outbreak in Hong Kong, January 2009. Photo by Frédéric Keck.
Price Potato cultivation in Lahore, Pakistan. Photograph by Abdul Razzaq.
Probiotic Forest regrowth at the Knepp Wildland Project in Sussex in the UK. Image courtesy of Charlie Burrell.
Quotidian Architectural renderings of a Bangkok canal-side community hang above the high water mark of the 2011 floods. Photo by Eli Elinoff.

Recalcitrance Kirby-Bauer antibiotic sensitivity test. Photograph by author.

Riddle Esther Ruiz, New Stone Age, 2012. Cement, blue marble, neon, Plexiglas, hardware. Photo courtesy of the artist.

Relationships Moss on pavement. Photo by Zoe Todd.

Rivers Waime Canyon, Kauai Island, Hawaii. Photo by Galyna Andrushko.

Seeds Seed samples prepared by Seed Savers Exchange for backup storage at Svalbard and Fort Collins. Photograph courtesy of Tracey Heatherington.

Shit A tractor hauls a large mound of biosolids (treated sanitation sludge) across a field near Mansfield, Washington (USA). Photo by Nicholas C. Kawa.

Slavery Beatriz Cortez, Cosmic Bed, 2019. Installation view of Trinidad: Joy Station at Craft Contemporary Museum. Courtesy of the artist and Commonwealth and Council, Los Angeles. Photo by Gina Clyne.

Smugglers Migrant Trail, Pakal Na, Chiapas, Mexico (Nikon F3, Ultramax 400). Photo by Jason De León.

Species A scanning electron micrograph of MRSA, an antibiotic-resistant bacteria that has generated new human categories as practitioners grapple with difficult-to-treat infections. Image courtesy of the National Institutes of Health (NIH).

Stability 2018 United States seismic hazard forecast, including anthropogenic and non-anthropogenic earthquakes. Source: U.S. Geological Survey.

Steps SONO, Sion, 2012, *The Land of Hope* [film still, 55.27].

Suburbs Post-capitalist suburb? Photo by RCB.

Surprise Frontispiece to the 1906 edition of *The Coal Question* by Stanley Jevons, showing the remarkable rise in coal consumption per capita.

Sustainability Maize dries on a rooftop in highland Guatemala. Photo by Emily Yates-Doerr.

Surreal Negative space of a removed warning sticker on the window of a former FEMA trailer. Photo by Nicholas Shapiro.

Terrain A windy day in Salta Forestal, province of Salta, Argentina. Photo by Gastón Gordillo.

Thermodynamics Energy at Work, circa 1870. Courtesy of the Wellcome Collection.

Thresholds Chukchi Sea Ice at Kivalina, May 17 2019. Photo by P. Joshua Griffin.

Timely Glacier. Fláajökull, East Iceland. Photo by author.

Turtle Eve. Photo by Zach Stone.

Trump Artifact of the Trumpocene. Photo by R. Nial Bradshaw.

Unknowns MEDIUM MEDIAN, Alicja Kwade, 2016. Image courtesy of Whitechapel Gallery, London.

Unseens Photo and artworks by Luke Jerram.

Vulnerability A typical Sophia home. Photo by author.

Wildness Lichen growing on a brick wall in Massachusetts. Photo by Dana J. Graef.

Zoonosis Child receiving a rabies vaccination after a dog bite at Moramanga Hospital, Madagascar. Photo by Genese Sodikoff, 2015.

www.ingramcontent.com/pod-product-compliance
Lightning Source LLC
Chambersburg PA
CBHW050327270326
41926CB00016B/3352